Q
647.94
G

GRAND BY NATURE

SKIRA

PREFACE BY SUSAN SARANDON   7
A SHORT HISTORY OF FAIRMONT   9

*O*RIGINS   13

ROMANTIC TRENDS	14
IRON DREAM	20
PRISTINE THRILLS	28
WILD WONDERS	37
ALFRESCO LUXURY	48
LIGHTHOUSES	58
NEW HORIZONS	68
EPICENTERS	84
GRAND RAILWAY HOTELS	98

*A*RCHITECTURE   113

RUSTIC STYLE	116
CHÂTEAU STYLE	124
ART DECO	132
MOCK TUDOR	134
SPANISH REVIVAL	136
NEOCLASSICISM & ROCCOCO	138
INDIAN STYLE	148
ORIENTAL STYLE	152
ASIAN STYLE	158
MODERN TIMES	162
GREAT ARCHITECTS	172

*S*OUL   189

ROYALTY	191
POLITICS	199
SUSTAINABILITY	211
VISUAL ARTS	217
LITERATURE	235
CINEMA	247
MUSIC	270
FASHION	286
PARTIES	300

"In Fairmont, there is 'fair' and 'mont'. What a beautiful idea: an ambitious destiny inspired by fairness. Fairmont castles have a soul: A fairy tale as I like them— sweetened by rooftop hive honey.

When you think about it, these landmarks have shaped the skyline and social life of our American and Canadian cities.

Fairmont has so many stories to tell: the reminiscence of its national parks' pristine origins, the echo of Hitchcock's muses down the corridors, the end planning of World War II or even Queen Elizabeth's favorite breakfast…

Lose yourself, feel the stories which pulse beyond the stones."

— *Susan Sarandon*

A Short History of Fairmont

IN THE BEGINNING, THERE WAS A MAN CALLED JAMES GRAHAM FAIR (1831–1894). IRISH BY BIRTH, HE EMIGRATED TO THE UNITED STATES AND HEADED WEST, WORKING AS A MINER FIRST IN CALIFORNIA, THEN IN NEVADA. THERE, IN 1873, HE STRUCK GOLD.

AS A YOUNG PROSPECTOR, FAIR AND THREE OTHER IRISHMEN CHANCED ON WHAT BECAME KNOWN AS THE BIG BONANZA, THE LARGEST SINGLE DEPOSIT OF GOLD AND SILVER EVER LOCATED. SOON, THEY BECAME KNOWN AS THE SILVER KINGS.

FAIR WAS NOT JUST WEALTHY. WITHIN THE DECADE, HE HAD BEEN ELECTED TO THE US SENATE. BUT POLITICS INTERESTED HIM LESS THAN BUSINESS, AND HE USED HIS WEALTH—HE WAS SAID TO HAVE BEEN WORTH 50 MILLION DOLLARS—TO INVEST IN THE RAILROAD AND IN REAL ESTATE. AMONG THE ACQUISITIONS HE MADE IN THE YEARS BEFORE HIS DEATH WAS THE PRIME SAN FRANCISCO LAND ON WHICH THE FIRST FAIRMONT HOTEL WAS BUILT. HOWEVER, FAIR DID NOT LIVE LONG ENOUGH TO SEE IT. THAT WAS LEFT TO HIS DAUGHTERS, WHO INHERITED BOTH THE LAND AND THEIR FATHER'S NOSE FOR BUSINESS. FAIR AND HIS ELDEST CHILD, THERESA, WERE NOT CLOSE. HE HAD DIVORCED HIS WIFE, AND THEIR CHILDREN HAD BEEN RAISED BY THEIR MOTHER, RESULTING IN AN ACRIMONY BETWEEN HIM AND THERESA THAT MEANT SHE DID NOT INVITE HIM TO HER WEDDING TO THE STEAMSHIP TYCOON HERMANN OELRICHS. EVEN SO, FAIR HAD GIVEN HER A MILLION DOLLARS AS A PRESENT. HER SISTER, VIRGINIA, MEANWHILE, MARRIED WILLIAM K. VANDERBILT II, PRESIDENT OF THE NEW YORK CENTRAL RAILROAD.

DESPITE THEIR WEALTHY MARRIAGES, THE SISTERS WERE DETERMINED TO MAKE MONEY OF THEIR OWN SO THEY DECIDED TO BUILD A HOTEL ON THE LAND THEIR FATHER HAD LEFT THEM. THEY CALLED IT THE "FAIRMONT," A CONFLATION OF THEIR MAIDEN NAME AND THE FASHIONABLY FRENCH WORD FOR MOUNT—MONT—BECAUSE IT STOOD NEAR THE SUMMIT OF NOB HILL, IN THE MOST SOUGHT AFTER PART OF THE CITY.

BUT JUST BEFORE THEY HAD PLANNED TO OPEN THE HOTEL IN APRIL 1906, THEY SUDDENLY SOLD IT. FIVE DAYS LATER, SAN FRANCISCO WAS HIT BY THE 7.9-MAGNITUDE EARTHQUAKE THAT RAVAGED THE CITY. THEY HAD INHERITED THEIR FATHER'S LUCK TOO.

FORTUNATELY, THE BUILDING SURVIVED MORE OR LESS INTACT—THE SISTERS HAD NOT STINTED ON THE QUALITY OF ITS CONSTRUCTION—BUT ITS STATELY INTERIORS WERE DESTROYED BY THE FIRE THAT FOLLOWED THE EARTHQUAKE. ITS NEW OWNERS COMMISSIONED JULIA MORGAN, THE FIRST FEMALE LICENSED ARCHITECT IN CALIFORNIA, TO RESTORE THEM. (SHE WENT ON TO DESIGN HEARST CASTLE, 250 MILES SOUTH ALONG THE PACIFIC COAST AT SAN SIMEON.) AND HER DESIGNS WERE MORE IMPRESSIVE STILL, SO SPLENDID IN FACT, THAT ON ITS COMPLETION, THERESA FAIR OELRICHS, BY THEN A WIDOW, BOUGHT IT BACK.

THE LAST DECADES OF THE NINETEENTH CENTURY HAD SEEN THE CREATION OF A COAST-TO-COAST RAILWAY NOT JUST IN THE UNITED STATES, BUT IN CANADA TOO, AND WITH IT A GROWTH IN THE NUMBER OF GRAND HOTELS.

HAVING STARTED WORK ON THE ILLINOIS CENTRAL RAILROAD AT THE AGE OF FOURTEEN, WILLIAM VAN HORNE HAD BECOME GENERAL MANAGER OF THE THEN-UNFINISHED CANADIAN PACIFIC RAILWAY IN 1881. ENTREPRENEURIAL BY NATURE, HE SAW POTENTIAL IN THE COMPANY THAT WENT FAR BEYOND TRACK AND TRAINS.

THE RAILROAD HAD MADE ACCESSIBLE SOME OF THE MOST DRAMATIC MOUNTAIN LANDSCAPES IN THE AMERICAS, A TERRAIN TO RIVAL THE ALPS (WHERE TOURISM WAS ALREADY ESTABLISHED), RICH IN HOT SPRINGS AND POTENTIAL FOR WINTER SPORTS. IF PEOPLE WERE TO TRAVEL TO THE CANADIAN ROCKIES, THEY WOULD NEED PLACES TO STAY. BUILD SPLENDID HOTELS, AND THEY WOULD BECOME DESTINATIONS IN THEMSELVES, ATTRACTING TRAVELERS IN SEARCH OF THE SUBLIME. "IF WE CAN'T EXPORT THE SCENERY, WE'LL IMPORT THE TOURISTS," VAN HORNE SAID. AND HE DID. IN 1887, THE CANADIAN PACIFIC RAILWAY OPENED THE BANFF SPRINGS HOTEL IN THE HEART OF WHAT WAS TO BECOME CANADA'S FIRST NATIONAL PARK.

VAN HORNE HAD AMBITIONS FOR FURTHER HOTELS: PALACES AT ONCE REMINISCENT OF SCOTTISH CASTLES AND FRENCH CHÂTEAUX, LUXURIOUSLY APPOINTED WITH ALL AMENITIES, AND ARCHITECTURALLY SO MEMORABLE THAT THEY WOULD BECOME LANDMARKS FOR THEIR RESPECTIVE LOCATIONS. JUST AS THE EIFFEL TOWER HAD COME TO REPRESENT PARIS, SO THEY TOO WOULD BECOME SIGNIFIERS FOR THEIR SETTINGS.

OVER THE COURSE OF THE TWENTIETH CENTURY, CANADIAN PACIFIC HOTELS, AS THE SUBSIDIARY WAS NAMED, EXPANDED, GOING ON TO ACQUIRE PROPERTIES ESTABLISHED BY ITS RIVAL, THE CANADIAN NATIONAL RAILWAY. AND SOON, THERE WOULD BE STEAMSHIPS TOO, ENABLING GUESTS TO TRAVEL EFFORTLESSLY FROM EUROPE AND THE UNITED STATES, TO QUEBEC; THENCE BY TRAIN ACROSS CANADA TO VANCOUVER; AND FROM THERE ACROSS THE PACIFIC TO HONG KONG. SUDDENLY THE WORLD WAS ACCESSIBLE TO TRAVELERS—AND TO TRADE—IN A WAY IT HAD NEVER BEEN BEFORE.

MEANWHILE, FAIRMONT HOTELS HAD GROWN GLOBALLY TOO. IN 1999, THE TWO COMPANIES MERGED TO FORM FAIRMONT HOTELS AND RESORTS.

OPPOSITE: VIRGINIA FAIR VANDERBILT PAINTED BY GIOVANNI BOLDINI, CA. 1900 (DETAIL), FOLLOWING HER MARRIAGE TO WILLIAM K. VANDERBILT II. — ABOVE: WILLIAM VAN HORNE PHOTOGRAPHED BY W.A. COOPER, CA. 1900.

So splendid, it was said, they built the city around it, the Fairmont opened in San Francisco at the top of Nob Hill in 1907, with a party at which 13,000 oysters and a "river" of champagne were consumed.

FAIRMONT SAN FRANCISCO, THE FIRST FAIRMONT HOTEL

A Natural Sanctuary
BANFF SPRINGS HOTEL, CANADA

DEEP IN THE HEART OF THE ROCKIES AT AN ALTITUDE OF 4,600 FEET, CLOSE TO THE CONFLUENCE OF SPRAY AND BOW RIVERS, THE SITE OF THE BANFF SPRINGS HOTEL WAS PERSONALLY SELECTED BY WILLIAM VAN HORNE FOR THE FORESTED BEAUTY OF ITS SURROUNDINGS AND ITS PROXIMITY TO NATURAL HOT SPRINGS.

IT STRUCK HIM AS THE PERFECT SETTING FOR A STATE-OF-THE-ART HOTEL THAT WOULD JUXTAPOSE LUXURY, SOPHISTICATION, AND THE LATEST IN THERAPEUTIC BATHING AND SPA CULTURE WITH PRISTINE NATURE AT ITS WILDEST AND MOST MAGNIFICENT—AND ALL ACCESSIBLE BY TRAIN.

THE BANFF SPRINGS HOTEL OPENED IN THE SUMMER OF 1888 WITH 250 BEDS AND, BY THE STANDARDS OF THE TIME, A VERTIGINOUS RATE OF 3.50 DOLLARS A NIGHT, IN A MONUMENTAL BUILDING CONSTRUCTED FROM TIMBER. BUT DUE TO A FIRE THE ORIGINAL STRUCTURE WAS SOON REPLACED, AND THE PRESENT CASTLE, NOW A NATIONAL HISTORIC SITE OF CANADA, DATES BACK TO 1928.

OPPOSITE: THE BOW VALLEY, BANFF, FROM A PAINTING BY ADAM SHERRIFF SCOTT PICTURED IN A 1929 CANADIAN PACIFIC RAIL PAMPHLET. — ABOVE: FAIRMONT SAN FRANCISCO POSTCARD, CA. 1900.

YRI
RI
GIN
S

"Worldwide in scope, international in activities, the Canadian Pacific is pre-eminently the expression of a progressive nation's character."
INTRODUCTION TO AN EARLY BROCHURE FOR THE BANFF SPRINGS HOTEL.

THE WESTERNMOST STRETCH OF RAILWAY THAT CONNECTED BRITISH COLUMBIA AND THE PACIFIC SEABOARD TO THE REST OF CANADA, THUS UNIFYING THE COUNTRY, WAS A STUPENDOUS FEAT OF ENGINEERING, "WEBBING PRAIRIES AND MOUNTAINS, REACHING OUT TO CITIES, FARMS, FORESTS, RANCHES AND MINES, SCATTERED OVER A MILLION SQUARE MILES."
BUT THOSE LAST 500 OR SO MILES WERE TREACHEROUSLY DIFFICULT TO BUILD THROUGH THE ROCKIES. IN 1881, A SYNDICATE OF SCOTTISH-CANADIAN BUSINESSMEN, THE CANADIAN PACIFIC RAILWAY COMPANY, HAD BEEN INCORPORATED, BUT THAT YEAR ONLY 131 MILES OF TRACKS WERE LAID.
THE ARRIVAL FROM THE UNITED STATES OF A NEW GENERAL MANAGER, WILLIAM VAN HORNE, NOT ONLY GOT THINGS MOVING, BUT WITHIN THE DECADE HE WAS OPENING HOTELS TO INSPIRE THE TRAVELING PUBLIC, ATTRACTING GUESTS FROM NORTH AMERICA AND BEYOND. THE RAILWAY NOW CONNECTED THE ROCKIES WITH THE ATLANTIC SEABOARD TOO, WHICH MEANT THAT CANADIAN PACIFIC STEAMSHIPS, WHICH SAILED "ON ALL THE WORLD'S SEVEN SEAS" COULD FERRY GUESTS "FROM ALL THE CONTINENTS" TO CANADIAN PACIFIC HOTELS, THE COLLABORATION "A GIGANTIC SYMBOL OF THE VISION, ENTERPRISE AND SPIRIT OF THE PEOPLE OF CANADA."

ABOVE: CANADIAN PACIFIC RAILWAY POSTER FROM AN OIL PASTEL BY ALFRED CROCKER LEIGHTON, CA. 1924. — OPPOSITE (INSET): POSTCARD PROMOTING THE SCENERY SURROUNDING THE TRACKS OF THE CANADIAN PACIFIC RAILWAY, CA. 1900.

The Origins of Canadian Spa Culture

In the winter of 1883–84, two brothers, William and Tom McCardell, and their friend, Frank McCabe, workers on the Canadian Pacific Railway, went prospecting for gold. After crossing the Alberta Bow River by raft, they came across a split in the rock through which hot steam was rising. Following it to its source, they came upon an underground pool of hot, sulphurous mineral-rich water fed by springs deep within the mountain. It was a find that was to have a major impact on the area.

Realising that people might want to pay to use the springs, they built a hut and began to charge visitors who came to bathe there. Although profitable, there was potential to develop the springs further. Lacking sufficient means to build, they took the idea to their boss, William Van Horne. Judging the springs to be "worth a million dollars," he bought the three men out for 675 dollars apiece and named the area Banff Hot Springs.

This was only the start. If Van Horne could persuade the Canadian government to designate the springs and their surroundings a national reserve, they could become a magnet for tourists prepared to travel long distances by train to bathe in the thermal waters and marvel at the scenery. So, he began to lobby the federal government.

Two years later, Canada's first nature reserve was created in November 1885, the result of Van Horne's campaigning and an early example of pressure brought by conservationists, backed by Canada's then prime minister, John A. Macdonald, to prevent commercial exploitation of a natural resource. In 1902, Banff became Canada's first National Park, a mountainous area that extended over more than 2,500 square miles of forest, glaciers, and ice fields, and home to grizzly bears, black bears, lynxes, mountain lions, wolverines, wolves, coyotes, elks, moose, deer, bighorn sheep, and hoary marmots.

Above: Underground pool of thermal water of Cave and Basin, Canadian historical site discovered in 1883. — Opposite (inset): Lantern slide showing early bathers in the Banff hot springs (external temperature around -30°C / -22° F).

"He who ascends to mountain-tops, shall find
The loftiest peaks most wrapt in clouds and snow;
He who surpasses or subdues mankind,
Must look down on the hate of those below.
Though high above the sun of glory glow,
And far beneath the earth and ocean spread,
Round him are icy rocks, and loudly blow
Contending tempests on his naked head,
And thus reward the toils which to those summits led."

Lord Byron
CHILDE HAROLD'S PILGRIMAGE, 1812.

In Search of the Sublime: An Alternative Grand Tour

THE CULT OF ROMANTICISM AND THE URGE AMONG EUROPEANS TO COMMUNE WITH NATURE AND CONTEMPLATE THE SUBLIME HAD BEEN GROWING SINCE THE END OF THE EIGHTEENTH CENTURY. INFLUENTIAL WRITERS LIKE LORD BYRON OR VICTOR HUGO WOULD TRAVEL TO THE ALPS AND PYRENEES MOUNTAINS AND SHARE THEIR FASCINATION WITH THE WORLD. "IT IS THE MOST MYSTERIOUS EDIFICE FROM THE MOST MYSTERIOUS OF ARCHITECTS; IT'S THE COLOSSEUM OF NATURE – IT'S GAVARNIE," READ VICTOR HUGO'S 1855 POEM *GOD* WHICH BROUGHT AN EVERGREEN FAME TO THE PYRENEAN CIRQUE. THE SWISS ALPS HAD BEEN A POPULAR DESTINATION AMONG THE ARISTOCRACY SINCE QUEEN VICTORIA SPENT A RESTORATIVE FIVE-WEEK HOLIDAY THERE IN 1868. ALTHOUGH AMERICA'S UPPER CLASSES ALSO LONGED FOR CLEAN AIR, HEALTH-GIVING WATERS AND SENSATIONAL SCENERY, EUROPE WAS A JOURNEY TOO FAR FOR MANY OF THEM. NOW ACCESSIBLE BY TRAIN AND OFFERING STATE-OF-THE-ART ACCOMMODATION, THE CANADIAN ROCKIES OFFERED AN IDEAL AND MUCH MORE CONVENIENT ALTERNATIVE.

ABOVE: LANTERN SLIDE SHOWING EARLY HIKERS AT THE LAKE OF THE HANGING GLACIER, CA. 1900. — OPPOSITE (INSET): *WANDERER ABOVE THE SEA OF FOG*, CASPAR DAVID FRIEDRICH, CA. 1818.

"What would you do with a magic carpet if one were lent you?
I ask because for a month we had a private car of our very own—
a trifling affair less than seventy foot long and thirty ton weight.
'You may find her useful,' said the donor casually, 'to knock about the country.
Hitch on to any train you choose and stop off where you choose.'
So she bore us over the [Canadian Pacific Railway]
from the Atlantic to the Pacific and back,
and when we had no more need of her,
vanished like the mango tree after the trick."

Rudyard Kipling
LETTERS OF TRAVEL, 1899.

By Royal Appointment
Princess Louise, an early influencer

Queen Victoria's sixth child and fourth daughter, Princess Louise, Duchess of Argyll (1848–1939), was the first member of the royal family to visit British Columbia, arriving in Victoria in 1882.
A talented artist, she had studied sculpture at the National Art Training School in London and was the first British princess to be educated at a public college.
Her mother had appointed her husband, the Marquess of Lorne, Governor General of Canada, then part of the British Empire, and Louise its Vice-Regal Consort. Their mission was, at least in part, "to arrest" Canada's "drifting into the Republic of the United States."
Lorne later traveled more widely through western Canada, writing a slim volume entitled *Our Railway to the Pacific* to promote the coming of the railway, not least for its potential to boost trade within the Empire. They proved a popular couple, participating enthusiastically in Canada's national sports: skating, tobogganing, and curling. They in turn loved their time there, especially the weeks spent painting and fishing by Quebec's Cascapédia River. They stayed in a log cabin named Lorne Cottage—said to have been the first prefabricated home in Canada—and sent boxes of iced salmon back to Queen Victoria in England, where the fish arrived "cold, pink and perfect."
For Louise, this was a time of both exceptional freedom and influence. She had made it her role to promote the arts in Canada, through institutions such as the National Gallery of Canada in Ottawa and the Royal Canadian Academy of Arts, both of which she played a part in establishing. So, like her husband, she also became a figurehead. As Lorne acknowledged in a speech he made in Halifax, "Although the sons of the sovereign have before this day visited these shores, this is the first occasion on which a daughter of the reigning house has seen the New World."
Indeed, the princess gave her name to Lake Louise and in turn the hotel that was built on its shore. But in 1880, their visit was cut short when she suffered a concussion and injured her ear in a sleighing accident, during which she was dragged 1,300 feet. Seeking a warmer climate in which to convalesce, she sailed to Bermuda, where two years later another palatial hotel was named in her honor, the Hamilton Princess. Like Chateau Lake Louise, it too is now a Fairmont hotel.

Opposite: *View from the Window of the Governor-General's Quarters, the Citadel, Quebec* (detail), a watercolor by H.R.H. the Princess Louise (above), painted in 1882 just a few hundred yards north of the promontory where Château Frontenac's construction would start ten years later.

Picture This: The Role of the Artist

By 1886, William Van Horne, then general manager of the now-complete Canadian Pacific Railway, realised that if visitors (and settlers) were to come to Western Canada, the company would need to promote the area. An accomplished amateur artist, who went on to collect works by El Greco, Mary Cassatt, Cézanne, Pissarro, and Toulouse-Lautrec, as well as a connoisseur of Japanese ceramics, Van Horne saw art as means to build his brand.

By sponsoring established painters, such as Lucius O'Brien, then president of the Royal Canadian Academy of Arts, along with John Arthur Fraser, John Colin Forbes, Frederic Marlett Bell-Smith, and Thomas Mower Martin, to travel west to paint the dramatic wildernesses of the Rockies, public curiosity was piqued when their work was exhibited, not just in Canada but internationally.

Esteemed foreign landscape artists such as the German-American Albert Bierstadt then began to approach the company, proposing tours. (Bierstadt was invited to bring along his wife, her maid, and a party of friends from Europe, though in the end he made his journey with just one companion.) In return for free first-class accommodation on its trains and at its hotels, the Canadian Pacific Railway had first refusal on buying the works they produced and retained the right to use them for promotional purposes.

Above: *Sunrise at Glacier Station*, painting by Albert Bierstadt, 1889. — Opposite: *Summit Lake near Lenchoile, Bow River* (detail), watercolor by John A. Fraser, 1886.

The Power of Photographs, Still and Moving

THE 1880S SAW TREMENDOUS DEVELOPMENTS IN PHOTOGRAPHY. (KODAK'S FIRST BOX CAMERA WAS LAUNCHED IN 1888, WITH THE SLOGAN: "YOU PRESS THE BUTTON, WE DO THE REST.") AND THE EVER-INNOVATIVE WILLIAM VAN HORNE SAW THE MEDIUM AS ANOTHER WAY THROUGH WHICH HE COULD PROMOTE THE CANADIAN PACIFIC RAILWAY, BY MEANS NOT JUST OF IMAGERY, BUT MAGIC LANTERN SHOWS, AN EARLY PRECURSOR OF CINEMA.

WILLIAM NOTMAN, A SCOT WHO HAD EMIGRATED TO CANADA IN 1856 AND ESTABLISHED A SUCCESSFUL STUDIO IN MONTREAL, WAS HIRED BY THE COMPANY TO SUPPLY PHOTOGRAPHS FOR ITS PROMOTIONAL PUBLICATIONS, THOUGH, RATHER THAN TRAVEL HIMSELF, HE SENT HIS SON, WILLIAM MCFARLANE NOTMAN, WHO MADE EIGHT TRIPS ON THE RAILWAY BETWEEN 1884 AND 1909. AS WITH THE ARTISTS WHO HAD BEEN INVITED TO PAINT THE LANDSCAPE, HE ENJOYED FREE TRAVEL AND LODGING, AS WELL AS HIS OWN RAIL CAR THAT HAD BEEN ADAPTED TO ACCOMMODATE A DARKROOM SO THAT HE COULD DEVELOP HIS PLATES AND MAKE PRINTS EN ROUTE.

TO MAKE THE IMAGES AN EVEN MORE COMPELLING ADVERTISEMENT FOR CANADA'S BIG COUNTRY, VAN HORNE HAD THEM TINTED, EMPLOYING ARTISTS AS RENOWNED AS JOHN ARTHUR FRASER, WHO WORKED FOR NOTMAN AND LATER BECAME HIS BUSINESS PARTNER, TO COLOR THE PRINTS.

PERHAPS THE MOST CELEBRATED PHOTOGRAPHER TO CAPTURE THE CANADIAN ROCKIES WAS BYRON HARMON, WHO MOVED TO BANFF AND IN 1906 BECAME THE OFFICIAL PHOTOGRAPHER OF THE ALPINE CLUB OF CANADA (SEE P.20-21).

THREE CLIMBERS ON A GLACIER, LAKE OF THE HANGING GLACIER, HAND-COLORIZED PHOTOGRAPH BY BYRON HARMON, CA. 1900. — RIGHT: *BYRON HARMON AND HIS CAMERA ON CLIFF*, BANFF, PHOTOGRAPH NEGATIVE, CA. 1900.

PRIS TINE THRILLS

"The tourist never had such an opportunity to witness anything half so grand or impressive as the Rocky passes through which the lines run."

The Marquess of Lorne
GOVERNOR GENERAL OF CANADA AND QUEEN VICTORIA'S SON-IN-LAW

"Lake Louise,
the hotel for outdoor adventurers
and alpinists."

William Van Horne

The Diamond in the Wilderness
Fairmont Chateau Lake Louise

"As God is my judge, I never in all my exploration saw such a matchless scene," exclaimed Thomas Wilson, an employee of the Canadian Pacific Railway, where he was charged with packing supplies and equipment for the construction team on Kicking Horse Pass, and who became the first European to see what he called the Emerald Lake. This was later named Lake Louise, after Princess Louise, Vice-Regal Consort of Canada.
The year was 1882, and Wilson was using his vacation to explore the area in the company of some Iyahe Nakoda (or Stoney), the indigenous people of Western Canada. One night, as they camped in the mountains, in what is now Banff National Park, he heard the distant roar of an avalanche. Communicating using his scant command of their language, he learned that the noise was coming from "snow mountains above the lake of little fishes."
The next day, he set out on horseback with two guides to find the "blue and green waters" of that lake. Word of his "discovery" reached Van Horne, who thought it the perfect site for "a hotel for the outdoor adventurer and alpinist."
In 1890, the first hotel, a single-story log cabin opened as the Chalet Lake Louise, the first of a succession of buildings—latterly châteaux rather than chalets—to have stood here. It became so popular that the present hotel runs with more than 500 rooms and suites.

Above: Two women enjoy the view from the lounge of Chateau Lake Louise, Hand-tinted slide lantern, ca. 1920. — Opposite (inset): Interior of a restaurant wagon, Etching by John Henry Walker, ca. 1890.

"If one wishes a still higher climb, one can venture across Abbot Pass (9,000 feet above sea level) and down the Victoria glacier to Lake Louise.

But this is only safe with an experienced Swiss guide, as the pass is frequently traversed by avalanches on its northern side."

Mary Vaux Walcott
CANADIAN ALPINE JOURNAL, 1907.

The Mountains Were There to Be Climbed

THE FIRST SUCCESSFUL ASCENT OF THE MATTERHORN IN THE SWISS ALPS MAY HAVE ENDED IN TRAGEDY FOR FOUR MEMBERS OF THE TEAM, BUT IT SPARKED A FASHION FOR ALPINISM OR MOUNTAINEERING AS AN ADVENTUROUS LEISURE ACTIVITY. ONCE THE COMPLETION OF THE CANADIAN PACIFIC RAILWAY HAD MADE THE CANADIAN ROCKIES ACCESSIBLE, EUROPEAN AND AMERICAN CLIMBERS, MEMBERS OF LONDON'S ALPINE CLUB, OR THE APPALACHIAN MOUNTAINEERING CLUB OF BOSTON, BEGAN TO TRAVEL TO CANADA, DETERMINED TO SCALE PEAKS IN THE ROCKIES AND THE SELKIRK RANGE IN BRITISH COLUMBIA. INDEED, EDWARD WHYMPER, THE ENGLISH MOUNTAINEER WHO LED THE CONQUEST OF THE MATTERHORN, DECLARED THE CANADIAN ROCKIES "FIFTY SWITZERLANDS IN ONE."
BUT THESE MOUNTAINS WERE MOSTLY UNCONQUERED BY CLIMBERS. FOLLOWING A FATAL CLIMBING ACCIDENT ON MOUNT LEFROY NEAR LAKE LOUISE IN 1896, CLIMBERS IN THE AREA BEGAN TO SEEK THE SERVICES OF GUIDES. CONSCIOUS OF THIS AND CONCERNED THAT ITS GUESTS SHOULD NOT TAKE UNNECESSARY RISKS, THE CANADIAN PACIFIC RAILWAY BEGAN TO RECRUIT ITS FIRST PROFESSIONAL GUIDES, AND, IN 1899, CHRISTIAN HAESLER AND EDWARD FEUZ, PICTURED WITH A CLIENT IN THE ROCKIES, NEAR LAKE LOUISE, LEFT THEIR NATIVE INTERLAKEN IN SWITZERLAND TO JOIN ITS STAFF.
OVER THE NEXT HALF-CENTURY, THE CANADIAN PACIFIC RAILWAY EMPLOYED ABOUT THIRTY-FIVE SWISS MOUNTAINEERS, AS WELL AS OTHERS FROM AUSTRIA AND CANADA, ON SEASONAL CONTRACTS TO KEEP ITS CLIENTS SAFE. ALL OF THEM WERE ALSO SKIERS (AND AFTER 1940, CERTIFIED SKI INSTRUCTORS), AND PLAYED A SIGNIFICANT ROLE IN INTRODUCING SKIING TO CANADA AND IN DEVELOPING IT AS A RECREATIONAL SPORT, NOT LEAST IN THEIR CREATION OF A RELIABLE MOUNTAIN SAFETY SYSTEM.

OPPOSITE: WOMEN IN BATHING SUITS ON THE SMALL 'ICEBERG' OF A CANADIAN ROCKIES GLACIAL LAKE, LANTERN SLIDE, CA. 1930. — ABOVE: SWISS GUIDE EDWARD FEUZ WITH THE WIFE OF NEW YORK'S FIRE CHIEF ON SADDLEBACK, CA. 1910. — LEFT: BEAR CUBS BY THE EXPLORER MARY SCHÄFFER WARREN, LANTERN SLIDE, CA. 1900.

32 — 33

> "If Lake Louise is a pearl,
> Maligne is the entire pearl necklace [...].
> There burst upon us [...] the finest view
> any of us had ever beheld in the Rockies.
> This was a tremendous assertion,
> for of that band of six of us,
> we all knew many valleys in that country,
> and each counted his miles of travel
> through them by the thousands."
>
> *Mary Schäffer Warren*
> AFTER HER EXPLORATION OF MALIGNE LAKE BY HORSE AND RAFT, 1908.

El Dorado for Naturalists and Two Pioneering Women

MARY VAUX WALCOTT (1860–1940) WAS AMONGST THE CANADIAN PACIFIC RAILWAY'S VERY FIRST PASSENGERS. SHE FIRST JOINED THE CANADIAN ROCKIES FROM PHILADELPHIA AS EARLY AS 1887, JUST A FEW MONTHS AFTER THE CANADIAN PACIFIC RAILWAY WAS INAUGURATED. TOGETHER WITH HER FATHER AND BROTHERS, SHE WOULD STAY IN THEIR HOTEL, GLACIER HOUSE, NEWLY OPENED BESIDES THE TRACKS AND NO LONGER EXISTS TODAY.

MESMERISED BY THE ILLECILLEWAET GLACIER NEARBY, SHE STARTED TO PHOTOGRAPH, SKETCH, AND MEASURE THE GLACIERS IN THE ROCKIES, PROVIDING TODAY'S SCIENTISTS WITH THE MOST PRECIOUS CLIMATE RECORDS. TO DEVELOP THE NEGATIVES OF HER LARGE AND HEAVY CAMERAS, MARY WOULD OFTEN USE THE HOTEL'S CLOSETS AS A DARKROOM.

FROM THE THEN-CALLED CHALET LAKE LOUISE, WHICH SHE PHOTOGRAPHED AS WELL, SHE MEASURED THE VICTORIA GLACIER SEVERAL YEARS IN A ROW. "DURING THE PAST TEN YEARS, I HAVE SPENT FROM THREE TO FOUR MONTHS EACH SEASON IN THE CANADIAN ROCKIES, COVERING IN ALL MORE THAN 5,000 MILES ON MOUNTAIN TRAILS."

VAUX WALCOTT'S PHOTOGRAPHS AND DISCOVERIES WERE PUBLISHED IN NUMEROUS CANADIAN PACIFIC RAILROAD PAMPHLETS TO PROMOTE TOURISM IN THE AREA. NICKNAMED "THE AUDUBON OF BOTANY", VAUX WALCOTT WAS ALSO AN ACCOMPLISHED ARTIST WITH A KEEN INTEREST AND KNOWLEDGE OF FLORA. HER FIVE-VOLUME WORK OF REFERENCE, *NORTH AMERICAN WILD FLOWERS*, SPONSORED BY THE CANADIAN PACIFIC RAILWAY, WAS PUBLISHED IN THE 1920S BY THE SMITHSONIAN INSTITUTION.

VAUX WALCOTT 'S DEAR FRIEND, MARY SCHÄFFER WARREN (1861–1939), WAS ANOTHER HIGHLY SKILLED BOTANICAL ARTIST, PHOTOGRAPHER, AND NATURALIST USING CHALET LAKE LOUISE AS A BASE CAMP. SHE WAS THE FIRST EUROPEAN-AMERICAN TO LAY EYES ON MALIGNE LAKE IN THE JASPER NATIONAL PARK IN 1908, WHICH SHE LATER SURVEYED FOR THE GEOGRAPHICAL BOARD OF CANADA. HAVING CARRIED THE ELEMENTS OF A RAFT ON HORSEBACK THROUGH THE MOUNTAINS, SHE COULD EXPLORE THE BORDERS OF MALIGNE LAKE FROM THE WATER TO COLLECT BOTANICAL SAMPLES (OPPOSITE).

HER BOOK *IN THE HEART OF THE CANADIAN ROCKIES WITH HORSE AND CAMERA*, IS AN ACCOUNT OF HER EXPLORATIONS ACCOMPANIED BY LANTERN SLIDES WHICH SHE TOOK, COLLECTED, AND THEN TINTED BY HAND.

ABOVE: MARY SCHÄFFER WARREN'S *PRAIRIE CROCUS* HAND-TINTED LANTERN SLIDE, CA. 1900 & CALYPSO ORCHID WATERCOLOR, 1891. — OPPOSITE: *BUILDING A RAFT AT MOUTH OF MALIGNE LAKE*, HAND-TINTED LANTERN SLIDE FROM MARY SCHÄFFER WARREN'S DISCOVERY EXPEDITION IN 1908.

"The glaciers must be measured, and I shall hope to use the camera seriously, and get all I can. Last summer's work was such a disappointment in photographic results."

Mary Vaux Walcott
IN A LETTER TO CHARLES WALCOTT, 1912.

WILD WONDERS

Photograph from Agathe Bernard's documentary *Carving Landscapes*, in which she retraces 100 years later Mary Vaulx's priceless measurements of the glaciers, 2018.

"Like an eagle in his eyrie, high above Bow Valley, you lounge on sunny terraces
and let your spirits soar to the shining peaks that kiss the radiant skies. [...]

Hours you could dream here,
watching the orchid and rose cloud nymphs
dance across the gigantic stage and tint the mighty back drop of the Fairholme range."

BANFF SPRING ADVERTISING PAMPHLET, 1932.

A Castle in the Wild
BANFF SPRINGS HOTEL

WHEN IT OPENED, THE BANFF HOT SPRINGS HOTEL DREW WATER DIRECTLY FROM THE GEOTHERMAL SPRINGS TO FILL ITS SWIMMING POOL AND SUPPLY THE ROOMS IN ITS SANATORIUM WHERE THE CANADIAN PACIFIC RAILWAY'S DOCTOR, ROBERT GEORGE BRETT, TREATED VISITORS WITH ITS MINERAL-RICH WATERS, HERALDING THE BIRTH OF BALNEOLOGY IN CANADA.

THE WATER IN ITS SPA IS NO LONGER DRAWN DIRECTLY FROM THE EARTH. BUT SINCE THE HOTEL'S DEVELOPMENT IN THE EARLY 1990S OF A MOUNTAIN HERITAGE PROGRAM TO DEMONSTRATE ITS RESPONSIBILITY TOWARD PROTECTING AND SHARING THE NATURAL AND CULTURAL HERITAGE OF THE BANFF NATIONAL PARK, IT HAS TAKEN A NUMBER OF STEPS TO REDUCE ITS CARBON EMISSIONS AND PROTECT ITS ENVIRONMENT ABOVE AND BEYOND THE NOW STANDARD CONSERVATION MEASURES IT PIONEERED.

TODAY, FOR EXAMPLE, HEAT IN ITS OUTDOOR SWIMMING POOL IS RETAINED THANKS TO A LIQUID POOL COVER, AN INVISIBLE LAYER JUST ONE MOLECULE THICK THAT NEVERTHELESS BOTH PREVENTS EVAPORATION AND REDUCES THE RATE AT WHICH TEMPERATURE CHILLS. IT ALSO USES OUTDOOR AMBIENT TEMPERATURES TO COOL ITS CHILLED WATER SYSTEM, WHICH IT ESTIMATES SAVES IT ALMOST 370,000 KILOWATT-HOURS OF ENERGY A YEAR.

ABOVE: WAITER SERVING TEA ON THE TERRACE OVERLOOKING THE BOW VALLEY, CA. 1920. — OPPOSITE (INSET): PHOTOGRAPH OF THE BANFF SPRINGS HOTEL, CA. 1924.

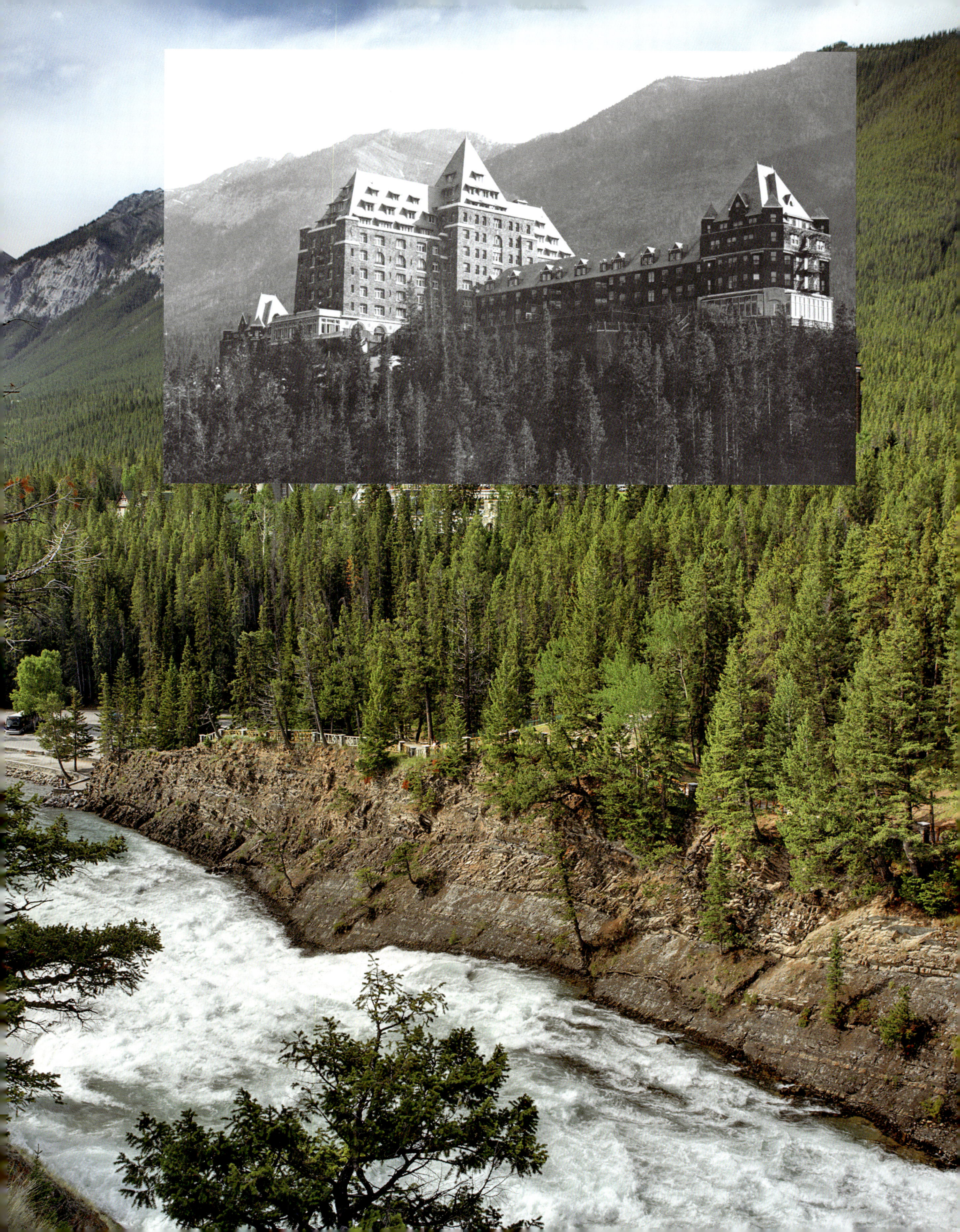

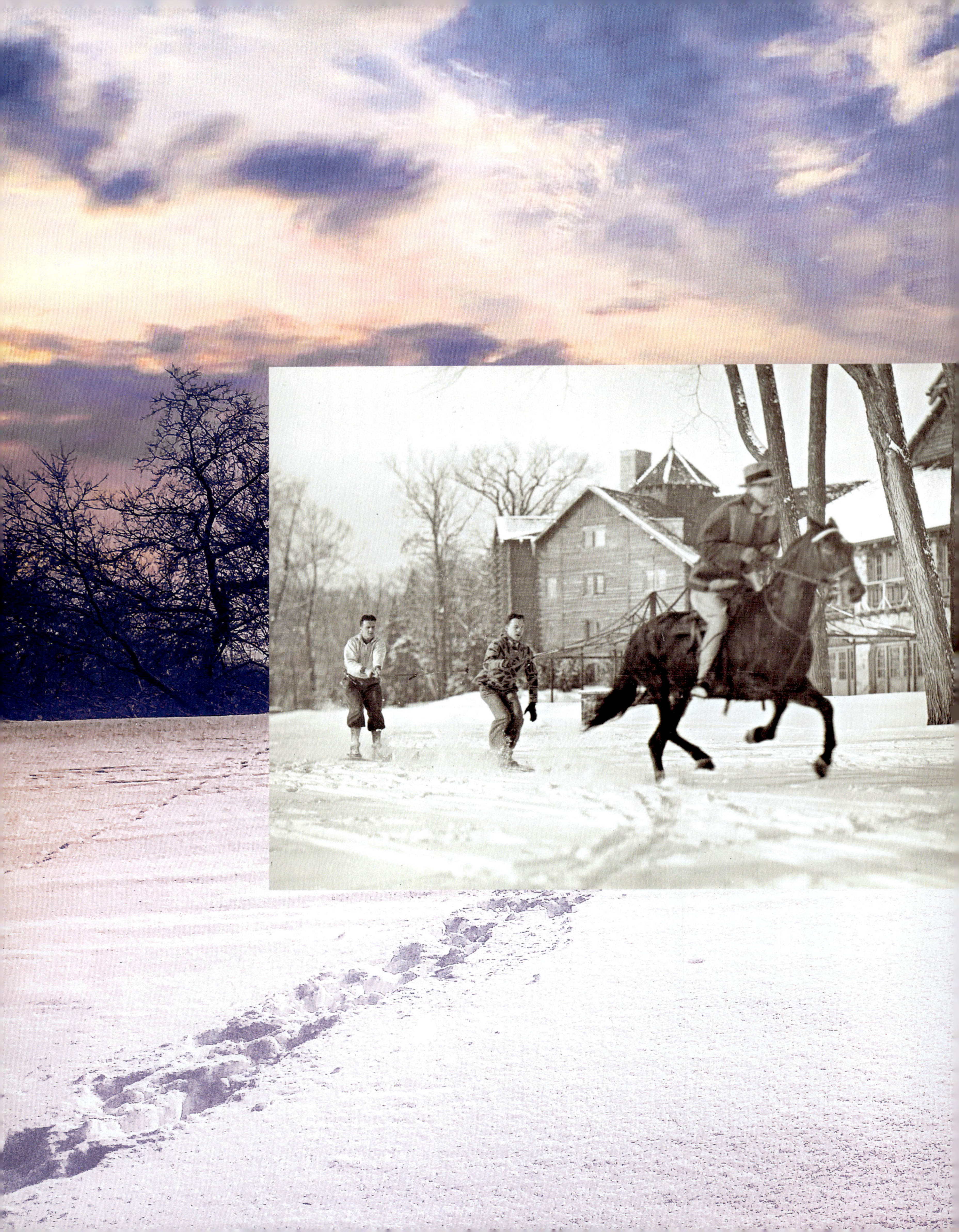

The Largest Log Cabin in the World
Fairmont Château Montebello

Halfway between the cities of Ottawa and Montreal on the banks of the mighty Ottawa River (hence its yacht club), Château Montebello was built by a team of 3,500 men in just four months, opening in 1930, the culmination of an ambition by the Swiss-American entrepreneur, Harold M. Saddlemire, to create what he called Lucerne in Quebec.

Incorporating more than 10,000 cedar logs and half a million hand-cut cedar shingles on its roof (along with a certain amount of granite, not least for its fireplaces), the star-shaped building is still probably the largest log cabin in the world. Even the swimming pool is encased in a timber structure.

Montebello started life as the Seigniory Club, a private members' club with a now-fabled golf course, it went on to become a hotel hosting a succession of world leaders, among them Helmut Schmidt, François Mitterrand, Margaret Thatcher, Prince Rainier III and Princess Grace of Monaco, Emperor Akihito and, among a handful of US presidents, Harry S. Truman, who praised the spectacular trout fishing.

Opposite (inset): Winter sports at the Seigniory included high-speed, horse-powered skijoring, ca. 1930. — Above: Château Montebello's seventy-five-foot-long indoor swimming pool is housed in a separate log cabin linked in the winter to the hotel by a tunnel.

A Royal Retreat
FAIRMONT JASPER PARK LODGE

OVERLOOKING LAC BEAUVERT IN JASPER NATIONAL PARK, JASPER PARK LODGE BEGAN AS AN ENCAMPMENT OF TEN TENTS ESTABLISHED BY THE GRAND TRUNK PACIFIC RAILWAY, WHICH CONNECTED WINNIPEG WITH THE PACIFIC PORT OF PRINCE RUPERT. IT DIDN'T THRIVE AND THE RAIL COMPANY WENT BUST, BUT ITS ASSETS WERE ACQUIRED BY THE GRAND NATIONAL RAILWAY, WHICH REPLACED THE TENTS WITH EIGHT LARGE LOG CABINS, WHICH OPENED IN 1923.

THERE FOLLOWED DOZENS OF NEW BUILDINGS AND CABINS THAT DOT THE 700-ACRE SITE, NOT LEAST THE OUTLOOK, A SECLUDED CHALET WHERE KING GEORGE VI AND HIS WIFE, QUEEN ELIZABETH (ABOVE, LEFT), STAYED DURING THEIR OFFICIAL TOUR OF CANADA IN 1939. BOTH THEIR DAUGHTERS, QUEEN ELIZABETH II AND PRINCESS MARGARET, HAVE STAYED THERE SUBSEQUENTLY TOO, AS RECENTLY AS 2005 IN QUEEN ELIZABETH II'S CASE.

RECONSTRUCTED ACCORDING TO ITS ORIGINAL 1930 PLANS (BUT BETTER INSULATED AND MORE COMFORTABLE), IT REMAINS A RUSTICALLY STYLED SIX-BEDROOM LOG CABIN, WITH A FOOTPRINT OF 6,000 SQUARE FEET, THAT STANDS ALONE NEAR THE SOUTHERN TIP OF A PENINSULA THAT EXTENDS INTO LAC BEAUVERT.

AND OF COURSE, THE SERVICE REMAINS FIT FOR ROYALTY. BEARS, HOWEVER, ARE NO LONGER ADMITTED AND FEEDING THEM IS FORBIDDEN, THOUGH THIS POPULAR POSTCARD (ABOVE, RIGHT), DATING BACK TO 1941 AND CAPTIONED "ROOM SERVICE" STILL RAISES A SMILE.

OPPOSITE (INSET): POSTCARD OF A DEER ON GROUNDS OF JASPER PARK LODGE, CA. 1930.

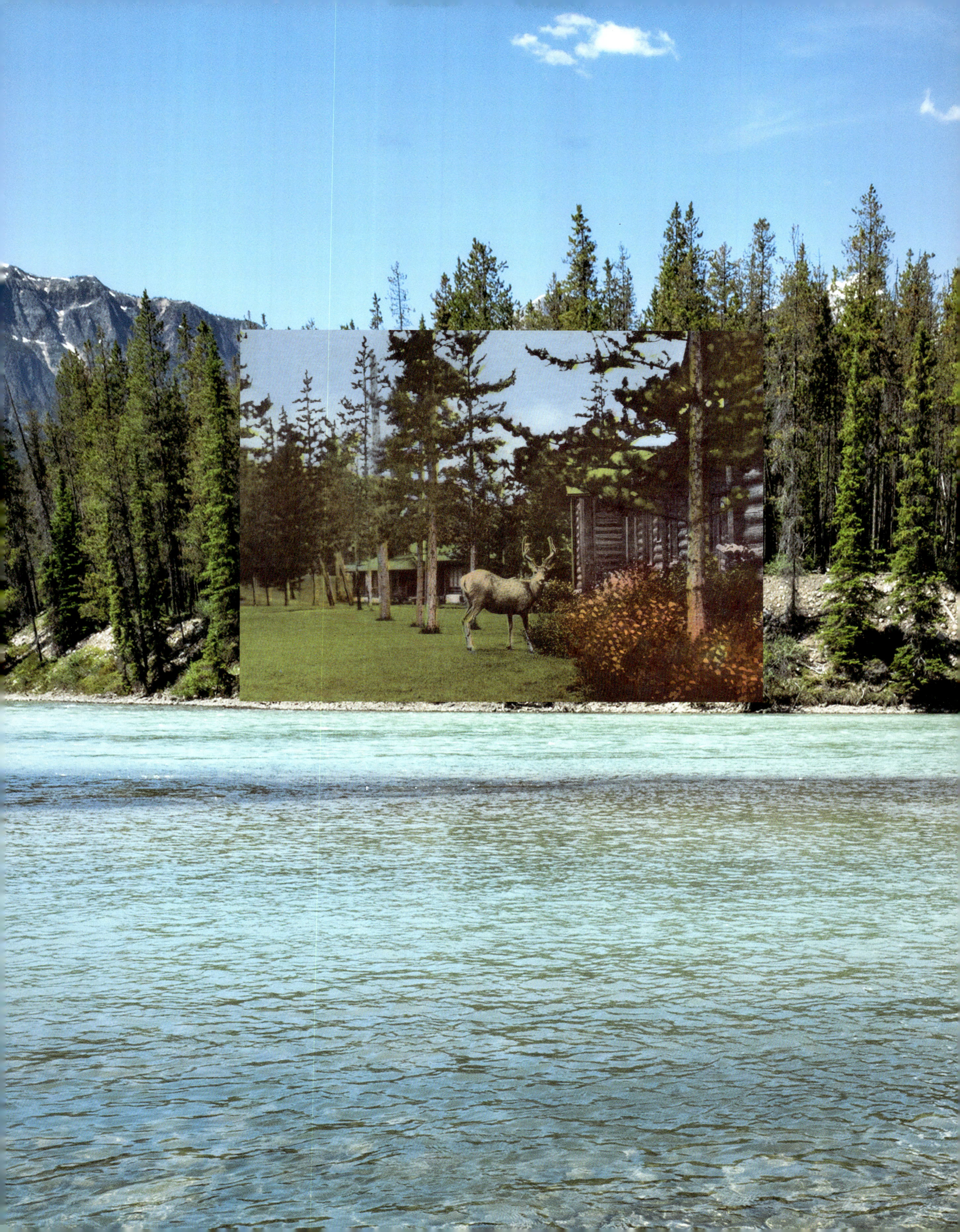

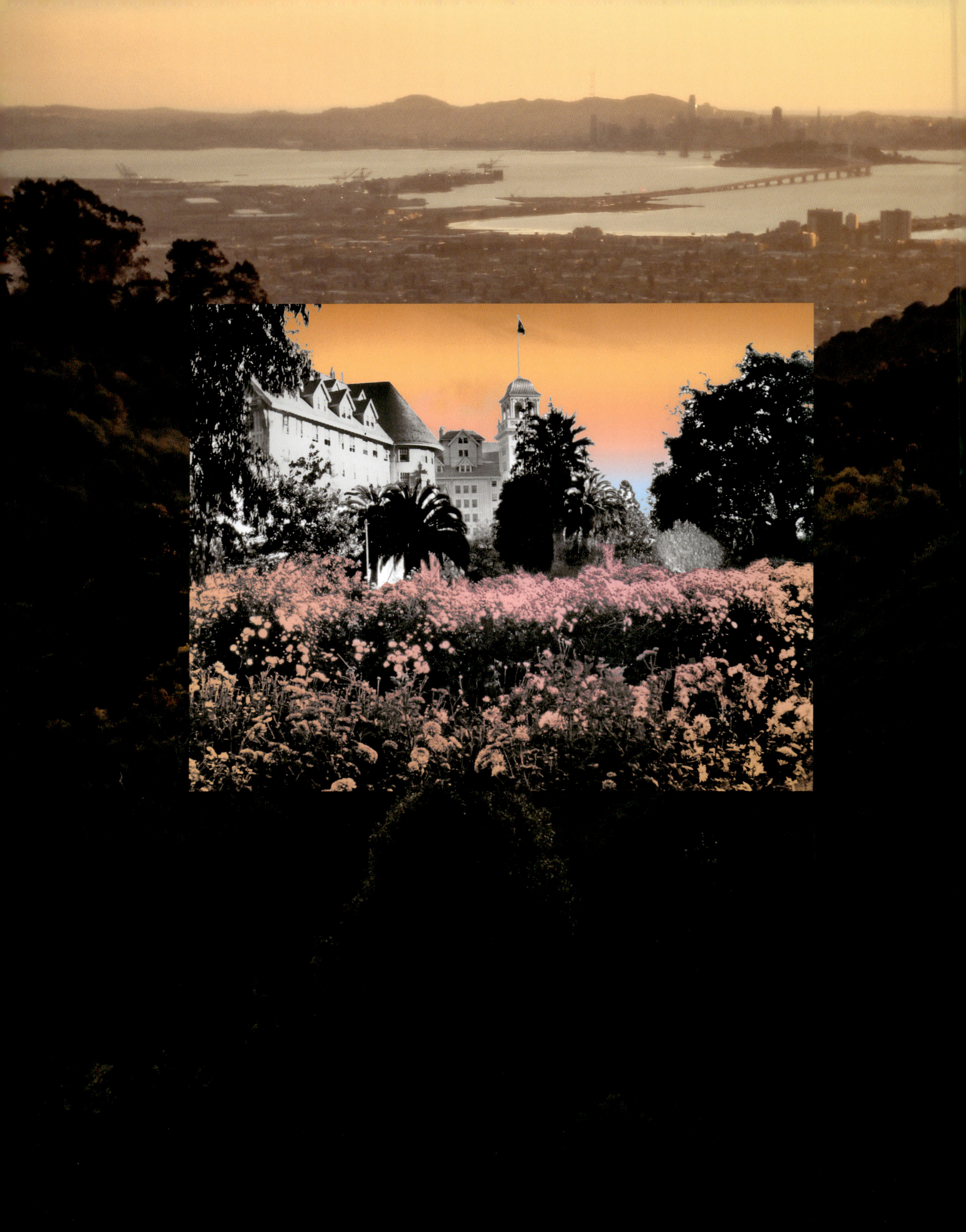

"One of the few hotels in the world with warmth, character and charm."

Frank Lloyd Wright

The White Castle on the Hill
Claremont Club & Spa, A Fairmont Hotel, Berkeley, California

Like the very first Fairmont in San Francisco, the Claremont Hotel, twelve miles northeast across the bay in Berkeley, was financed from the proceeds of a lucky strike during the gold rush. It stands on an estate originally developed by a farmer from Kansas, whose wife dreamed of living in what she imagined an English castle would be. But the castle burned down, the estate was sold, and the site acquired by another former miner, whose ambition was to build a resort hotel into whose lobby trains would run directly. Sadly, that is no longer the case. But until 1958, the Transbay Key railway line (later the E line) ran past what were the hotel's tennis courts (and is now the Berkeley Tennis Club) right to the steps of the main hotel. (Today the hotel has its own tennis club, with ten courts, on another part of its estate.)

When the Claremont Club finally opened in 1915, the present property, which sits amid twenty-two rolling acres and looks toward the Golden Gate Bridge, was the largest hotel on the Pacific, a development so substantial that it incorporated a school and its own radio station.

The only disincentive to staying there was its lack of a licence to serve alcohol. Even after prohibition its proximity to the Berkeley campus of the University of California meant the sale of liquor was banned—at least until 1936, when an enterprising student calculated that the distance from the bar to the college was actually over a mile, so the ordinance did not apply. She was rewarded with free cocktails for the rest of her life.

Built atop the Berkeley Hills, overlooking the cities of Oakland and Berkeley, the Claremont Hotel boasts the most breathtaking panoramas over the Golden Gate and San Francisco's iconic bay.

Wellness in Wine Country
Fairmont Sonoma Mission Inn & Spa

In 1895, drilling a well on the land developed in the 1840s as the Agua Rica Farm, Captain H.E. Boyes discovered a very promising 112-degree water spring. Five years later, he built the Boyes Hot Springs Hotel around it. The fame of its geothermal waters quickly turned the destination into the most glamorous hot mineral resort in California. By 1920, wealthy guests could even reach Sonoma via its own railroad station.
In 1923, however, a fire started by a beekeeper destroyed the hotel, which was rebuilt four years later as the Sonoma Mission Inn, "an architecturally accurate replica of a California mission" as described by its architects. Constructed at a cost of 600,000 dollars, it was luxurious and so popular in its early days that it could command a room rate of 7.50 dollars. (The going rate at its neighboring properties was nearer one dollar a night.)
But the Mission Inn did not survive the Depression, and during World War II it became a rest home for military personnel serving in the Pacific. Sold after the war, however, it "underwent extensive remodeling and redecorating," according to a front-page splash in the Californian newspaper *The Press Democrat*, and was transformed into such sophisticated fitness facilities that the San Francisco Seals and Chicago Cubs baseball teams came here for their spring training.
Today, its hot spring still feeds the hotel's Willow Stream Spa.

Above: "Boating at Boyes Hot Springs" postcard, 1912. — Opposite (inset): "Beautiful Sonoma Mission Inn in the Valley of the Moon" postcard, ca. 1930.

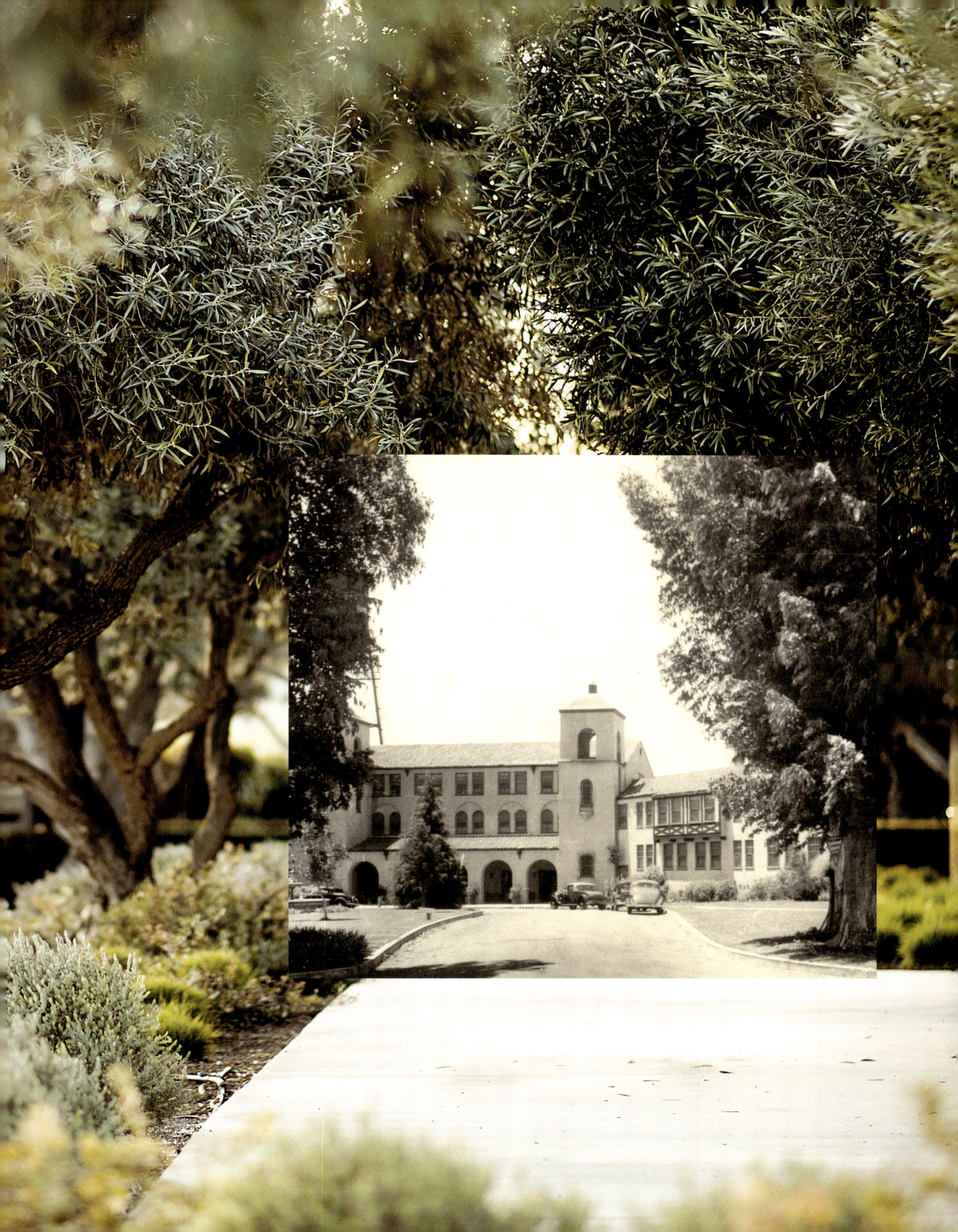

AL FRESCO LUXURY

APERITIFS ON THE ICE RINK AT CHÂTEAU FRONTENAC, QUEBEC, IN THE EARLY 1960S

The Flourishing of Canadian Winter Sports

By the 1930s, Château Montebello in Quebec had the largest winter-sports complex in Canada, a world-class facility designed by some of the biggest names in the business. A bobsleigh run had been created by the German engineer Stanislaus Zentzytzki, who had designed the runs for the Winter Olympics at Lake Placid in New York State in 1932 and at Garmisch-Partenkirchen in Bavaria. The 300-feet ski jump (top) was designed by the Norwegian ski champion Herman "Jackrabbit" Smith-Johannsen, who is also credited with introducing cross-country skiing to Canada. There are, to this day, indoor and outdoor skating rinks too. The figure skater pictured right is executing an arabesque spiral in Banff, ca. 1935.
Direct heir of Lake Louise, the Fairmont Chateau Whistler (middle) was built in 1989 seventy-five miles north of Vancouver. Crowned top Ski Resort in North America by both Condé Nast Traveler and Skiing magazine, the hotel stands at the doorstep of Whistler-Blackcomb, one of the finest ski resorts in North America: two side-by-side majestic mountains and an average snowfall of thirty feet per year.
Fairmont Tremblant (left) was built in 1996 below the Mont-Tremblant National Park. The Canadian Pacific Railway had promoted this accessible area in the Quebec province as early as 1915. The company had indeed built a station in pure rustic style in Mont-Tremblant and was encouraging tourism in the surroundings. "In the autumn, the woods about shelter deer and moose [...] The lake suddenly glitters into view, stretching for seven miles its surface studded with dark green islands. Here the beauty of the mountains cannot be surpassed with Mont-Tremblant towering majestically over all," read *The Montreal and the Laurentians* Canadian Pacific Railway Pamphlet, ca. 1915.

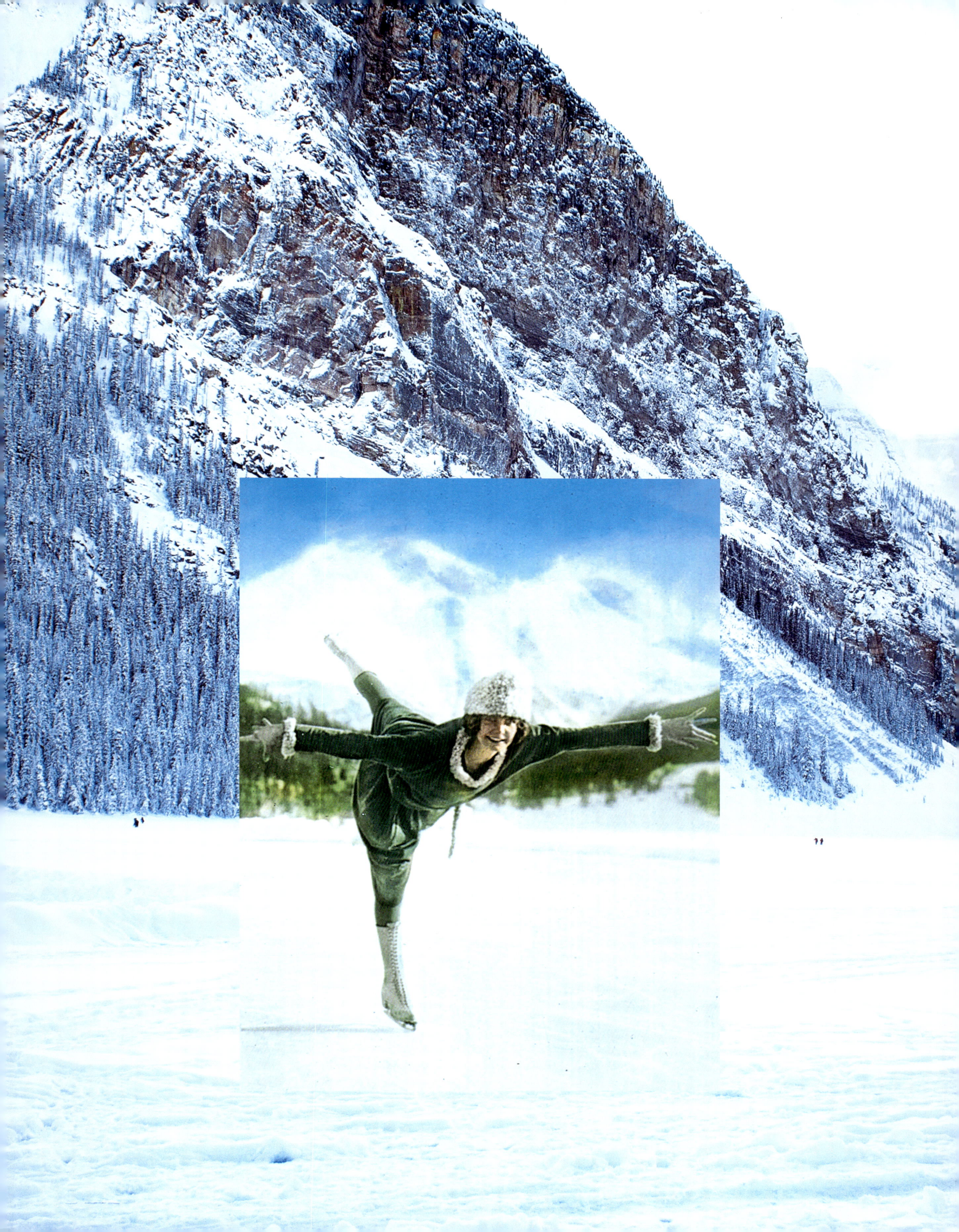

Panoramic Golf Courses

Born in Toronto in 1893 to Scottish immigrant parents, Stanley Thompson grew up a keen golfer, spending his spare time caddying at the Toronto Golf Club. During World War I, he served in Europe with the Canadian Expeditionary Force. Periods of leave were few, but he was able to travel to Great Britain and visit its renowned golf courses, places such as St. Andrews in Scotland, the fabled "home of golf."
Returning to Canada after the war, he resolved to become a designer of golf courses, and among the greatest he configured are those at Banff Springs—which opened in 1929 and was reportedly the first course to cost a million dollars—and Jasper Park Lodge (opposite, inset). Both are notable for what was called the "natural artistry" with which he planned and oriented the fairways and greens to focus on and complement the dramatic landscape including its resident bears!
But Thompson, who also designed the course at Château Montebello in Quebec, was not the only exceptional golf-course architect working in Canada.
Born in 1880, Herbert Strong was an English golfer, who finished ninth in the US Open in 1913. In the mid-1920s, he designed the 27-hole court at Le Manoir Richelieu, which William Howard Taft, the 27th President of the United States, opened in 1925. Given the constraints of the undulating site, where the elevation rises by more than 400 feet, it's a remarkable achievement.
Today, guests at Fairmont hotels have access to some of the most beautiful golf courses in the world, from the Club de Golf Murray Bay at La Malbaie, Charlevoix (P.62), the third-oldest course in North America, to the famously challenging Par 72 Montgomerie Links Golf Course at Carton House in Ireland (top), named after Colin Montgomerie (who designed it), host of three Irish Opens, and visible for miles, thanks to its Prospect Tower. Fairmont St. Andrews Bay (bottom), a 520-acre estate on the east coast of Scotland, is home to two spectacular links courses, the world-famous Torrance championship course, designed by Sam Torrance; and the fractionally shorter Kittocks course, designed by Bruce Devlin with assistance from Gene Sarazen. Not only is Mount Kenya Safari Club's Golf Course (opposite, background) located at the foot of the highest summit in Kenya, and second highest in Africa, its course is bisected by the Equator. Golfers cross from the Northern to the Southern Hemisphere surrounded by the most stunning view.

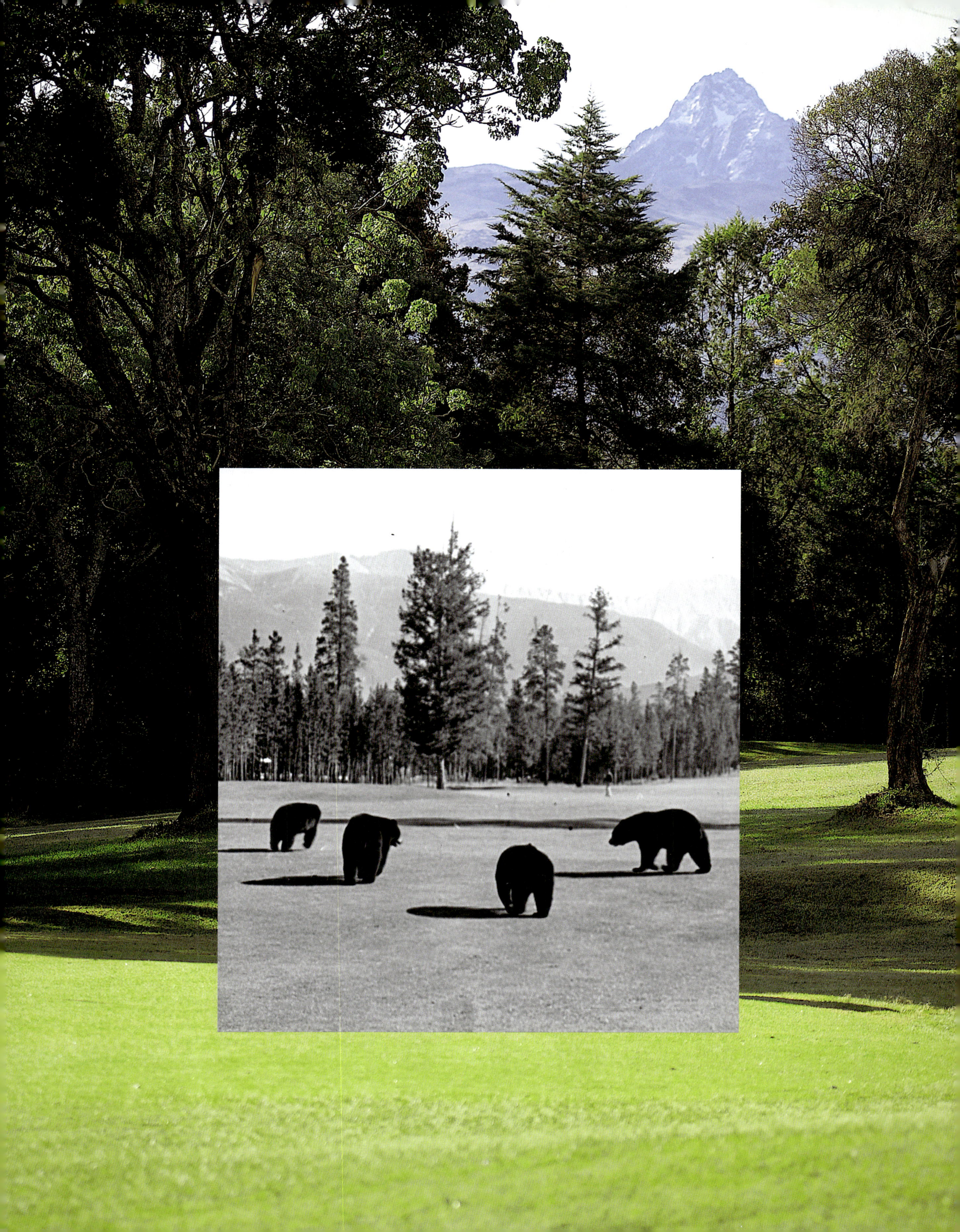

Sensational Swimming Pools

In June 1925, the Empress hotel, which had opened in Victoria on Vancouver Island in 1908, unveiled its Crystal Garden. This was a vast conservatory inspired by London's Crystal Palace, enclosing luxuriant gardens, a dance floor, gymnasium, concert hall, and tearoom. Its glory, however, was its heated saltwater swimming pool, then the largest in the British Empire, which contained more than 250,000 gallons of water, which flowed from the ocean via the laundry, where it was warmed by its boilers.

The following year, Chateau Lake Louise opened a pool (opposite, inset) that, at 100 by 40 feet, was filled with water from nearby Lake Agnes (opposite, background) and heated to a comfortable seventy-seven degrees Fahrenheit.

The hotel in Banff Springs also had pools fed and heated by the natural springs. "Diving off the top of the world into a warm sulphur pool is one of Banff's unique joys," read an advertisement for the hotel in 1930. "Plunging from the sulphur pool into an invigorating warmed glacial pool is another joy. The radioactive mineral waters, with the ultra-violet rays of an Alpine sun, make the outer pool a perfect health resort."

Château Montebello also has a splendid 1930s pool in its Aquatic Centre, accessed from the main building via a tunnel. The historic structure has a vaulted ceiling of latticed beams constructed from timber and glass, and at seventy-five feet, the swimming pool it encloses is believed to be the largest hotel indoor heated pool in North America.

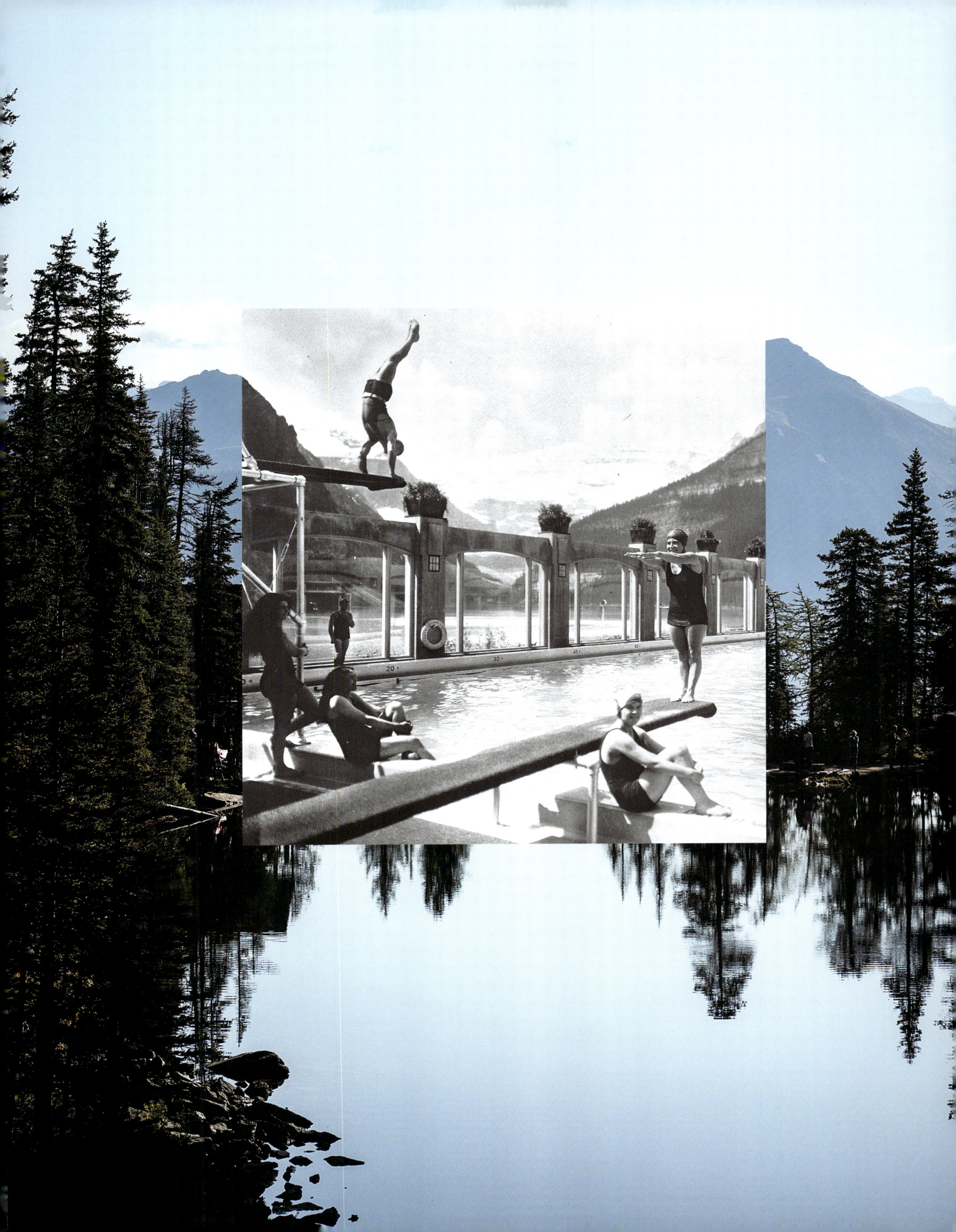

"What marvels the mountains
hold for those who motor, climb, ride!

Skyline trails where you look out across a sea of peaks
rippling away into tinted infinity. [...]

Exhilarating, glacier-cooled atmosphere
that is wine to spirits and tireless energy to the body."

BANFF SPRINGS HOTEL PAMPHLET, 1932.

Transports of Delight

"YOU'LL SEE MORE OF MAGNIFICENT CANADA FROM THE SCENIC DOMES OF THE CANADIAN," READ A 1950S ADVERTISEMENT FOR THE CANADIAN, "CANADA'S ONLY DOME TRAIN, A STAINLESS-STEEL STREAMLINER" WITH GLASS-ROOFED CARRIAGES "THAT TAKES YOU ON THE BANFF LAKE-LOUISE ROUTE THROUGH 2,881 MILES OF EVER-CHANGING SCENERY" (TOP).
OTHER GUESTS, HOWEVER, PREFERRED TO EXPLORE BY CAR, HENCE THIS PHOTOGRAPH OF GUESTS FROM CHATEAU LAKE LOUISE DRIVING OUT ON THE ICEFIELD HIGHWAY, FEATURED IN A CANADIAN PACIFIC BROCHURE CALLED *GRACIOUS LIVING IN THE CANADIAN ROCKIES*, 1949 (MIDDLE).
BUT SOMETIMES THE DEMANDS OF THE ROCKY MOUNTAIN TERRAIN WERE SUCH THAT ENTIRELY NEW MODES OF TRANSPORTS NEEDED TO BE DESIGNED. WITNESS THESE ECCENTRIC GOLF BUGGIES ON A FAIRWAY AT JASPER PARK LODGE (BOTTOM). OR THE BOMBARDIER "SNOW COACH," A TYPE OF EARLY SNOWMOBILE (OPPOSITE, INSET), PHOTOGRAPHED IN THE COLUMBIA ICEFIELDS OF THE JASPER NATIONAL PARK BY HARMON BYRON AROUND 1940.

5

LIGHT HOUSES

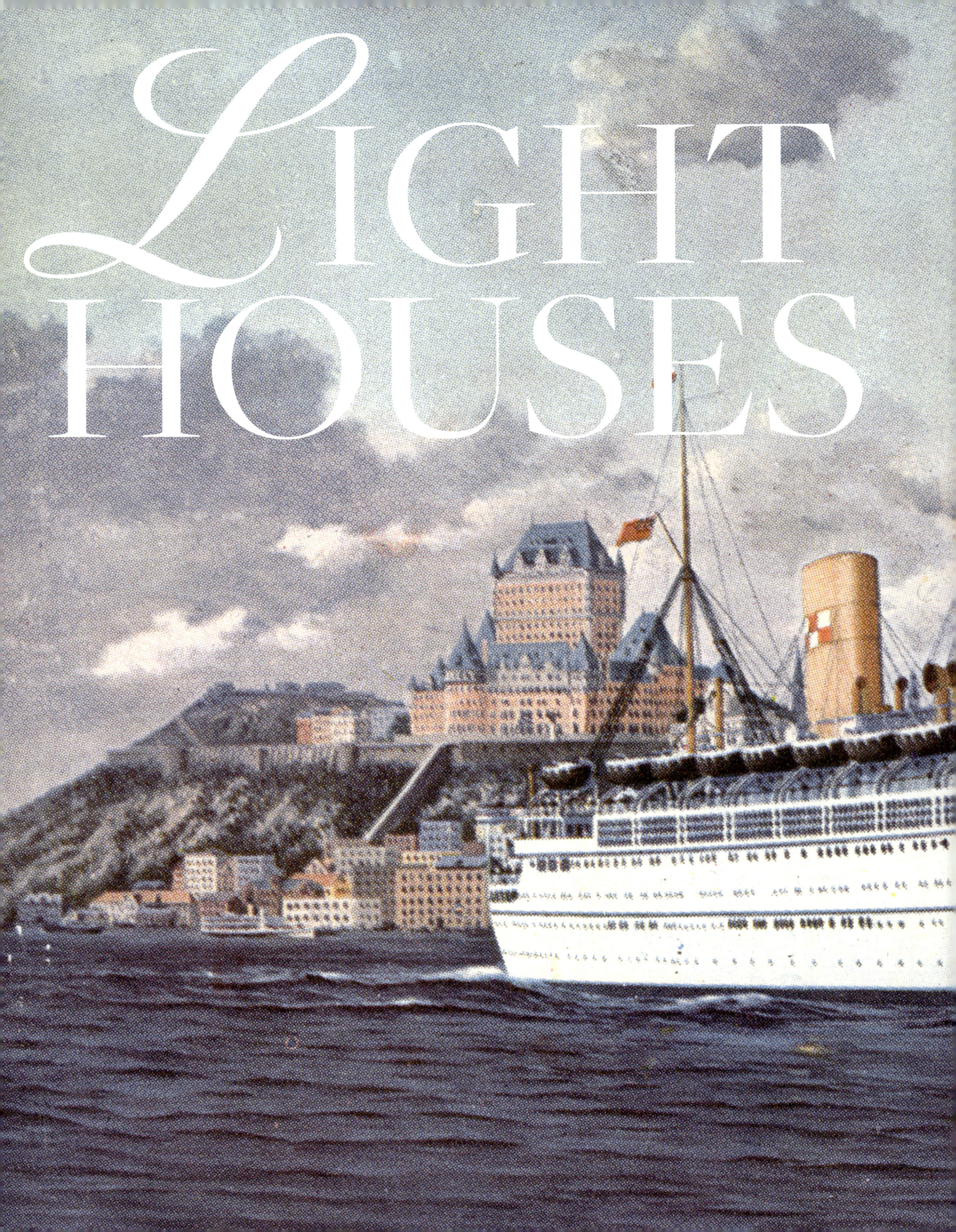

"The clerk at Château Frontenac beamed kindly upon us
and gave us a large and comfortable room overlooking the terrace promenade.
The place rather overwhelmed us, so much so that we thought we'd better dress for dinner..."

Cornelia Otis Skinner

THE AMERICAN ACTRESS AND AUTHOR, ON SAILING FROM MONTREAL TO LIVERPOOL, ENGLAND, ON THE CANADIAN PACIFIC PASSENGER STEAMER
RMS MONTCALM, WHICH RAN AGROUND JUST BEFORE IT REACHED QUEBEC IN JUNE 1922. SHE SAILED TEN DAYS LATER ON THE EMPRESS OF FRANCE.

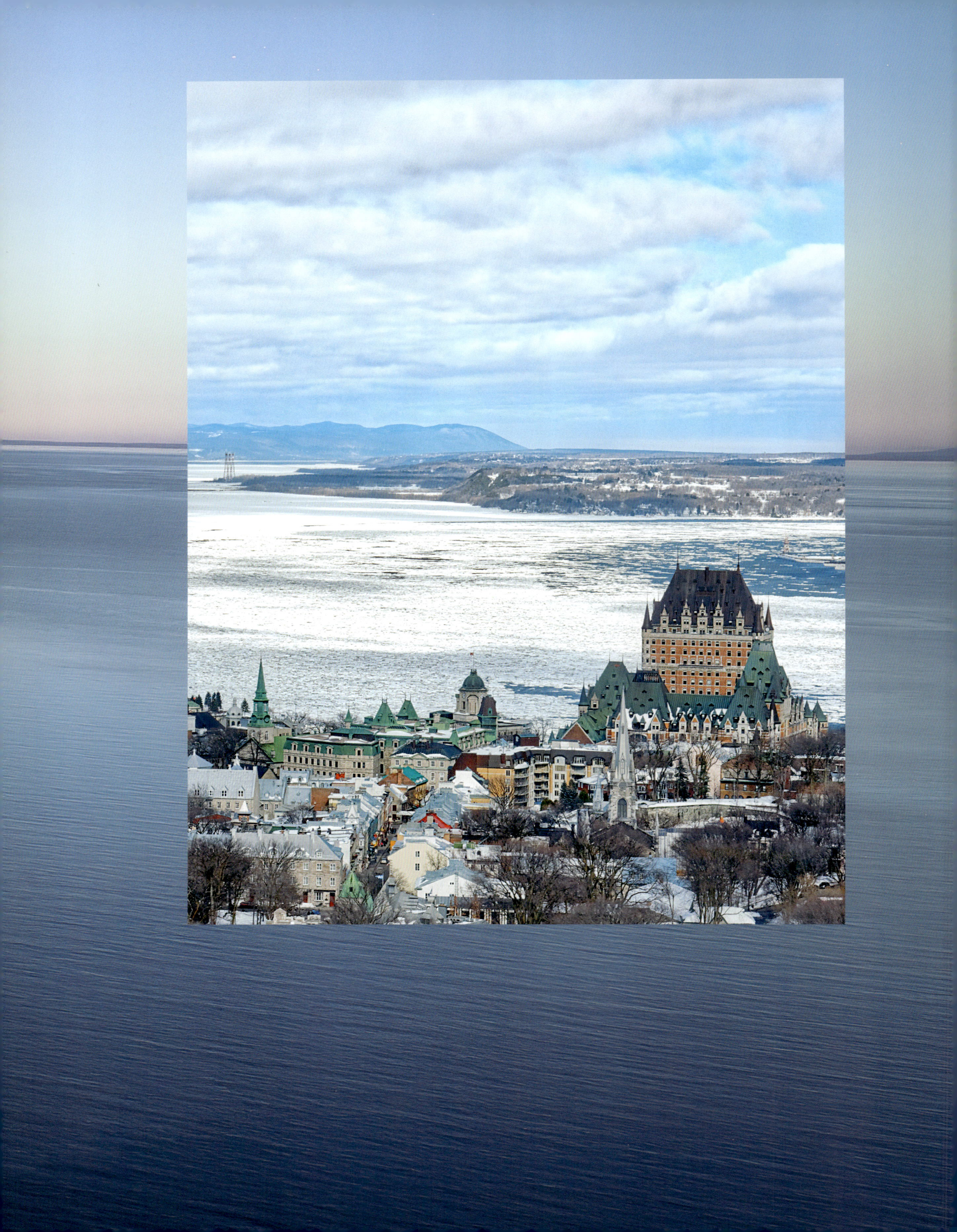

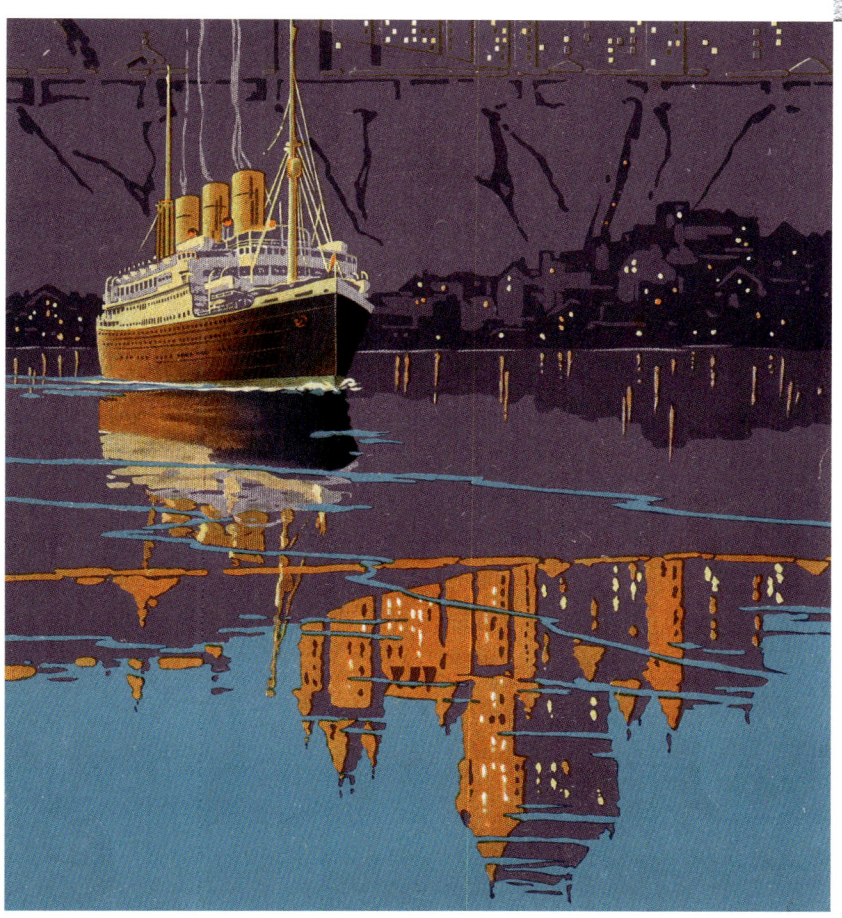

The Lantern That Lights Quebec
Château Frontenac, Quebec City

Named after Louis de Buade, Comte de Palluau et Frontenac, a seventeenth-century French courtier who became Governor General of New France, as francophone Canada was once known, Château Frontenac stands on the elevated site of the former governor's fortress, rising majestically above the St. Lawrence River, from which the steamships would depart for Europe.
Completed in 1893, the eighteen-story landmark rises 260 feet and is visible from as far as the Atlantic. For those making the long passage from Europe by steamship, on a clear day it was visible for miles, a welcome sign that they would soon be on dry land. It remains an unmissable landmark, its copper roof a fantastical mash up of cupolas, turrets, towers, and spikes, combining Gothic, Italian, and French Renaissance and revivalist architectural styles. The bas-relief pictured above had been carved as early as 1647 by the Priory of the Knights of Malta; formerly part of Château Saint-Louis of Quebec in 1834, it was inserted in the walls of Château Frontenac in 1920.

Above left: the cover of a Canadian Pacific ships pamphlet advertising travel to Europe via the St. Lawrence Seaway, ca. 1920.

60 — 61

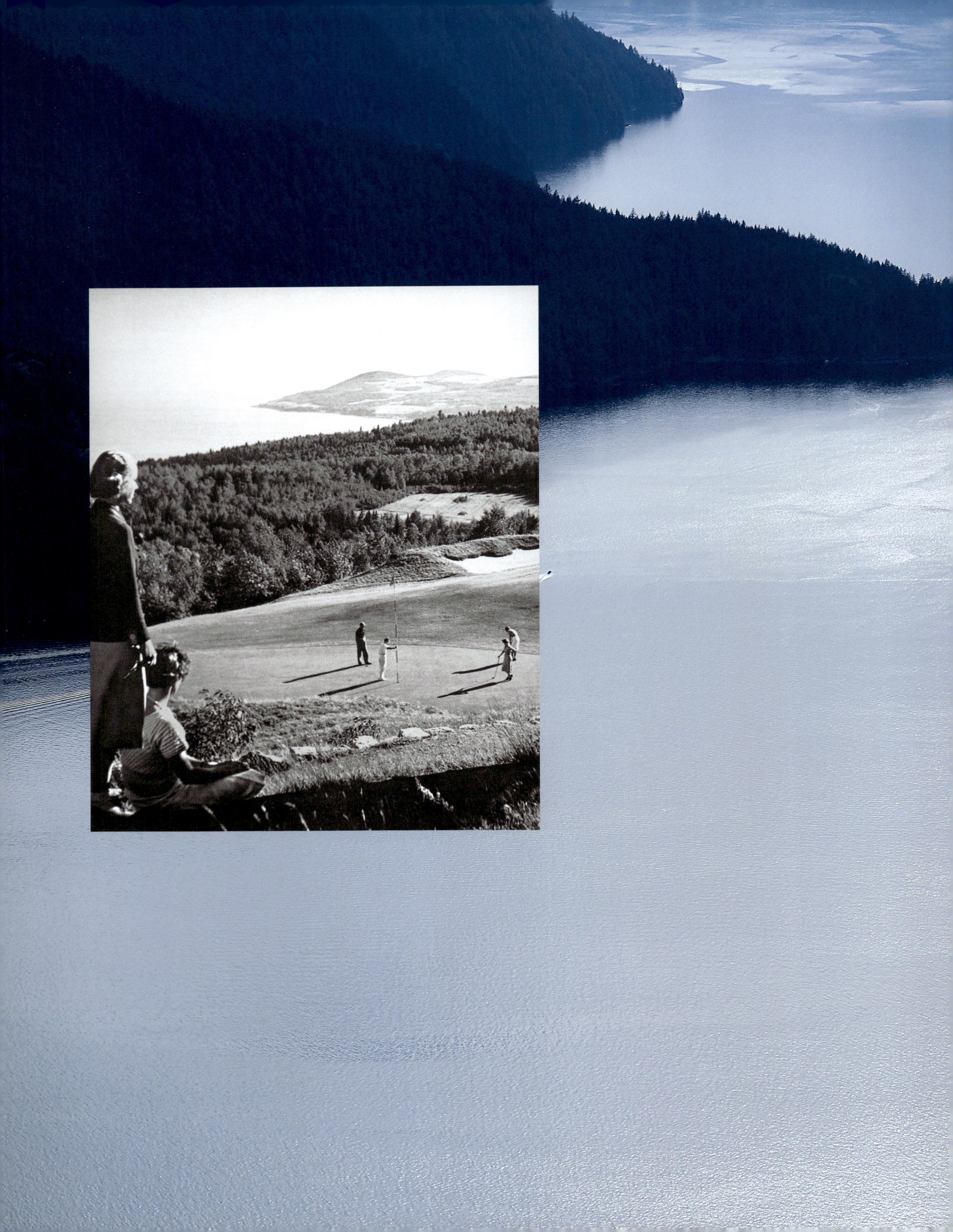

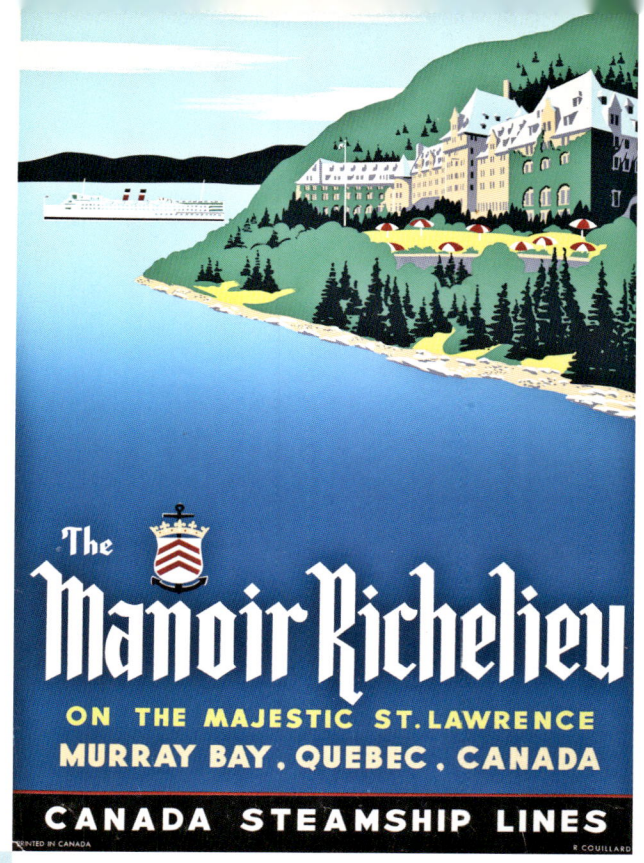

The Castle on the Cliff
LE MANOIR RICHELIEU, CHARLEVOIX

JUST AS MANY OF THE EARLIEST HOTELS IN CANADA WERE BUILT BY THE CANADIAN PACIFIC RAILWAY FOR TRAVELERS TO HAVE COMFORTABLE PLACES TO STAY EN ROUTE, NOT TO MENTION DESTINATIONS TO TRAVEL TO IN THE FIRST PLACE, SO THE ONTARIO NAVIGATION COMPANY, WHICH OPERATED PASSENGER STEAMSHIPS ON THE ST. LAWRENCE RIVER AND GREAT LAKES, BEGAN TO DIVERSIFY INTO HOSPITALITY. HIGH ON THE POINTE-AU-PIC BLUFFS ABOVE THE ST. LAWRENCE RIVER ON THE ESTUARY KNOWN AS LA MALBAIE, NOW DUBBED "THE CRADLE OF RESORT VACATIONING IN CANADA," LE MANOIR RICHELIEU WAS ORIGINALLY CONSTRUCTED IN 1899 AS A FIRST STOP FOR SHIPS SAILING FROM MONTREAL, THOUGH THE PRESENT CHÂTEAU-STYLE RESORT DATES BACK TO 1929. THE SUCCESS OF THE HOTEL WAS IMMEDIATE, ATTRACTING POLITICIANS LIKE THE US PRESIDENT WILLIAM TAFT, CANADA'S PRIME MINISTER SIR WILFRID LAURIER AND CINEMA CELEBRITIES LIKE DOUGLAS FAIRBANKS, JEAN HARLOW, CHARLIE CHAPLIN, AND MARY PICKFORD.

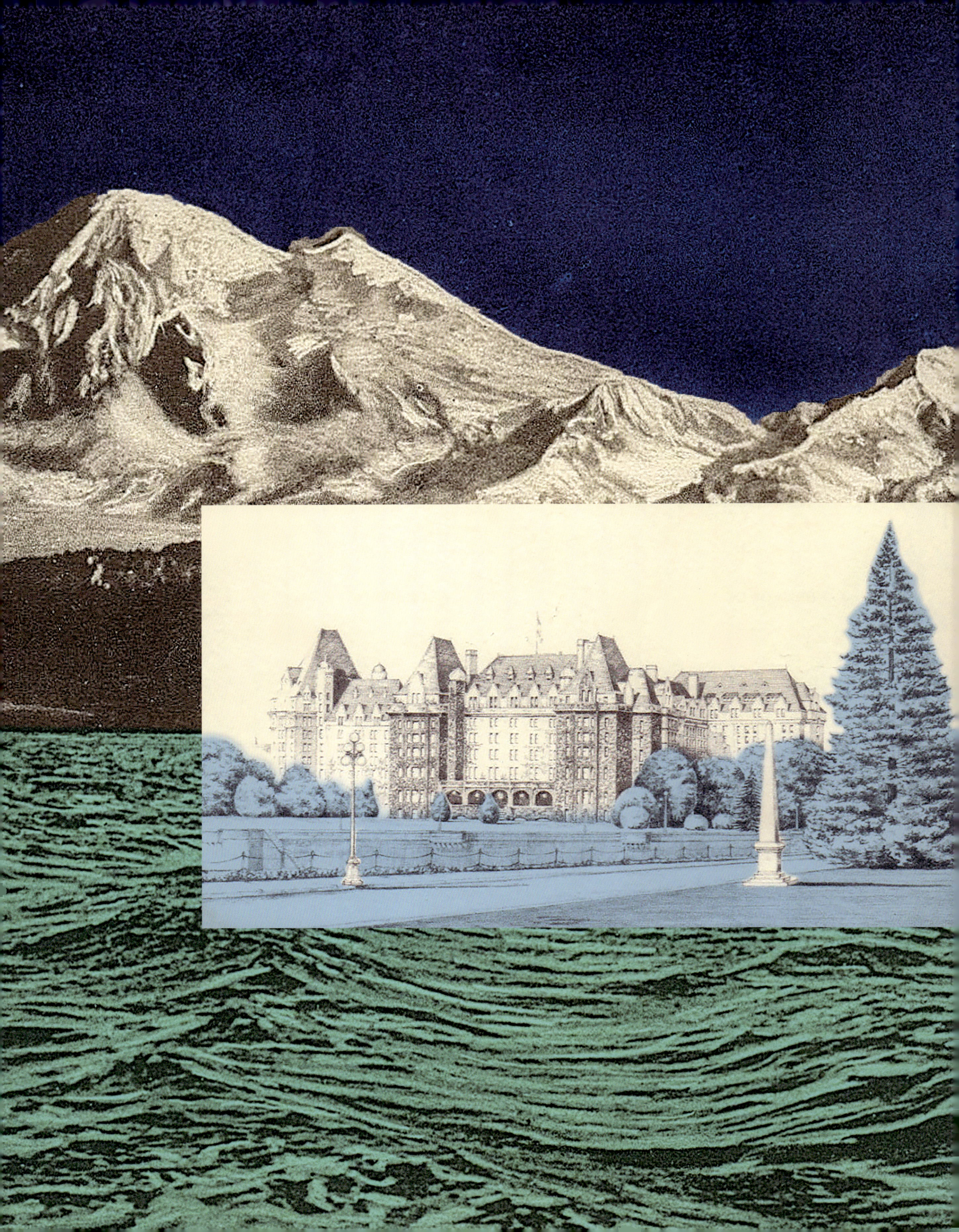

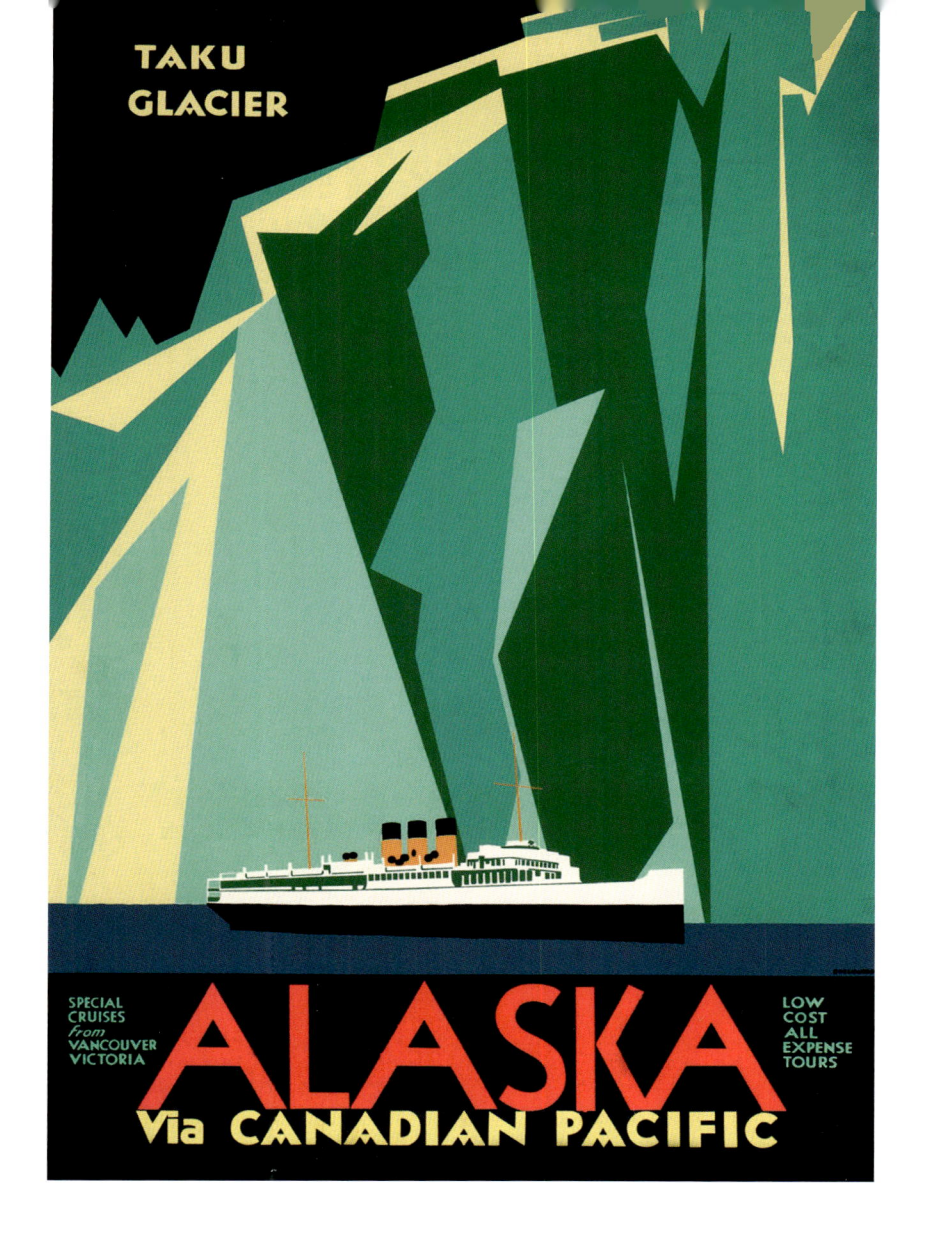

"A meeting place for world travellers"
FAIRMONT EMPRESS, VICTORIA

ONE OF CANADA'S GREAT RAILWAY HOTELS, THE EMPRESS (LEFT) OPENED IN 1908, SITUATED CLOSE TO VICTORIA'S INNER HARBOUR AND THE CANADIAN PACIFIC RAILWAY STEAMSHIP TERMINAL.

IN 1903, SIR THOMAS SHAUGHNESSY, THEN PRESIDENT OF THE CANADIAN PACIFIC RAILWAY HAD VISITED THE CITY, AND SEVERAL PROMINENT LOCAL BUSINESSMEN HAD ASKED HIM TO CONSIDER BUILDING A HOTEL THERE. HE DROVE A HARD BARGAIN: "IF THE CITY WILL SUPPLY THE SITE AND EXEMPT US FROM TAXATION AND GIVE US FREE WATER FOR TWENTY YEARS, WE WILL BUILD A HOTEL AT A COST OF NO LESS THAN $300,000," HE WROTE. THE CITY PUT IT TO A VOTE; ITS CITIZENS VOTED 1,205 TO 46 IN FAVOR OF ACCEPTING HIS DEMANDS; AND WITHIN A FORTNIGHT WORK HAD BEGUN ON ITS CONSTRUCTION.

VICTORIA CONSEQUENTLY BECAME MUCH MORE THAN A PLACE FOR TRAVELERS—"BOUND OUT TO THE ORIENT OR HOME FROM THE SEVEN SEAS" AS AN EARLY ADVERTISEMENT READ—TO SPEND THE NIGHT BEFORE EMBARKING ON OR ALIGHTING FROM A VOYAGE OR TRAIN TRIP.

CLOSE TO THE CITY'S GOVERNMENT BUILDINGS, THE EMPRESS DESCRIBED ITSELF AS "ONE OF THE FIVE GREATEST WORLD HOTELS" AND WAS A SOCIAL HUB FOR THE CITY TOO. THOUGH IT STROVE NOT TO "SEEM LIKE A HOTEL, BUT RATHER LIKE A BIG ENGLISH COUNTRY HOUSE. IT IS SET IN AN EIGHT-ACRE GARDEN, FULL OF RARE VARIETIES, WITH ROSES IN BLOOM ALMOST EVERY DAY OF THE YEAR. ALL THROUGH THE HOTEL THERE IS QUIET … LOW ENGLISH VOICES, RESTRAINED ENGLISH MANNERS, EFFICIENT ENGLISH SERVICE."

IT PROMISED "VARIED YEAR-ROUND RECREATIONS, GOLF, POLO, TENNIS, RIDING, SWIMMING, SAILING CANOEING, FISHING, HUNTING AND CAMPING" TOO. BUT ABOVE ALL, IT ADVERTISED ACCESS TO THE WORLD, A MEETING POINT FOR EAST AND WEST, AN EPICENTER OF COSMOPOLITANISM IN A CITY FEW OUTSIDE CANADA HAD HITHERTO HEARD OF.

OPPOSITE (INSET): THE EMPRESS HOTEL, VICTORIA, BY EDWARD GOODALL, CA. 1910.
OPPOSITE (BACKGROUND): MOUNT BAKER FROM OAK BAY, VICTORIA, 1910 — ABOVE: CANADIAN PACIFIC STEAMSHIPS POSTER, CA. 1930.

Ghirardelli

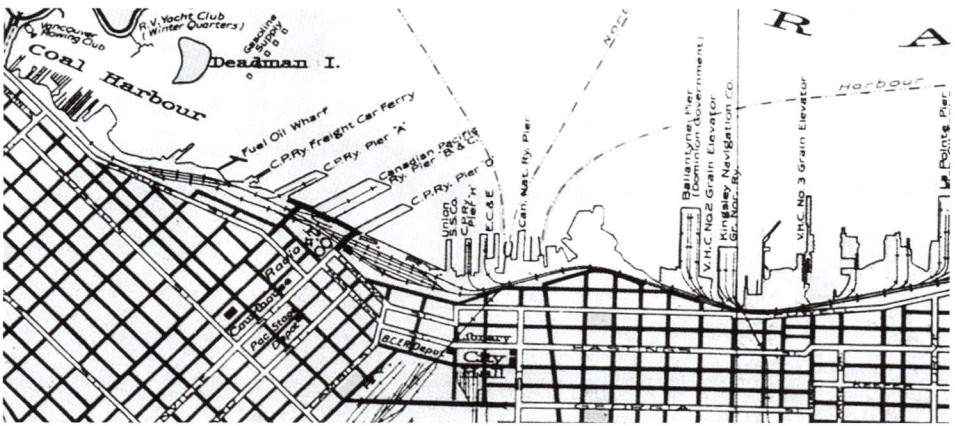

The Importance of Ports
Fairmont Hotel Vancouver and Fairmont Heritage Place, Ghirardelli Square

Raw silk was such a valuable commodity in the nineteenth and early twentieth centuries that, in its early days, the Canadian Pacific trains that conveyed it east from Vancouver (imported from Asia by Canadian pacific steamships) carried armed guards. Raw silk is a fragile commodity, liable to deteriorate, so speed was critical too in order not to lose value. Indeed, a train carrying Prince Albert, later King George VI, was once held in a siding, to let the silk train pass.

Although the Canadian Pacific Railway's original hotels in Vancouver were demolished, the present Fairmont Hotel Vancouver (top) opened in 1939 just in time for a state visit by George VI and his wife, Queen Elizabeth. It remains a landmark, very much the city's grande dame, though it now has two younger offsprings: Fairmont Waterfront overlooking Vancouver Harbour, which opened in 1991, just a two-minute walk away, and, since 2010, Fairmont Pacific Rim on the exact location where the Canadian pacific docks and trains used to be filled directly from the ships (see map above).

800 miles south of Vancouver, also on the Pacific seaboard, San Francisco, home of the original Fairmont, is another port city. If that hotel is inland, at the top of Nob Hill, its sibling in the city is close to the water, right by Hyde Street Pier, in what is now part of the city's Maritime National Historical Park.

Like silk, chocolate was a valuable commodity, but an export rather than an import. By the end of the nineteenth century, San Francisco's Ghirardelli Chocolate Factory (left) was shipping to China, Japan, and Mexico, and was on course to become one of the largest confectioners in the world.

By the 1960s, Ghirardelli had expanded considerably and left its original base on the city's waterfront, and its buildings were redeveloped as Ghirardelli Square, now a National Historic Landmark. In 2008, Fairmont transformed its distinctive red-brick chocolate factory into a hotel.

New Horizons

Fairmont Waterfront

"This Pacific Railway fulfilled its primary purpose when it connected the Atlantic with the Pacific seaboard. But its still greatest importance to the Empire at large, and to Canada also, lies in the possibilities of extended trade between England, Japan, China, India and Australia. Services by this route will compare with those using the Suez Canal."

The Marquess of Lorne
Governor General of Canada, in *Our Railway to the Pacific* (1886)

Fairmont Pacific Rim

In Linking the Pacific with the Atlantic, the Railway Made Canada a Rival to Suez

When Jules Verne's novel *Around the World in Eighty Days* was published in 1872, the contention that the globe could be circumnavigated in so short a time would have seemed fantastical.
But the completion of the Canadian Pacific Railway in 1885, which made it possible to sail to Quebec, traverse the country by train, a journey of about a week, and pick up a ship to China, via India, at Vancouver, made it almost a possibility.
It was not until 1924, however, that the dream of a round-the-world cruise became a reality, when Canadian Pacific Steamships announced the *Empress of Scotland* would embark on a circumnavigation, setting sail from New York on December 3, 1925.

See this World before the Next by The World's Greatest Travel System

Canadian Pacific

"THE CATHAY"—the most modern Hotel in China

The Pearl of the East
Fairmont Peace Hotel, Shanghai

Back in 1935, *Fortune* magazine described Shanghai as "the megalopolis of Asia... inheritor of nineteenth-century London and twentieth-century Manhattan," a roaring mercantile center that was already home to the tallest towers outside America. Among these was the Cathay Hotel (now Fairmont Peace Hotel), which opened in 1929, rising 250 feet from its base on the Bund, the sweeping esplanade that runs along the Huangpu River. Its ten stories were topped by a penthouse with a steep pyramid roof clad in copper—now a distinctive green—so as to be visible from miles away. Its creator, Sir Victor Sassoon, spared no expense on white marble, Lalique crystal and solid silver taps. There were telephones in the rooms and air conditioning, both then unheard of in Europe.

The hotel was a place every bit as intriguing and exotic as its original owner. In May 1936, Jean Cocteau met Charlie Chaplin and his wife Paulette Goddard on the steamship heading to Shanghai. Upon arrival, the three of them went directly to the Cathay hotel to have lunch. As Jean Cocteau recalled in *Mon premier voyage*, "If I ended up writing about Victor Sassoon [...] it would be thrilling. [He] drives China as if it were a Rolls-Royce, [his] cane (he limps thanks to a war wound) reveals treasures and his eye undertakes calculations behind an icy monocle."

A Castle in the Savanna
Fairmont The Norfolk, Nairobi

The Norfolk Hotel in Nairobi opened its doors on Christmas Day 1904, boasting forty rooms (there are now 170), a billiard table and a French chef and claiming to be the only stone building in East Africa.
Among its early guests at this improbably pastiche Tudor manor were Theodore Roosevelt, who had just finished his second term as US President, and his son, Kermit.
Baron Bror von Blixen-Finecke stayed there too, ahead of the arrival of his future wife, the writer-to-be Karen Blixen, en route to the coffee plantation he had bought near the Ngong Hills, which they ran and she wrote about as Isak Dinesen in her 1937 memoir *Out of Africa*.
Among the characters in her book is Lord Delamere, an aristocratic English expatriate and early settler in Kenya, who reportedly rode his horse into the dining room at the Norfolk, jumping the tables as though it was a dressage event. He was prominent among the notoriously scandalous and hedonistic Happy Valley set, as was the American heiress Alice, Comtesse de Janzé (pictured with her pet lion cub), who arrived in Kenya in 1921 and had a string of affairs, not least with the Earl of Erroll, another British aristocrat, who was shot dead in 1941—the subject of the movie *White Mischief*—for which she was a suspect and after which she committed suicide.
She also shot and wounded another lover from Kenya, Raymond de Trafford, this time in Paris, an incident that inspired a scene in F. Scott Fitzgerald's novel *Tender Is the Night*.

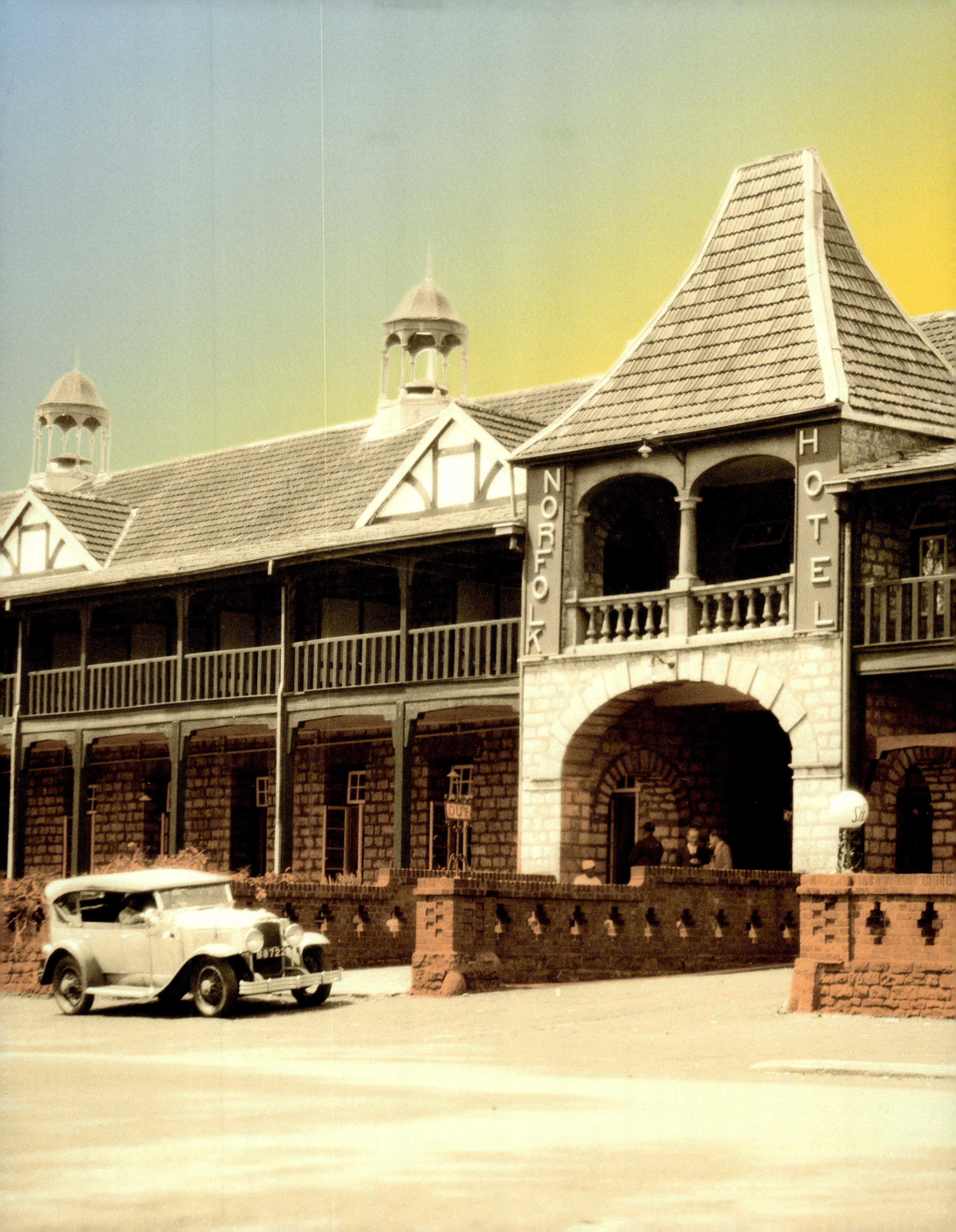
NORFOLK
HOTEL
OUT

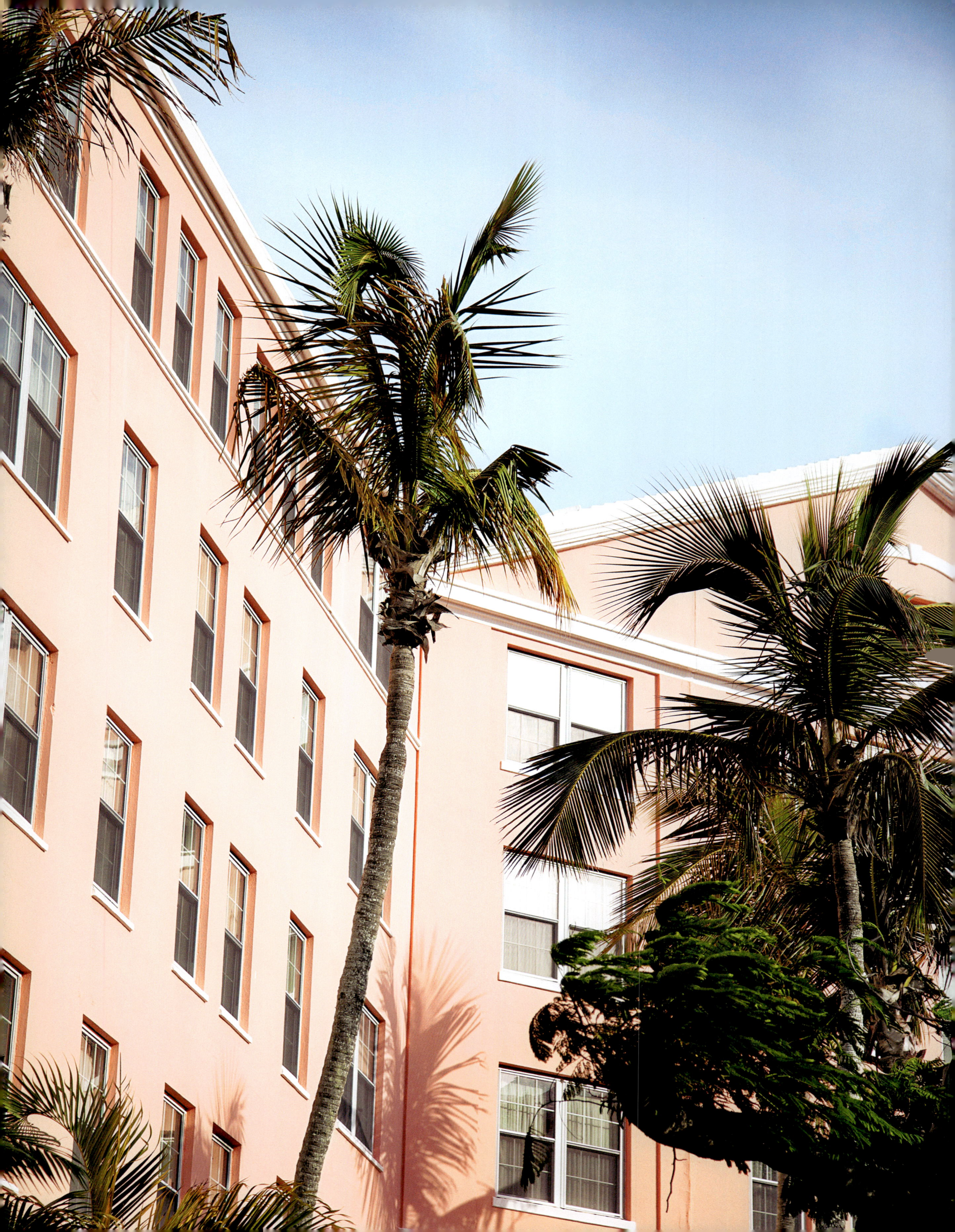

Bermuda's Pink Palace and Big Pink Lady on the Hill
The Hamilton Princess & Beach Club and Fairmont Southampton

When Queen Victoria's daughter Princess Louise arrived on the island of Bermuda, a mid-Atlantic outpost of the British Empire, to convalesce from her sleigh accident in Canada in 1883, there was not yet a grand hotel. But her ten-week stay was widely reported, notably by *The New York Times*, and did much to promote tourism to the island. The princess loved her time there, praising its "frank and genial people," painting its subtropical landscapes and, alluding to the English metaphysical poet Andrew Marvell's poem *Bermudas* (1653), writing that she would always remember "my sojourn on these islands in 'this Eternal Spring, which here enamels everything'."

The hotel pictured opposite, named The Princess in her honor, opened two years later. It was later renamed The Princess Hamilton to be consistent with the naming of the second Fairmont to open in Bermuda, Fairmont Southampton, which was built in another parish about six miles southwest in the 1970s, and soon became known as the Big Pink Lady on the Hill. Thanks to the hotel's appeal—it was, by the standards of the time, fabulously modern: its rooms supplied with hot and cold running water and lit by gas lights—Bermuda soon became a popular staging post for ocean liners on the transatlantic crossing, among them Canadian Pacific's Duchess of Atholl and Duchess of York, as well as cruise ships en route to the Caribbean.

Above, four New Yorkers dressed in bathing suits, enjoy the beach in Bermuda, 1932.

Islands of Enduring Summer
Fairmont Kea Lani, Maui, and Fairmont Orchid Hawaii, Kohala Coast

William Van Horne founded what became the Canadian Pacific Steamship Company in Vancouver in 1887, and soon it was Canada's largest operator of steamships, plying both the Atlantic and Pacific oceans, operating services not to Europe but to Hong Kong.
In time, Honolulu became a stop on the Pacific route. And thus, tourism to Hawaii and its islands began to grow. In 1903, when a bureau to promote tourism to the then kingdom (it did not become a US state until August 1959) was established, 2,000 visitors alighted there. In 1925, it was advertised as a stop on Canadian Pacific Cruise's inaugural round-the-world itinerary.
Fairmont now operates two hotels in the archipelago: Fairmont Kea Lani (1) on Maui and Fairmont Orchid (5) in Hawaii, both popular with "snowbirds," residents of cooler climates, who travel to spend the winter somewhere warmer, whether it's Americans heading west to Hawaii, east to Bermuda and the Fairmont Southampton (4), or south to Mexico and Fairmont Heritage Place Acapulco (3), or residents of Asia heading to Sanya—the Hawaii of China—home of Fairmont Sanya Haitang Bay (2), or Bali and the white sands of Fairmont Sanur Beach (6).

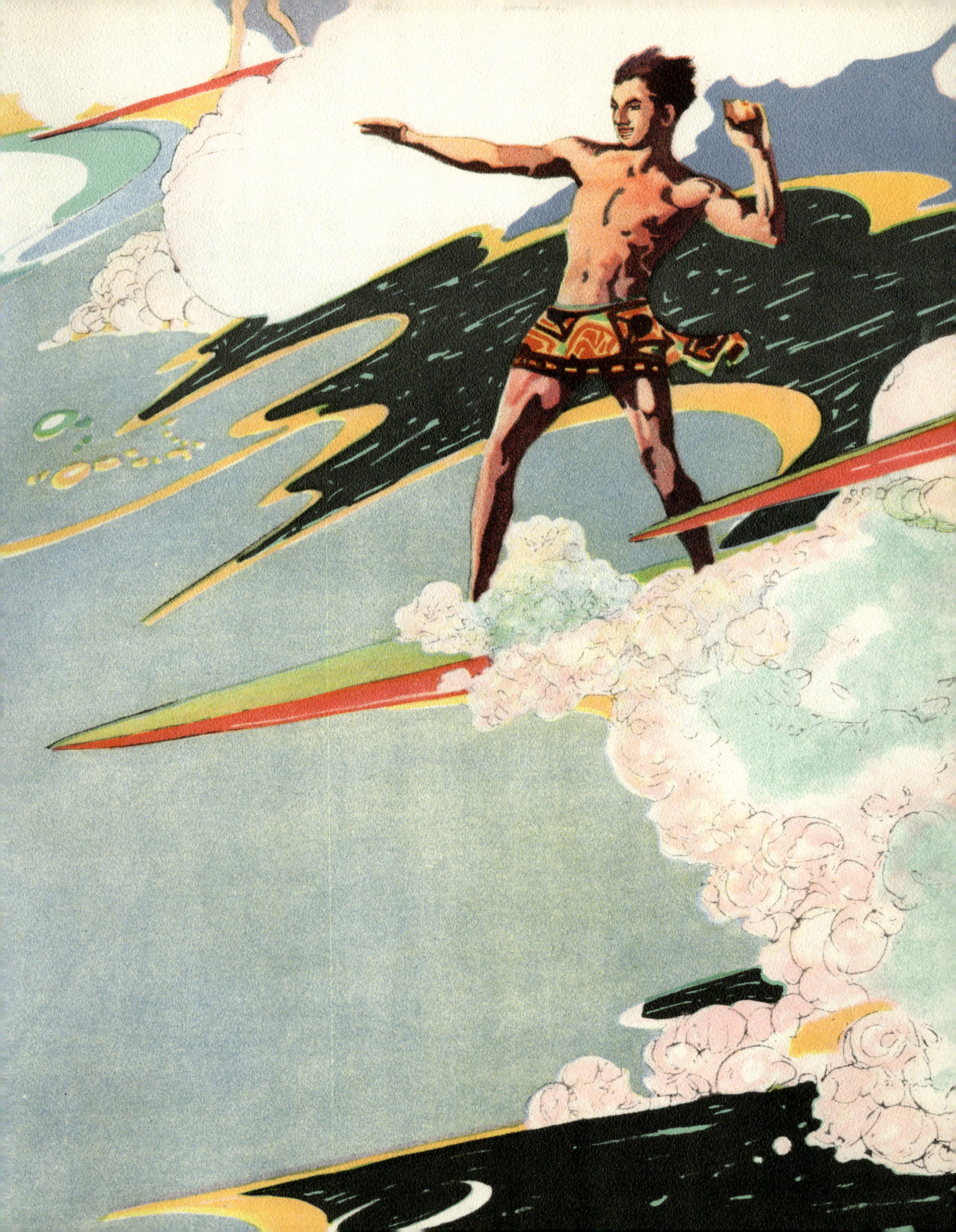

Stories of the Skies
THE LAUNCH OF CANADIAN PACIFIC AIR LINES

HAVING LAUNCHED CANADIAN PACIFIC HOTELS AS A SUBSIDIARY COMPANY, THE CANADIAN PACIFIC RAILWAY DIVERSIFIED NEXT INTO AVIATION, LAUNCHING CANADIAN PACIFIC AIR LINES IN 1942, WHICH OPERATED OUT OF VANCOUVER INTERNATIONAL AIRPORT, LATTERLY AS CP AIR, UNTIL 1987, WHEN IT WAS SOLD.
IT FOLLOWS THEN THAT THERE SHOULD BE A HOTEL AT THE AIRPORT, A LOW, LINEAR, GLASS-AND-STEEL STRUCTURE BUILT IN 1999 (ABOVE, RIGHT), THAT OFFERS VIEWS BOTH OF THE RUNWAY (EACH ROOM HAS A PLANE SPOTTER'S GUIDE TO DIFFERENT AIRCRAFT) AND THE MOUNTAINS BEYOND. UNUSUALLY FAIRMONT VANCOUVER AIRPORT ALSO HAS A 575-CUBIC-FOOT FREEZER, WHERE GUESTS CAN STORE SALMONS THEY'VE CAUGHT IN ADVANCE OF THEIR FLIGHT HOME. THERE IS EVEN A FISH VALET TO TAKE CARE OF IT.
A LEGACY—AT LEAST A TANGENTIAL ONE—OF CANADIAN PACIFIC AIR LINES ENDURES AT FAIRMONT MALDIVES SIRRU FEN FUSHI (OPPOSITE), WHICH CHARTERS A DE HAVILLAND TWIN OTTER SEAPLANE TO FERRY GUESTS THE FIFTY-FIVE-MINUTE FLIGHT FROM THE INTERNATIONAL AIRPORT AT MALÉ TO ITS ISLAND, 143 MILES NORTH IN SHAVIYANI ATOLL.

Two Intrepid Aviators
TWO WORLD FIRSTS

SEVERAL SIGNIFICANT AVIATORS HAVE CONNECTIONS WITH FAIRMONT HOTELS TOO. IN JULY 1909, LOUIS BLÉRIOT CELEBRATED HIS FIRST-EVER FLIGHT ACROSS THE ENGLISH CHANNEL AT THE SAVOY IN LONDON.
IN JULY 1927, THE AMERICAN AVIATOR CHARLES LINDBERGH FLEW HIS SINGLE-ENGINE, SINGLE-SEAT MONOPLANE SPIRIT OF ST. LOUIS, IN WHICH HE HAD MADE THE FIRST NONSTOP TRANSATLANTIC FLIGHT FROM NEW YORK TO PARIS, TO OTTAWA, STAYING AT CHÂTEAU LAURIER, TO CELEBRATE THE SIXTIETH ANNIVERSARY OF CANADA'S INDEPENDENCE AS A NATION.
AND THE ENGLISH AVIATRIX BERYL MARKHAM (ABOVE, LEFT), THE FIRST PERSON TO FLY NONSTOP ACROSS THE ATLANTIC FROM THE UNITED KINGDOM TO THE UNITED STATES IN 1939—AN EVENT SHE TOO CELEBRATED AT THE SAVOY—WAS ALSO A REGULAR AT THE NORFOLK IN NAIROBI, DURING THE YEARS SHE SPENT WORKING AS A BUSH PILOT IN KENYA.

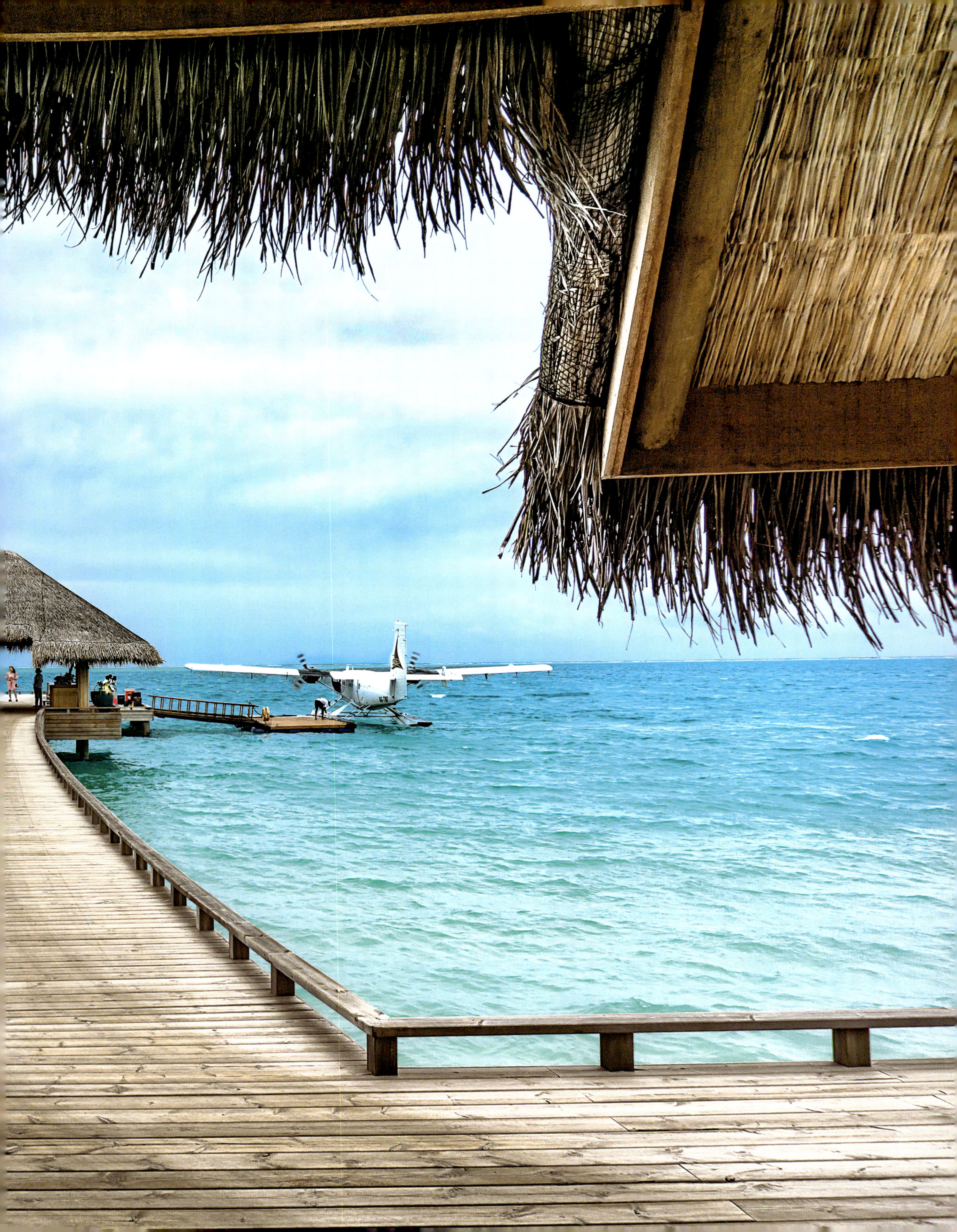

A Footnote in the Story of the Moon Landing
Stars, bars and cocktails: The Savoy

Back from their mission to the moon in 1969, the American astronauts Neil Armstrong, Buzz Aldrin, and Michael Collins traveled to several cities to mark their gigantic step for mankind at hotels that are now part of Fairmont. In Los Angeles, they were celebrated at the Century Plaza (left), in Montreal at the Queen Elizabeth, and in London there was a dinner at The Savoy.
In anticipation of their arrival in London Joe Gilmore, head bartender at The Savoy's American Bar created a special cocktail, the Moonwalk, a mix of grapefruit juice, Grand Marnier Cordon Rouge, and rosewater, shaken over ice, and topped up with champagne. To be sure they would like it, he sent a flask ahead to NASA's Johnson Space Center in Houston, where they were quarantining in a converted Airstream (top). It's said it was the first thing Armstrong drank on his release.
So, it is appropriate that when Star Wars: The Empire Strikes Back opened in London in 1980, the press call, at which Carrie Fisher was photographed in the arms of two Stormtroopers, was held at The Savoy (opposite).

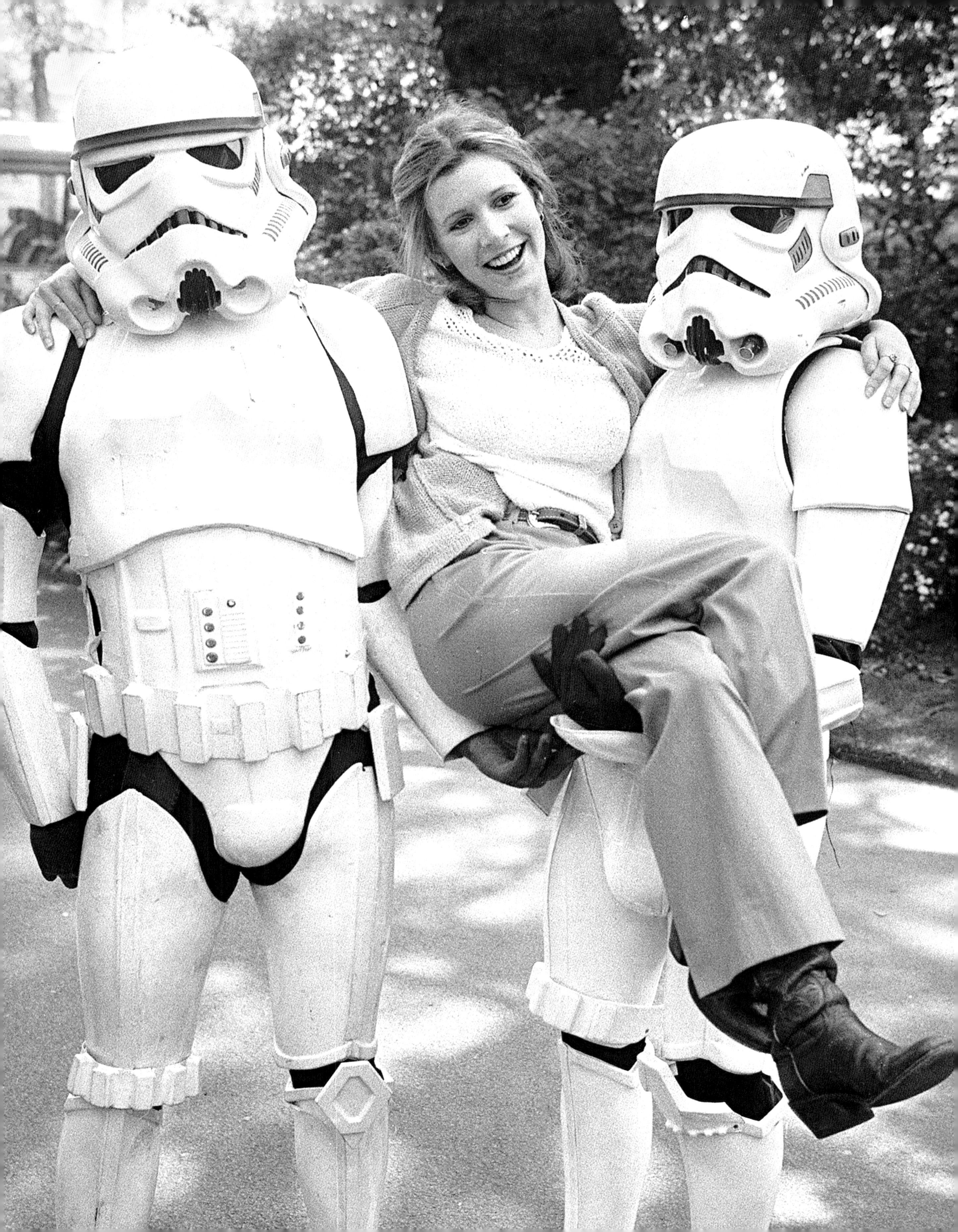

EPICENTERS

The Birth of the Brand and of the United Nations

The Fairmont in San Francisco was not just the first Fairmont hotel, it was also the birthplace of the United Nations. On October 24, 1945 the UN Charter, establishing its purpose, principles and framework, was drafted in the Garden Room of the hotel. Flags from the fifty countries that signed it are flown at the hotel to this day.

Where "nothing unimportant ever happens"
The Plaza, A Fairmont Managed Hotel, New York

The architect Henry Janeway Hardenbergh began to build hotels in the United States, notably The Plaza in New York, to which he "brought fresh ideas and a sophisticated approach to design in the skyscraper age" as Elaine Denby writes in her authoritative study of the origins of the hospitality industry Grand Hotels (1998). The hotel opened in 1907, with a "radiating glamour and excitement to New Yorkers and visitors alike". That was certainly its intention. "The Plaza is in a class by itself," read one early advertisement.

There were 800 rooms, 500 bathrooms, seventeen apartments (though they could be combined to form fewer larger ones), ten elevators and five marble staircases. The chandeliers in the Terrace Room, inspired by those at Versailles, were made by Charles Winston, brother of the celebrated jeweler, Harry Winston. But what really secured the hotel's stellar reputation, then as now, were its guests. The very first to sign the register was Alfred Gwynne Vanderbilt, who moved into an apartment there at 9 a.m. on the day it opened in October 1907, even though the Vanderbilt mansion was literally next door, on the northwest corner of Fifth Avenue and East 57th Street. He set the tone, and from Hollywood royalty (Greta Garbo liked to be alone there; Marlene Dietrich took up residence; Marilyn Monroe caused a sensation in the Terrace Room) to actual royals such as the Duke and Duchess of Windsor, its guestbook continues to trace the history of modern celebrity.

Above: "American Autumn. Three women and a man standing in the Persian Room at The Plaza, wearing evening gowns and a tuxedo. People having dinner in the background," Jean Pages for *Vogue*, September 1, 1935. — Opposite: *The Plaza*, oil on canvas by William R. Derrick, ca. 1907–11.

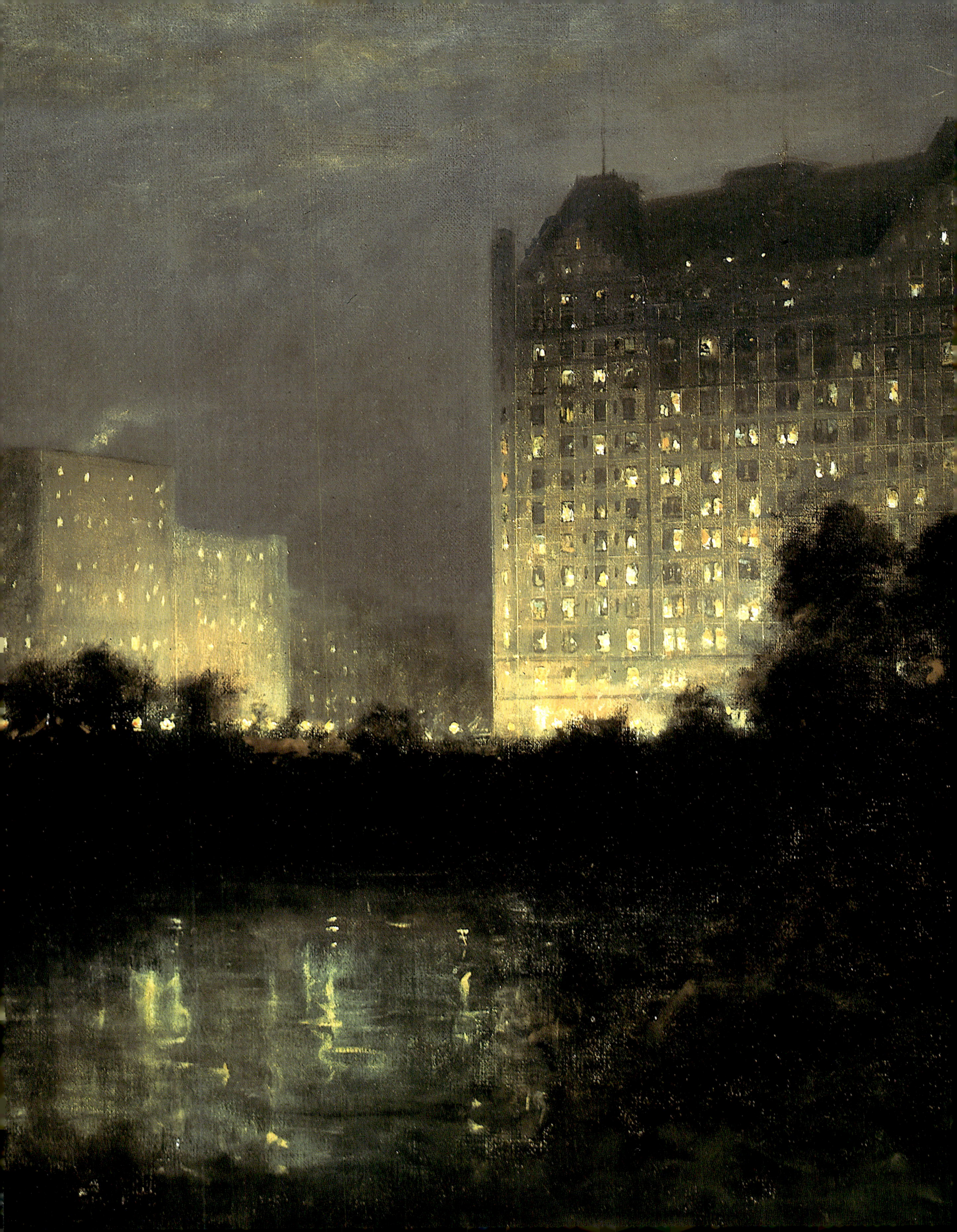

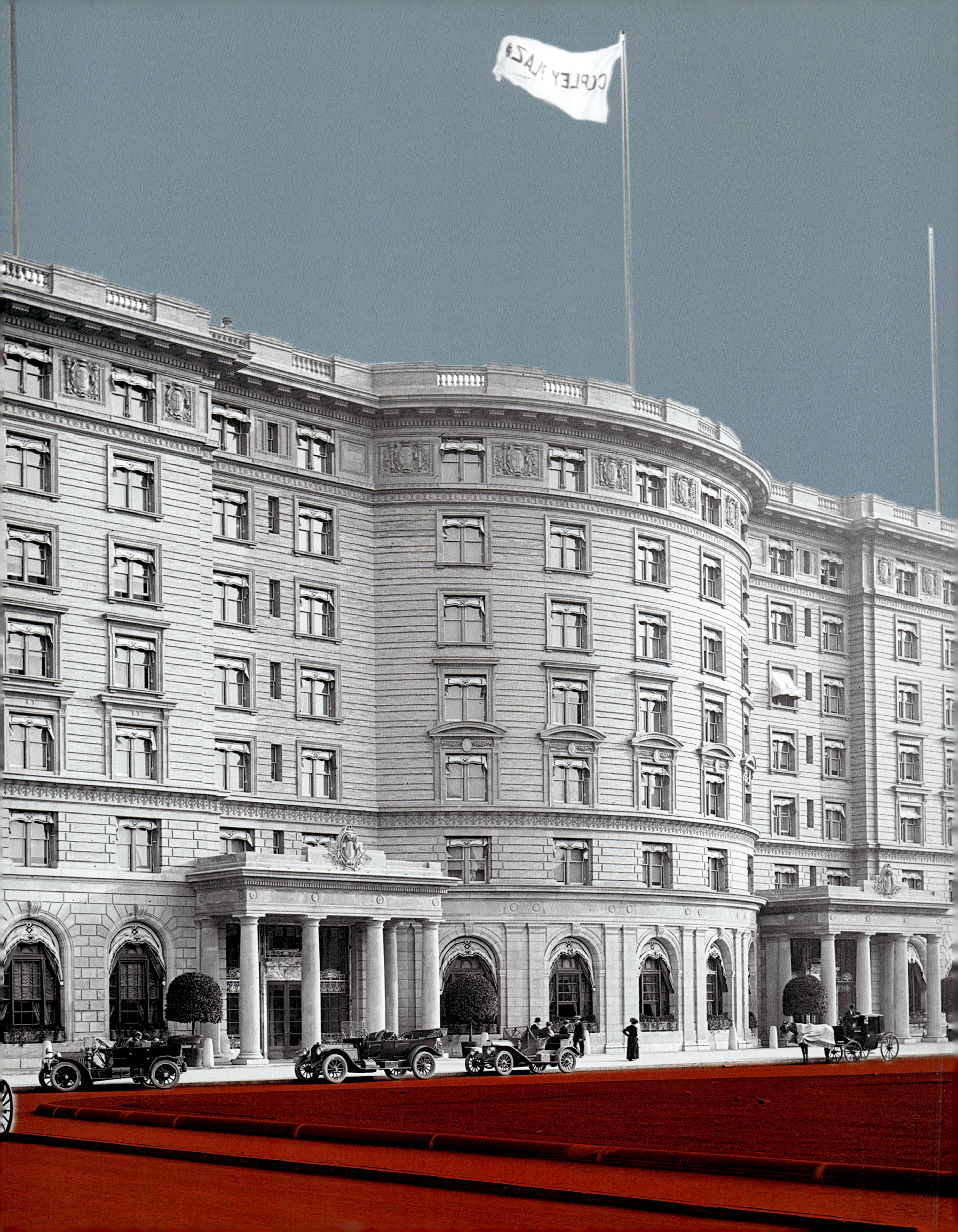

A Kennedy Favorite
FAIRMONT COPLEY PLAZA, BOSTON

ON AUGUST 19, 1912, THE MAYOR OF BOSTON, JOHN F. FITZGERALD, WHOSE GRANDSON, JOHN FITZGERALD KENNEDY (PICTURED IN THE HOTEL IN 1958 WITH FORMER PRESIDENT HARRY S. TRUMAN AND ATTORNEY GENERAL EDWARD F. MCCORMICK JR.) WOULD GROW UP TO BE PRESIDENT, THREW A PARTY FOR A THOUSAND PEOPLE AT THE NEWLY OPENED COPLEY PLAZA HOTEL. "THE MAGNIFICENT GREAT BALLROOM, THE LARGEST IN BOSTON, WAS CROWDED TO ITS UTMOST CAPACITY BY DINERS," REPORTED THE *BOSTON GLOBE*, NOTING TOO THAT THE WOMEN WORE "COSTLY DECORATIONS, AND FEW WORE PICTURE HATS, WHICH WERE IN EVERY CASE STRIKING AND BEAUTIFUL."
THE HOTEL WAS TO BECOME AN IMPORTANT PLACE FOR FITZGERALD AND KENNEDY FAMILY CELEBRATIONS, AND THERE'S A JFK SUITE TO THIS DAY.

One usually thinks of a hotel as designed
to care for the needs of visitors only temporarily in the city.
And in this respect the Olympic has already begun to fulfill its mission [...]
But it is destined to be no less a factor in the lives of Seattle's own citizens.
It will inevitably be a social center.

THE TOWN CRIER, DECEMBER 6, 1924

The Making of a City
FAIRMONT OLYMPIC HOTEL, SEATTLE

AFTER THE END OF WORLD WAR II, SEATTLE'S CHAMBER OF COMMERCE DECIDED THAT IF IT WAS TO ASSERT ITSELF AS A MAJOR INTERNATIONAL CITY, IT NEEDED A GRAND HOTEL. THE ARCHITECTURE FIRM SELECTED WAS GEORGE B. POST & SONS, DESIGNERS OF THE NEW YORK STOCK EXCHANGE AND THE CORNELIUS VANDERBILT HOUSE (CORNELIUS VANDERBILT WAS THE FATHER OF ALFRED GWYNNE VANDERBILT, FIRST GUEST OF THE PLAZA HOTEL). THE OLYMPIC HOTEL OPENED IN 1924, IN WHAT PURPORTED AT THE TIME TO BE A EUROPEAN RENAISSANCE STYLE. THE 1920S PICTURE ABOVE SHOWS ITS ASSEMBLY LOUNGE (NOW SPANISH FOYER).
THE HOTEL QUICKLY BECAME THE PLACE FOR PRESIDENTS AND HEADS OF STATE, SUCH AS FRANKLIN D. ROOSEVELT IN 1932, OR HARRY TRUMAN, JOHN KENNEDY, OR CROWN PRINCESS MICHIKITO, AND CROWN PRINCE AKIHITO OF JAPAN IN THE 1960S. IT ALSO ATTRACTED VISITING HOLLYWOOD STARS LIKE LANA TURNER, BING CROSBY, OR STEVEN SPIELBERG AND TOM CRUISE. THE HOTEL PROVED ALSO TO BE A MAJOR FACTOR OF THE ECONOMIC RENAISSANCE OF THE CITY. IN 2015, BLOOMBERG RATED SEATTLE—NOW HOME TO AMAZON, BOEING, MICROSOFT, STARBUCKS, AND MANY OTHER MAJOR CORPORATIONS—THE FOURTH-RICHEST CITY IN THE UNITED STATES, THOUGH IN TERMS OF POPULATION IT BARELY MAKES THE TOP TWENTY.

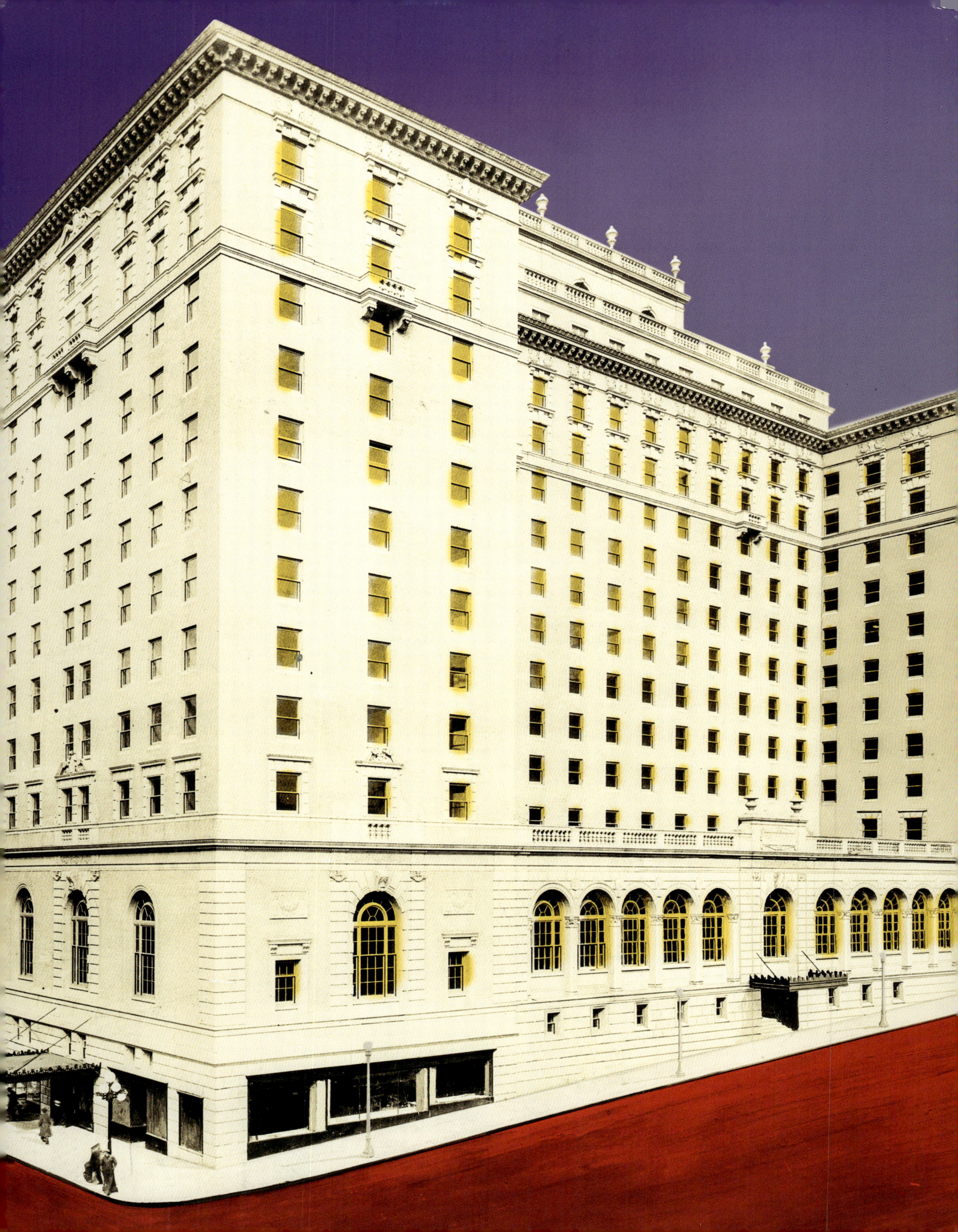

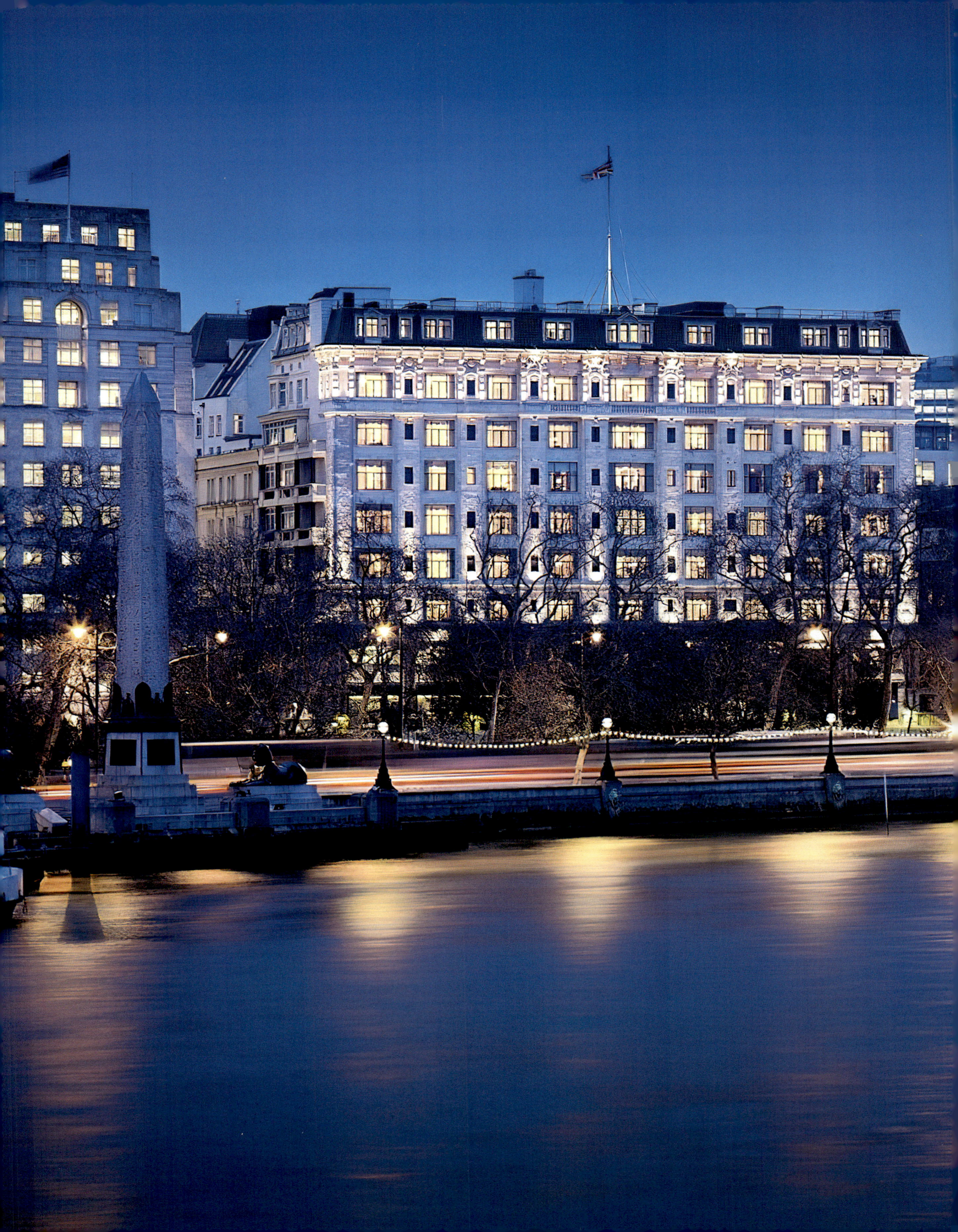

Where Royalty Might Mingle with the Merely Rich
The Savoy, A Fairmont Managed Hotel, London

Having made his fortune producing the light operas of Gilbert & Sullivan, the impresario Richard d'Oyly Carte resolved to build a hotel next to the theatre, also called The Savoy, on a piece of land overlooking the Thames.

The Savoy Theatre had been the first to be electrically lit, and the hotel, which opened in 1889, was another outlier when it came to technology. The structure was made from fire-resistant steel encased in concrete; there were six lifts; electric lights throughout; and hot and cold running water, but only seventy bathrooms for its 400 rooms.

It soon became a high-society favorite. "The place is a regular whispering gallery," wrote Arnold Bennett in his 1930 novel *Imperial Palace*, which was inspired by the hotel, just as his 1902 novel, *The Grand Babylon Hotel* had been.

Some guests were drawn by the food in its dining room and the promise of the fabled chef Auguste Escoffier's cooking. "Much as Eve tasted the first apple, I tasted the first *pêche melba* in the world. It's delicious," Dame Nellie Melba recalls asking what he had prepared as a dessert.

Others came for the parties. Witness the fancy-dress ball, pictured above, held in 1912 in aid of the Middlesex Hospital, and attended by Prince Alexander of Teck, later the Earl of Athlone, younger brother of George V's wife, Queen Mary, and a great uncle of Queen Elizabeth II.

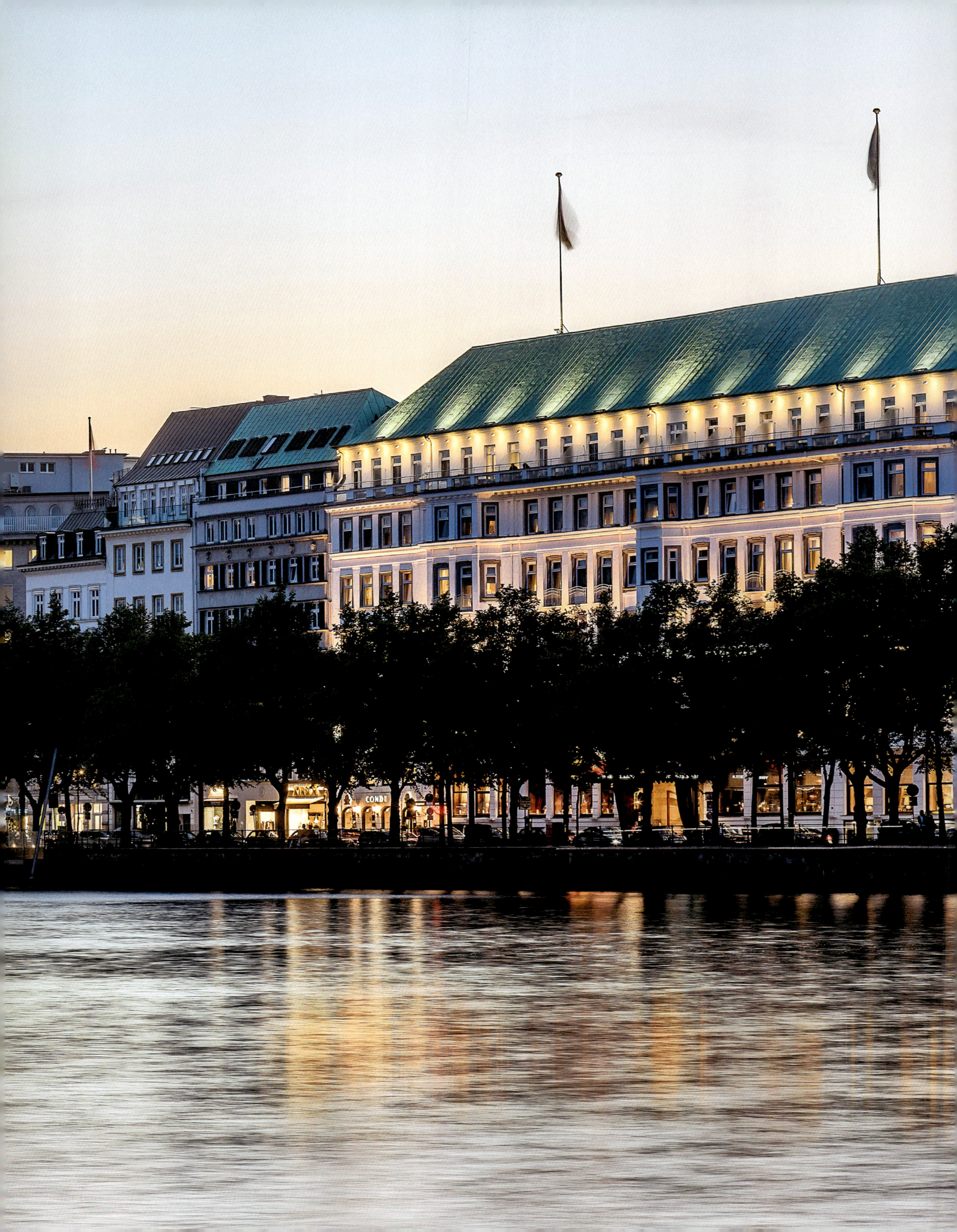

Contemporary Belle Époque
Fairmont Grand Hotel Kiev

Overlooking the Dnieper river in the Ukrainian capital's historic Podol district, Fairmont Grand Hotel Kyiv resembles a great baroque palace but has actually stood here only since 2012. From the crystal chandeliers hanging from the highest ceilings, to the splendiferous build of the glass canopy, everything echoes to the opulence of the grand hotels of the nineteenth century.

The Inner Alster's Great Grande Dame
Fairmont Hotel Vier Jahreszeiten, Hamburg

Having begun life as a waiter, Friedrich Haerlin moved into hotel-keeping and in 1897—the year he turned forty—he saw an opportunity to have one of his own. The owners of the Vier Jahreszeiten, then an eleven-room establishment overlooking the Inner Alster, had been bankrupted. Haerlin raised the money, bought them out on his birthday and began to buy up the neighboring buildings, eventually acquiring the whole street (opposite). Over time, he developed them, each in a different style—neo-Jacobean, new Renaissance, and later Jugendstil and art deco—but all within a unifying neoclassical shell. By 1911, the eclectically designed hotel had 140 rooms and 50 bathrooms. There are now 156, each one en suite it goes without saying.

It was famous, too, for its Café Condi (right), which served forty-two types of praline, a delicacy so delectable that Prinz Heinrich von Preussen appointed Haerlin a purveyor to the royal court of Prussia.

Montreux-Palace-Hotel Montreux

Music on the Lake
Fairmont Le Montreux Palace, Montreux

A palatial presence on Lac Léman facing the French Alps, Le Montreux Palace opened in 1906, with luxurious rooms and private bathrooms. The Palace's first guests were indeed early international tourists following the steps of the Empress Sissi or Sarah Bernhardt, joining Montreux on steamships crossing the Geneva lake or with the newly inaugurated electric train line linking Montreux to Gstaad.
Realizing its guests would enjoy entertainment in the evenings, it also incorporated a Salon de Musique, not merely an auditorium, but a suite of ballrooms where galas and concerts were held regularly.
Today, they are still highly prized locations during the prestigious annual Montreux Jazz festival.

GRAND RAILWAY HOTELS

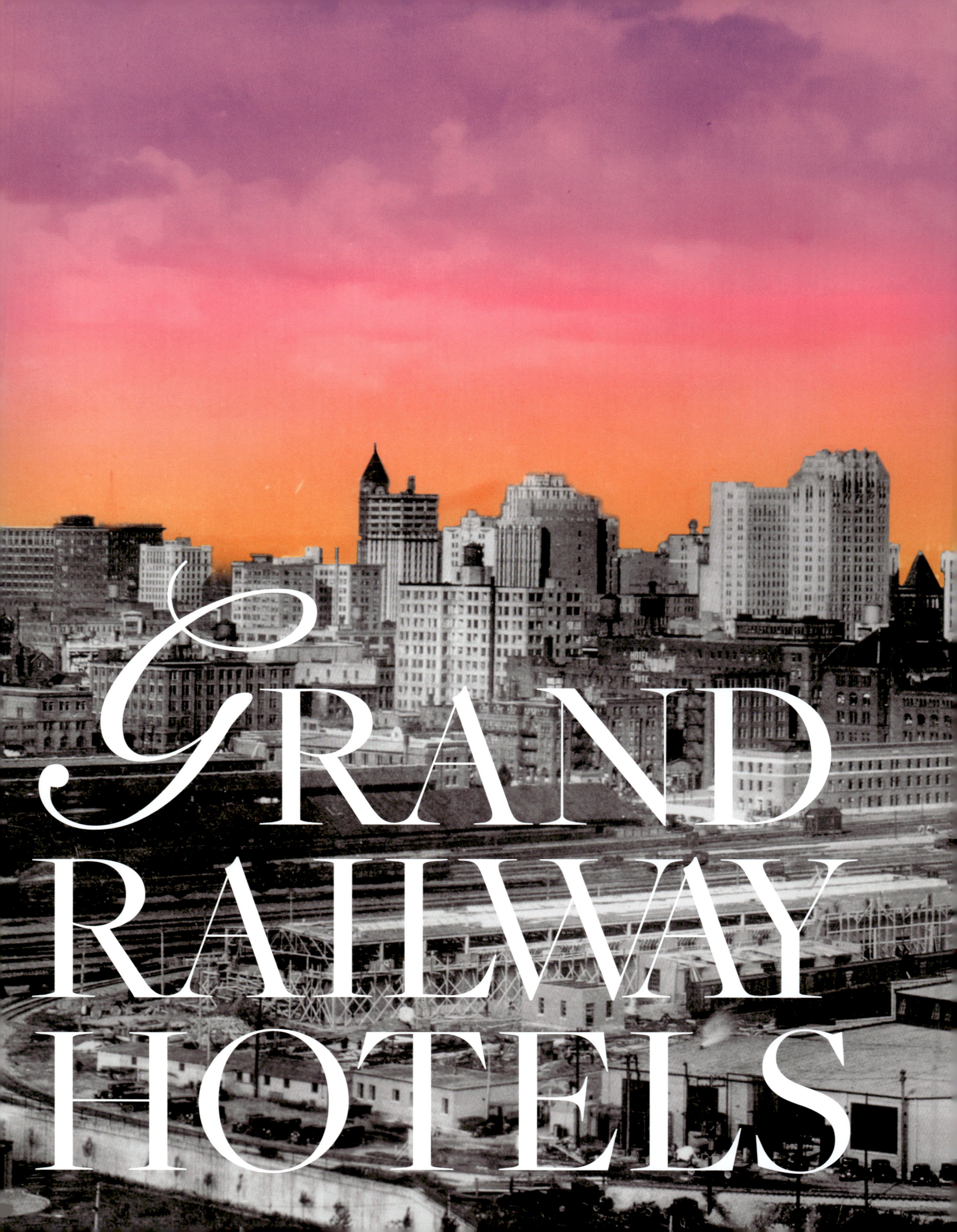

Roundhouse at the railway yard with the Royal York Hotel in the background, as seen from the waterfront, Toronto, 1933.

The "Third Chamber" of Canada's Parliament
Fairmont Château Laurier, Ottawa

Château Laurier opened in 1912, named after Sir Wilfred Laurier, Canada's first French-Canadian Prime Minister. Built by Canada's Grand Trunk Railway (rather than the Canadian Pacific), it was directly connected to the city's railway station by a tunnel, as painted by Richard Rummell in *Chateau Laurier, Grand Trunk System*, 1911 (opposite).
Its architecture was influenced as much by the château-style hotels in western Canada as French châteaux such as Chantilly and Carcassonne. No expense was spared on its interiors either. Sadly though, the furniture that its founder, Charles Melville Hays, President of Canada's Grand Trunk Railway, traveled to London to buy was lost, as was Hays and the ship he was traveling on, the Titanic. For all its grandeur, however, its Tiffany stained-glass rotunda, coffered ceilings and Belgian marble staircase and floors, the hotel contained dormitories as well as suites to make it accessible to less wealthy railway passengers. There were even inexpensive rooms for traveling salesmen, furnished with display tables for their wares.
Thanks to its proximity to the Canadian parliament, the Château Laurier became enduringly popular with politicians, welcoming international leaders such as Winston Churchill (left) or Ronald Reagan in 1982 (right). Pierre Trudeau lived at Château Laurier for three years from 1965, and he is said to have particularly enjoyed the hotel's splendid art-deco swimming pool.

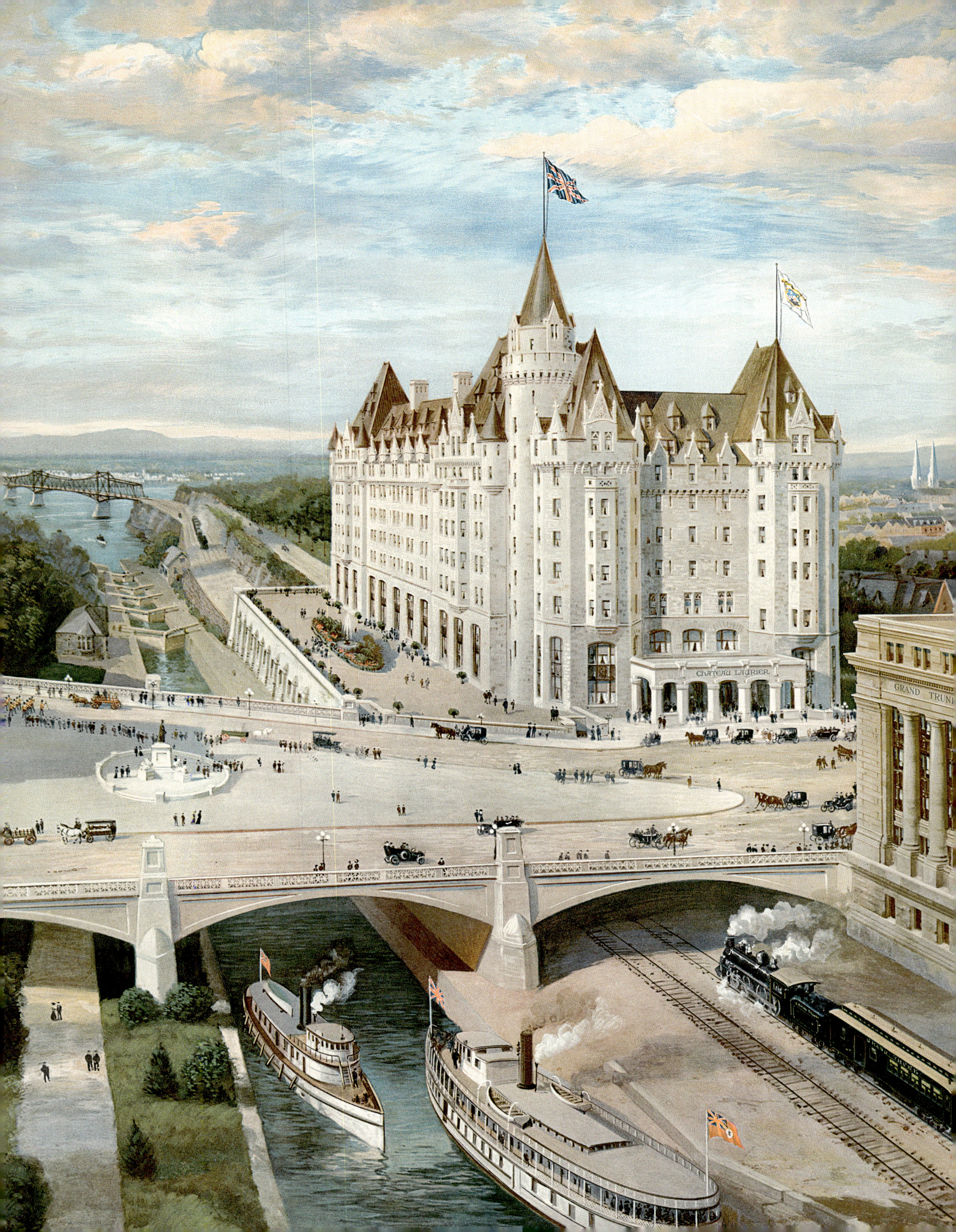
CHATEAU LAURIER
GRAND TRUN

A French Castle over the Saskatchewan River
Fairmont Hotel MacDonald, Edmonton

Overlooking the wide valley of the North Saskatchewan River, flowing from the ice fields of the Canadian Rockies, the MacDonald Hotel was built in 1915 by the Grand Trunk Railway three years after Château Laurier in Ottawa. Named like its counterpart after a major Canadian prime minister, it was also designed by Ross and MacFarlane.
The architects preferred a luminous limestone that could be delicately chipped and carved in a French Renaissance style, to the warm shade of bricks used by the Canadian Pacific Railway hotels. When the "Mac," as it has become affectionately known, closed its doors in 1983, the strong protests of the Edmontonian community led to its careful restoration and a highly expected public reopening in May 1991. Very soon, this centerpiece for royal visits (Queen Elizabeth II stayed twice) started to welcome again prestigious guests like Brad Pitt, Celine Dion, or the Rolling Stones.

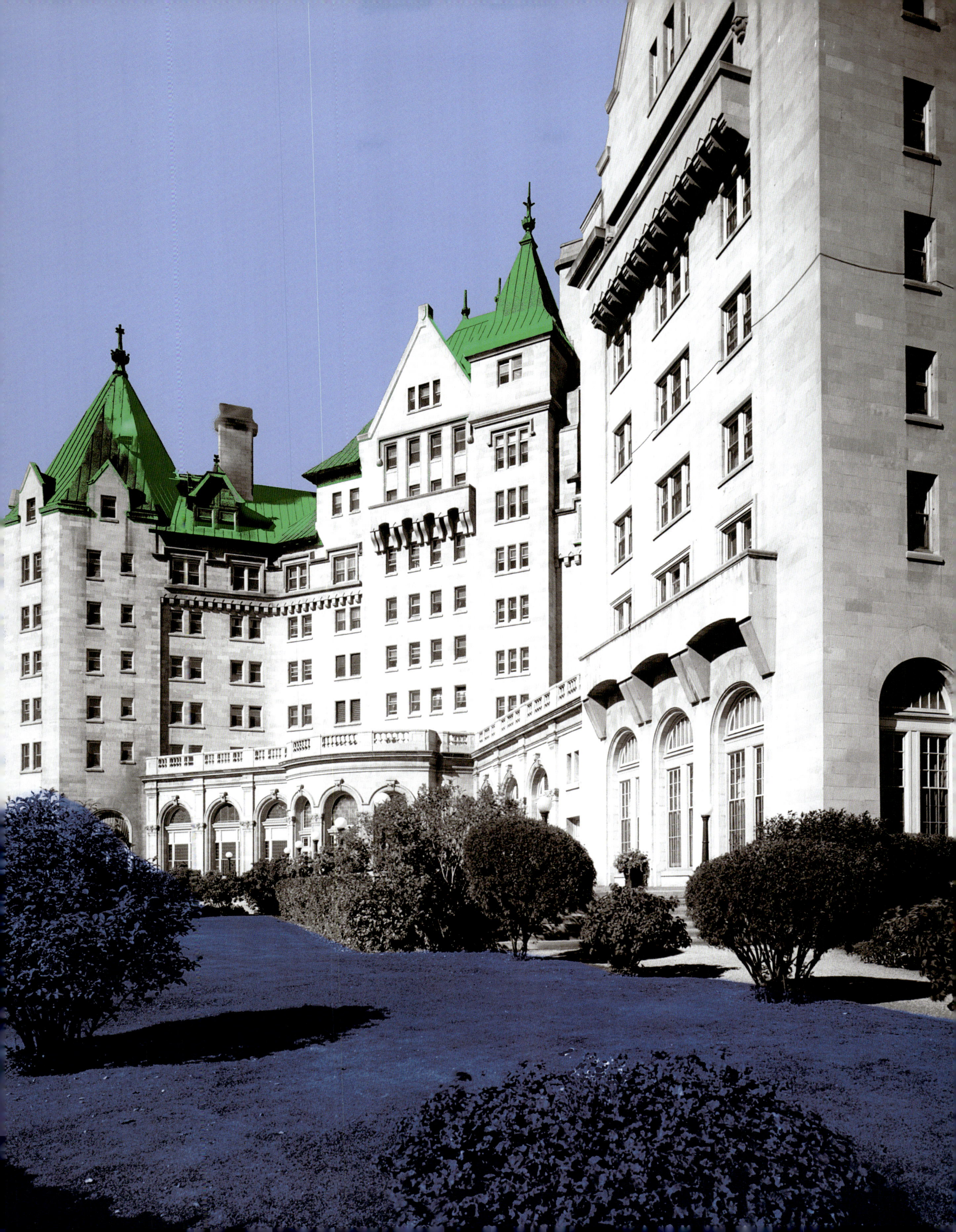

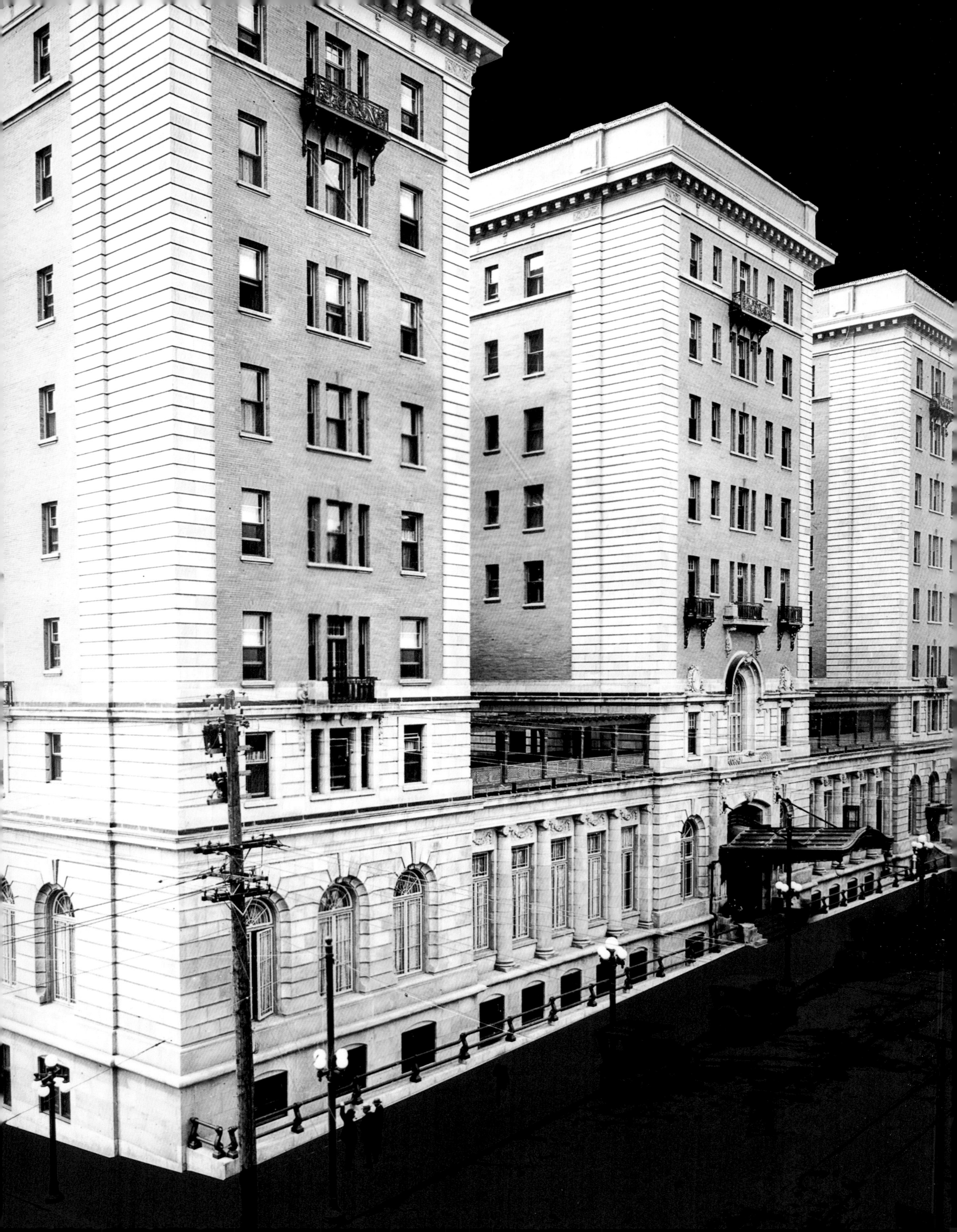

Gateway to the Rockies
Fairmont Palliser, Calgary

Built by the Canadian Pacific Railway at the request of the city's council, which waived taxes on the build, the Palliser opened in 1914. The city, which had branded itself the Gateway to the Rockies, hoped it would encourage tourism, and so named it after Captain John Palliser, the Irish-born leader of the British North American Exploring Expedition that surveyed western Canada's prairies and wilderness between 1857 and 1880. The crystal chandelier above, weighing approximately 2,450 pounds, was made of 2,800 multifaceted polished crystals.

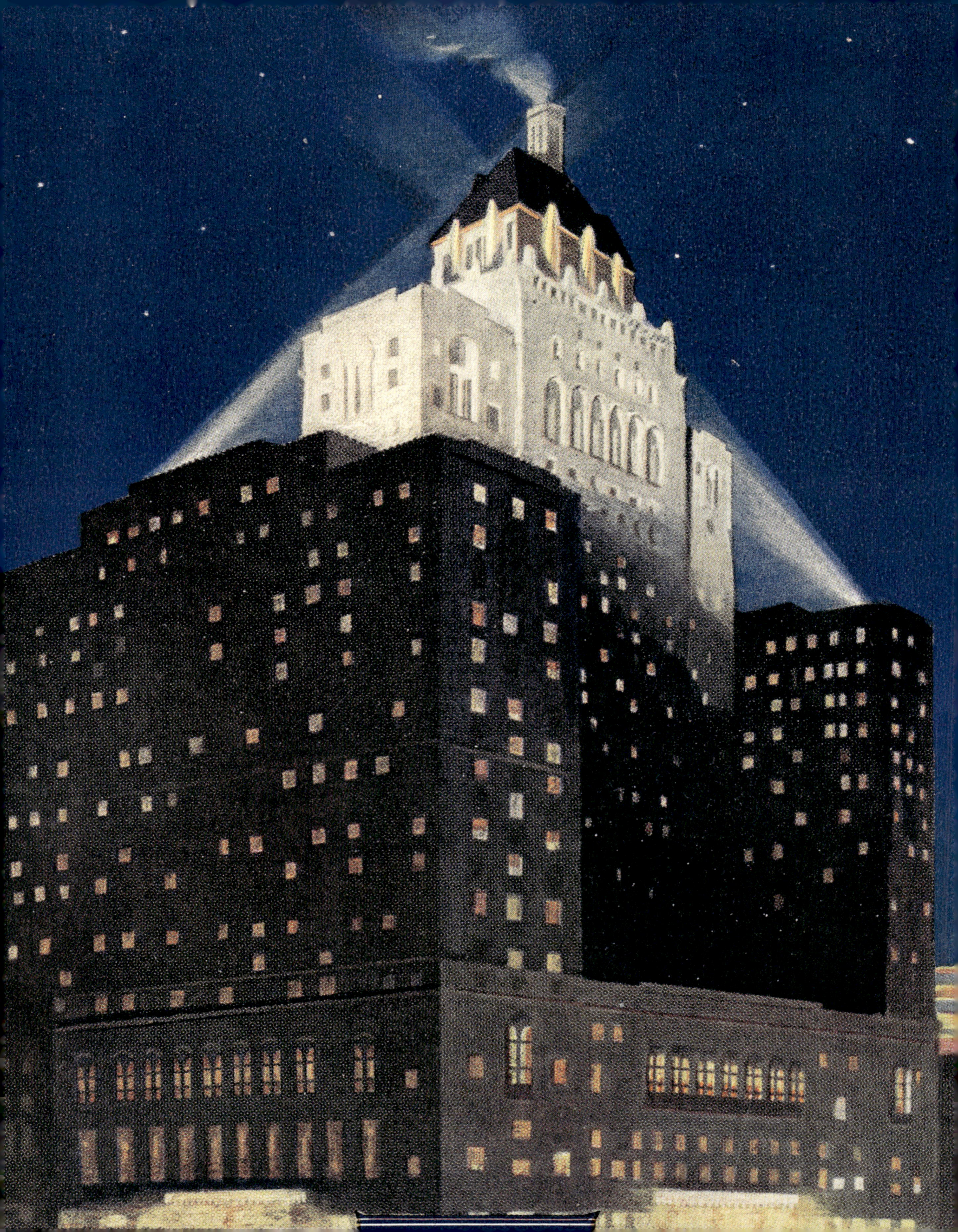

The Tallest Tower in the British Empire
FAIRMONT ROYAL YORK, TORONTO

MORE THAN 400 FEET HIGH, THE ROYAL YORK WAS, WHEN IT OPENED IN 1927, THE TALLEST BUILDING NOT JUST IN CANADA BUT IN THE WHOLE OF THE BRITISH EMPIRE. (CANADA'S BANK OF COMMERCE, TO ITS RIGHT IN THE 1930 PHOTOGRAPH OF AN R-100 AIRSHIP OVER THE CITY, ECLIPSED IT A YEAR LATER.) THERE WERE MORE THAN A THOUSAND ROOMS (THERE STILL ARE) AND THE TELEPHONE SWITCHBOARD WAS SIXTY-SIX FEET LONG. IT HAS LONG BEEN POPULAR WITH HEADS OF STATE, (THE HOTEL WAS SELECTED TO HOLD THE 2010 G20 SUMMIT). FOR DECADES, THE HOTEL HAS BEEN THE EPICENTER OF THE CITY'S CULTURAL LIFE, HOSTING THE SHOWS OF ELLA FITZGERALD, MARLENE DIETRICH, OR JOSEPHINE BAKER. THIS ARTISTIC COMMITMENT IS STILL ALIVE TODAY. AMONGST OTHERS, SUCH AS THE TORONTO INTERNATIONAL FILM FESTIVAL AND NUMEROUS MOVIE SETS, THE HOTEL CONTINUES TO WELCOME INTERNATIONAL STARS LIKE MERYL STREEP, ISABELLE HUPPERT, EVA LONGORIA, AND LADY GAGA. OPPOSITE, AN ILLUSTRATION EXTRACTED FROM A 1930 CANADIAN PACIFIC RAILWAY PAMPHLET.

The Last of the Châteaux Hotels
FAIRMONT HOTEL VANCOUVER

THE HOTEL VANCOUVER WAS THE THIRD OF THREE CANADIAN PACIFIC HOTELS TO BEAR THAT NAME. IT SUBSTITUTED AN ITALIAN RENAISSANCE-STYLE HOTEL BUILT JUST TWENTY-THREE YEARS EARLIER, PICTURED ABOVE, LEFT, DURING AN EVENING PARTY, CA. 1930, WHICH ITSELF HAD SUCCEEDED A MODEST FIVE-STORY BRICK FARMHOUSE-LIKE STRUCTURE, WHICH OPENED IN 1888 (I.E. TWO YEARS AFTER THE ARRIVAL IN THE CITY OF THE CANADIAN PACIFIC RAILWAY AND ITS NEW FLOW OF TRAVELERS TO VANCOUVER).
DESIGNED BY ARCHITECTS ARCHIBALD AND SCHOFIELD, THE CURRENT VANCOUVER HOTEL IS ONE OF THE LAST BUILDINGS IN BRITISH COLUMBIA TO BE ORNAMENTED WITH STONE CARVINGS. GOTHIC GARGOYLES, AND A CARVED CHIMERA (ABOVE, RIGHT), HERMES GOD OF TRAVEL, ALL CLASSICAL PATTERNS MIXED SURPRISINGLY WITH BAS-RELIEFS OF LOCOMOTIVES AND OCEAN LINERS. INSIDE THE HOTEL, NEOCLASSICISM, ROCOCO, AND THE THEN HIGHLY FASHIONABLE ART-DECO STYLE REIGN.
THE NEW HOTEL'S CONSTRUCTION WAS STALLED, HOWEVER, BY THE GREAT DEPRESSION. IT FINALLY OPENED IN MAY 1939, JUST IN TIME FOR KING GEORGE VI'S AND QUEEN ELIZABETH'S ROYAL TOUR OF CANADA THAT YEAR.

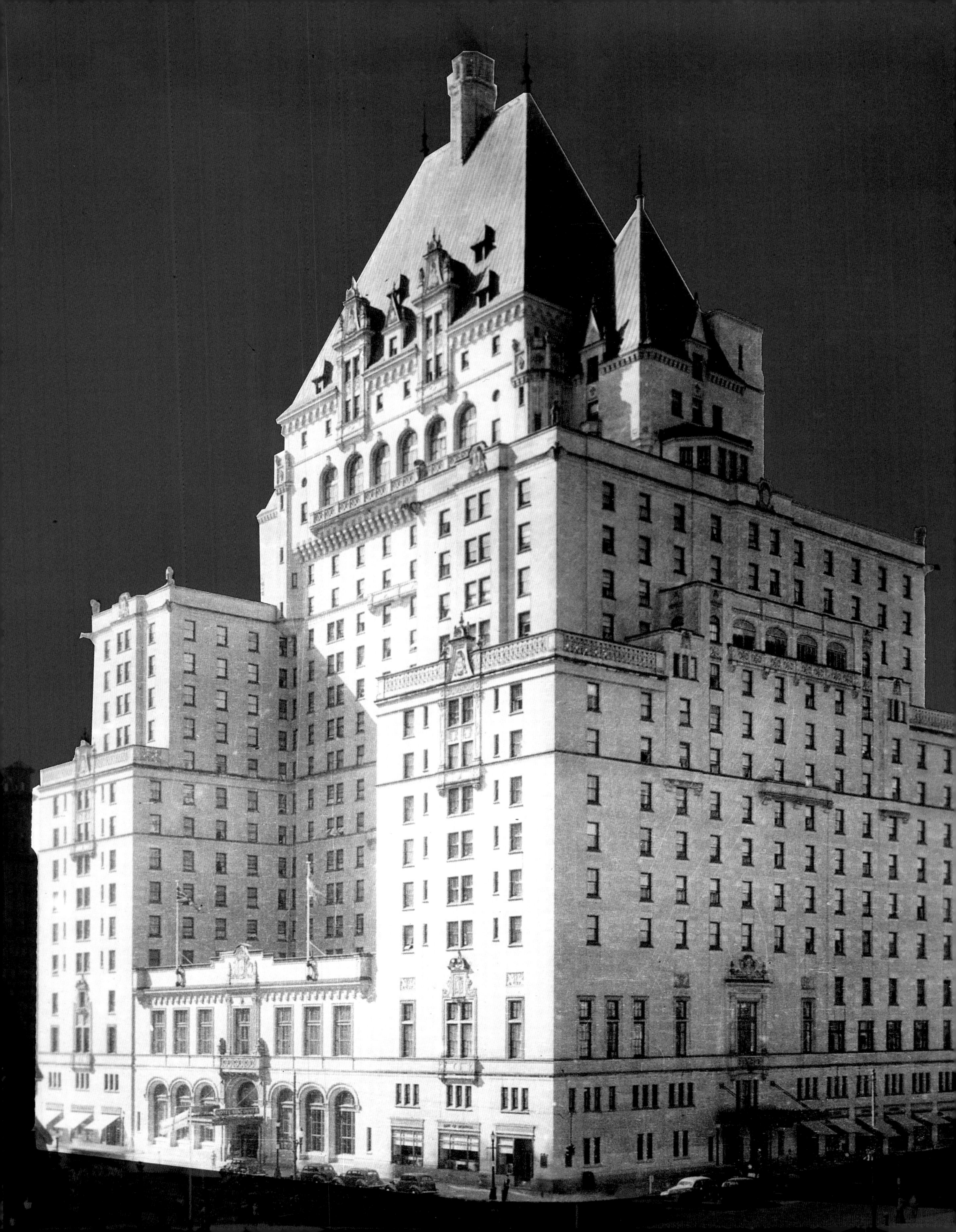

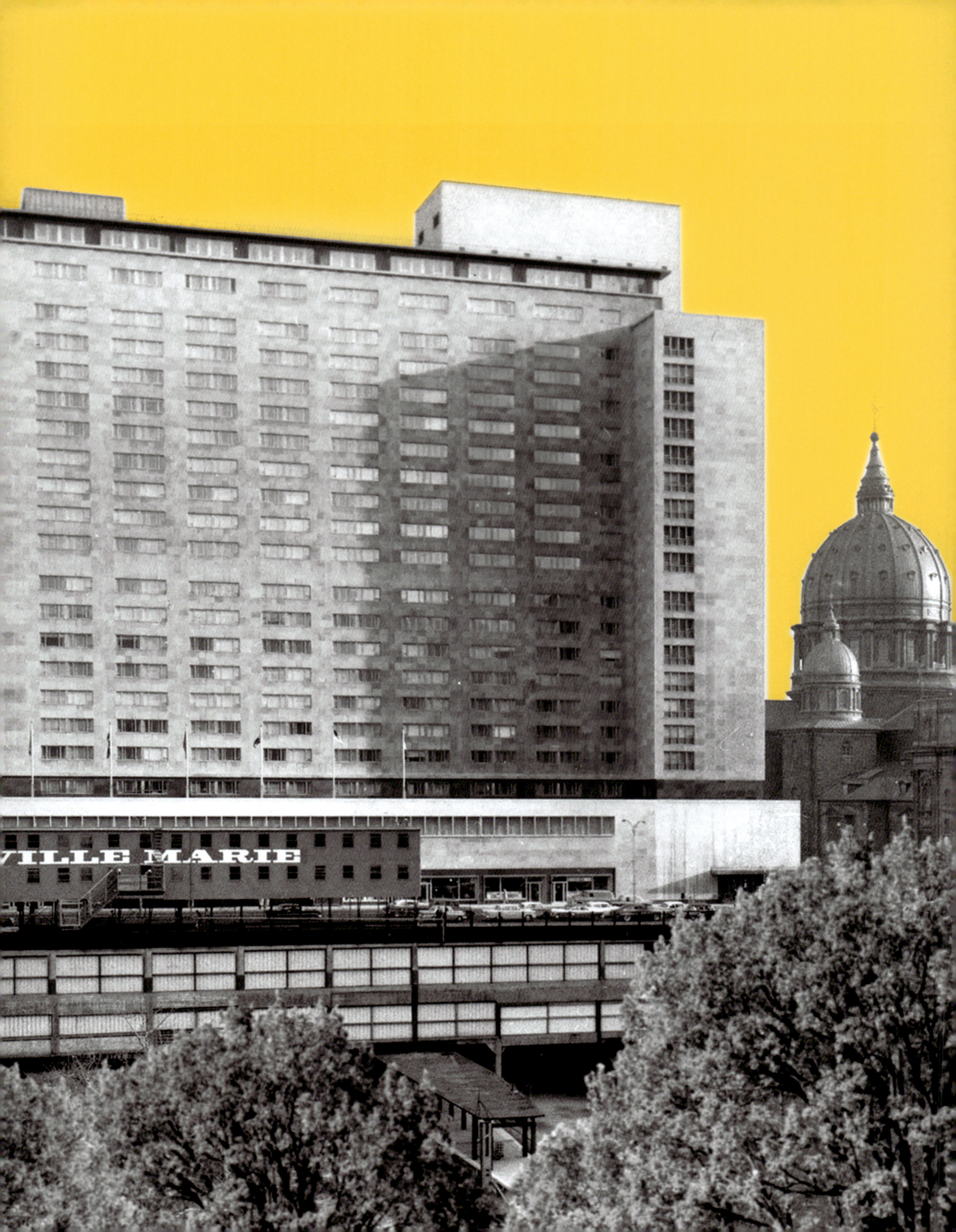
VILLE MARIE

Metropolitan Wonders
Fairmont Mayakovskaya, Moscow

Fairmont Moscow stands directly on top of the Mayakovskaya metro station, a palatial building, as well as an important interchange, designed by the influential Soviet-era architect Alexey Dushkin, whose style has informed the design of the newly built hotel and residences.

The station's vaulted ceiling is best known for its thirty-four domes, each one of which is lined with a circular mosaic by the revered artist Aleksandr Deyneka. They depict twenty-four hours in the life of the Moscow sky: kite flying, construction sites with cranes, airplanes, sunflowers, high-jumping athletes, factories with smokestacks, searchlights, parachutists ... all as seen from below. "The thousands of people who crowded the platforms day and night went crazy with delight," Dushkin wrote after its opening in 1938. "It was difficult to believe that one was [108 feet] beneath the soil." No wonder a reconstruction of two sections of it won the Grand Prix at the following year's World's Fair in New York.

Grand Tour Railways
Monte-Carlo Fairmont Hotel

The Monte-Carlo Fairmont Hotel was built in the exact same location where the Belle-Époque train station used to stand. The Société des Bains de Mer (SBM) had indeed built the whole infrastructures to attract wealthy grand tourists to their casino. A lift had even been installed directly linking the station to the game rooms. The soul of this period has been immortalized in Stefan Zweig's novel *Twenty-Four Hours in the Life of a Woman*, where the Monte-Carlo station is mentioned several times. Rebuilt forward on the hill, the original station no longer exists, only a piece of the original wall is hidden within the offices of what is today Monte-Carlo Fairmont Hotel.

Right by the Railway, but Fit for a Queen
Fairmont The Queen Elizabeth, Montreal

Built by the Canadian National Railway and connected to both the Central railway station and the RESO or Underground City, The Queen Elizabeth opened in 1958, its name a source of some local controversy in Francophone Montreal. Though the British monarch remains Canada's head of state, there had been a campaign to call it Château Maisonneuve (left).

ART

Paris may have the Eiffel Tower and Sydney its Opera House, but as William Van Horne predicted when he built Château Frontenac in Quebec, there are also cities that are known by their landmark hotels: the belle-epoque Montreux Palace, the Flame Towers in Baku, and the Katara Towers in the new Qatari city of Lusail. All are also Fairmont hotels.

Such buildings matter. When, in 1965, there was a plan to pull down the by-then moribund Empress in Victoria, the westernmost of Canada's great railway hotels, the British Colonist, a local newspaper, warned that "Without this splendid relic of the Edwardian era, literally tens of thousands of tourists will never return. This is the Mecca, the heart and soul of the city." The decision to demolish was rescinded. The hotel, once known as the Queen of the Pacific had been described by that same newspaper as "a distinct and important landmark" for the city when it opened in 1908. And so, it remains.

But, for a building to become a landmark, it needs to be architecturally significant. When Van Horne began to build hotels in Canada in the late nineteenth century, for example, he opted for a style that fused French Renaissance traditions found in the Loire châteaux with Scottish baronial style—an expedient, even political choice insofar as it unified the French and British elements of Canada's colonial heritage by fusing their traditions—resulting in a chain that was unified by the splendor and magnificence, not to mention the state-of-the-art facilities, of its buildings.

It's a commitment that endures. Fairmont now counts more than eighty hotels worldwide, a portfolio that embraces almost 300 years of architectural history from the exquisite eighteenth-century neoclassicism of Carton House in Ireland to twenty-first-century landmarks by the likes of Skidmore Owings & Merrill (Nanjing), Richard Rogers (Seoul), and Jean Nouvel (Geneva), by way of twentieth-century star architects such as Minoru Yamasaki (Los Angeles) and I.M. Pei (Singapore).

CHI
ECT
URE

1886

1894

1899

1901–1911

1908

ca. 1912

ca. 1926

The Evolution of Chateau Lake Louise

No hotel in Canada combines quite so many of the architectural styles that came to typify Canadian Pacific Hotels as Chateau Lake Louise, which began life as a log cabin and by the mid-1920s had morphed gradually into a huge and magnificent turreted castle.

The first building to occupy this site in 1886 was little more than a rustic cabin, offering meals and a place to sleep.

It was destroyed by a fire in 1893 and replaced by a chalet-like dining room, which opened the following year, catering principally to day trippers from Banff.

A second hotel subsequently opened, another timber building this time set further back from the lake, with long verandas facing the water. It did not conform to the style of a castle, but it was named Chateau Lake Louise nevertheless.

Over time, it was extended by the British-born architect Francis Rattenbury, and by 1908 it had become a three-story building, with 500 beds. Its original, essentially neoclassical form was enveloped in a half-timbered frame with stucco infill in accordance with the then-fashionable style known as Mock Tudor, after the royal family that ruled England and Wales from 1485 to 1603.

Its roofline, however, was made spiky with gables. Towers, admittedly quite stunted ones, were added at each corner. It was becoming a castle.

In 1912, W.S. Painter, the architect of the Banff Springs Hotel, was brought in to modernize the hotel further, adding a new wing in what was purportedly the Italian villa style, and replacing the shared veranda with an arcade of private balconies on the lower floors.

After a second terrible fire that destroyed Rattenbury's additions in 1924, a new architectural practice, Barott and Blackader, was hired. It designed a new nine-story wing, this time in brick, with 400 bedrooms, most facing the lake, and in 1926, added a 100-feet heated swimming pool, then the second-largest in Canada.

Though parts of the existing building date back to 1913, the surviving hotel is essentially a Renaissance-revival château. A row of pointed dormers gives the roof line a jagged faintly gothic quality and harks back to the dormers Rattenbury had designed, as do the pyramid-roofed towers he placed at each corner.

In combining so many different design tropes—from Canadian mountain vernacular to alpine chalet to cod-Elizabethan to Renaissance French château—it represents not only most of the prevailing fashions of its age, but all the key architectural features of the earliest Canadian Pacific Hotels.

Rustic Style
Little Switzerland

A short hike from Chateau Lake Louise brings you to Lake Agnes and its little tea house (above) built by the Canadian Pacific Railway in 1901 as a refuge for walkers and a resting place from which to admire the view. Architecturally, it is a modest rustic construction, a log cabin dressed in wood shingles and uncut stone, intended to evoke both North American vernacular and, in the pitch of its roof, an alpine chalet. For just as the Canadian Pacific Railway wanted its splendid hotels to recall noble French châteaux, so it wanted to build more modest structures that resembled alpine villages—none more blatantly than the one it named Edelweiss, near the town of Golden, where the Swiss guides it recruited were invited to settle permanently with their wives and families, in the hope that it might remind them of home.
Jasper Park Lodge (right) and Château Montebello, respectively built in 1922 and 1930 fully embrace the rustic style to create a refreshing version of luxury in the wild.

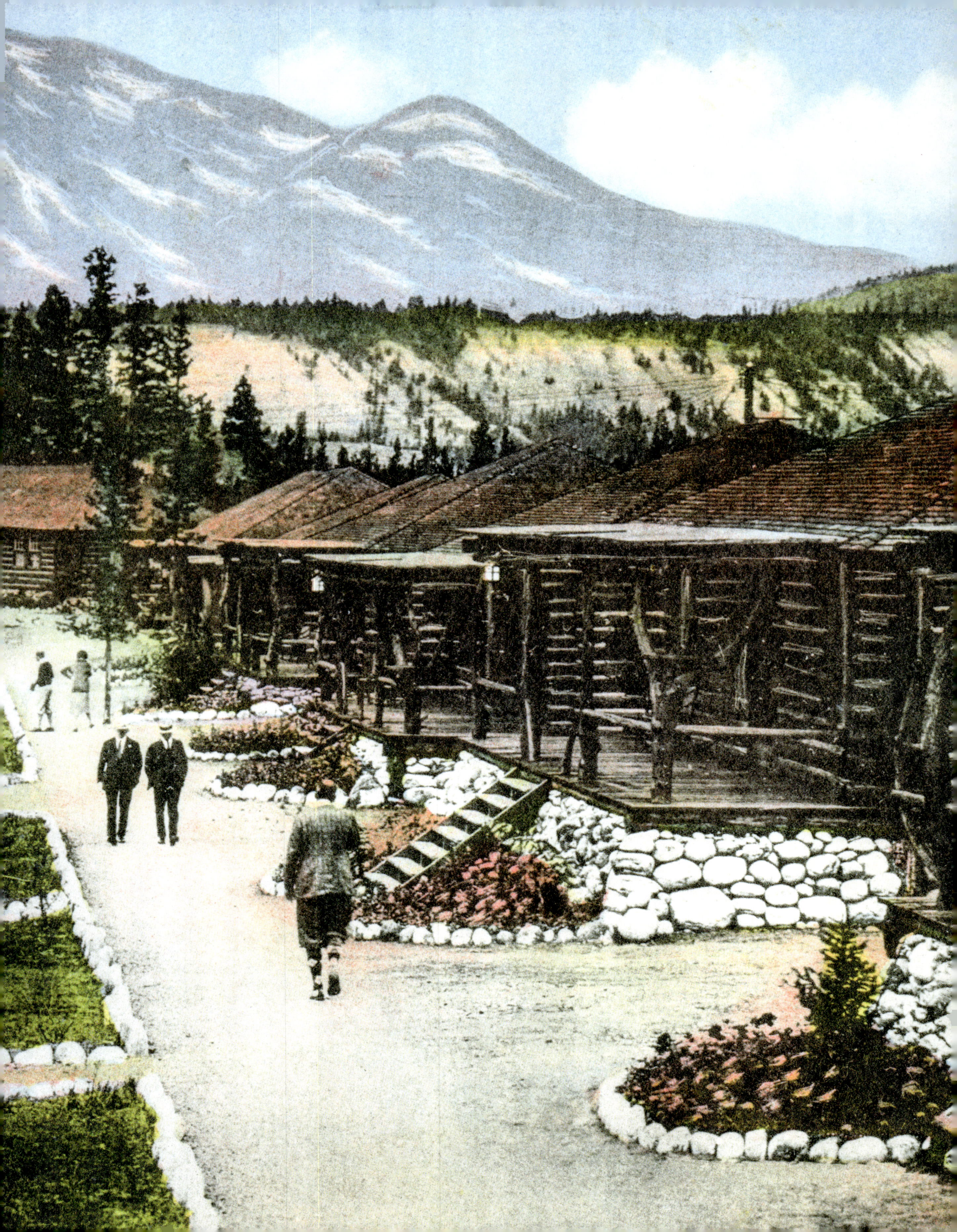

WHITE SAND, LUSH JUNGLE, TURQUOISE SEA: THE VILLAS AT FAIRMONT MALDIVES, SIRRU FEN FUSHI (LEFT) AND FAIRMONT MAYAKOBA ON MEXICO'S CARIBBEAN COAST IS ROOFED RESPECTIVELY WITH CANVAS AND THATCH (RIGHT).

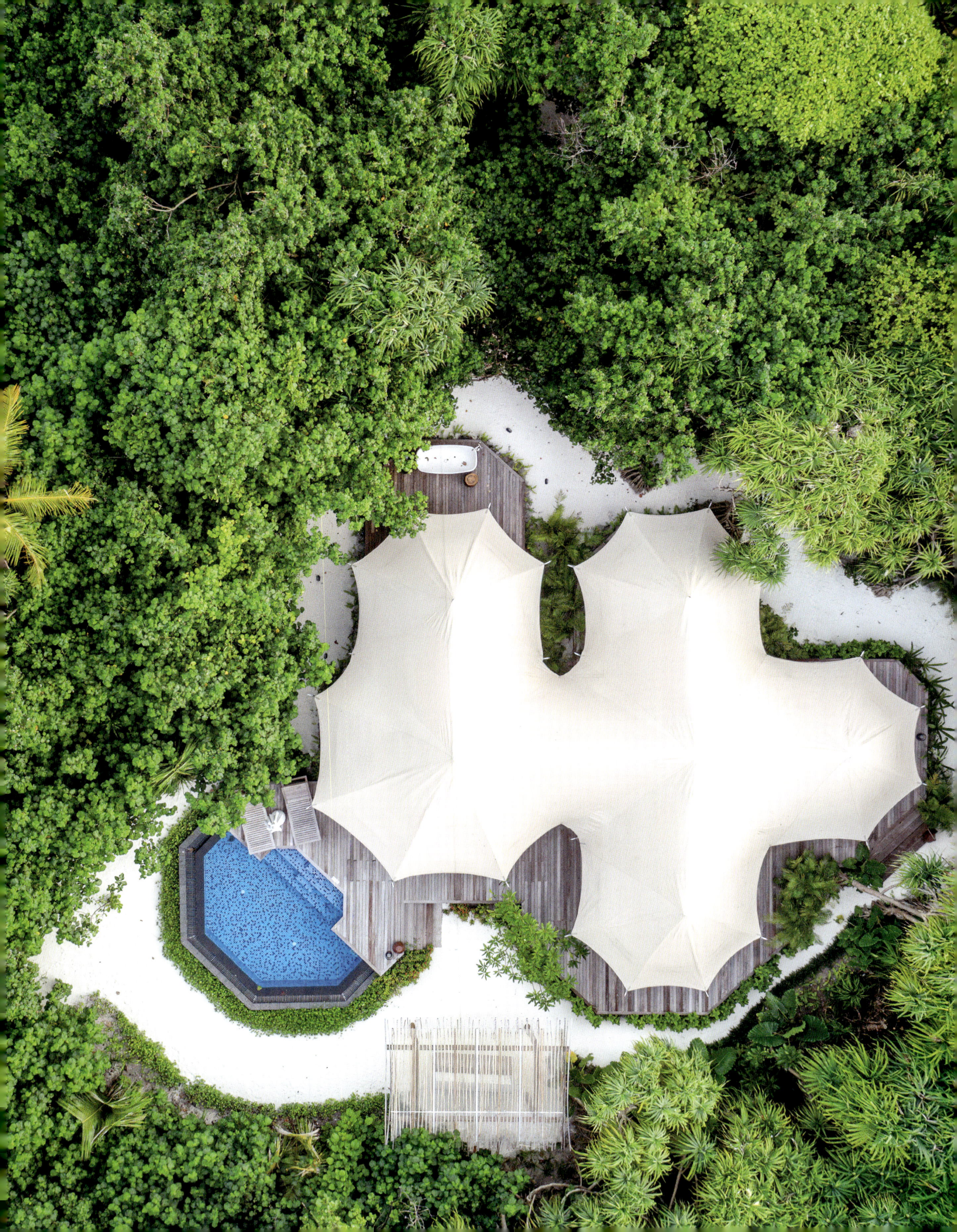

As a natural heat and humidity regulator, compacted earth or mud has been used for millennia all over the planet. Pisé, as it is known in Morocco, was selected among other natural traditional materials (cedar wood, taddelak...) to build Fairmont Royal Palm Marrakech (opposite & bottom), in an enchanting century-old olive and lemon tree grove under the snowy mounts of the Atlas. In Fairmont Taghazout Bay as well (above left), built on the shores of the Atlantic Ocean, traditional techniques and materials were chosen. Adobe, a Spanish word derived from the Arab طوب for unfired brick, was used at Fairmont Scottsdale Princess in the desert Arizona (right).

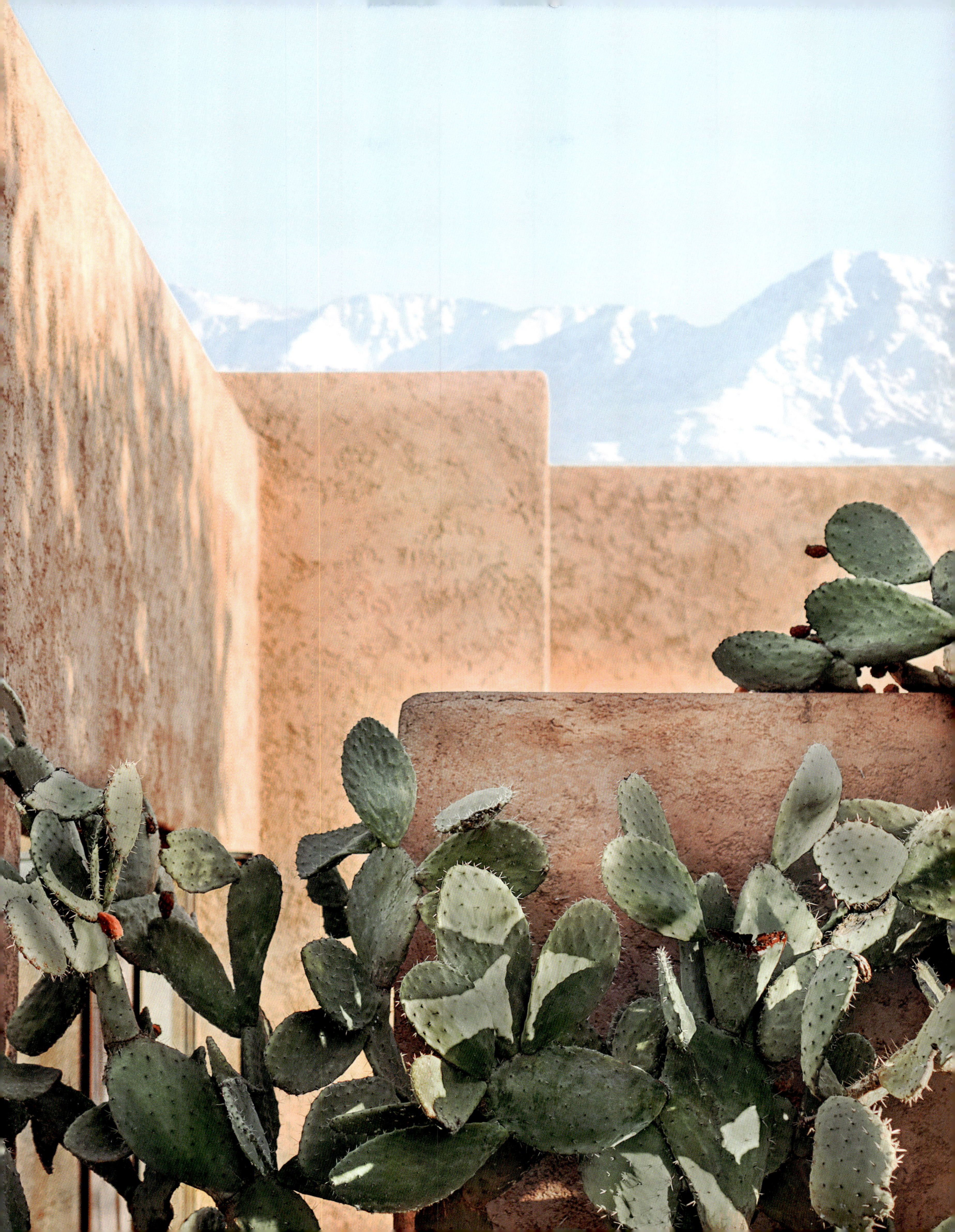

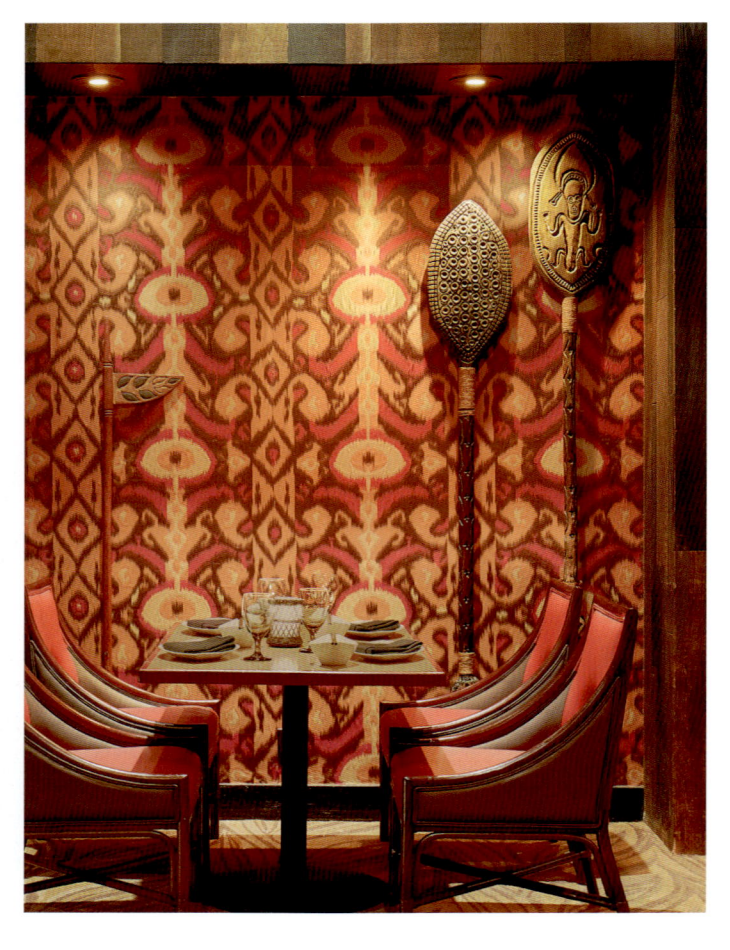

In 1929, the Fairmont in San Francisco had a seventy-five-foot indoor swimming pool, "the Fairmont Plunge," attracting actors such as Ronald Reagan and Helen Hayes. By 1945, Mel Melvin, Metro-Goldwyn-Mayer's leading set director, was commissioned to transform it into something more exotic, a kitsch extravaganza of thatched tiki huts, palm fronds, and nautical accessorizing. Inspired by the idea of a tropical lagoon, the result was the Tonga Room (left). A floating platform on which a band could play was even installed on the water.
Located in the renowned Masai Mara Game Reserve—home to the great wildebeest migration—the Fairmont Mara Safari Club's luxurious tents (right) and their private wooden decks overlook the hippo-filled Mara River. Its smooth red huts (opposite) are direct heirs of the Masai traditional constructions.

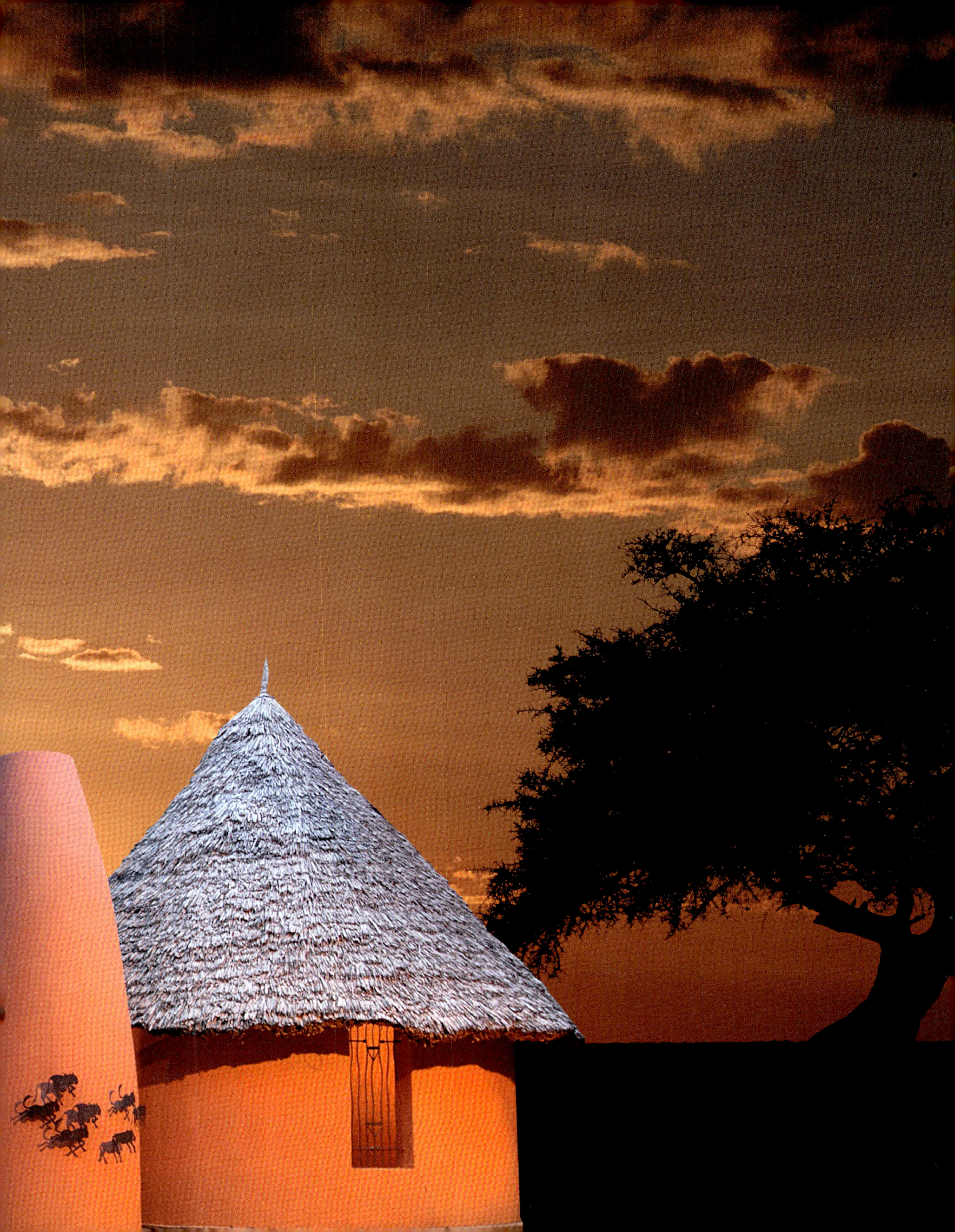

"Broad effects,
rather than ornamentation and detail
[like] marble and frills."

William Van Horne
IN A LETTER TO HIS PREDECESSOR LORD MOUNT STEPHEN
ABOUT HIS PLANS FOR CHÂTEAU FRONTENAC

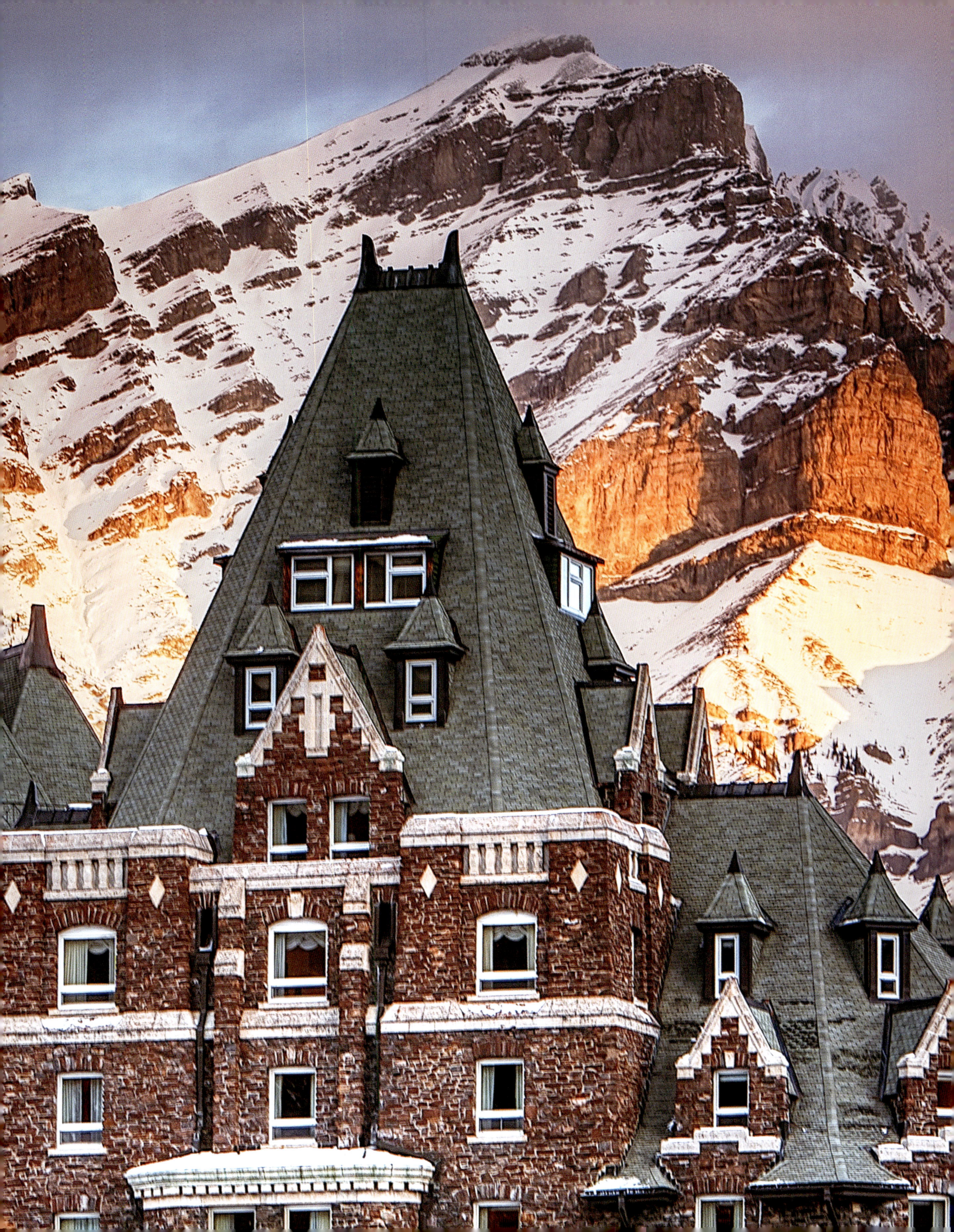

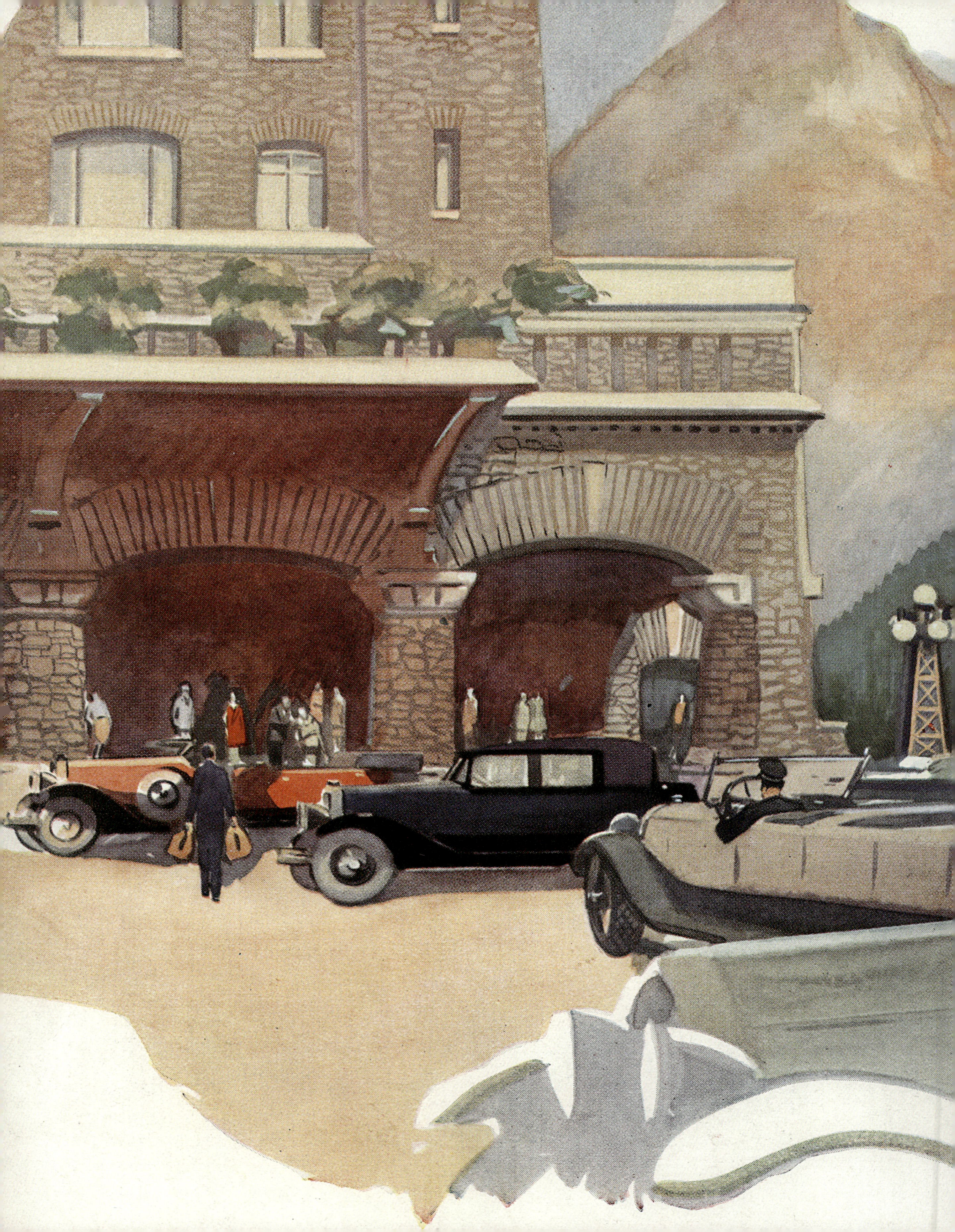

Château Style

If Banff Springs (opposite & above left) was the first hotel in Canada to aspire to the architecture of a French château, then Château Frontenac in Quebec was to take the idea and run with it. Its principal architect, Bruce Price, acknowledged a debt to the lesser-known Château de Jaligny, and several of his colleagues borrowed from various Loire châteaux. Look at the pitch of its roof (previous page), with its asymmetrical crowd of spiky towers, and one cannot help being reminded of Amboise, even Chambord. Canadian Pacific's château style informed more than the roofs of its hotels. It borrowed from medieval and Renaissance architecture in other ways too: note the heavily dressed stonework; rusticated architraves; fan vaulting; coffered ceilings or theatrical outlines that came to be found even in contemporary hotels across the world from Fairmont Chateau Whistler, Château Tremblant (top), Hotel Fairmont Heritage Place Franz Klammer Lodge in Telluride (bottom).

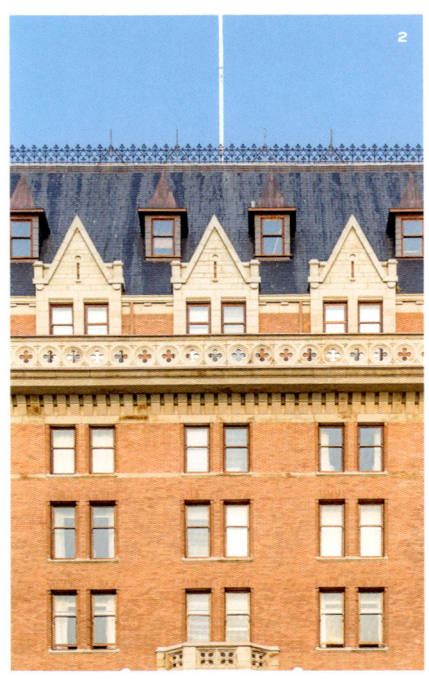

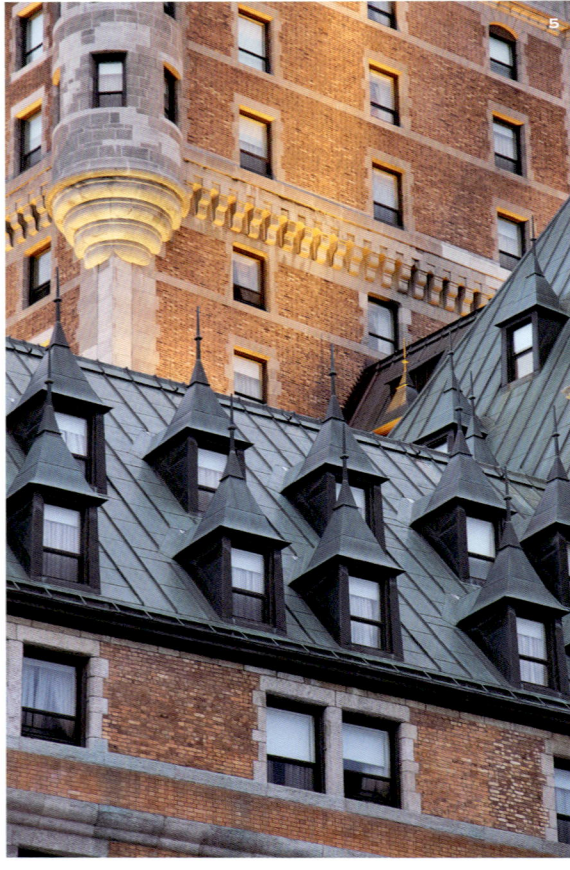

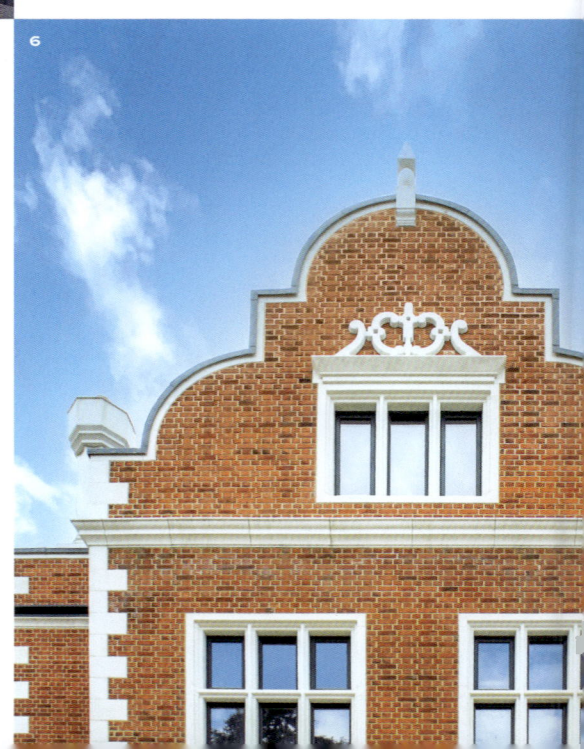

The Château-Style Design of the Canadian Pacific Railway's Hotels

Château Laurier (3 & 4), Château Frontenac (5 & opposite) and the Empress Victoria (2) for example, may ultimately be pastiche, but the new-build Fairmont Windsor Park (6), close to Windsor Castle in England, evokes the Dutch-gabled facade of the seventeenth-century Jacobean mansion that originally stood here. In the same way, the tower of the Ghirardelli chocolate factory in San Francisco, originally the Pioneer Woollen Mill and now Fairmont Heritage Place (1), Ghirardelli Square, is a copy of the Gothic Louis XII tower of the fifteenth-century Loire Château of Blois in France.

"Would Paris be the same without the Eiffel Tower, and Quebec without Château Frontenac, would it still be Quebec?"

William Van Horne
JULY 3, 1893

From Château Style to Art Deco

The Canadian "Château" trademark has smoothly evolved since the end of the nineteenth century, influenced both by the needs of the local urban density and more general international trends.
Canadian Châteaux like Le Manoir Richelieu in Charlevoix (1), or Chateau Lake Louise (3), overlooking amazing scenery, could afford a wide structure of low buildings. During the same period, the most dense cities would introduce their tallest versions, like New York and The Plaza Hotel (4).
The MacDonald Hotel (2), in the city center of Edmonton, though overlooking the escarpment of the North Saskatchewan River, is rightly between those two extremes.
Gradually the Châteaux would integrate geometric Art-Deco lines–Chateau Lake Louise (3), Royal York Toronto (5), and The Vancouver Hotel (opposite)–meeting the international trend of the most precursory skyscrapers of the time, such as the Shanghai Peace Hotel (7).
Contemporary Fairmont hotels carry the heritage of this evergreen architecture: geometric shapes crowned by pyramidal roofs as in the Fairmont Chicago Millenium Park (8). Fairmont Dubai (6) mixes international architecture with its traditional Arabic roots, with an overall shape inspired by the traditional wind tower "Barajeel."

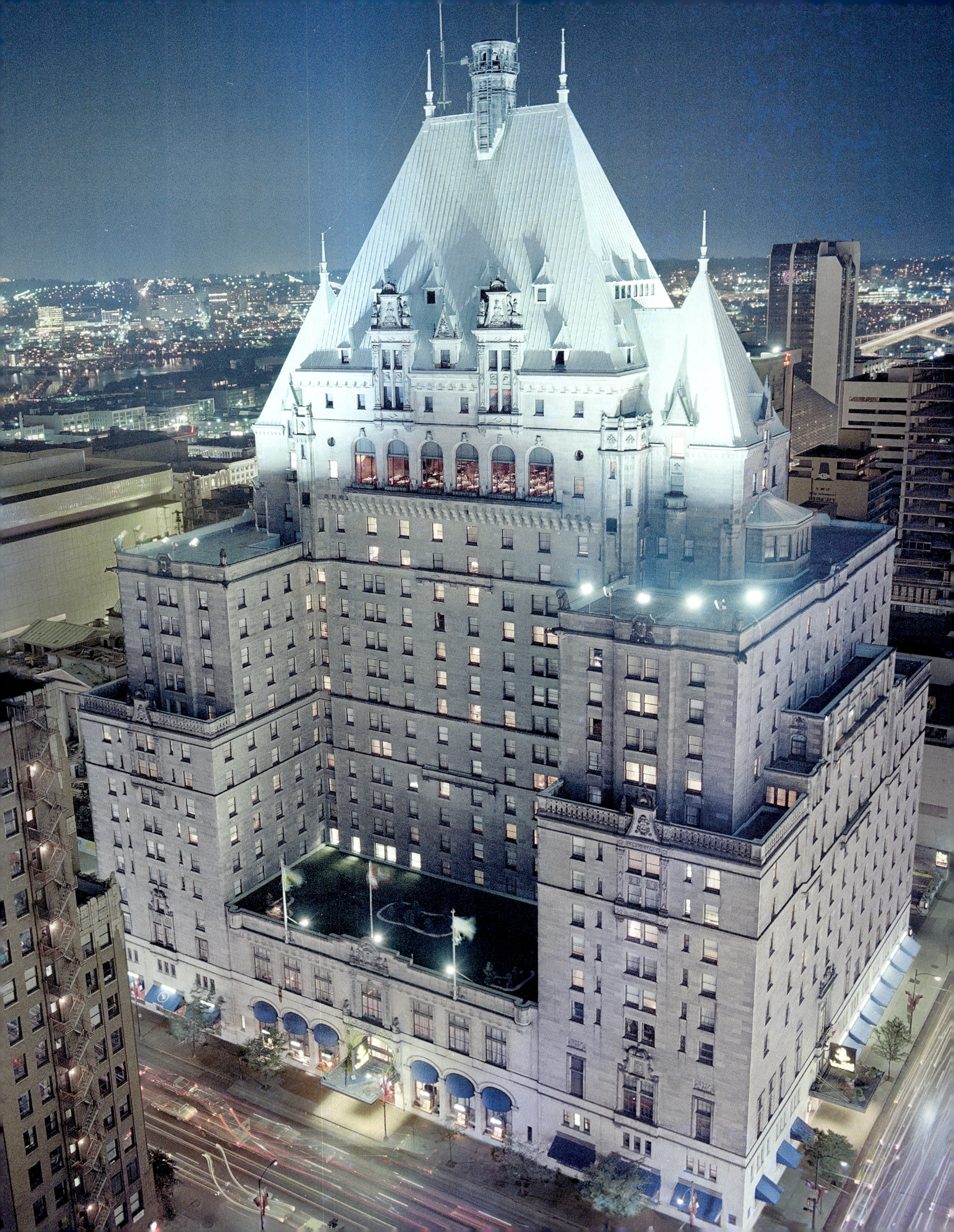

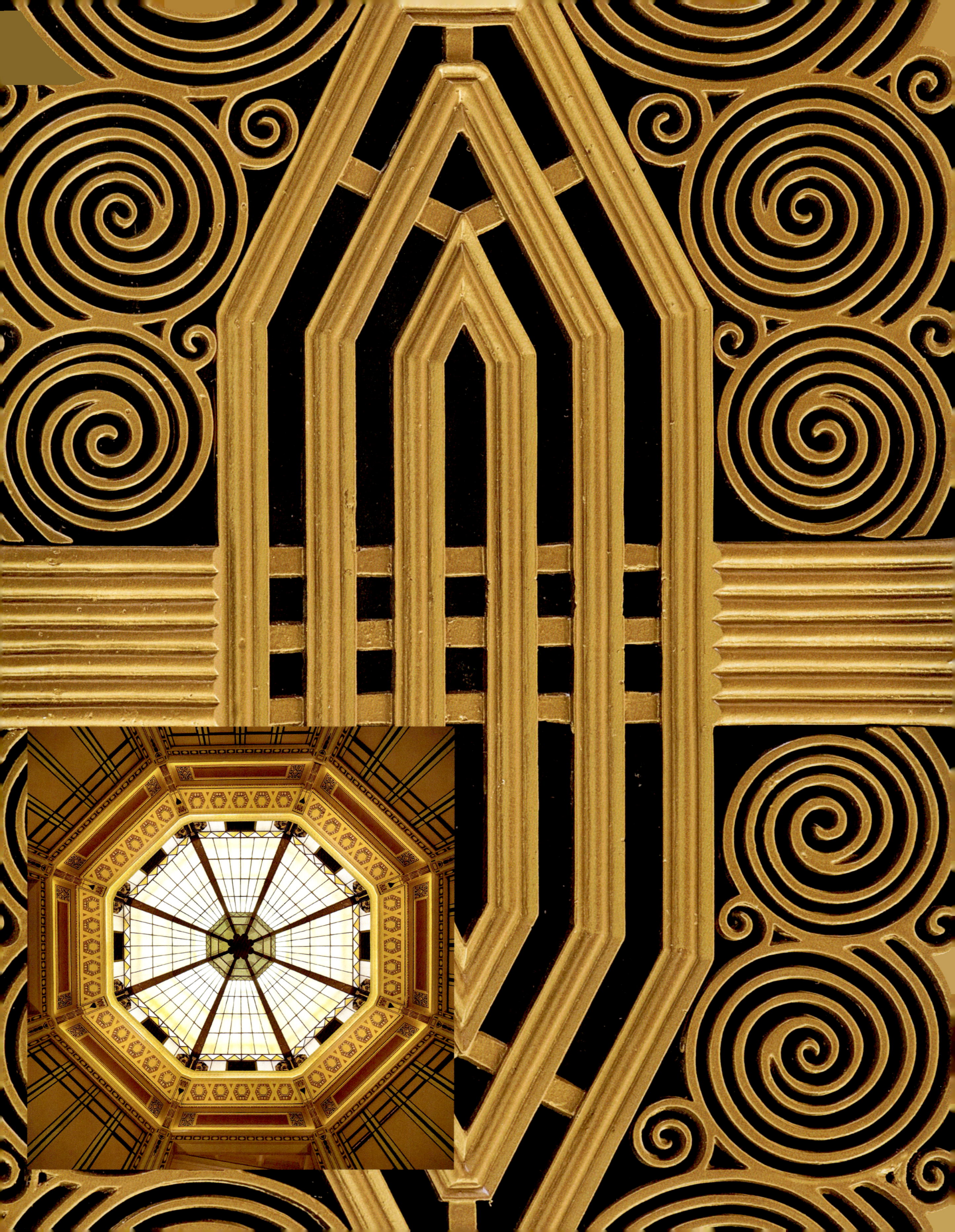

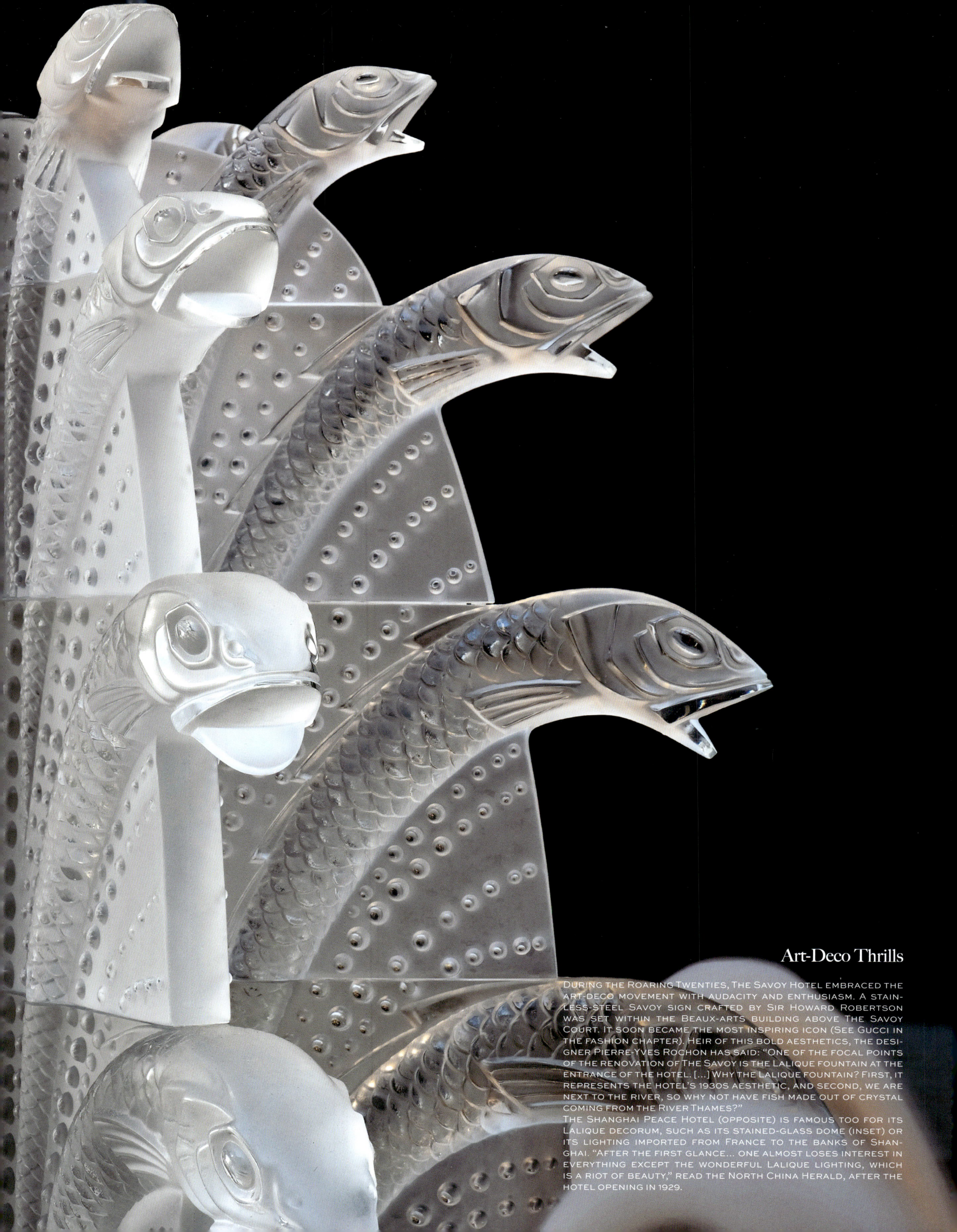

Art-Deco Thrills

During the Roaring Twenties, The Savoy Hotel embraced the art-deco movement with audacity and enthusiasm. A stainless-steel Savoy sign crafted by Sir Howard Robertson was set within the Beaux-arts building above The Savoy Court. It soon became the most inspiring icon (See Gucci in the fashion chapter). Heir of this bold aesthetics, the designer Pierre-Yves Rochon has said: "One of the focal points of the renovation of The Savoy is the Lalique fountain at the entrance of the hotel. [...] Why the Lalique fountain? First, it represents the hotel's 1930s aesthetic, and second, we are next to the river, so why not have fish made out of crystal coming from the River Thames?"
The Shanghai Peace Hotel (opposite) is famous too for its Lalique decorum, such as its stained-glass dome (inset) or its lighting imported from France to the banks of Shanghai. "After the first glance... one almost loses interest in everything except the wonderful Lalique lighting, which is a riot of beauty," read the North China Herald, after the hotel opening in 1929.

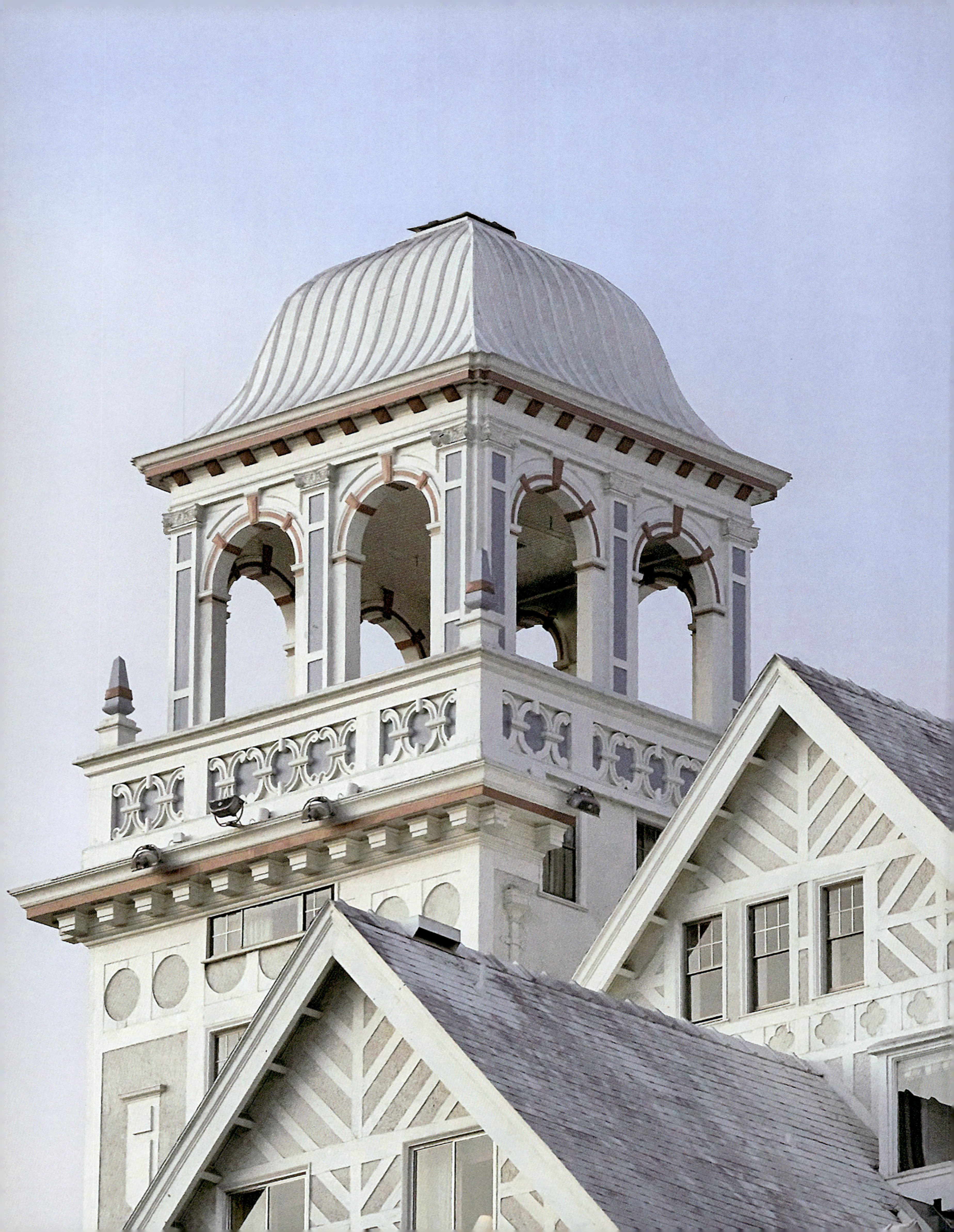

Mock Tudor

Rooted in the English vernacular architecture of the sixteenth century, the Mock Tudor style, also known as Tudor Revival or half-timbered, became fashionable toward the end of the nineteenth century. If the timbers were usually black as they were at The Norfolk in Nairobi (1904, top) and in an early but no-longer-extant wing of Chateau Lake Louise (1910, bottom), they nowadays are white at the Claremont Club in Berkeley (1915, opposite).

Spanish Revival

FAIRMONT MISSION INN (LEFT), SONOMA, AND FAIRMONT GRAND DEL MAR (RIGHT), SAN DIEGO, ARE BOTH EXAMPLES OF THE SPANISH REVIVAL STYLE FOUND THROUGHOUT CALIFORNIA, RECALLING THE COLONIAL BUILDINGS BUILT BEFORE 1848, WHEN THE STATE BECAME PART OF THE UNITED STATES, HAVING FORMERLY BEEN PART OF MEXICO AND, UNTIL 1821, GOVERNED BY SPAIN.
OPPOSITE, THE FLUSHED FACADES OF THE HAMILTON PRINCESS, BERMUDA (OPPOSITE, BACKGROUND), AND FAIRMONT ROYAL PAVILION, BARBADOS (OPPOSITE, INSET).

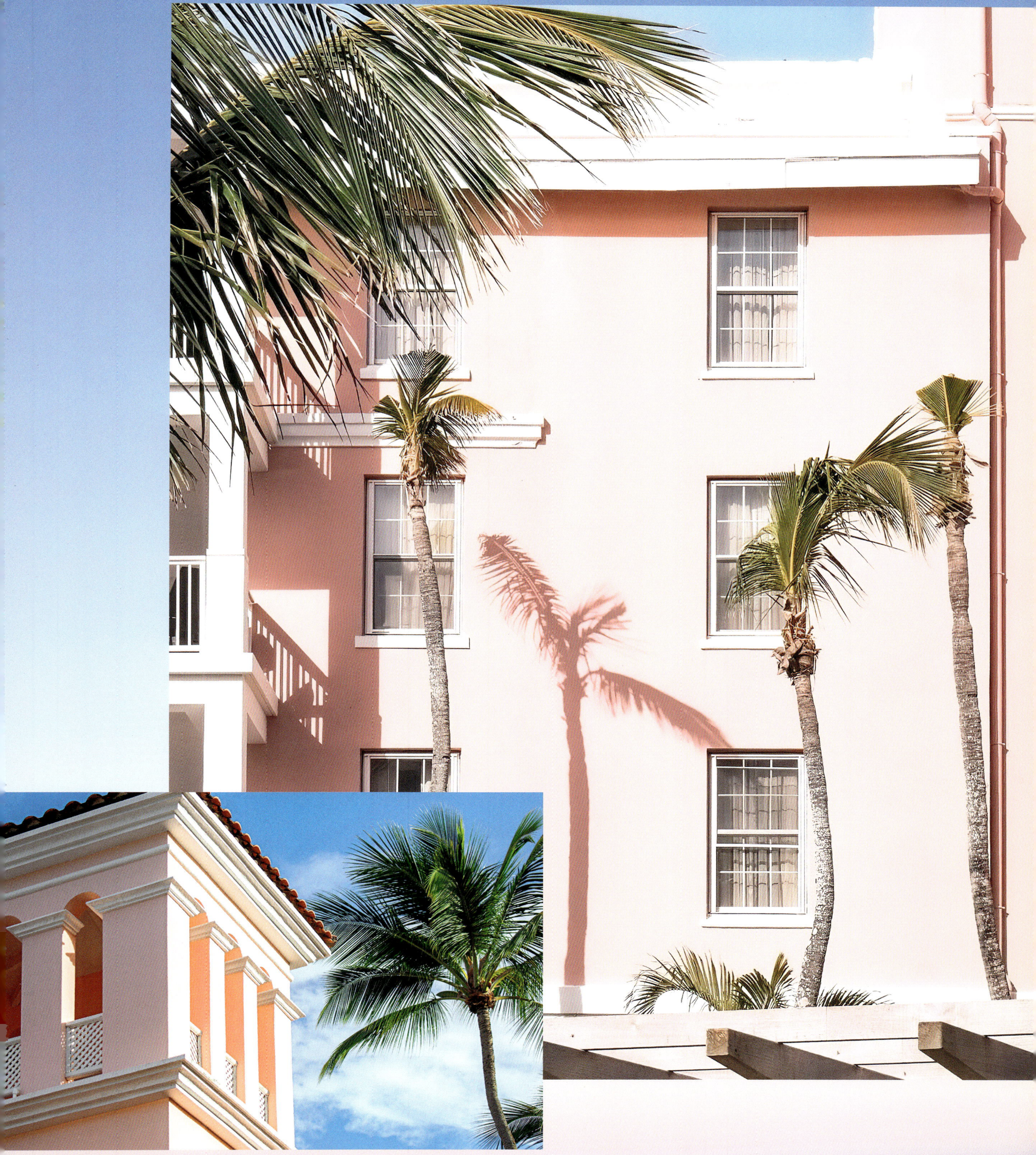

The ceiling of the Gold Salon at Carton House, a Fairmont Managed Hotel

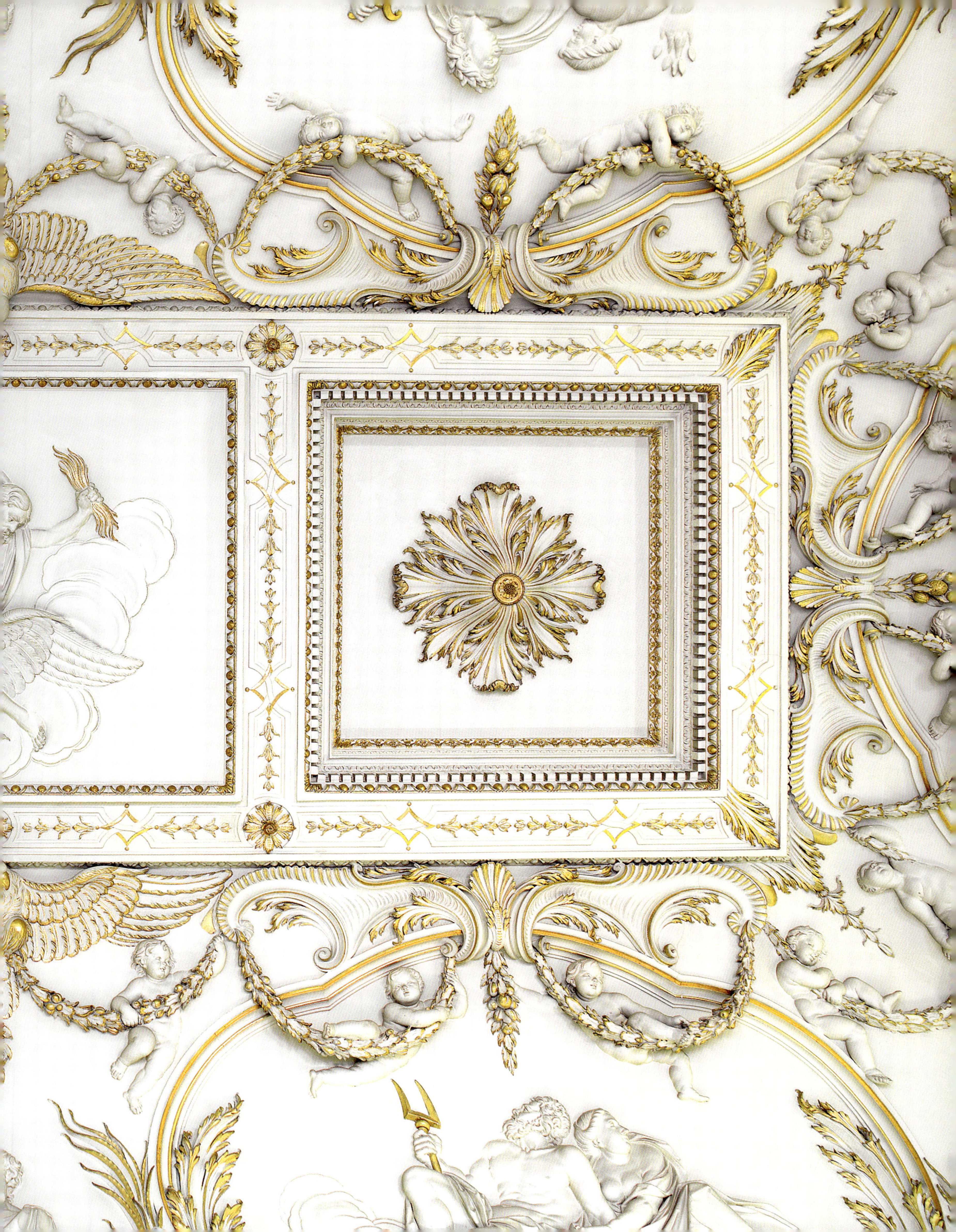

Neoclassicism and Rococo

Ancestral home of the Earl of Kildare and the Dukes of Leinster, Carton House (top) was built in the 1740s at a cost of £26,000 by Richard Cassels (also known as Richard Castle), an architect originally from Kassel in Germany, who went on to build Leinster House in Dublin, which now houses the Irish Parliament.
A fine example of Irish neoclassicism, its sober exterior conceals rococo interiors that are as lavish as the facade is austere. Its double-height Gold Salon, for example, has a coved ceiling decorated in gilded plasterwork, a work entitled The Courtship of the Gods by the fabled Lafranchini brothers from Switzerland, whose masterpiece this is reckoned to be. At its eastern end, there is an organ encased in richly ornamented housing designed by a son of the third duke and installed in 1857.

Like Carton House, Fairmont San Francisco is essentially neoclassical in style, though it was built a century and a half later (opposite). Like the ceiling of the Gold Salon, the Oval Room at Fairmont Copley Plaza in Boston (bottom) has an elaborately decorated ceiling, in which the artist John Singer Sargent had a hand.
Sargent was a regular guest at the hotel (which was named after the American artist John Singleton Copley), during the years in which he worked on the murals at the Boston Public Library. One day, while lunching at the hotel, he was observing the artists who had been hired to paint a trompe-l'oeil sky for the ceiling of the Oval Room, when one of them asked if he would like to add to it. Sargent inscribed an angel, but sadly, it was painted over in the 1940s and has never since been revealed.

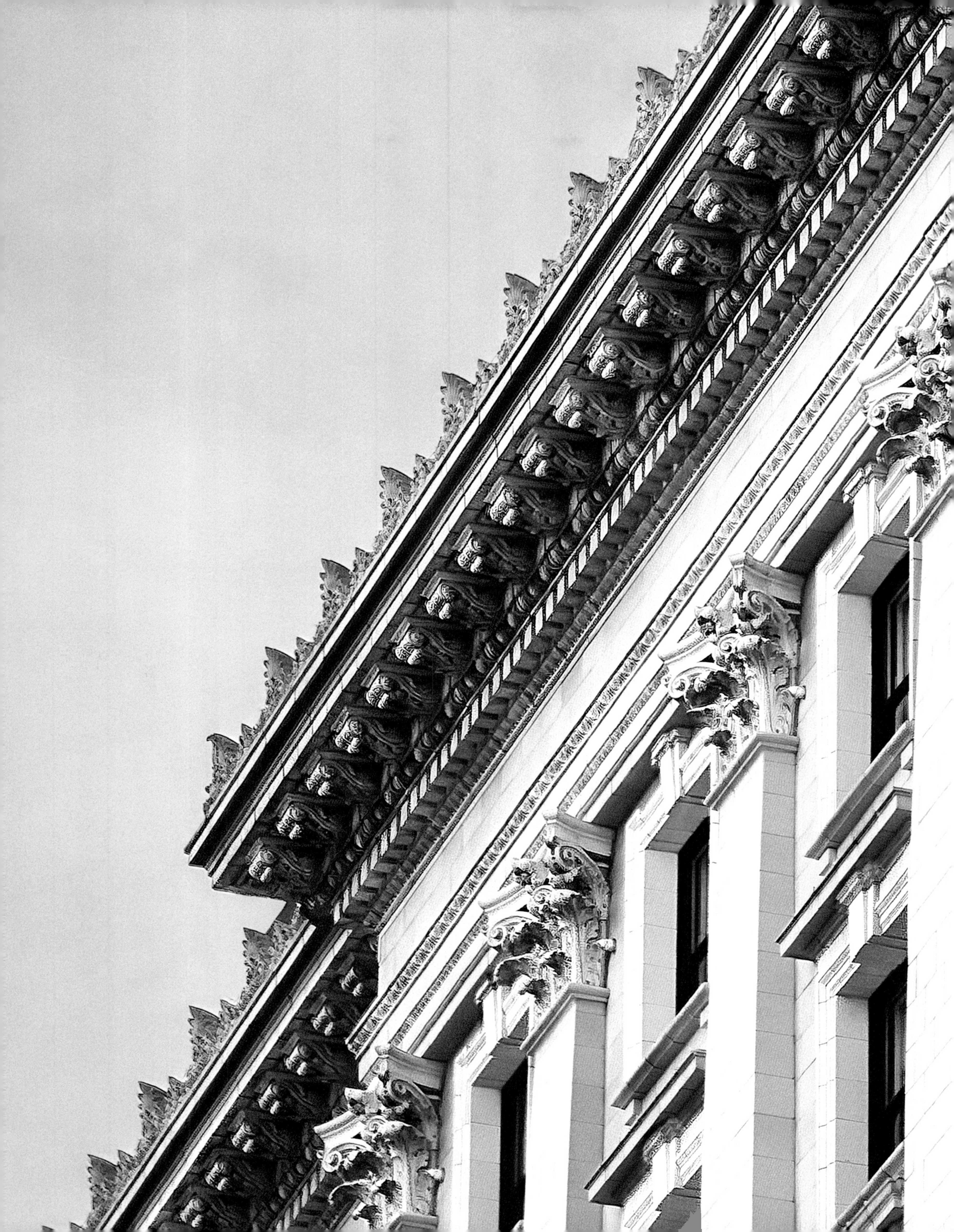

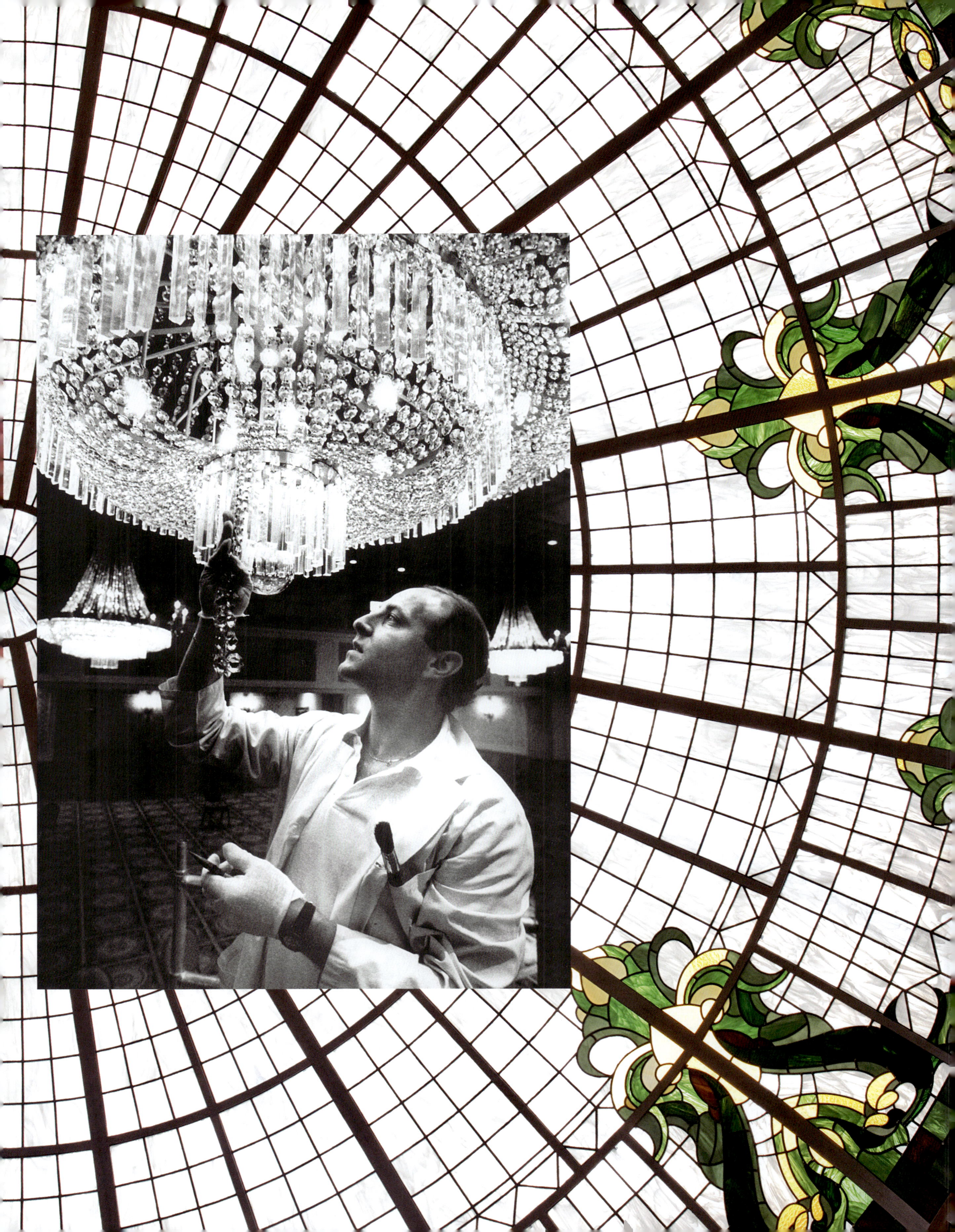

Luminous Masterpieces

Cleaning the chandeliers in the concert hall of the Royal York, Toronto, required gloved maintenance expert Gary Rochon three months of work to complete in 1988. (opposite, inset) The Palm Court at The Plaza New York (above) is famous for its stained-glass canopy, reminiscent of the historical stained-glass lay-light installed in 1907. At The Savoy, London, the glass dome of the Thames Foyer (opposite, background) and the gazebo were created by the architect Pierre-Yves Rochon during the three-year renovation of the hotel started in 2003. As he declares "When I first walked into the Thames Foyer, I found it huge and without life unless the room was full. So I decided to put a gazebo in the middle. It creates smaller corners, so you never feel alone."

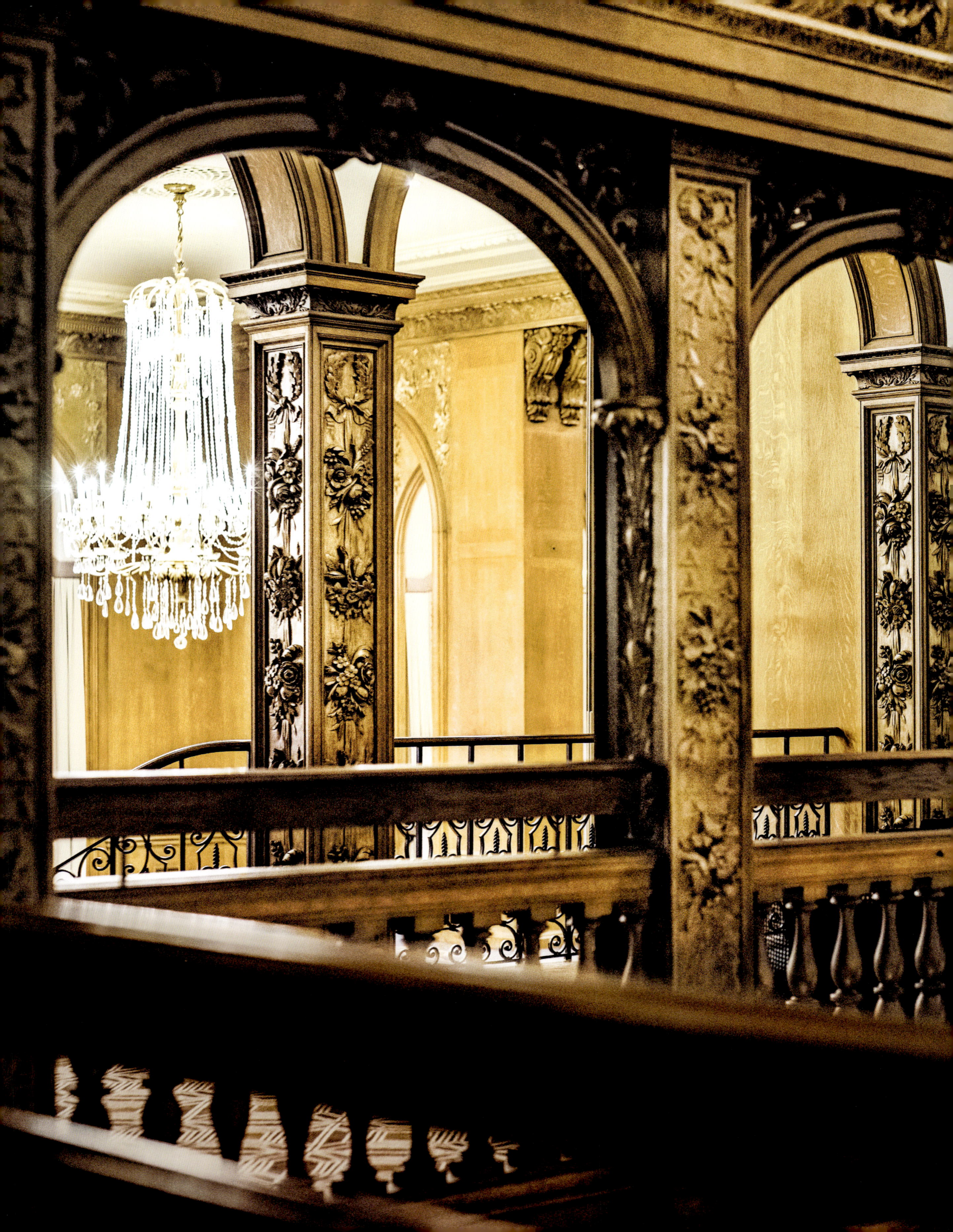

Belle-Époque Rococo

The oversize mirror of the Montreux palace's ballroom, dating from the origins of the hotel in 1906 (above). In front of it was filmed the love scene of Sophia Loren and David Niven in Peter Utsinov's *Lady L* movie, 1965. Beaux Arts loggia in carved American oak built in 1929 overlooking the lobby of the Fairmont Olympic hotel (opposite) lavishly restored in 2021.

1930s Frescoes

In May 1935, seventeen months after Prohibition was repealed, the Cirque Room at the Fairmont in San Francisco (above) became the first major bar to open in the city. Guests flocked not just for the cocktails, but to see the circus-themed murals, the work of Esther Bruton and her sisters, Margaret and Helen.

Opposite, the ballroom at the Royal York, Toronto. Painted in 1929, its ceiling featured three topless women. Mindful of the offence this might cause, the hotel recalled the artist and instructed him to paint in some clothing, but a compromise was reached, and each figure was left with one exposed breast.

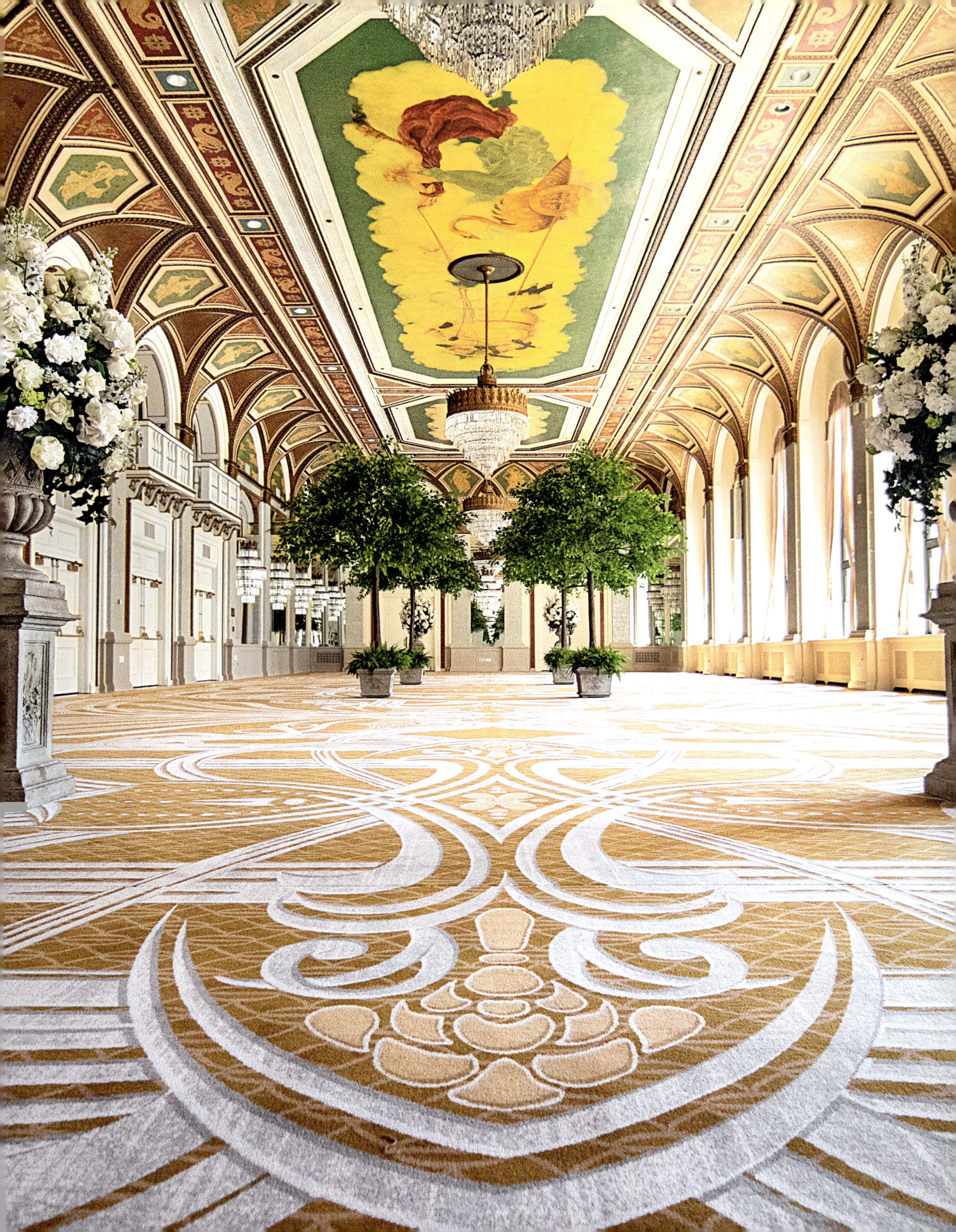

Rajasthani Indo-Saracenic or Mughal-style domed pavilions, known as chhatris, after the Urdu word for umbrella, decorate the roof of Fairmont Jaipur

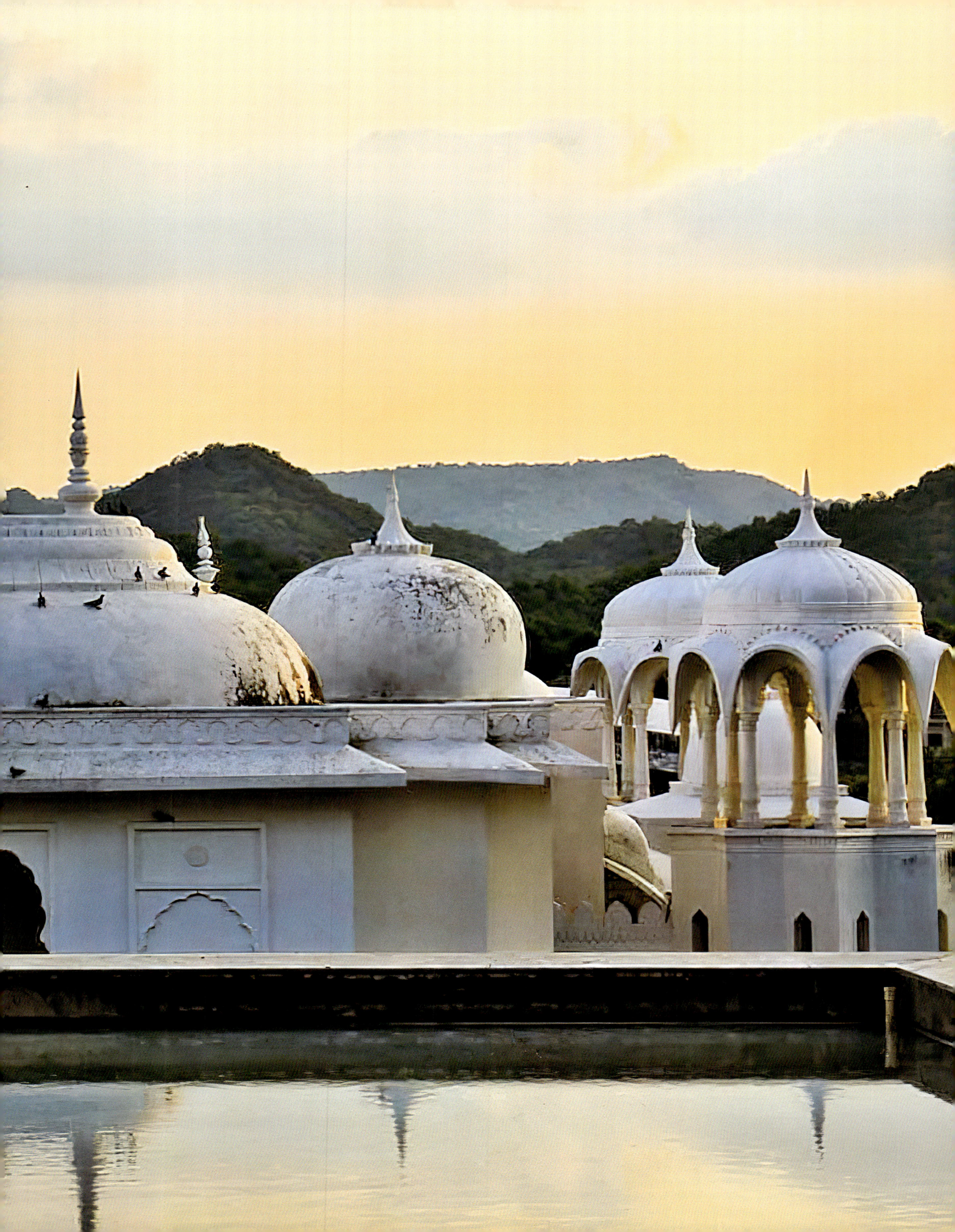

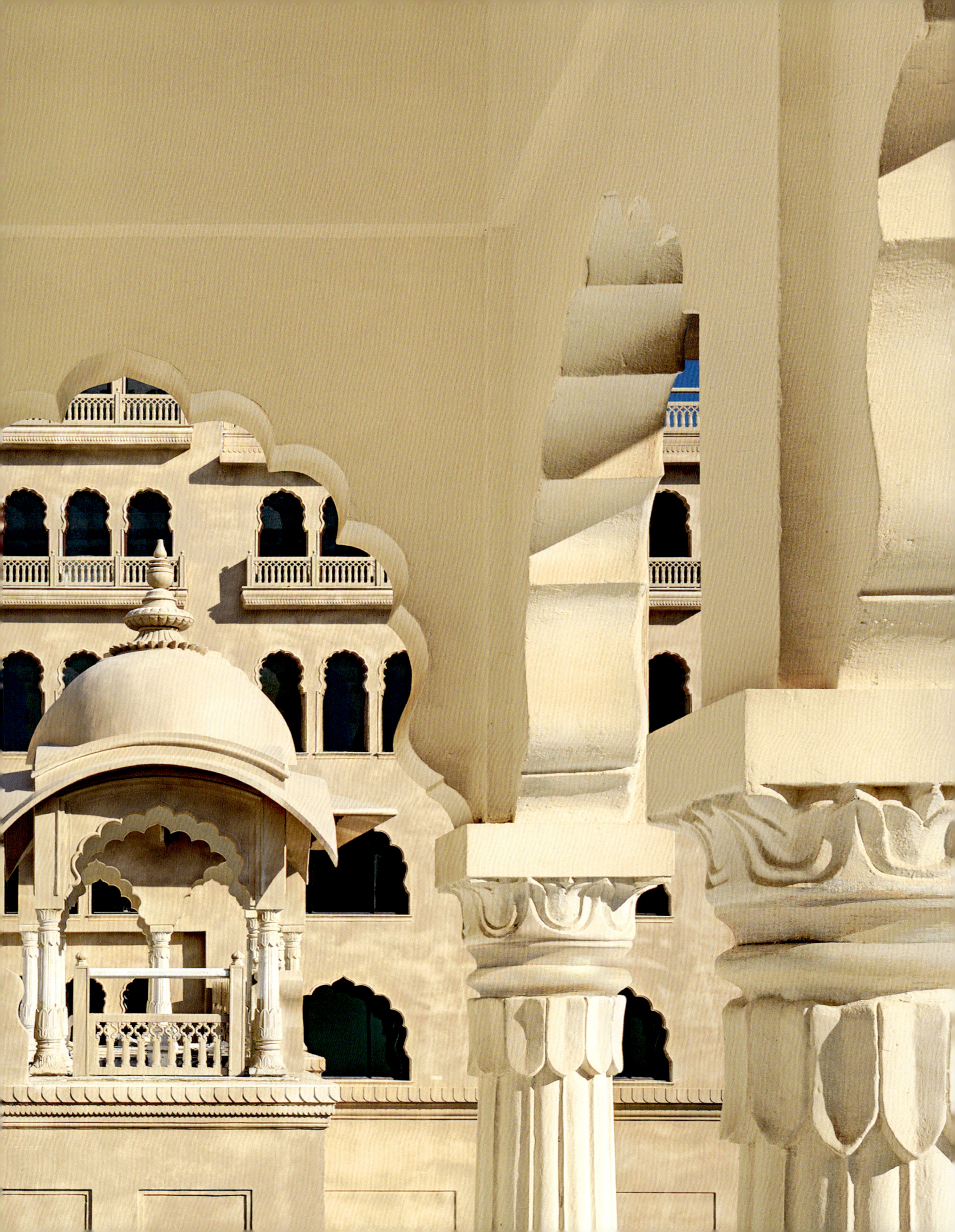

Fascinating India

Ornate woodcarving has a long and distinguished tradition in the Maldives. Witness the doorway, shaped like a Mughal arch, at Fairmont Maldives, Sirru Fen Fushi (left).
The architecture of Fairmont Jaipur also incorporates many defining motifs of Mughal architecture, from the chhatris, or domes, and decorative finials on its roof, to the stained glass and friezes on its ceilings (opposite).
More incongruously Mughal accents were also employed in the decorative scheme at the Fairmont Peace Hotel in Shanghai (right), when it opened in 1929. Far from wanting to evoke anything obviously Chinese, its original decor strove to be as cosmopolitan as the city was. There was glass by Lalique, marble from Italy, and each of its nine premium suites recalled a different national culture, this one Indian.

Arabian Nights

The mosaic floor of the swimming pool at Fairmont Fujairah Beach Resort, in the United Arab Emirates (above, right), was inspired by a Persian rug. The Floet light sculpture that hangs in the lobby of Fairmont Ajman (above, left), was designed to reflect the emirate's fishing culture; a sweeping net of tiny handblown glass beads suspended above a shoal of little translucent fish, while the interior design of Fairmont Marrakech is accurately drawn from Moroccan traditional arts and crafts (p.120, bottom).
Opposite, Arthur Upham Pope, a former professor of art history at UC Berkeley who went on to establish the American Institute for Persian Art and Archaeology (now the Asia Institute), first visited Iran in 1925. A speech he made had caught the attention of the Shah, who—assured that his interest was genuine—permitted him to visit and photograph its most important mosques. The following year, he organized the first international congress on Persian art, and in 1927 was invited, along with his wife, Phyllis Ackerman, to design the interiors of the penthouse at San Francisco's Fairmont Hotel in the style of a Persian palace, complete with billiard room.

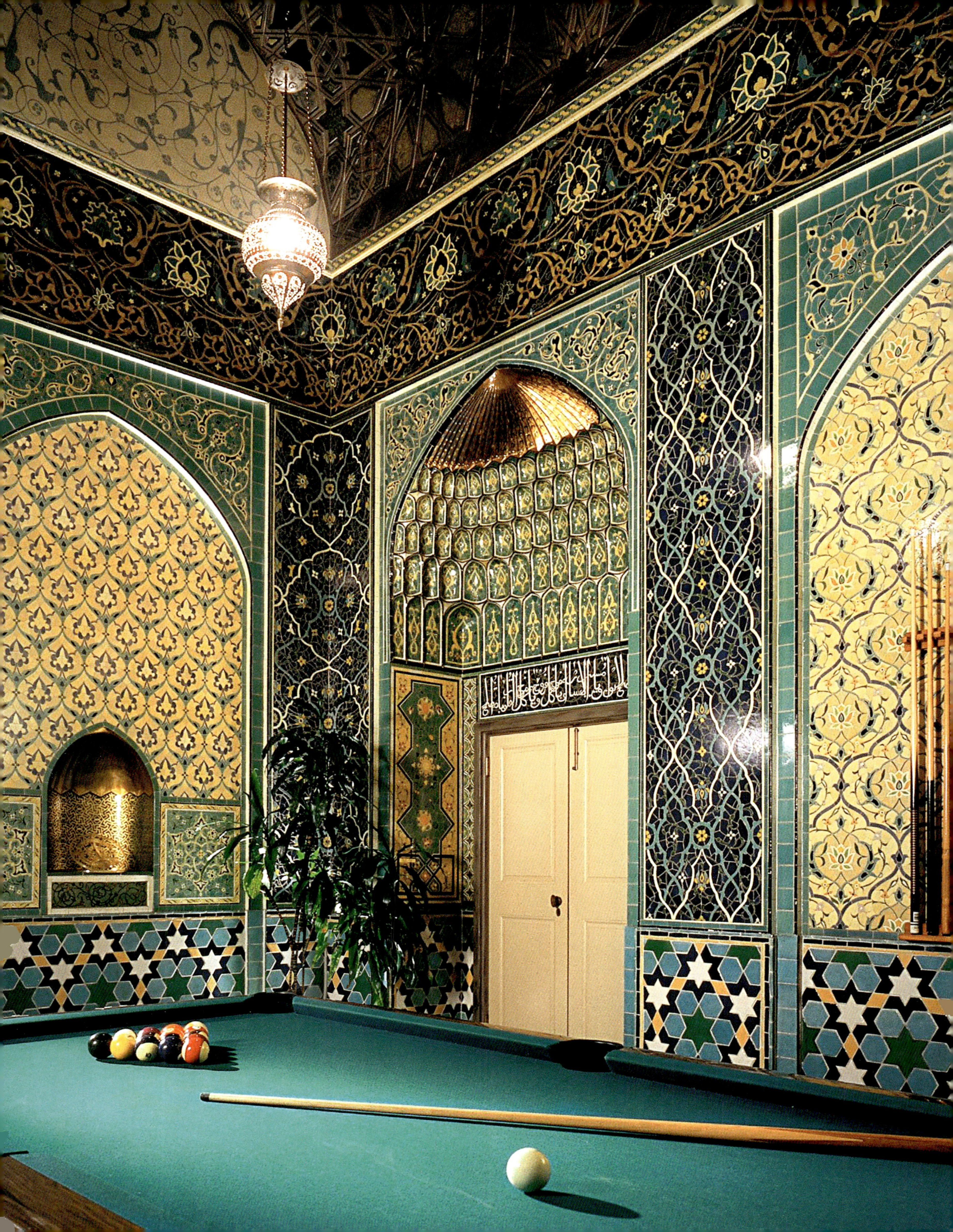

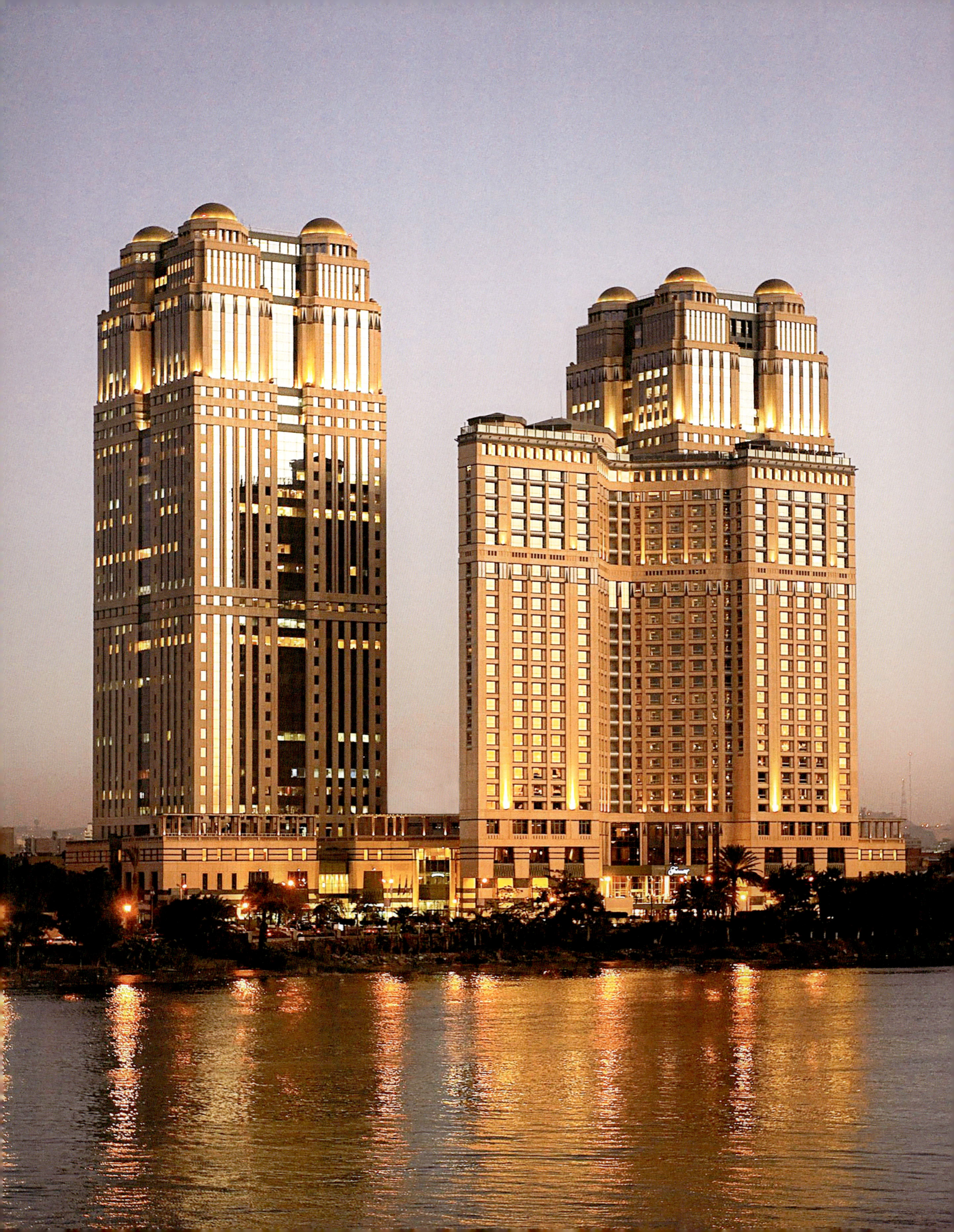

Contemporary Alcazars

Opulent golden cupolas, slender trefoil arches, Arabic traditions may also be discerned in the contemporary architecture of Fairmont Nile City in Cairo (opposite), Fairmont Riyadh (left) and Fairmont The Palm in Dubai (right).

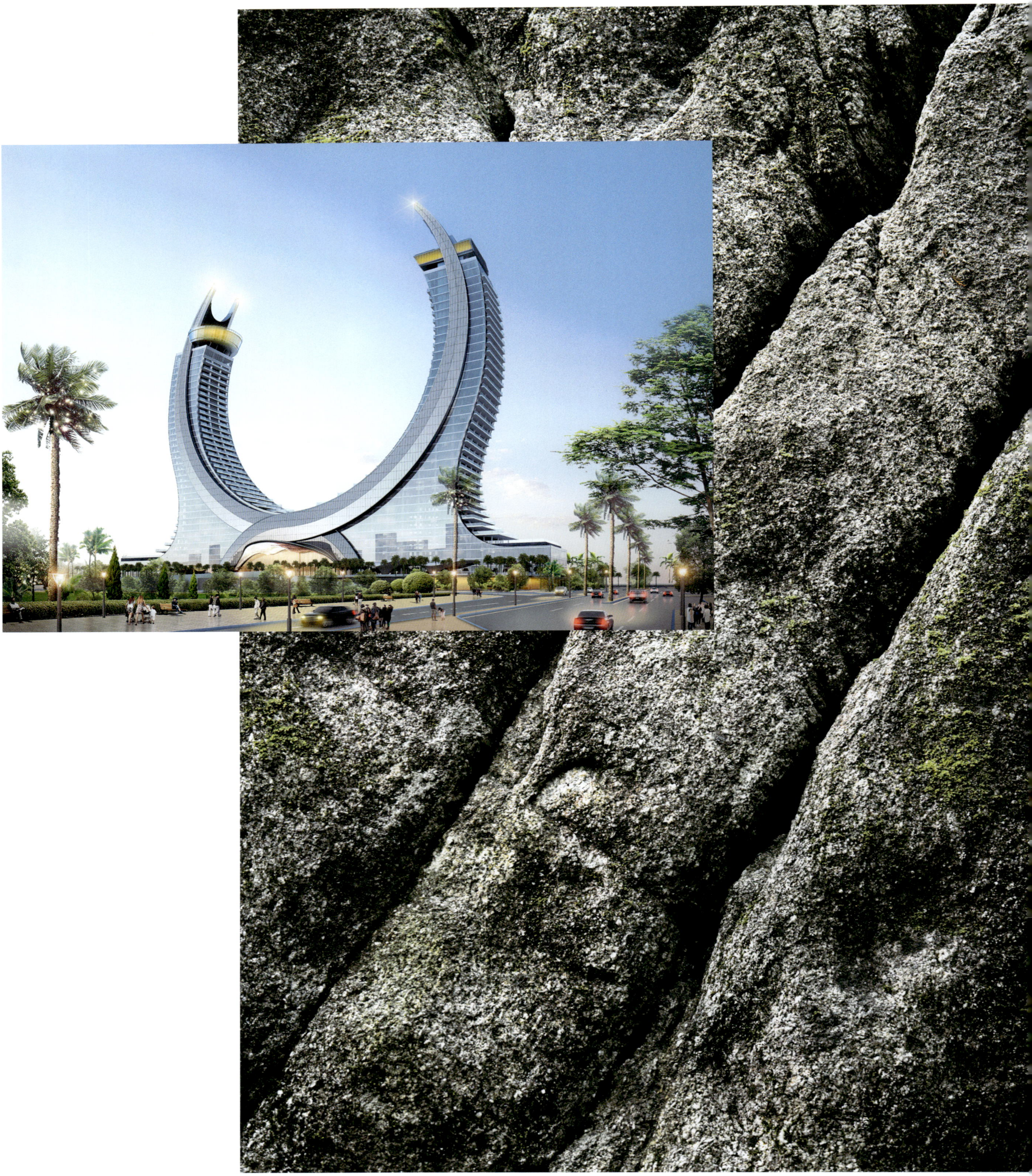

Architectural Utopias

Fairmont will open a hotel in one of the forty-story Katara Towers, which overlook the marina in the new city of Lusail, immediately north of Doha (opposite, inset). Due to open in time for the 2022 FIFA World Cup in Qatar, the towers have been designed to represent two scimitars curving toward each other.

Across the border with Saudi Arabia 930 miles west of Doha, lies the holy city of Mecca, site of the Makkah Clock Royal Tower, which at 1,972-feet high (including its spire) is the tallest building in the kingdom. Within it, rising from the ground to just below the clock face—itself an astonishing 141 feet in diameter—there is a 1,618-room hotel, Fairmont Makkah Clock Royal Tower, with breathtaking views of Masjid al-Haram and the Holy Kaaba (above).

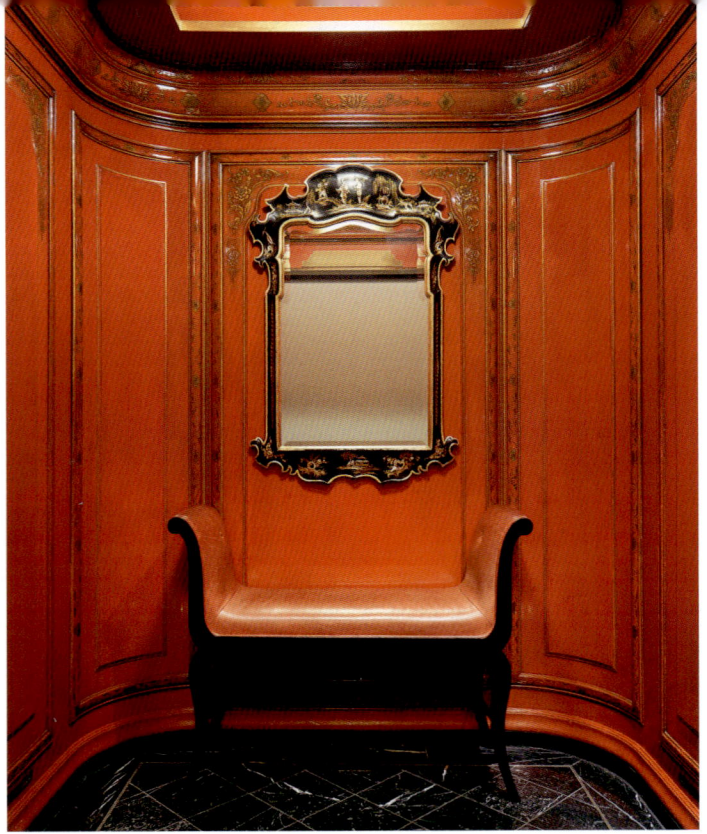

"The hotel has three elevator cabs completely lacquered in Chinese design.
One is red, one is blue and gold, and one is a deep green.
It's very unusual to find this level of ornamentation in a hotel elevator.
I was so impressed that we decided to keep them.
Even today, they are in very good condition."

Pierre-Yves Rochon
INTERIOR DESIGNER IN CHARGE OF THE SAVOY HOTEL RENOVATION

Asian Design

DESIGNED BY US ARCHITECTS SKIDMORE, OWINGS & MERRILL, FAIRMONT NANJING (ABOVE, LEFT) OCCUPIES THE TOP TWENTY-SEVEN FLOORS OF NANJING KEYNE CENTRE, ITSELF A HOMAGE TO BRANCUSI'S *ENDLESS COLUMN* SCULPTURE AND ALREADY A LANDMARK IN THE CITY.
ITS INTERIORS, THE WORK OF BRAYTON HUGHES, ARE NO LESS TRANSFIXING. INSPIRED BY A TRADITIONAL CHINESE LANTERN, THE WALLS OF ITS TWENTY-SEVEN-STORY ATRIUM ARE LINED WITH FACETED, BACKLIT METALLIC PANELS, ENGRAVED TO EVOKE PLUM BLOSSOM AND THE CHANGE OF COLOR ACCORDING TO THE SEASONS.
FAIRMONT BEIJING (OPPOSITE), MEANWHILE, WAS DESIGNED IN THE FORM OF A TRADITIONAL CHINESE GATE, ITS FACADE CLAD IN A CURTAIN OF ROSE-GOLD GLASS, SO THAT THE WHOLE STRUCTURE GLOWS RED, AN AUSPICIOUS COLOR IN CHINA.
HENCE, THE RED-LACQUERED WALLS OF THE CHINOISERIE LIFT AT THE SAVOY (ABOVE, RIGHT) IN LONDON, AN ORNAMENTAL STYLE THAT TOOK REFERENCES FROM A VARIETY OF ASIAN APPLIED ARTS, THAT FIRST BECAME FASHIONABLE IN ENGLAND IN THE EIGHTEENTH CENTURY.
FAIRMONT AMBASSADOR SEOUL (RIGHT) OCCUPIES THE SHORTEST OF THE THREE TOWERS THAT COMPRISE THE PARC 1 COMPLEX IN YEOUIDO, A MIXED-USE DEVELOPMENT INCLUDING OFFICES AND RETAIL THAT WAS ORIGINALLY DESIGNED BY RICHARD ROGERS'S PRACTICE, ROGERS STIRK HARBOUR + PARTNERS (IN CONJUNCTION WITH SAMOO ARCHITECTS), A STRUCTURE AT ONCE CONTEMPORARY AND INTERNATIONAL, BUT INFORMED BY TRADITIONAL KOREAN DESIGN.

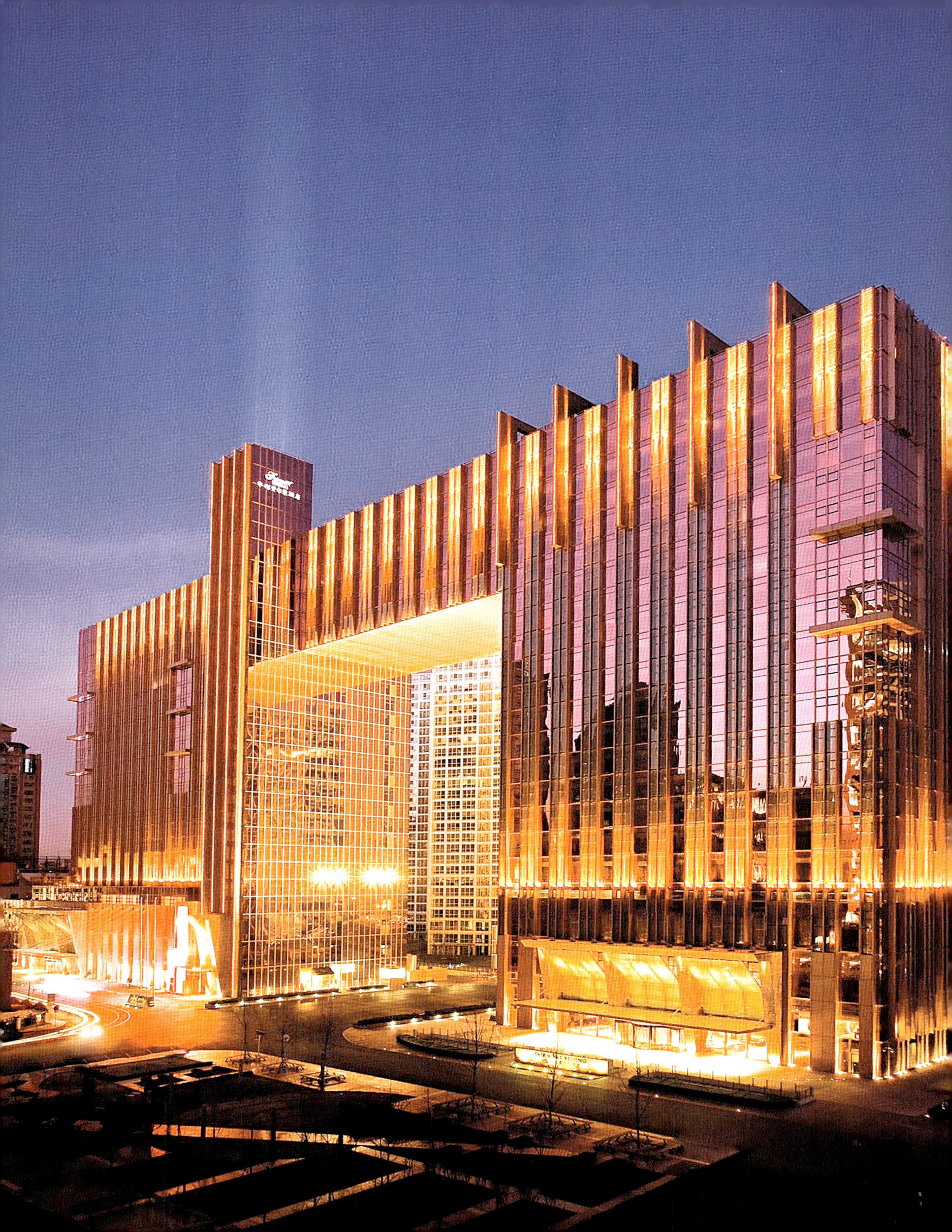

Chinese Ink

The exterior of Fairmont Chengdu is resolutely twenty-first century. Enter its lobby, however, and one encounters ancient crafts as well as new ones. Though contemporary with the architecture, the giant Shu embroidery that hangs here speaks of centuries of traditional Chinese ink painting and artisanal skill. The picture on which it is based was created by the digital ink artist Lu Jun by dropping colored pigments into water. Depicting an abstracted landscape of waterfalls, her work on paper was then turned into an embroidery by Yang Dequan, former director of the Sichuan Embroidery Workshop, along with a team of twenty embroidery artists, who worked with 546 different colors of silk thread.

Opposite, when Queen Victoria stayed at Carton House in 1849, she slept in the Chinese Boudoir. Her four-poster bed is there to this day, draped in silks imported from China, as was the specially commissioned hand-painted wallpaper, which has hung here since 1759 and inspired many of the bespoke wallpapers commissioned for the newer rooms of the hotel. The extravagantly ornate rococo frame of the overmantel mirror is by Thomas Chippendale.

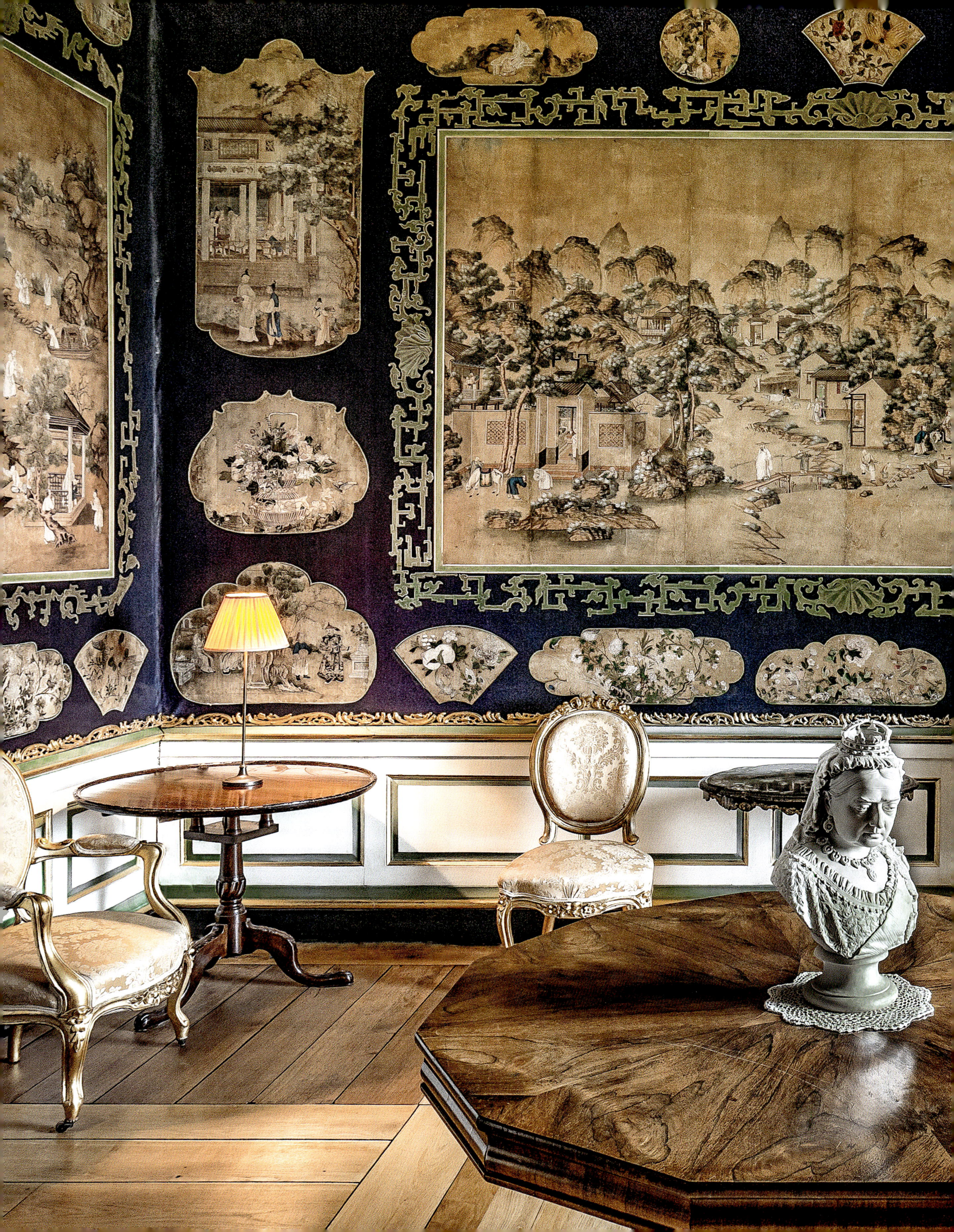

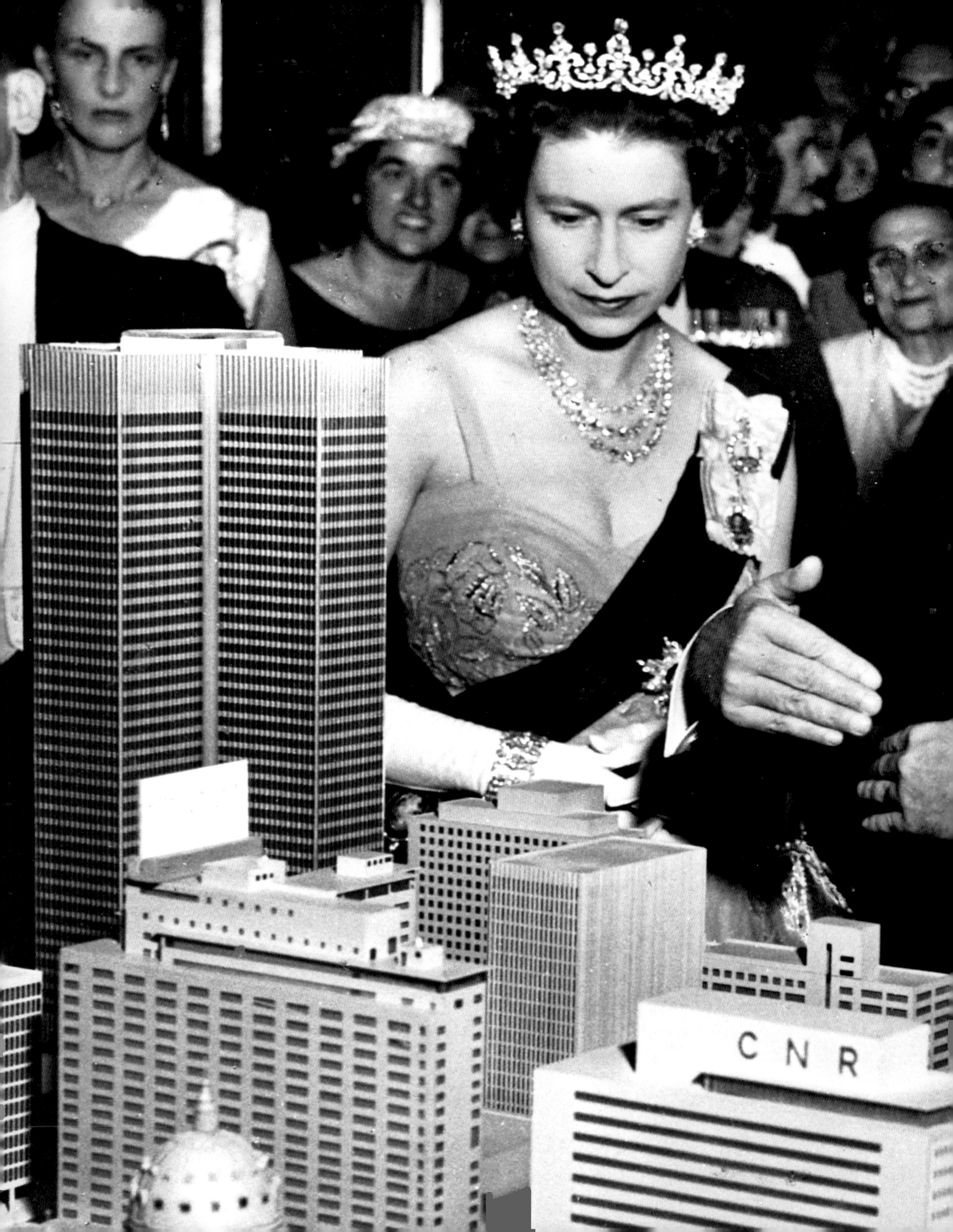
CNR

Queen Elizabeth II inspects a model of the proposed Place Villa-Marie in downtown Montreal, in June 1959. The hotel, which was built by the Canadian National Railway Company, had opened a year earlier, one of the first in North America to have escalators, centralized air-conditioning, and direct-dial telephones in its guest rooms.

Modern Places for Modern Ideas

Located on the beach in Santa Monica, Fairmont Miramar Hotel & Bungalows (1) occupies the site of what used to be an estate belonging to the senator and businessman John Perceval Jones. One of the Silver Kings of Nevada, he represented the state as a senator before going on to establish the city of Santa Monica and build its first railroad to Los Angeles. His house, named Miramar, became a hotel in 1921, only to burn down in 1938. Only a six-story wing added in 1924 known as the Palisades, survived the fire; it is now at the heart of the hotel. Its geometric structure, a typical example of Modern style, is free from any ornamentation to showcase its raw construction materials. So does Fairmont Winnipeg (5), originally the Winnipeg Inn, a brutalism gem constructed four decades later demonstrates similar techniques. Here the reinforced, site-cast concrete of the facade even includes visible aggregate on the overhanging entranceway.

Playing with pure glass surfaces, hotels over the world have since emulated uncluttered architecture. Take Fairmont Bab al Bahr, which overlooks the Arabian Gulf in Abu Dhabi (4). The same style that informs urban high-rises too: witness Fairmont Pittsburg built in 2009 (3), or Fairmont Makati (2) built in Manila in 2012.

Opposite, Fairmont Austin opened in 2018, as the largest Fairmont property in the USA and second largest Fairmont hotel globally. Its contemporary architecture is at once compellingly modern and integrated with nature, in this instance in the way it reflects the Texan sky and sunset. Designed by the San Francisco-based architects Gensler and attached to the Austin Convention Center by a sky bridge, the 1,068-room hotel has panoramic views across the Lady Bird Lake.

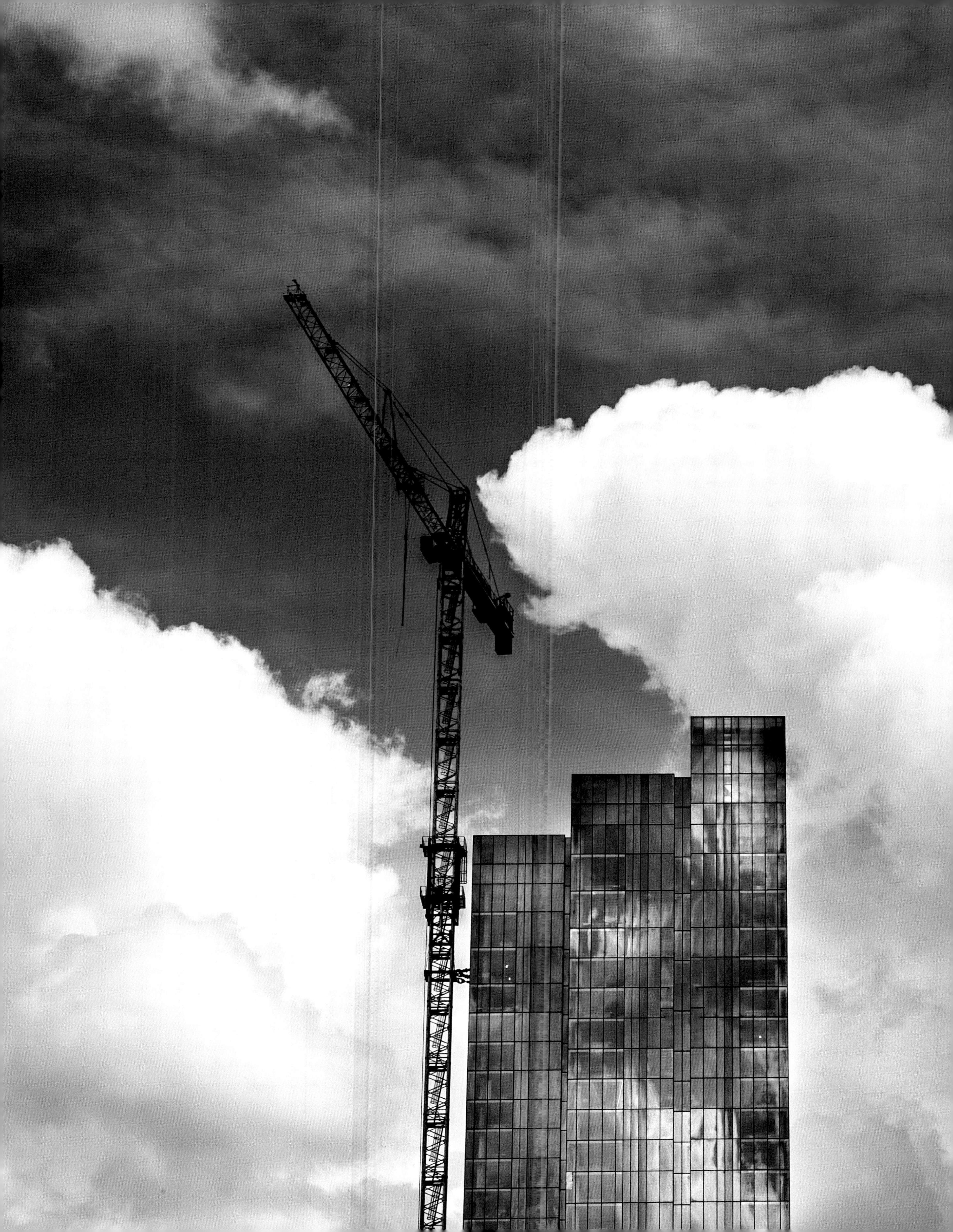

Inspiring Traditions

"Nothing ages more quickly than newness, so I decided long ago that all of my designs would embody respect for the past," said Dutch designer Marcel Wanders.
To enhance the area around the glass-walled swimming pool at Fairmont Qasar Istanbul, he created these fantastical golden tree-like structures (left). Reminiscent of the bulb of Turkish incense burners, they are also made of traditional perforated brass. In Rabbat, Fairmont was inspired by the Moroccan plaster work of the arches, the rough sobriety of the Berber carpet patterns, and the opulence of the metal and mother-of-pearl marquetry (right).
Fairmont Wuhan's magnificent interior design is deeply rooted by the city's cultural heritage, including its historic Yellow Crane Tower, or the most sober design of traditional Chinese wood screens (opposite). The architecture of Fairmont Nanjing's building (inset) is inspired by the folding lines of the traditional Chinese square paper lantern.

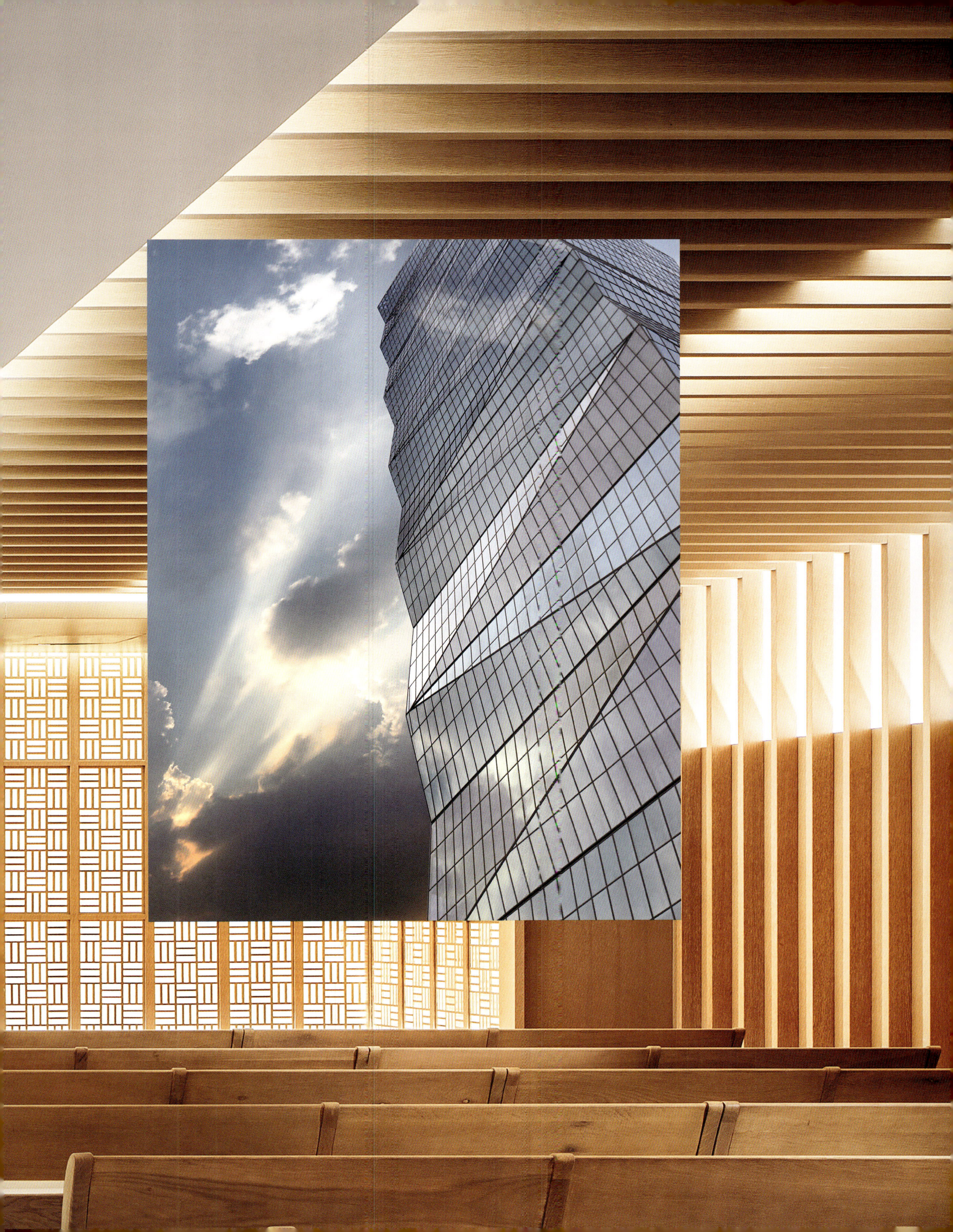

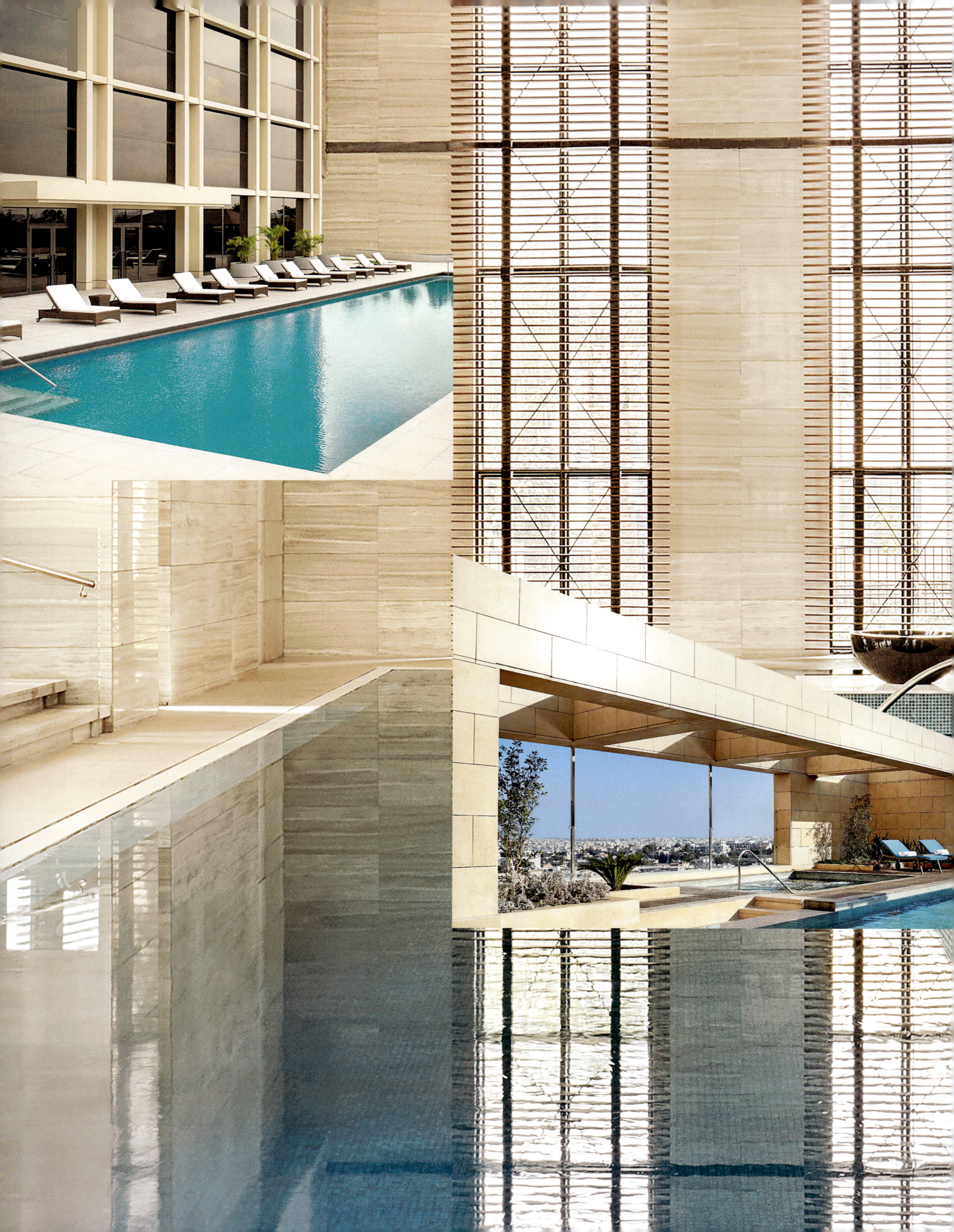

Liquid Gems

Sirru Fen Fushi, the little island that Fairmont's Maldivian property has to itself, is just a kilometre long and barely 820 feet wide, a total area of forty acres on which there are just 120 villas. The challenge for the architect was how to distribute them.
Inspired by land art projects by artists such as Christo and Jeanne-Claude (*Surrounded Island* and *Floating Piers*), Andy Goldsworthy (*Gold Rock*), Donald Judd (*Concrete Windows*), and Robert Smithson (*Spiral Jetty*), STX Landscape Architects, the Singapore studio that won the competition to design the resort, bisected the island with a narrow channel. This Water Axis, as they named it, is 650 feet long and 33 feet wide, and cuts across the land from east to west, so that the sun rises at one end and sets at the other.
Rather than assuming guests would only want to lock out from the island toward the horizon, it provides an alternative focal point to draw the eye in, the better to appreciate the beauty of its interior landscape and its trees. The shadows cast by the coconut palms on the water also allow it to function as a kind of giant sundial, by which guests can learn to tell the time of day.

Opposite, examples of swimming pools inseted within the architecture of the hotels: Fairmont Jakarta (left), Fairmont Amman (bottom), Fairmont Riyadh (background).

168 — 169

Suspended Pools

Designed by Tokyo-based architect Nikken Sekkei as a vertical oasis over the city, Fairmont Ramla Riyadh, integrates in its structure natural materials such as plants and wood (above).
Located under the majestic Sugar Loaf Mountain, Fairmont Rio de Janeiro offers the best view over the sublime Copacabana beaches from its two suspended pools located on the sixth floor (opposite).

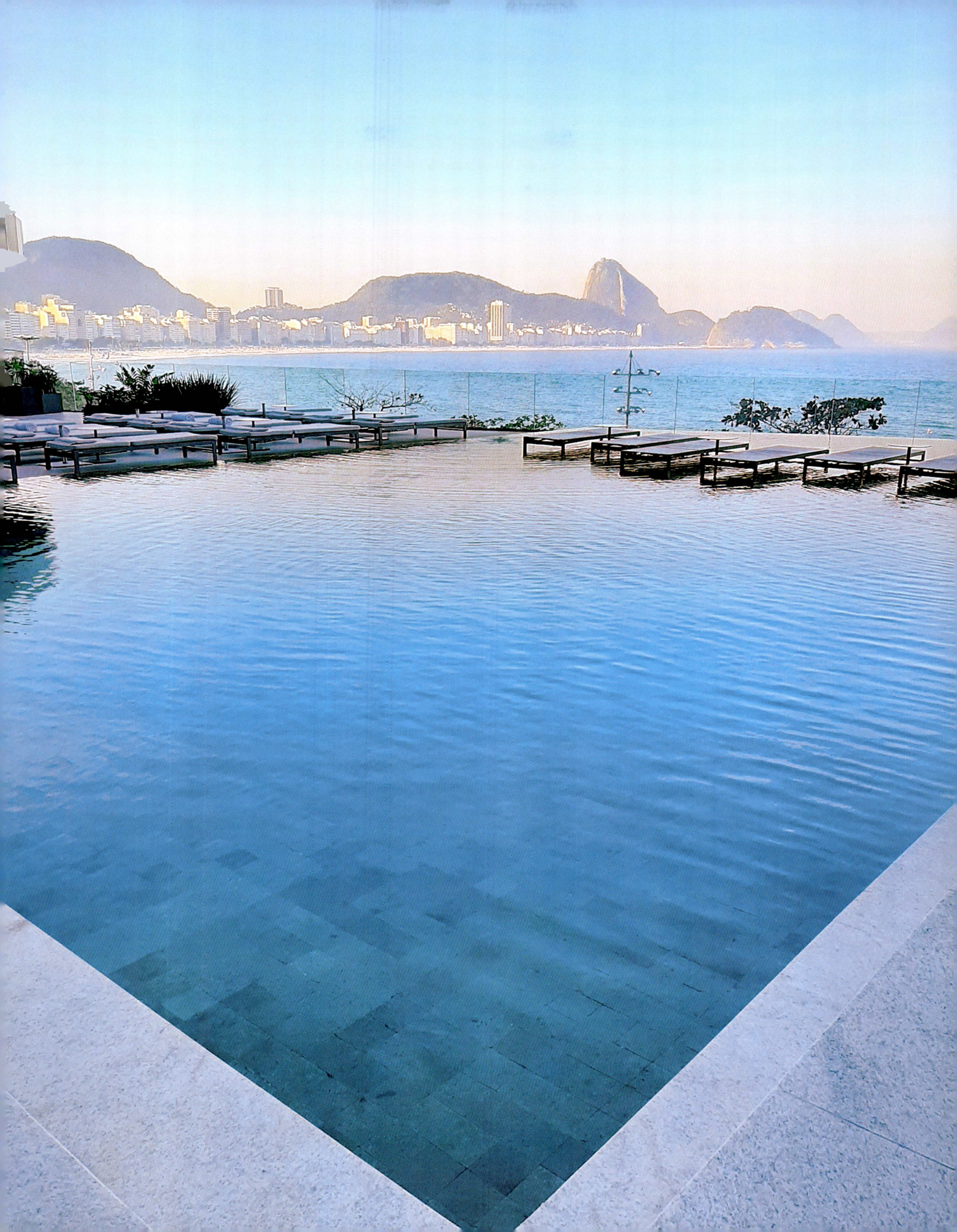

GRAND HOTEL GEN[EVE]

GRAND HOTEL GENEVE

Jean Nouvel in Geneva

Best known for the Philharmonie de Paris, the Louvre Abu Dhabi, and the National Museum of Qatar in Doha, the world-renowned French architect Jean Nouvel designed the striking exterior of Fairmont Grand Hotel Geneva (see rendering below), to complement two earlier projects in the city, notably the new stations on the CEVA (Cornavin–Eaux-Vives–Annemasse) orbital rail line and the restoration and expansion of its Museum of Art and History.

Facing Lac Leman and the Alps beyond, the hotel's existing building will be wrapped in a new glass facade that reflects its surroundings (rather as the glass walls of Nouvel's Fondation Cartier in Paris reflect trees), in order "to integrate it perfectly into its environment," hence the extravagant planting that promises to be integrated into its structure and contribute to its eco credentials.

But this project won't just be strikingly beautiful. It will also be energy efficient, using, for example, water from the lake to both cool and heat the building.

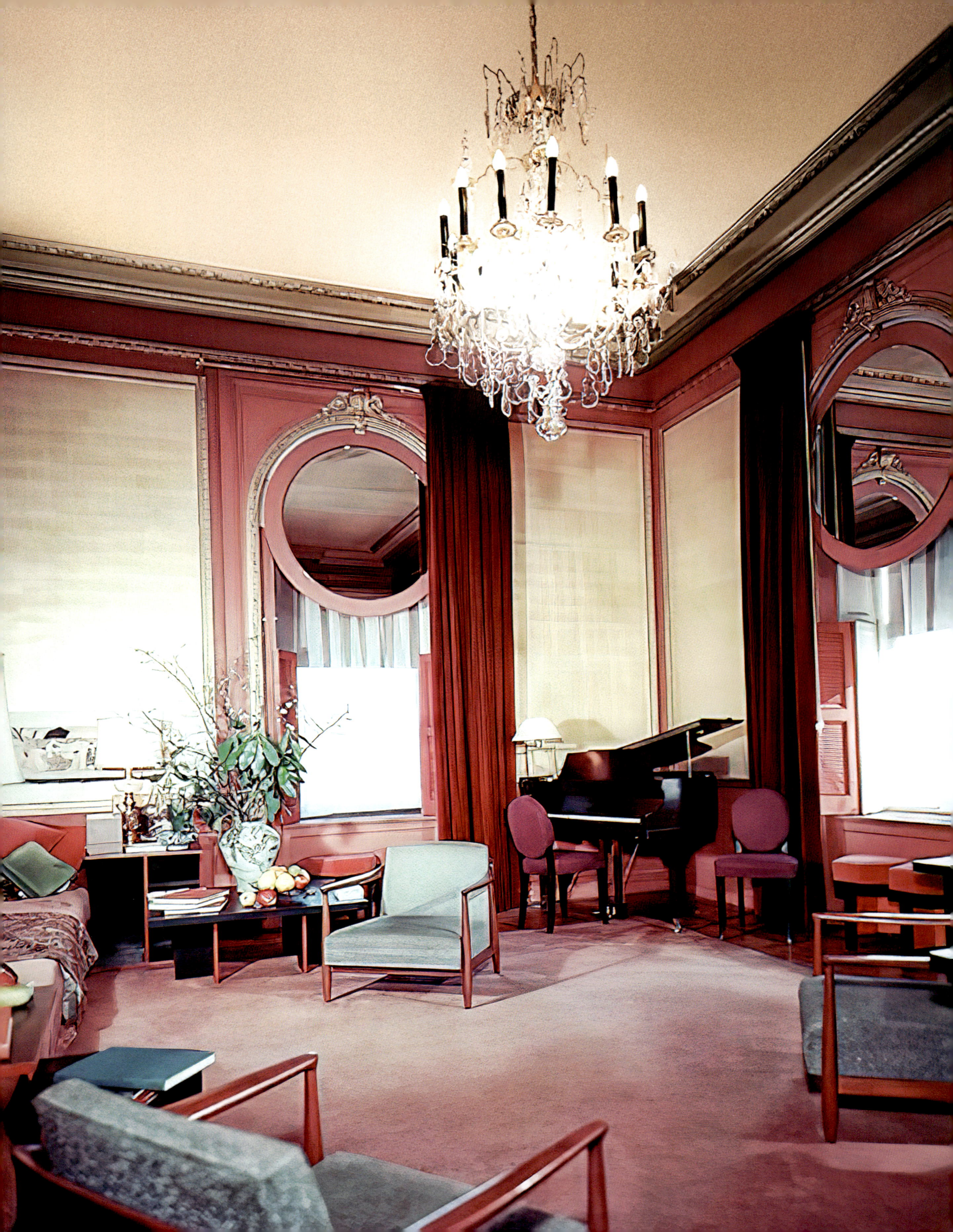

Frank Lloyd Wright at The Plaza

From 1954 to 1959, Frank Lloyd Wright (left) lived at The Plaza while working on the Solomon R. Guggenheim Museum, the striking spiral structure twenty-nine blocks north. As the architect John Rattenbury, who worked with Wright on the Guggenheim project, recalled: "Much of the furniture in the suite was Mr. Wright's design, including desks, hassocks [small ottomans] and display easels. The furniture was constructed of plywood and finished in black lacquer. The edges of the plywood were painted scarlet." The suite, he noted, became known as Taliesin III, after the house Wright built in Spring Green, Wisconsin. (Taliesin II was the name he gave his studio.)
Wright's suite had previously been decorated by Christian Dior in 1949, with beige toile-de-Jouy fabric on the walls (right). Wright retained the chandelier from that scheme, replacing Dior's olive carpet with a more modern mauve one.

WEDDING CHAPEL FOR CLAREMONT
BERKELEY, CALIFORNIA
FRANK LLOYD WRIGHT ARCHI

HOUSE FOR MR. AND MRS ARTHUR MILLER
FRANK LLOYD WRIGHT ARCHITECT

Among Frank Lloyd Wright's visitors at The Plaza were the Hollywood actress Anne Baxter, who was also his granddaughter, and Marilyn Monroe, or Mrs. Arthur Miller, as she styled herself privately at the time, pictured here with her husband Arthur Miller before her press conference at The Savoy for her movie *The Prince and the Showgirl*. Wright was designing a home for the couple in Roxbury, Connecticut (left), though it was never built.

While living at The Plaza, Wright also had the Claremont Club in Berkeley as a client, which he considered "one of the few hotels in the world with warmth, character and charm." In 1957, he was commissioned to build a wedding chapel (opposite), for which he proposed a glazed polygonal room on slits with a soaring spire, accessed via a glass corridor from the hotel's tower. He came to the hotel by helicopter to deliver the plans personally. Sadly, but perhaps not surprisingly, it was never built.

I.M. Pei in Singapore

Before the Louvre Pyramid in Paris and the Museum of Islamic Art in Doha made him a household name, the Chinese-American architect I.M. Pei (left) built what is now Fairmont Singapore. This twenty-six-story tower containing 778 rooms and suites, and thirteen restaurants, forms part of the Raffles City complex (right).
During this period of the construction work, which started in 1980 and ended in 1986, Pei was awarded the 1983 Pritzker Architecture Prize for his contributions to his field.
Pei's architectural signature is defined by the *New York Times* as "clean, reserved, sharp-edged and unapologetic in its use of simple geometries and its aspirations to monumentality," what the architect summarized as "crispy geometry." This very special quality is recognizable within the hotel in a series of details, including the star-shaped ceiling of the ballroom (opposite).

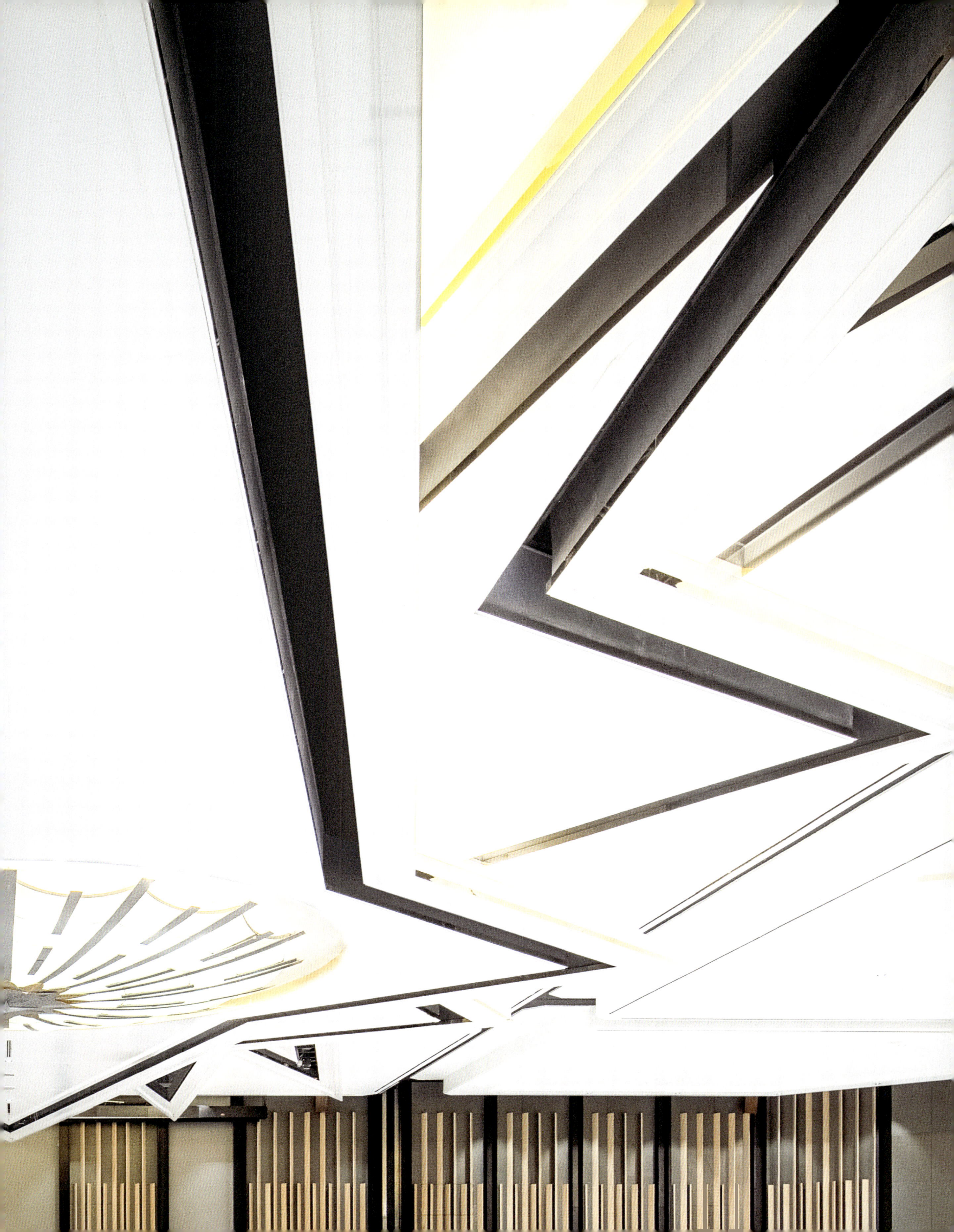

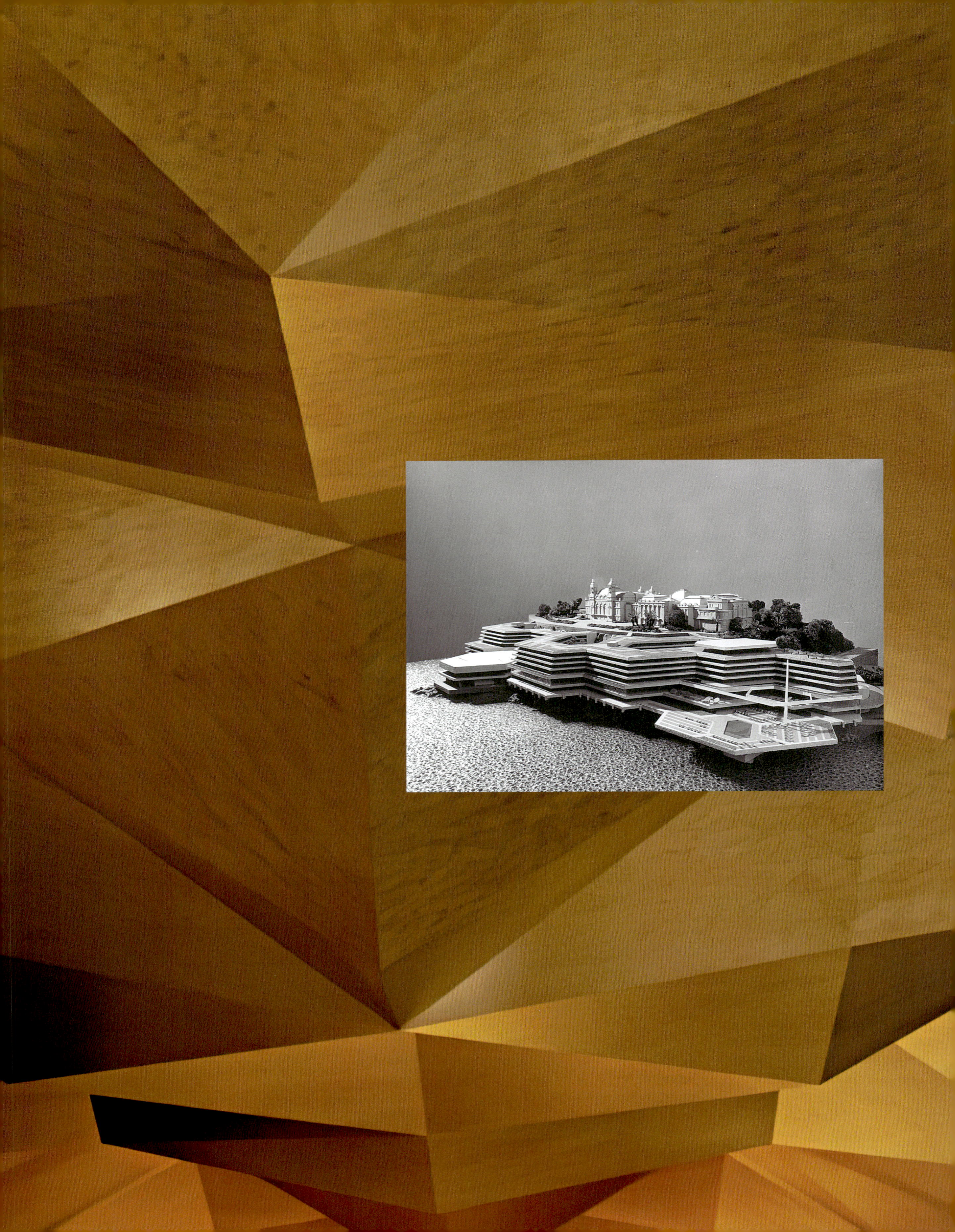

Fairmont Monte Carlo (opposite, inset) was a radically futuristic building when it opened in 1975 (as the Loews Hotel) built out from the cliffs and incorporating the site of the old railway station, it stands on fifty-feet stilts rooted in the seabed, so that it resembles a seven-story cruise ship berthed just below the Casino. It was groundbreaking for several reasons, not least that it was the first hotel to air-condition its interiors by means of "deep-sea water cooling," which draws water from the Mediterranean from a depth of 100 feet. Its aesthetic may be austere, but the multifaceted form of the arrangement of its balconies calls to mind something cellular that one might encounter in nature, a trope evident in the use of bookmarked marble at Fairmont Qasar Istanbul (above), in the central installation of the Lobby Lounge at Fairmont Washington, DC (right, background), and in the modular construction of Fairmont Pacific Rim (right).

Minoru Yamasaki in Los Angeles

In 1963, Twentieth-Century Fox released its epic movie *Cleopatra*. It flopped so badly that the studio was forced to sell off part of its back lot. But a project rose from that disaster: Century City, essentially a city within Los Angeles. Among its most striking buildings—an essay in 1960s modernism—is its hotel, now Fairmont Century City, designed by the Japanese architect Minoru Yamasaki (right).
Selected for the presidential celebration of the Apollo 11 moon landing, the curves of this futuristic building inspired masters of the precursory architectural photography, such as Balthazar Korab (opposite). In September 2021, the hotel reopened after a complete renovation signed by the International design firm Yabu Pushelberg.

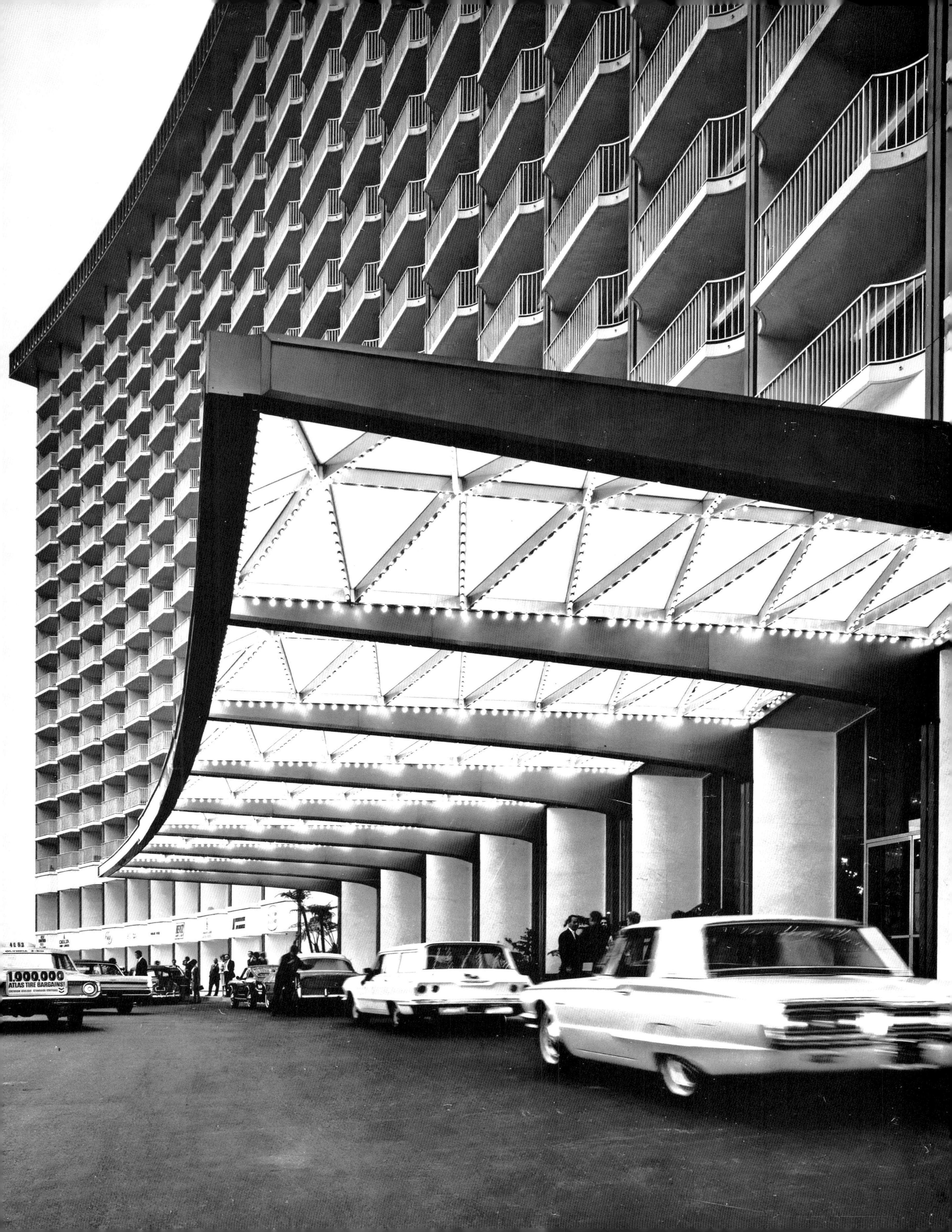
4083
1,000,000
ATLAS TIRE BARGAINS!
DELTA
HERTZ

Fairmont Waterfront   Fairmont Pacific Rim

Sustainable Hospitality

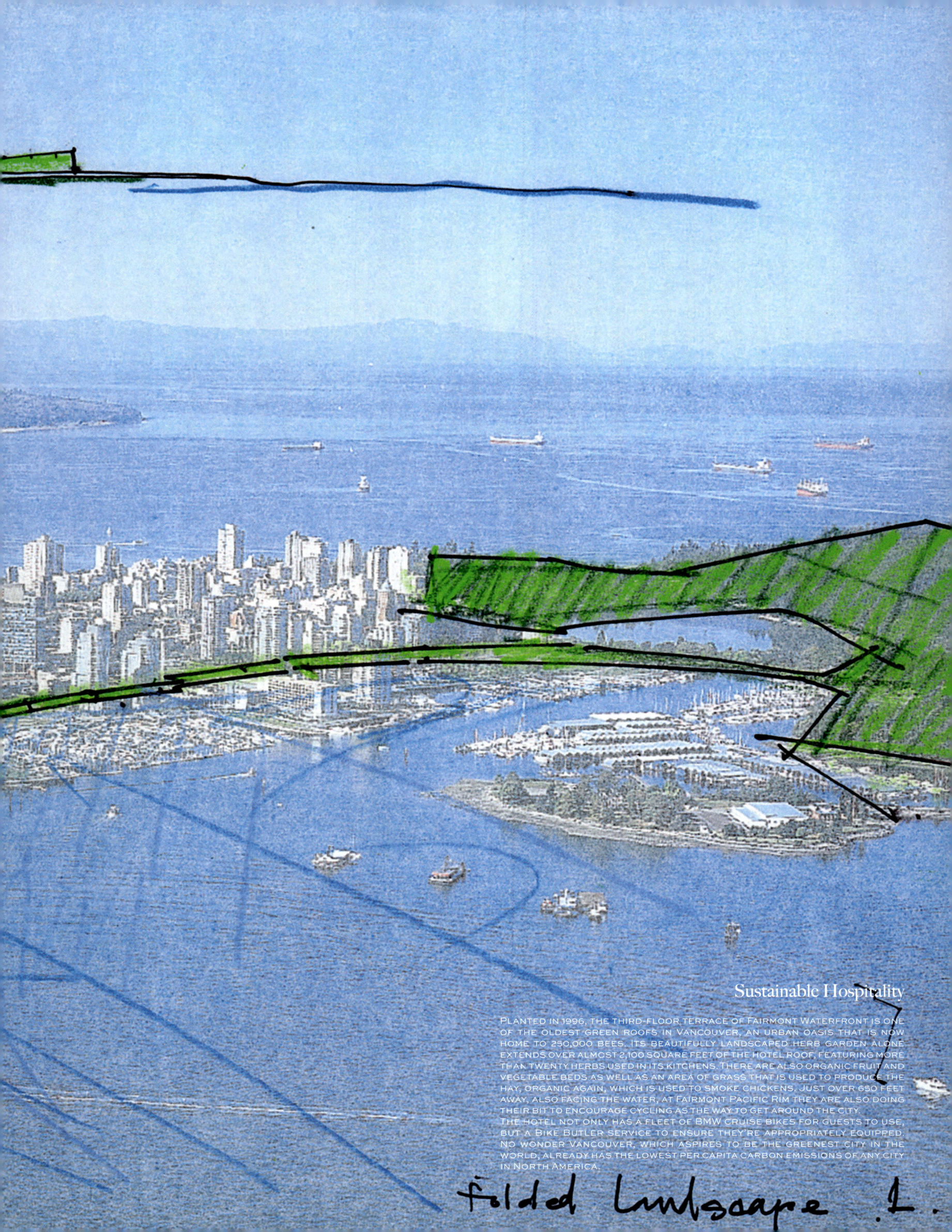

Planted in 1996, the third-floor terrace of Fairmont Waterfront is one of the oldest green roofs in Vancouver, an urban oasis that is now home to 250,000 bees. Its beautifully landscaped herb garden alone extends over almost 2,100 square feet of the hotel roof, featuring more than twenty herbs used in its kitchens. There are also organic fruit and vegetable beds as well as an area of grass that is used to produce the hay, organic again, which is used to smoke chickens. Just over 650 feet away, also facing the water, at Fairmont Pacific Rim they are also doing their bit to encourage cycling as the way to get around the city. The hotel not only has a fleet of BMW cruise bikes for guests to use, but a Bike Butler service to ensure they're appropriately equipped. No wonder Vancouver, which aspires to be the greenest city in the world, already has the lowest per capita carbon emissions of any city in North America.

folded landscape .1.

"'What hotel?'
'The Fairmont.'
'In the Flame Towers?'
The glass facades of these immense towers built on a hill overlooking the city are illuminated day and night by moving and colored projections.
They give the impression of burning like gigantic torches."

Jean-Christophe Rufin
DOUBLE WINNER OF THE PRIX GONCOURT

Prominently sited on the hill that rises behind the Gulistan Palace, Baku's three Flame Towers, one of which is a Fairmont hotel, have become the landmark, not just for the city, but for Azerbaijan. Their curving facades and tilted pinnacles are clad in more than 10,000 LED luminaires, which are programmed to flicker and change color, creating the illusion of flames, a reference to the nation's abundant oil and gas reserves and the importance of fire to Azerbaijani culture.

SOUL

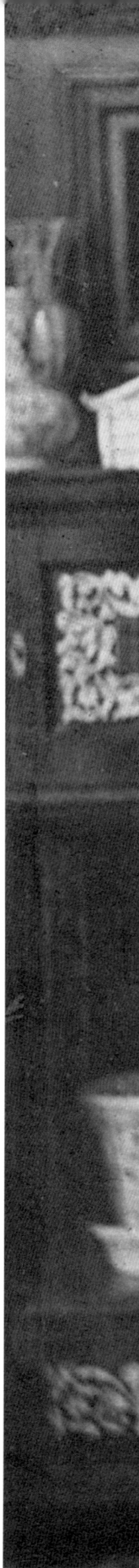

Queen Victoria and Her Descendants

Queen Victoria first visited Carton House, now a Fairmont hotel, the year she turned thirty, when she went to Ireland in 1849 with her husband, Prince Albert of Saxe-Coburg and Gotha. Sleeping in the Chinese Boudoir, she dreamt one night that she was rowing on a lake. There wasn't one on the 1,100-acre estate, only a river. So, anxious to please their sovereign, the FitzGerald family, which owned the estate, decided to create one, and a section of the Liffey, the river that flows through Dublin, was widened to form the body of water that stands there today. By the time the Queen returned in 1897, it was well established and filled with wild brown trout and pike, which guests can fish to this day. That first royal visit was the start of a long association between the British royal family and several of the properties that are now Fairmont hotels. Indeed, three of Victoria's children had associations with other hotels in the group.

Her eldest son, later Edward VII (pictured here with Victoria and his son, later George V, at the christening of the future Edward VIII in 1894) was a regular at The Savoy in London. Her sixth child, Princess Louise, Duchess of Argyll, gave her name to Chateau Lake Louise in Canada and the Hamilton Princess in Bermuda. Her seventh child, Prince Arthur, Duke of Connaught and Strathearn, visited The Norfolk Hotel in Nairobi in 1906.

It's a connection that continued down the generations. Victoria's great grandson, later George VI, became the first reigning monarch to visit Canada, accompanied by his wife, Queen Elizabeth, the Queen Mother in 1939, and staying at what is now Fairmont Hotel Vancouver, which was completed just in time for their visit, as well as at the Empress in Victoria, British Columbia (which was named after his mother), Château Frontenac, Chateau Lake Louise, Banff Springs and Jasper Park Lodge. His brother, the Duke of Windsor (briefly Edward VIII), also toured Canada and frequented The Plaza in New York.

Over the years, six royals have stayed at Banff Springs, hence its Royal Suite. Princess Diana praised Château Laurier in Ottawa. Elizabeth II made twenty-two official visits to Canada, the first as a princess in 1951, the last in 2010. Hence, for example, the Queen Elizabeth II Suite at Fairmont Hotel Macdonald, Alberta; the Royal Suite at Fairmont Banff Springs; Fairmont Royal York Toronto; and Fairmont The Queen Elizabeth in Montreal.

ROYALTY

"I have just left the magnificent train which has transported me across the Dominion and in which I have lived in such comfort for the last two and a half months."

Edward, Prince of Wales
PRAISING THE CANADIAN RAILWAYS FOR HIS 9,000-MILE JOURNEY.

WHILE THE PALLISER HOTEL IN CALGARY WELCOMED THE DUKE OF WINDSOR (FORMERLY EDWARD VIII), WHEN HE WAS STILL THE PRINCE OF WALES, IN ITS REGAL SUITE IN 1919, THE BANFF SPRINGS HOTEL'S 1932 PAMPHLET MENTIONS "THE VICE-REGAL SUITE OF FOURTEEN ROOMS, SEVERAL TIMES OCCUPIED BY THE PRINCE OF WALES." THE PAPARAZZI OF THE TIME HAD CAPTURED HIM ON THE TERRACE OF CHATEAU LAKE LOUISE, IN BANFF IN HIS DRESSING GOWN COMING BACK FROM THE POOL, GOING DOWN THE HOTEL'S STEPS, OR PLAYING GOLF IN 1919 AND AGAIN IN 1923. AT THE VICTORIA EMPRESS HOTEL IN 1919, THE PRINCE ATTENDED A CHARITY GALA IN THE CRYSTAL BALLROOM, WHICH BROKE ALL RECORDS OF PROFITABILITY.
THE DUKE AND DUCHESS OF WINDSOR DANCING AT THE DECEMBER BALL AT THE PLAZA, NEW YORK, ON DECEMBER 11, 1946. TEN YEARS EARLIER TO THE DAY, THE FORMER KING HAD ABDICATED THE BRITISH THRONE IN ORDER TO MARRY HER. HIS BROTHER ALBERT, MADE DUKE OF YORK IN THE 1920S, WAS THEN CROWNED GEORGE VI IN MAY 1937. TWO YEARS LATER, IN MAY AND JUNE 1939, HE AND HIS WIFE, QUEEN ELIZABETH, TOURED CANADA AND THE UNITED STATES. OPPOSITE, A PARLIAMENTARY DINNER WITH W.L. MACKENZIE WAS HELD IN THEIR HONOR AT CHÂTEAU LAURIER IN MAY 1939.

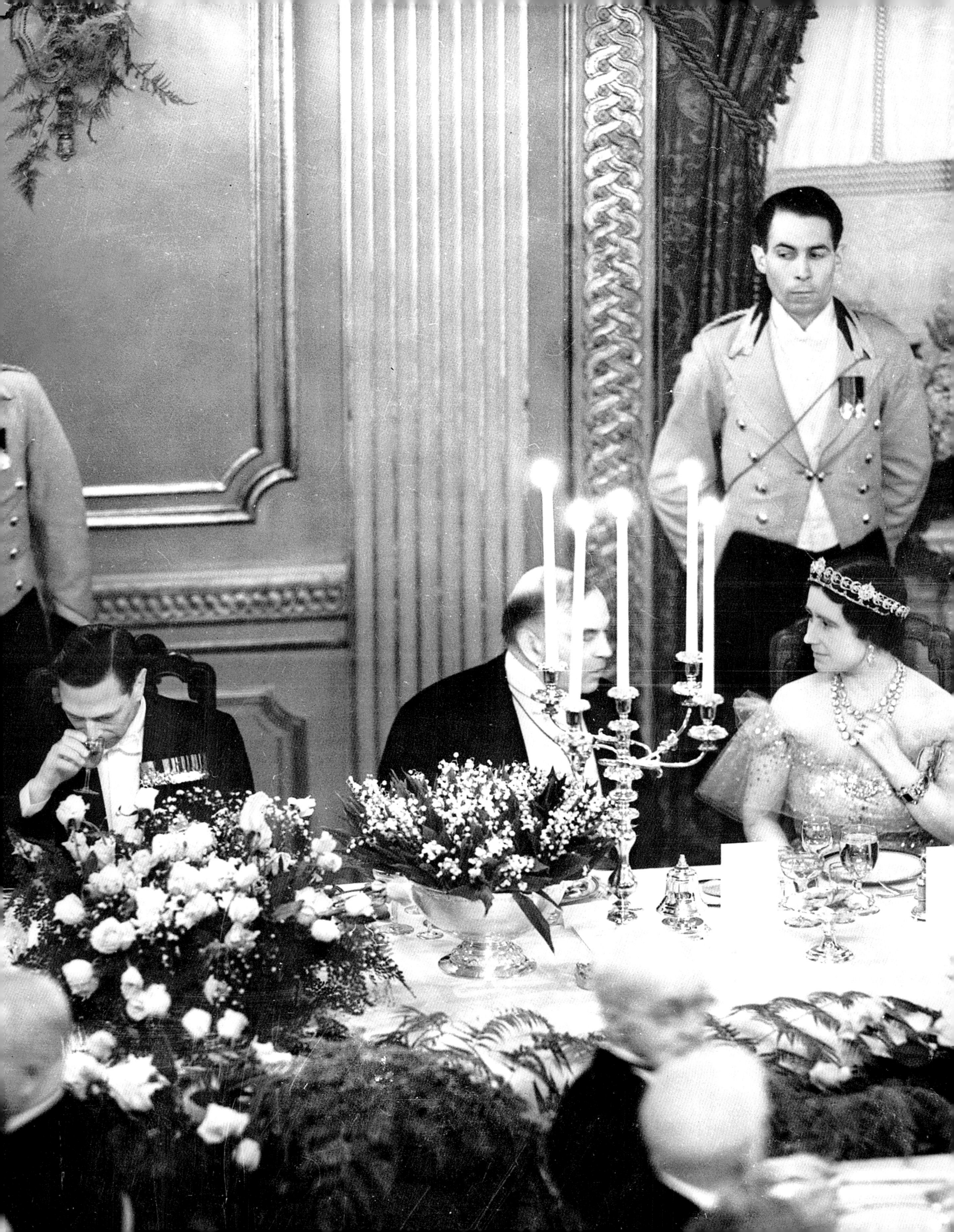

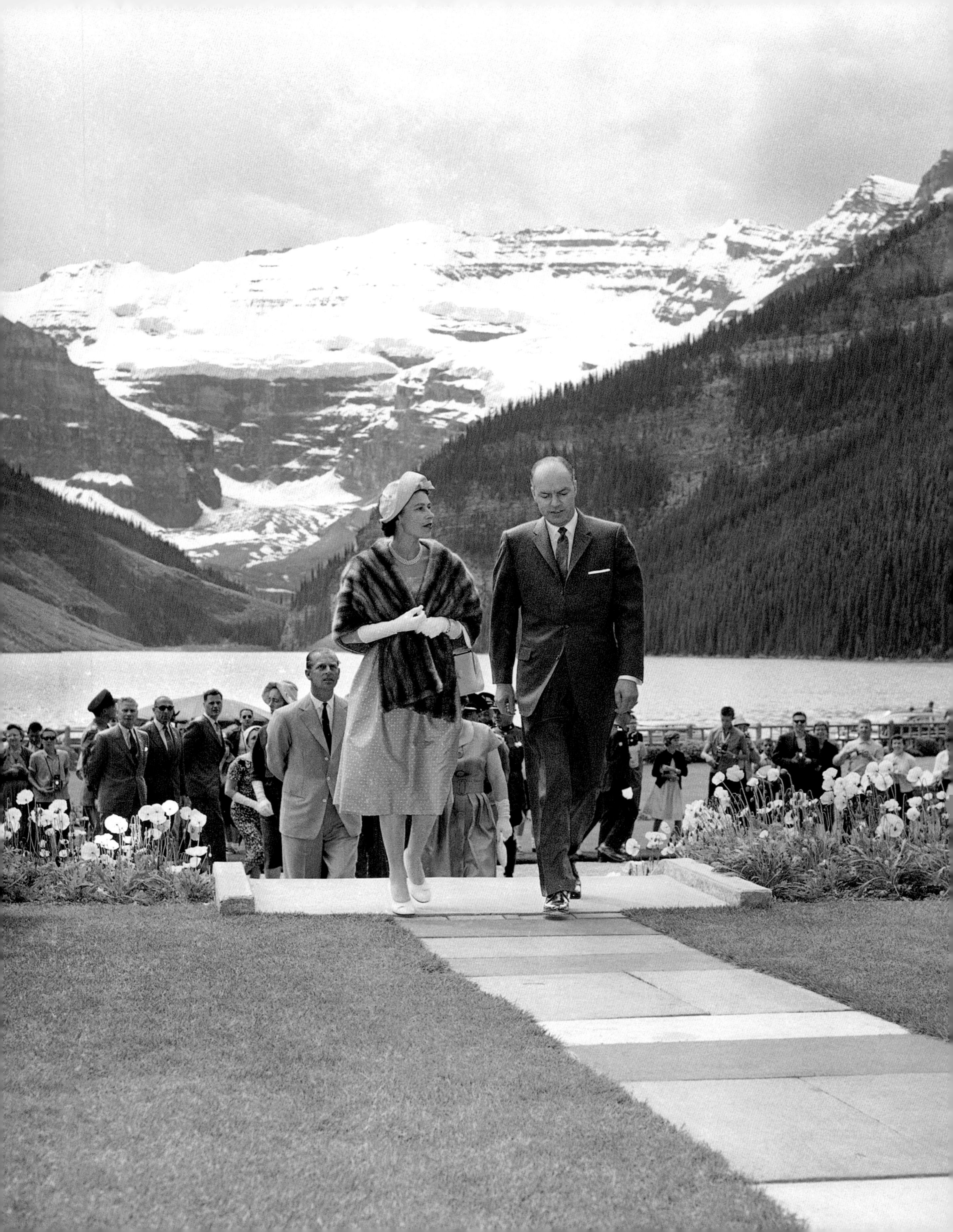

The twenty-year-old Princess Elizabeth was seen for the first time with her husband-to-be Lord Mountbatten in 1946, at the wedding of her cousin Captain Andrew Elphinstone at The Savoy Hotel.
Later crowned Queen, she followed in the footsteps of her parents in several Royal tours of Canada, along with Prince Philip, from the Atlantic to the Pacific coast. Starting from 1951, the Royal couple stayed in hotels such as the MacDonald in Edmonton, the Empress Hotel in Victoria, Château Frontenac, the Toronto Royal York, or Jasper Park Lodge.

Opposite, Queen Elizabeth with Don Williams at Chateau Lake Louise during her Royal tour of Canada, 1959.

Above, Diana, Princess of Wales, attends a gala dinner at the Royal York Hotel in Toronto during her official visit to Canada, October 27, 1991.

Above, left, Meghan Markle, photographed in April 2016, during the Canadian Arts and Fashion awards at the Royal York, the hotel where Prince Harry would stay when he visited her on set in Toronto. Meghan Markle played the character of the paralegal Rachel Zane in Suits, the TV drama that made her name. Her character dreamed of marrying Mike Ross (played by Patrick J. Adams) at The Plaza in New York, but the wedding episode was shot at Fairmont Royal York in Toronto, the city where Suits was filmed.
Right, Prince William on his graduation day in 2005 at the University of St. Andrews in Scotland where he and Kate Middleton, now the Duchess of Cambridge, were both students. According to the prince's biographer, Katie Nicholl, author of William and Harry, in 2002 the prince paid £200 for his front-row seat at a charity fashion show at Fairmont St. Andrews where Kate Middleton was modeling, and whispered, "Wow, Kate's hot," to his friend, Fergus Boyd.
Opposite, Prince Harry on May 2, 2016, with Canadian Prime Minister Justin Trudeau, and members of Canada's Invictus Games team, ahead of its official launch at Fairmont Royal York in Toronto.

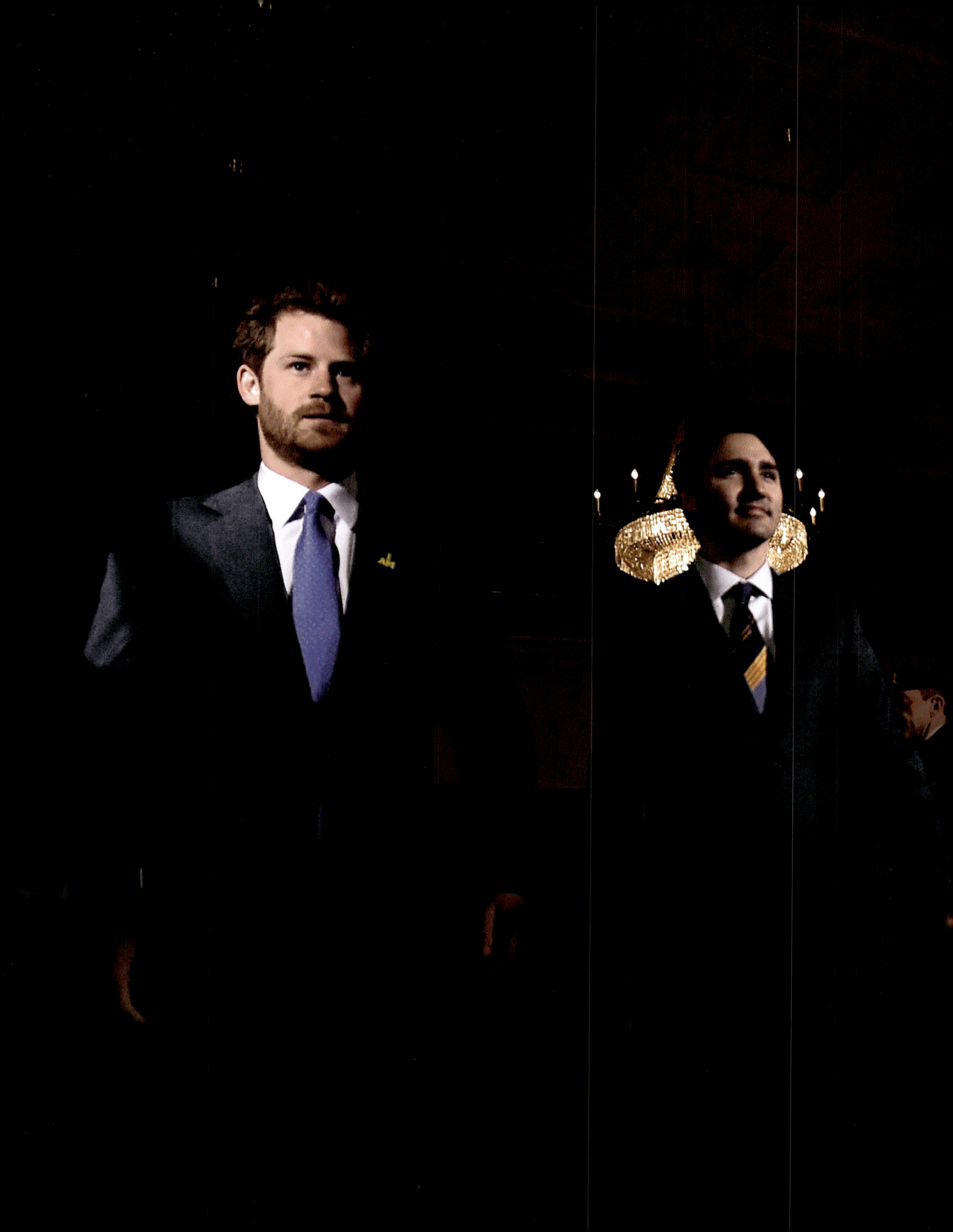

PO LIT ICS

Fairmont Hotels have long been popular with politicians, both as places to dine and drink, and venues for summits such as the G7. In Boston, Fairmont Copley Plaza has had a long association with the Kennedy family. In Ottawa, Fairmont Château Laurier is still regularly referred to as the third chamber both for its proximity to the Canadian parliament and its popularity with ministers.

In London, The Savoy has also historically been a political hangout. Less than a mile from the Houses of Parliament, it is close enough to walk to, but not so close as to be crowded with political insiders.

In 1911, Winston Churchill and the celebrated lawyer and politician F.E. Smith founded a dining society named The Other Club at The Savoy that met fortnightly when Parliament was in session in the Pinafore Room (named after HMS Pinafore, one of Gilbert & Sullivan's "Savoy operas"), to discuss the issues of the day. Originally the club's membership included twelve Liberals (then Churchill's party) and twelve Conservatives (Smith's)—the two major political parties of the day—along with twelve "distinguished outsiders." A diverse bunch, among them, over the years, Aristotle Onassis, whom Churchill suggested, the playwright Sir Tom Stoppard, and Prince Charles. There were twelve rules, the last of which stated that "Nothing in the rules or intercourse of the Club shall interfere with the rancour or asperity of party politics." At least there was always accord when it came to what they ate: the dish that was always served at these dinners was *pot-au-feu*.

Opposite, Churchill went to Washington soon after the Japanese attack on Pearl Harbor and America's entry into World War II. He traveled back via Canada, where he addressed Parliament on December 30, 1941. On his way back to Château Laurier where he was staying, Winston Churchill was immortalized by Turkish-born Canadian photographer Yusuf Karsh (right):

"The Prime Minister, Mackenzie King, invited me to be present. After the electrifying speech, I waited in the Speaker's Chamber where, the evening before, I had set up my lights and camera. The Prime Minister, arm-in-arm with Churchill and followed by his entourage, started to lead him into the room. I switched on my floodlights; a surprised Churchill growled, 'What's this, what's this?' No one had the courage to explain. I timorously stepped forward and said, 'Sir, I hope I will be fortunate enough to make a portrait worthy of this historic occasion.' He glanced at me and demanded, 'Why was I not told?' When his entourage began to laugh, this hardly helped matters for me. Churchill lit a fresh cigar, puffed at it with a mischievous air, and then magnanimously relented. 'You may take one.' Churchill's cigar was ever present. I held out an ashtray, but he would not dispose of it. I went back to my camera and made sure that everything was all right technically. I waited; he continued to chomp vigorously at his cigar. I waited. Then I stepped toward him and, without premeditation, but ever so respectfully, I said, 'Forgive me, sir,' and plucked the cigar out of his mouth. By the time I got back to my camera, he looked so belligerent he could have devoured me. It was at that instant that I took the photograph. My portrait of Winston Churchill changed my life. I knew after I had taken it that it was an important picture, but I could hardly have dreamed that it would become one of the most widely reproduced images in the history of photography."

The photographer lived and had his studio in the hotel.

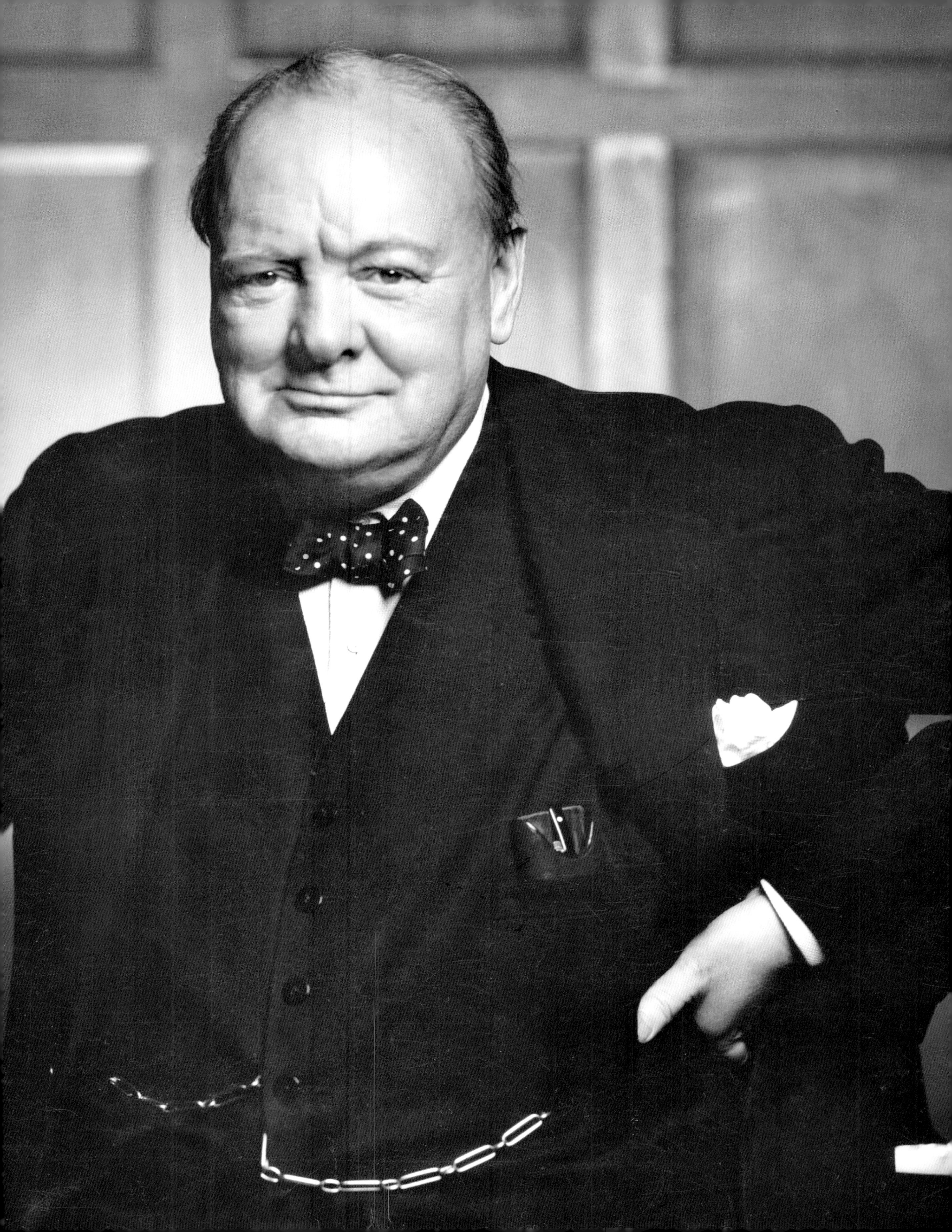

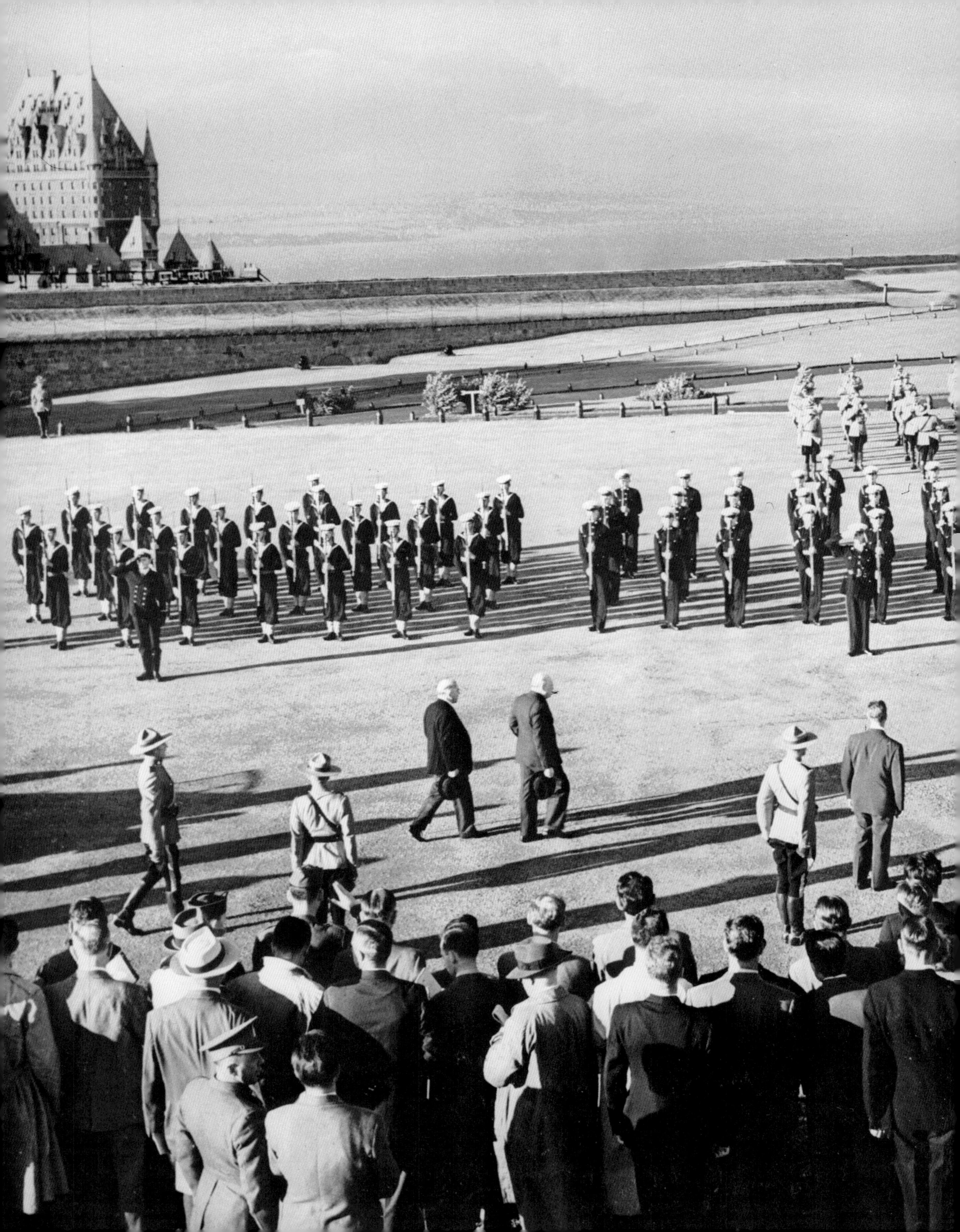

World War II

July 14, 1942, the French national holiday, General Charles de Gaulle receives the French Colonies Delegation at The Savoy Hotel, London, epicenter of the exiled French resistance (right).
In August 1943, the US President Franklin D. Roosevelt (top, left) and the British Prime Minister Winston Churchill met at Château Frontenac in Quebec, for the first of two conferences hosted by the Canadian Prime Minister, Mackenzie King, which had the code name Quadrant (opposite). The purpose of the first conference was to plan D-Day and the Normandy Landings and to finalize the Quebec Agreement, which outlined the Allies' terms for the coordinated development of nuclear weapons. Also among those who attended the 1943 conference was Ian Fleming, the creator of James Bond, who was then an intelligence officer in the British Naval Volunteer Reserve. The allies met in Château Frontenac again in September 1944 to discuss the demilitarization of Germany.
Bottom, left, on April 25, 1945, the music hall artist Josephine Baker, committed to the Resistance, arrives at The Savoy Hotel in London in her military outfit. "Born American and having chosen France, through her engagements and battles, Josephine Baker carried the motto of the French Republic high. On November 30, 2021, she will enter the Pantheon," declared French President Emmanuel Macron.

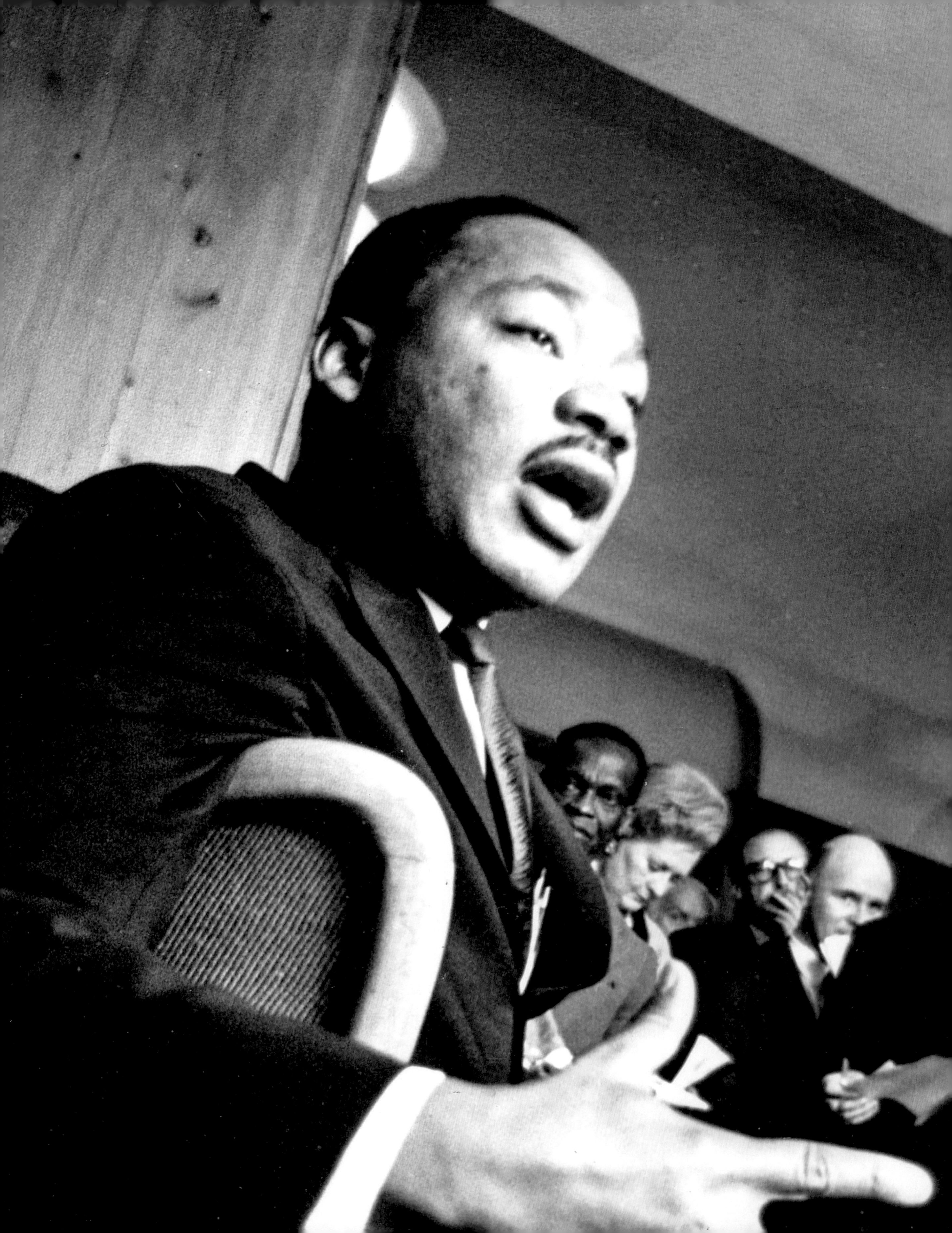

Civil Rights

In September 1964, the civil rights leader Martin Luther King (opposite) visited London and gave a press conference at The Savoy, just one month before he received the Nobel Prize for Peace "for his non-violent struggle for civil rights for the Afro-American population". The American author James Baldwin (top) attends a press conference at the Fairmont Hotel in San Francisco on a tour with the Congress of Racial Equality, May 1963. Awarded the 2001 Nobel Prize for Peace, Kofi Annan (bottom), the seventh Secretary-General of the United Nations at the Century Plaza Hotel in December 2003 for the fiftieth anniversary of the World Affairs Council.

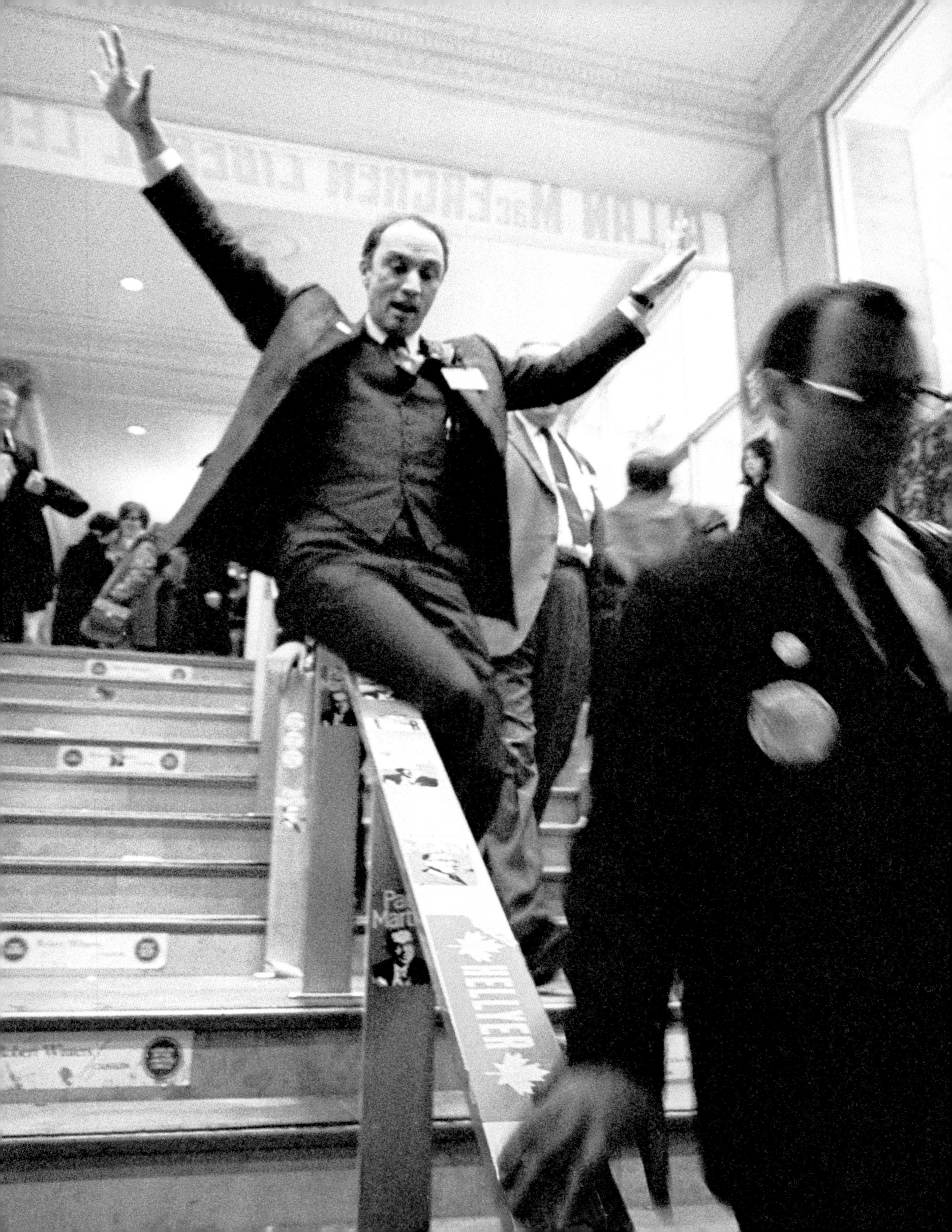
HELLYER

"[Bill Clinton] liked this hotel so much that ... you know how people on a road trip say: 'Let's stop in Fresno for a coffee.'

Well, when he traveled, he'd say : 'Let's stop at the Fairmont in San Francisco to smoke a cigar.'"

Tom Wolfe
FAIRMONT SAN FRANCISCO CHIEF CONCIERGE

Bill Clinton

PHOTOGRAPHED IN APRIL 1992 WHEN HE WAS A PRESIDENTIAL CANDIDATE, NEXT TO FAIRMONT SAN FRANCISCO (ABOVE).

Pierre Trudeau

THEN JUSTICE MINISTER, AND A GUEST AT THE HOTEL, PIERRE TRUDEAU (OPPOSITE) SLIDES DOWN A BANISTER AT CHÂTEAU LAURIER IN OTTAWA, APRIL 6, 1968. TRUDEAU WAS RUNNING AGAINST THE INCUMBENT PRIME MINISTER, LESTER PEARSON, FOR LEADERSHIP OF THE LIBERAL PARTY, AND THIS GESTURE, BEFORE AN ASSEMBLED PRESS CORPS, WAS RECKONED TO BE WHAT SPARKED *TRUDEAUMANIA*. TWO WEEKS LATER ON APRIL 20, HE WAS SWORN IN AS PRIME MINISTER AND WOULD REMAIN IN THIS ROLE FOR THE NEXT SIXTEEN YEARS.

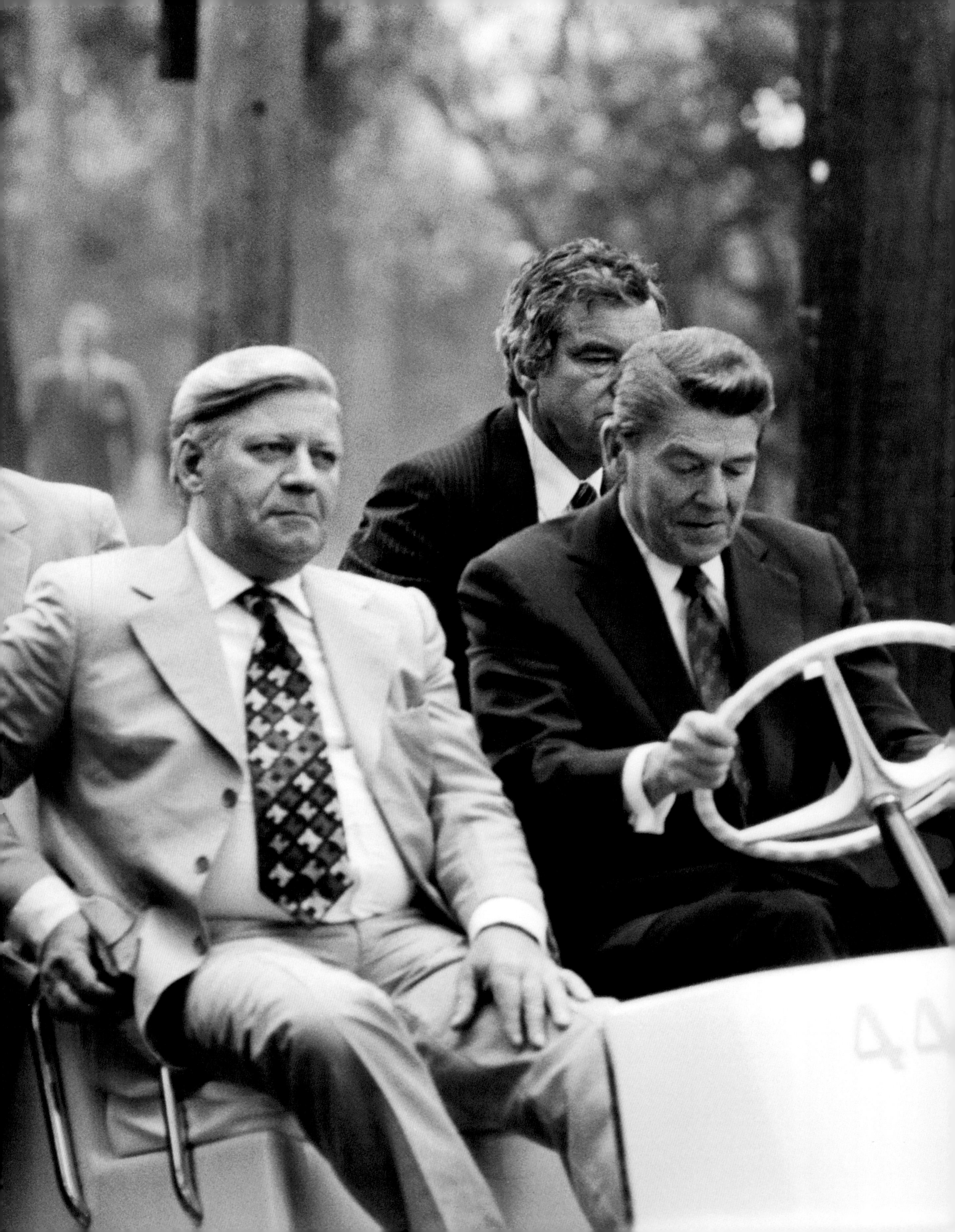

"We were at the Century Plaza Hotel in Los Angeles for a couple of days. President Reagan had a meeting scheduled with one of his primary speechwriters, Ken Khachigian.

At the appointed hour I walked into the President's suite; he was sitting on a sofa folding a piece of White House stationery into the shape of a paper airplane.

'I'll be right with you fellas,' he said to us, as he finished his creation.

He then walked out to the balcony and let his paper airplane fly. The three of us then leaned out over the balcony to watch as it landed on a hotel balcony some seventy floors below. None of us ever told the Secret Service about this little escapade."

Pete Souza
OFFICIAL WHITE HOUSE PHOTOGRAPHER FOR RONALD REAGAN, 1986

Ronald Reagan

IN LOS ANGELES, RONALD REAGAN SO FAVORED FAIRMONT CENTURY PLAZA, BOTH WHEN HE WAS GOVERNOR OF CALIFORNIA AND PRESIDENT OF THE UNITED STATES THAT THE MEDIA USED TO CALL IT THE "WESTERN WHITE HOUSE."
BOTTOM, CALIFORNIA GOVERNOR RONALD REAGAN TOGETHER WITH PRESIDENT GERALD FORD IN THE CENTURY PLAZA'S PRESIDENT'S SUITE IN 1974. IN 1980, HE WAS CELEBRATING HIS RE-ELECTION AS PRESIDENT ON THE STAGE OF THE ORIGINAL HOTEL'S LOS ANGELES BALLROOM. FOUR YEARS LATER, WHEN THE HOTEL OPENED IN NOVEMBER 1984, ADDING A FURTHER 322 ROOMS, RONALD REAGAN WAS THE FIRST GUEST TO CHECK IN TO THE TOWER AT CENTURY PLAZA. IN 1999, THE HOTEL NAMED ITS THIRTY-SECOND-FLOOR PENTHOUSE THE RONALD REAGAN SUITE.
OPPOSITE, PRESIDENT RONALD REAGAN AND HELMUT SCHMIDT, CHANCELLOR OF THE FEDERAL REPUBLIC OF GERMANY, RIDING A GOLF CART DURING THE 1981 SUMMIT AT FAIRMONT CHÂTEAU MONTEBELLO, CANADA.

"White house diaries, Sunday, July 19, 1981.
Air Force One to Ottawa & then Marine One to Montebello—
the largest log cabin [in] the world.

The hotel is a marvelous piece of engineering, totally made up of logs.

Had a one on one with Chancellor Schmidt.
He was really down & in a pessimistic mood about the world.
Following—met with Pres. Mitterrand—
explained our ec[onomic] program
& that high interest rates were not of our doing.

Merci Dinner that night was just the 8 of us. The 7 heads of State
& the Pres. (Thorn) of the European Community.
It became a really freewheeling discussion of ec[onomic] issues,
trade etc. due largely to a suggestion by P.M. Thatcher."

Ronald Reagan
WHITE HOUSE JULY 19, 1981

World Summits

Meeting of the Allied Nations, creation of the United Nations, G7, G20 … The exceptional locations of the Fairmont Hotels and resorts—be it in the heart of cities or in uncontaminated nature—have proven to be shelters for the most strategic political meetings. The leaders of the world can gather in the most relaxing yet highly protected luxury. Canada hosted the seventh G7 summit at Château Montebello in the state of Quebec in July 1981. Opposite, the leaders who attended were, from left to right, European Commission President Gaston Thorn, Zenko Suzuki (Japan), Helmut Schmidt (West Germany), Ronald Reagan (US), Pierre Trudeau (Canada), François Mitterrand (France), and Margaret Thatcher (UK).
In June 2018, Canada hosted the forty-fourth G7 summit, this time at Fairmont Le Manoir Richelieu at La Malbaie in Quebec, where the delegates were, above, from left to right, President of the European Council Donald Tusk, Theresa May (UK), Angela Merkel (Germany), Donald Trump (US), Justin Trudeau (Canada), Emmanuel Macron (France), Shinzo Abe (Japan), Giuseppe Conte (Italy), and Jean-Claude Juncker (President of the European Commission).

208 — 209

Obamas & Bidens

On november 6, 2012, US President Barack Obama and First Lady Michelle Obama were watching from the Fairmont Chicago Millennium Park the results of the elections, together with Vice President Joe Biden and Dr. Jill Biden. This photograph was taken by the official White House photographer Paul Souza, just moments after the television networks called the election in their favor.

210 — 211

SUSTAIN ABIL ITY

Protecting Nature since 1885

Direct heir of the creators of the first Canadian national park in 1885, Fairmont is a global leader in sustainability. It was the world's first luxury hotel brand to embrace environmental stewardship, when in 1991 (as Canadian Pacific Hotels) it launched its Green Partnership Guide. As early as 2006, it was offsetting greenhouse gas emissions through the purchase of wind-power energy. By 2015, it had reached its goal to reduce operational carbon emissions by twenty percent. Now part of Accor's Planet21 Program, the Fairmont Sustainability Partnership combines leading efforts to reduce the impact on the planet with innovative programs to promote responsible tourism and community outreach.

An Organic Farm
Fairmont Yangcheng Lake

Yancheng Lake is an eight-square-mile body of freshwater that teems with fish—salmon, eels, various whitefish—and crustacea, most famously hairy crabs, one of the great delicacies of Shanghainese cuisine. On its eastern shore stands Fairmont Yangcheng Lake and its thirty-three-acre organic farm, Yue Feng (Great Harvest), which supplies the kitchens of its three restaurants.
Given the farm's watery environs, it is no surprise there are paddy fields where rice is grown. But there are orchards, too, filled with loquat, peach, pomegranate and pear trees. And in its kitchen gardens and glass houses grow not just familiar fruits and vegetables—broccoli, pumpkin, strawberries—but esoteric edible varieties such as crystal ice plant (Mesembryanthemum crystallinum), a succulent that looks as though little pockets of dew or ice have crystallized on its subtly salty leaves (which can be steamed or stir-fried) and water lilies with edible bulbs.
From the Dong Ting Mountain of Tai Hu, *Bi Luo Chun* is a delicate green tea with a fruity taste and floral aroma whose culture dates back more than a thousand years. In Spring, it is picked from the hotel's organic farm, hand roasted and served in the Luwei Lounge overlooking the park and lakefront.

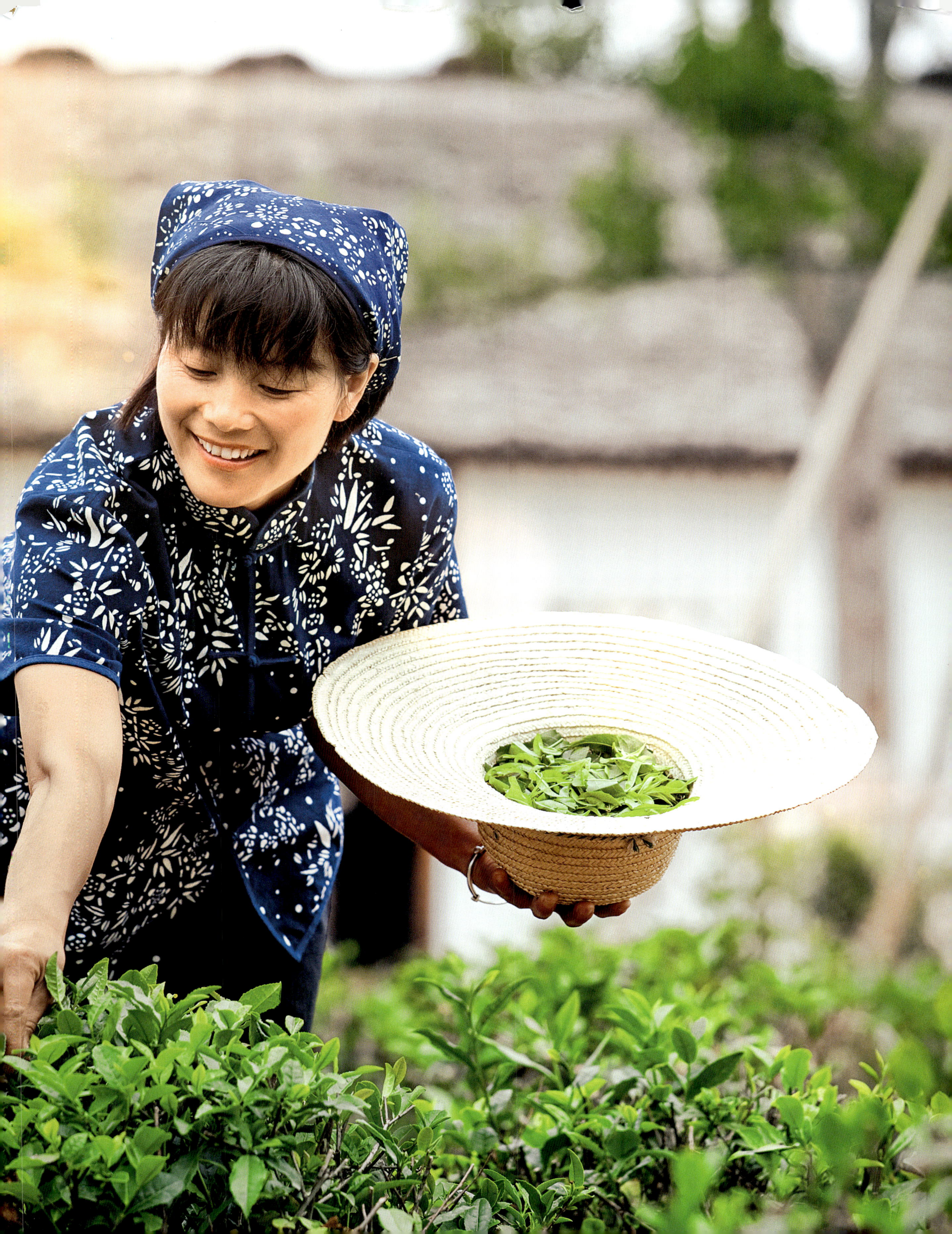

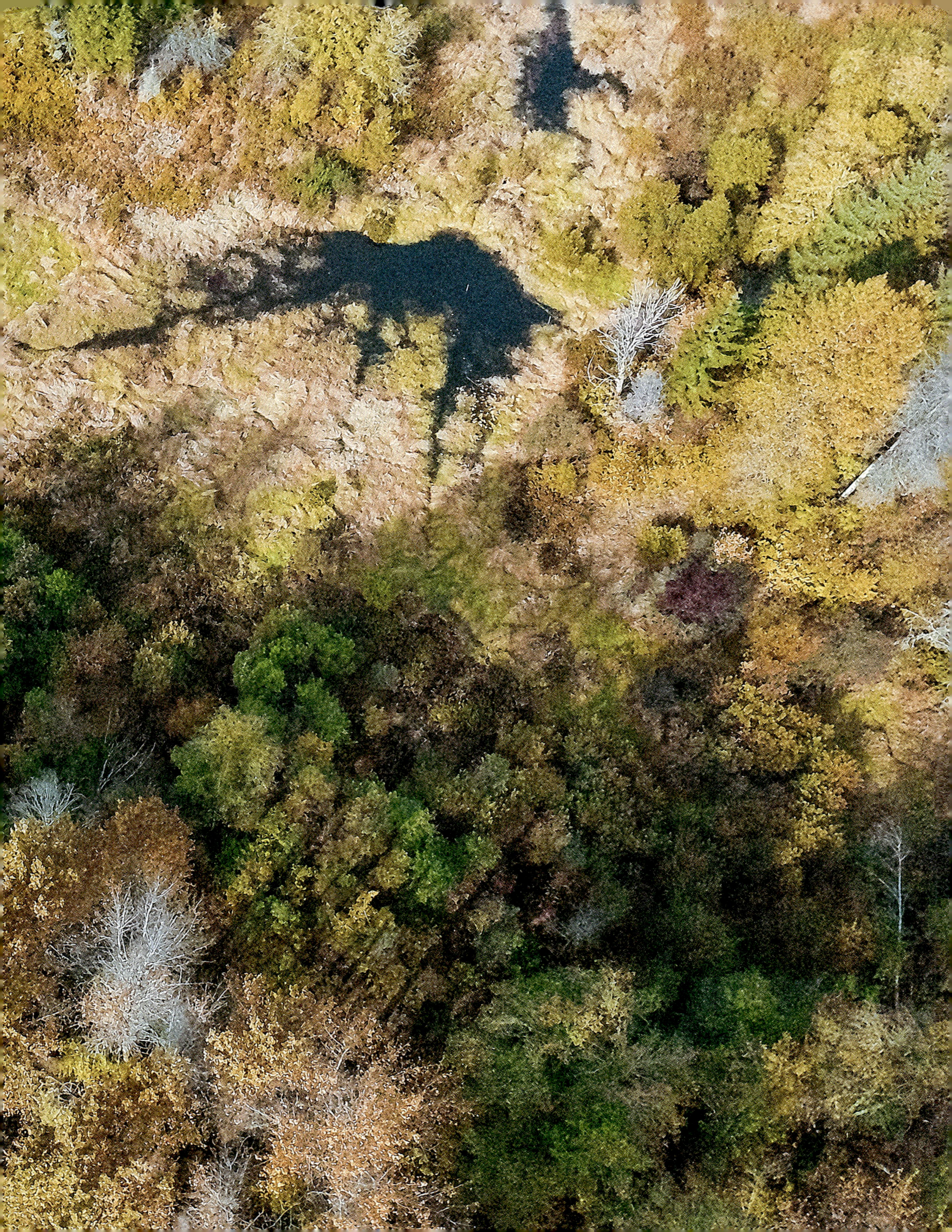

Carbon Compensation
Fairmont Château Frontenac, Quebec

In 2016, the Fairmont Château Frontenac in Quebec City launched a program called Château Boreal, in which it undertook to plant a tree for every guest who agreed to forgo housekeeping services during their stay. Over four years, thousands of individuals rose to the challenge, and the Montmorency Forest—a substantially wooded area of lakes and mountains covering almost 150 square miles in the province of Quebec, which is managed by the Laval University and serves as the largest "research forest" in the world—acquired a further 5,000 trees.
Four years later, the hotel made a yet more important announcement when it became the first historic hotel in Canada to achieve carbon neutrality, setting a new standard of sustainable tourism that it hopes will inspire others to reduce their emissions.
Thanks to a continuing partnership with Université Laval, it has introduced a raft of measures to offset its greenhouse gas emissions, notably a commitment to continue to plant trees in order to maintain and improve the carbon-capture capacity. To further this initiative, it has also created a support fund for training and research into how responsible forestry can combat climate change and a master's scholarship.

Bee Sustainable
Twenty-one Fairmont Hotels around the World

Fairmont was the first luxury hotel group to develop bee programs on its properties and is considered an industry leader in this area. The Royal York in Toronto was the first, installing bees on its property as early as 2008. Today Fairmont locations worldwide feature over twenty honeybee apiaries and more than twenty wild pollinator bee hotels in seven countries: Bermuda, Canada, China, Kenya, Mexico, Switzerland and the United States. In 2009, Fairmont Washington welcomed 105,000 honeybees in three dedicated rooftop beehives. The same year, The Fairmont Yangcheng Lake in China hired the local, seventh-generation beekeeper, Bao Beilei, to bring hives onto its thirty-three-acre organic farm. The forty colonies she had brought with her have now increased to sixty. Above, the 200,000 honeybees of Fairmont San Francisco dine on its lavender and aromatic herbs to produce 600 pounds of palatable honey yearly—a 100% local ingredient, invaluable for the hotel's chefs and the brewers of its own Honey Beer Series.

Coral Protection
Fairmont Mayakoba Mexico, Fairmont Fen Surri Maldives

Just off the Caribbean coast off Mexico's Riviera Maya (above), the Mesoamerican Reef extends for almost 620 miles, making it the largest colony of coral after Australia's Great Barrier Reef.
But corals the world over are threatened by rising sea temperatures and the bleaching events they give rise to. This reef has also been ravaged by white-band disease. In May 2015, Fairmont Mayakoba joined forces with the Mexican marine conservation non-profit Oceanus AC to rebuild the reef by creating nurseries for baby corals that can then be transplanted onto the reef. To date, it has successfully transferred more than 1,500 corals, with about eighty percent surviving, and it is working with local community groups both to train them in coral-conservation practices and to raise awareness of the issues facing reefs. Guests, meanwhile, can visit the nurseries on guided snorkelling tours.
The Coralarium is the first and only coral regeneration project in the Maldives. First installed in 2018 in the Fairmont Sirru Fen Fushi lagoon within the Shaviyani Atoll, it was created by the celebrated underwater naturalist Jason deCaires Taylor. Its non-toxic steel-and marine-grade structure (opposite) acts as a semi-immersed artificial reef. Quickly inundated with hard corals, sponges, and thousands of schooling fish, the installation has become an ever-changing museum.

Turtles Nestling
Fairmont Mayakoba Mexico, Fairmont Sanur Beach Bali, Fairmont Fen Surri Maldives

Every year between April and October, leatherback, green, hawksbill, and loggerhead turtles come to the beach at Mayakoba to nest, digging holes in the sand. Working with local conservation agencies, not least the Mexican government's Secretariat of Environment and Natural Resources, the resort works actively to protect the turtles and their young. And under the guidance of its resident naturalist, about 7,000 volunteer guests and staff have aided the release of more than 25,000 hatchlings when they emerged into the world after an incubation that lasted forty-five to sixty days.
In Bali, Fairmont Sanur Beach is not officially a turtle sanctuary, but every year, hundreds of turtles lay their eggs there, and when they hatch, guests can help return the hatchlings to the sea, sparing them the often hazardous and disorienting journey across the sand to the water.
In Fen Surri, fifty turtles of the critically endangered Hawksbill subspecies have been traced by the resort's marine biologist in the waters surrounding the resort, with ten permanently residing in the nearby reef. Identified, surveyed—including by trained little guests of the resort's Turtle Rangers program—their migration patterns are tracked in a non-invasive way.

"I wanted to create something that existed between two worlds, a bridge that allowed us to see through the surface of the sea. A way to re-imagine our interactions with the natural world and form a controlled space where marine life can come and go as it pleases."

Jason deCaires Taylor

Since the very early days of what has become Fairmont, visual arts have been a keystone of the brand's DNA. William Van Horne, founder of the Canadian Pacific hotels, was himself a talented painter and a passionate art collector. He immediately involved the most talented artists of the time in the creation of the Brand's imagery. To decorate the hotels themselves or to produce pamphlets, postcards and other communication tools.
Sending painters, illustrators, photographers, videographers on the Canadian tracks, he offered Canada the highest level and most prolific imagery since its very birth. While the artists were at the beginning still influenced by the European beauty canons, thirty years later they had founded the Canadian painting school.
Opposite, the mountain landscape (untitled) was painted in 1928 by Lawrence Stewart Harris, member of the pioneering *Group of Seven* who explored the Canadian National parks during the 1920s.

Visual Arts

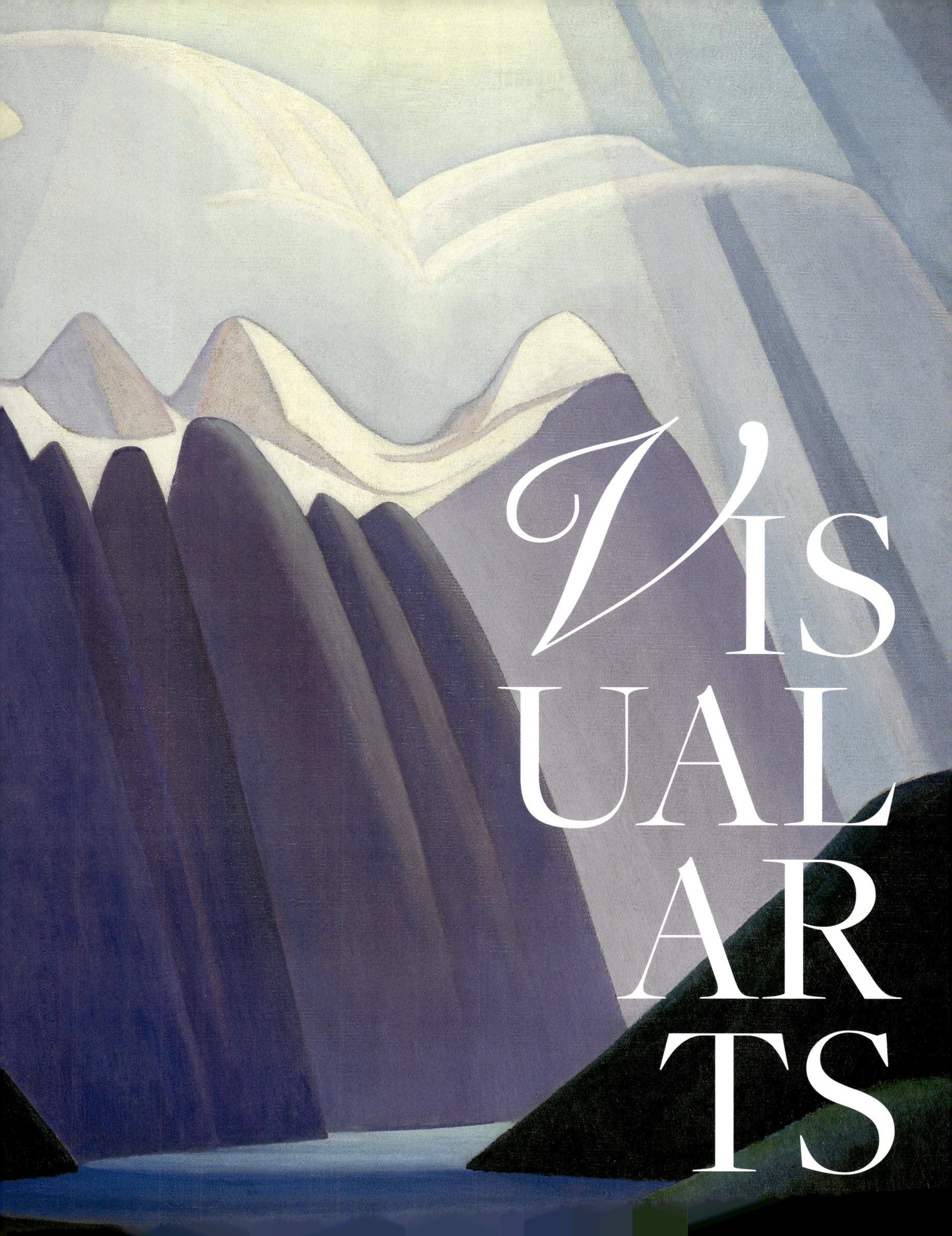

James McNeill Whistler

WHISTLER STAYED AT THE SAVOY, LONDON, IN A SIXTH-FLOOR CORNER ROOM FROM JANUARY TO MARCH 1896. HE WAS TRANSFIXED BY VIEWS OF THE THAMES AND MADE A SERIES OF LITHOGRAPHS NOT JUST OF THE FAMOUS BRIDGES AND LANDMARKS VISIBLE FROM THE HOTEL, BUT OF THE THEN INDUSTRIAL SOUTH BANK OF THE THAMES. WHERE HIS FRIEND MONET FAVORED COLOR, WHISTLER FAVORED A DULLER PALETTE THAT WAS ALMOST MONOCHROME

"The sun rose, and was dazzling ...
The Thames was all gold.
God it was beautiful,
so fine that I began to work in a frenzy,
following the sun and its reflections on the water."

Claude Monet

Claude Monet

When Monet came to England toward the end of January 1901, his painting materials were impounded by customs, preventing him from working. Rather than waste his precious time in London, he purchased a set of pastels and began to work with those instead. It took four days for his luggage to be returned to him, but during that period, he produced twenty-six superb, though by his own admission "promptly made," images of the Thames—west toward the Houses of Parliament and east toward Waterloo Bridge and the City beyond—as he saw it from his room on the sixth floor of The Savoy. Above, *The Thames at Charing Cross Bridge*, 1903.

Pablo Picasso

ALONG WITH HIS WIFE, THE FORMER BALLETS RUSSES BAL-
LERINA OLGA KHOKHLOVA, PABLO PICASSO STAYED AT THE
SAVOY FROM MAY UNTIL JULY 1919, CREATING FOR THE BAL-
LETS RUSSES THE STAGE SETS OF *THE THREE-CORNERED
HAT* (ABOVE, GOUACHE DRAWING, MUSÉE PICASSO PARIS
COLLECTION) ON STAGE AT THE ALHAMBRA OF LONDON ON
JULY 22, 1919. AT THE HOTEL, PICASSO WAS ALSO DRAWING
THE BALLERINA LYDIA LOPOKOVA, WIFE OF THE ECONOMIST
JOHN MAYNARD KEYNES.

Solomon R. Guggenheim

Before he opened his Museum of Non-Objective Painting in 1939, Solomon R. Guggenheim used to display works from his art collection in his apartment in The Plaza, which he would occasionally open to the public.
In 1937, when this photograph was taken, his bedroom was hung with several works by Wassily Kandinsky, among them *Composition 8* (to the left of the door).

"Garbo arrived wearing a biscuit-colored suit and polo-collared sweater, her hair's a lion's mane.
At first she stood stiffly to attention, facing my Rolleiflex full face as if it were a firing squad.
But, by degrees, she started to assume all sorts of poses and many changes of mood.
The artist in her suddenly came into flower. She was enjoying the return to an aspect of the métier
that had been her life's work. Could I believe my luck?
[...]

Every now and again Greta was saying:
'That's enough now – got to go.'
But by the time I took her word as gospel, a vast number of pictures had been made.
The result formed a prized collection."

Cecil Beaton

Cecil Beaton

IN 1945, SERGE OBOLENSKY, A RUSSIAN PRINCE BY BIRTH BUT POST-REVOLUTION OBLIGED TO EARN HIS LIVING AS THE PLAZA'S PUBLIC RELATIONS DIRECTOR, SUGGESTED THE HOTEL HIRE CECIL BEATON TO DESIGN SUITE 249–251.
HAVING VISITED PICASSO AT HIS HOME, BEATON DECIDED TO MAKE A WORK OF CONTEMPORARY ART—IN THIS INSTANCE FERNAND LÉGER'S *DIVERS, BLUE AND BLACK* (1942–43) NOW IN THE METROPOLITAN MUSEUM OF ART—ITS FOCAL POINT, PICKING UP LÉGER'S COLORS IN THE DECOR. THEY MAY NOT SEEM AS BRIGHT AS BEATON IMAGINED THEM IN THE WATERCOLOR HE MADE OF THE ROOM, BUT THE RED IN LÉGER'S OIL PAINTING IS ECHOED IN THE FABRIC BEATON USED FOR THE CURTAINS, THE UPHOLSTERY, AND IN THE LACQUERED CABINET.
CECIL BEATON OFTEN USED HIS SUITE AT THE PLAZA AS A STUDIO, PHOTOGRAPHING GRETA GARBO THERE IN 1946. THE GLACIAL SWEDISH MOVIE STAR MADE A PARTICULAR IMPRESSION ON HIM.
LATTERLY, HE ALSO PHOTOGRAPHED MICK JAGGER, WHOM HE DESCRIBED AS "A GOOD GUY, INCREDIBLY PHOTOGENIC," AT THE HOTEL.

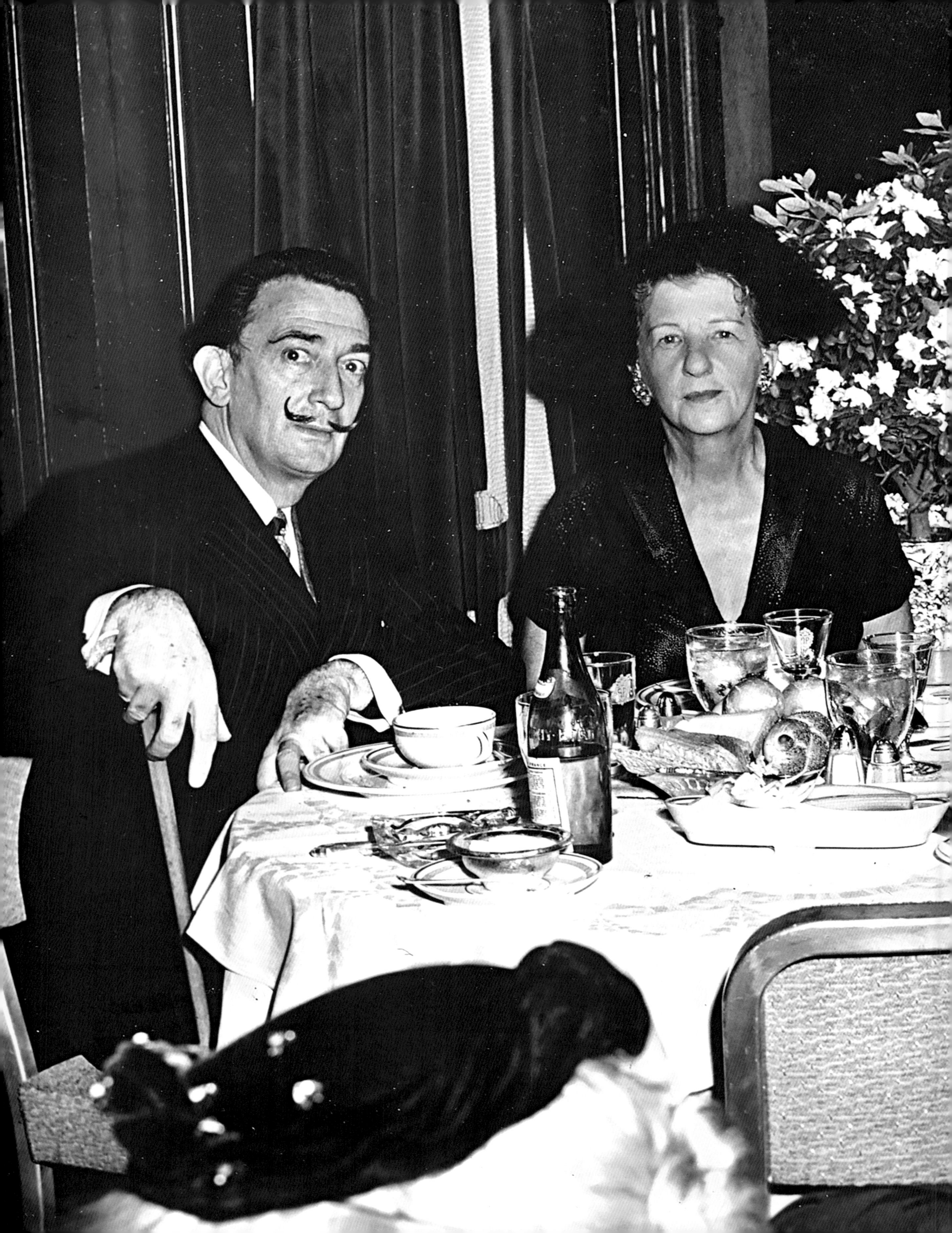

"Here I am,
living on the 8th floor
of the smartest hotel in Europe.
I have to live this high up
because from here I can paint
the broadest vista
of the Thames!"

Oskar Kokoschka

Oskar Kokoschka

HAVING SIGNED A CONTRACT IN 1923 WITH THE ART DEALER CASSIRER WHO UNDERTAKES TO PURCHASE ALL HIS UPCOMING WORKS, THE AUSTRIAN PAINTER OSKAR KOKOSCHKA LEAVES DRESDEN WHERE HE TEACHES ART TO EMBARK ON A NOMADIC LIFESTYLE THAT TAKES HIM THROUGH EUROPE, ASIA MINOR AND NORTH AFRICA.
VIEW FROM THE VIER JAHRESZEITHEN HOTEL OVER THE JUNGFERNSTIEG, 1926 (TOP).
LONDON, SMALL VIEW ON THE THAMES, 1926 (BOTTOM).

Salvador Dalí

SALVADOR DALÍ WAS HAVING DINNER WITH ART COLLECTORS MARY DALE AND CHESTER DALE AT THE PLAZA HOTEL IN 1958, ON "THE DAY OF THE ANNIVERSARY WHEN [CHESTER] INSPIRED IN [HIM] THE IDEA TO PAINT THE LAST SUPPER."

"Free countries are great, because you can actually sit in somebody else's space for a while and pretend you're a part of it. You can sit in The Plaza Hotel and you don't even have to live there. You can just sit and watch the people go by."

Andy Warhol

ANDY WARHOL WHO LIKED TO HAVE BREAKFAST AT THE PLAZA IS PHOTOGRAPHED HERE DURING THE BLACK AND WHITE BALL BY TRUMAN CAPOTE AT THE PLAZA, 1966.

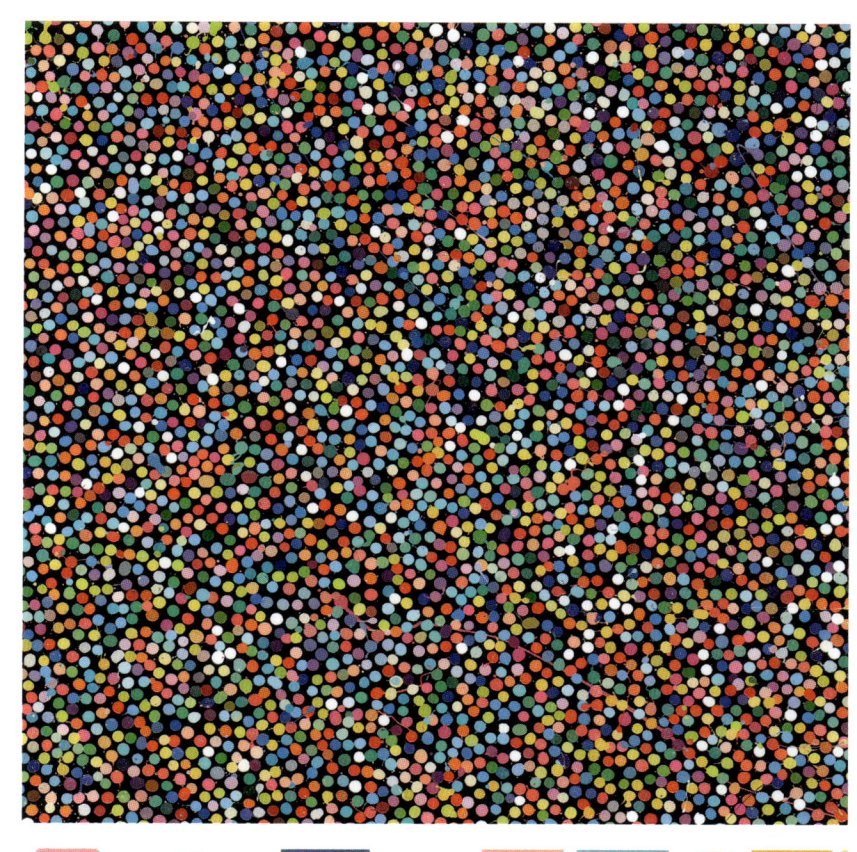

Damien Hirst

Damien Hirst, who has named works in his *Colour Space* series *Plaza*, 2018 (right) and *Savoy*, 2018 (top), is one of the artists whose work can be seen at the Hamilton Princess in Bermuda, where his spot print *Cineole*, 2004 hangs in the lobby.

Julian Opie

The art collection at the Hamilton Princess is even more remarkable, a museum-quality assemblage of works by the likes of Matisse, Magritte, Picasso, Roy Lichtenstein, Robert Rauschenberg, and Andy Warhol, as well works by contemporary artists, among them Ai Weiwei, Banksy, David Hockney, KAWS, Jeff Koons, Yayoi Kusama, Takashi Murakami, Bridget Riley, Tom Sachs, and Yoshimoto Nara, not to mention a series of lithographs of sketches by Nelson Mandela. While outdoors, Julian Opie's forty-two-feet-long limestone-and-bronze outdoor mural *Beach Walkers* (left) has become something of a landmark for its marina.

"Attractive people
doing attractive things
in attractive places"

Slim Aarons

Prince Rodrigue d'Arenberg playing backgammon by the pool on the roof of what is now Fairmont Monte Carlo, August 1975.

Victor Vasarely

Hexa Grace: Le Ciel, La Mer, La Terre, 1979
Stay in a sea-facing room at Fairmont Monte Carlo, and there's always the possibility that your view will also take in Victor Vasarely's huge rainbow-colored installation, which covers the roof of the Auditorium Rainier III below.

Martin Parr

TEACUPS AT THE SAVOY, 2016
THE OLD JAZZ BAND AT THE SHANGHAI PEACE HOTEL, 1985

Annie Leibovitz
Donald and Ivana Trump at The Plaza, 1988

This picture was shot the year Donald Trump bought the hotel, which he owned for seven years, having paid 407.5 million dollars for it.
"This isn't just a building," he said at the time. "It's the ultimate work of art. I was in love with it."

Nan Goldin
Marc Jacobs at The Plaza Hotel, 2010

"One is never so naked as when dressed for a party."

Jessica Craig-Martin
The Red Ball at The Plaza, 2000

"I derive
intense enjoyment
& transports of enthusiasm
from the balustrade of
[my] terrace at night fall."

Vladimir Nabokov

Vladimir and Vera Nabokov playing chess on a balcony at the Montreux Palace, 1964 (photo by Philippe Halsman). An accomplished chess player, Vladimir Nabokov believed that "Chess's problems demand from the composer the same virtues that characterize all worthwhile art: originality, invention, conciseness, harmony, complexity and splendid insincerity ... Problems are the poetry of chess."

LIT ERA TURE

"March 1893, Savoy Hotel

Dearest of All Boys,
Your letter was delightful, red and yellow wine to me; but I am sad and out of sorts. Bosie, you must not make scenes with me. They kill me, they wreck the loveliness of life. I cannot see you, so Greek and gracious, distorted with passion. I cannot listen to your curved lips saying hideous things to me. I would sooner be blackmailed by every renter in London than to have you bitter, unjust, hating. You are the divine thing I want, the thing of grace and beauty; but I don't know how to do it. Shall I come to Salisbury?

My bill here is 49 pounds for a week. I have also got a new sitting-room over the Thames. Why are you not here, my dear, my wonderful boy? I fear I must leave; no money, no credit, and a heart of lead.

Your own, Oscar"

Oscar Wilde

The Savoy was a favorite haunt of the writer Oscar Wilde and his lovers, among them Lord Alfred Douglas, with whom he is pictured.
Noted for his beauty, Bosie, as Wilde called him, was described by one of the chambermaids in a letter as "a common boy, rough looking, about 14 years of age." (In fact, he would have been twenty-two.)
Though homosexuality was illegal, he and Wilde did not feel the need to hide their sexuality in the hotel. As Wilde's friend the French writer Pierre Louÿs, the dedicatee of his play Salome, observed, they shared a room with "one bed and two pillows." .

Noël Coward

In December 1929, the English playwright, songwriter, and actor Noël Coward sailed from San Francisco to Yokohama, via Honolulu, and on to Shanghai, where, suffering from influenza, he was confined to his room at the Cathay (now Fairmont Peace) Hotel. Here, to pass the time, he wrote his sophisticated comedy of hotel balconies, *Private Lives*, in just four days.
"We stayed a fortnight in Shanghai and I wrote a light comedy for Gertie [the musical comedy star and his great friend Gertrude Lawrence] and me," Coward wrote to a friend on the voyage home. "It's completely trivial except for one or two slaps, but it will be fun to play. I have an uneasy feeling that you won't approve of it."
The idea had come to him one night earlier on the trip. "The moment I switched out the lights, Gertie appeared in a white Molyneux dress on a terrace in the South of France and refused to go again until four a.m., by which time *Private Lives*, title and all had constructed itself."
The play opened in London in 1930, starring Lawrence and Coward (top). It has been revived many times since, not least in 1983, when Richard Burton and Elizabeth Taylor (bottom) played the central characters, Elyot and Amanda. Prior to its Broadway run, that production had a short season at the Shubert Theatre in Boston, and Burton and Taylor stayed at the Copley Plaza.

Rudyard Kipling

"Canada possesses two pillars of Strength and Beauty in Quebec and Victoria," wrote Rudyard Kipling, the British author of, among many novels, *The Jungle Book*, in one of his *Letters of Travel*, published in 1899.
He traveled widely within Canada—not least on the Canadian Pacific Railway, meeting William Van Horne in Quebec, "head of the whole system"—and was particularly impressed by Victoria.
The city, he observed, combined all "the eye admires most in Bournemouth, Torquay, the Isle of Wight, the Happy Valley at Hong-Kong, the Doon, Sorrento, and Camps Bay; add reminiscences of the Thousand Islands, and arrange the whole round the Bay of Naples, with some Himalayas for the background [...] The high, still twilights along the beaches are out of the old East just under the curve of the world, and even in October the sun rises warm from the first. Earth, sky, and water wait outside every man's door to drag him out to play."
The Empress "hotel was just being finished," so he could not stay there. Though, on visiting the site, he was impressed by "the ladies' drawing room, 100ft by 40," and the fact that the plasterwork on its ceiling had been based on a photograph in the English magazine of rural pursuits, *Country Life*.

"The early twilight of a Sunday evening
in Hamilton, Bermuda,
is an alluring time.

There is just enough of whispering breeze,
fragrance of flowers,
and sense of repose to raise one's thoughts heavenward;

and just enough amateur piano music
to keep him reminded of the other place."

Mark Twain

Mark Twain

Mark Twain made eight trips to Bermuda between 1867 and 1910, many of them for the sake of his health, staying on occasion at The Princess in Hamilton, where he liked to smoke cigars on the veranda. He recorded his impressions in an extended piece for *The Atlantic* magazine entitled "Some Rambling Notes of an Idle Excursion." It's fair to say it wasn't his most captivating work, but it did encourage tourism to the island.
A tireless traveler he also stayed at The Savoy in London and at what is now the Fairmont Hotel Vancouver.

"We can take your liver
and give it to the Princeton Museum*,
your heart
to the Plaza Hotel,
one lung
to Max Perkins**
and the other
to George Horace Lorimer.***"

Ernest Hemingway
IN A LETTER TO F. SCOTT FITZGERALD, 1935

*FITZGERALD ATTENDED PRINCETON UNIVERSITY
**EDITOR OF HEMINGWAY AND FITZGERALD
***RENOWNED JOURNALIST WHO LAUNCHED
THE CAREER OF MANY MAJOR WRITERS

"It had been tradition of mine
to climb to the Plaza roof
to take leave of the beautiful city
extending as far as the eyes could see."

F. Scott Fitzgerald
MY LOST CITY: PERSONAL ESSAYS, 1920–40

F. Scott Fitzgerald

THE PLAZA HAS BEEN ENSHRINED IN ALL SORTS OF FICTION, BUT ITS MOST CELEBRATED LITERARY CREDENTIALS ARE TO BE FOUND IN F. SCOTT FITZGERALD'S NOVEL *THE GREAT GATSBY*, AFTER WHICH A SUITE IS NAMED.
INDEED, THE HOTEL PLAYS A CENTRAL ROLE IN CHAPTER SEVEN, WHEN GATSBY AND DAISY BUCHANAN IN ONE CAR, AND HER HUSBAND, TOM, JORDAN, AND NICK IN ANOTHER, SET OFF FOR MANHATTAN. ON ARRIVING AT THE PLAZA ONE HOT AFTERNOON, DAISY SUGGESTS THEY "HIRE FIVE BATHROOMS AND TAKE COLD BATHS." (INSPIRED, PERHAPS, BY THE LEGEND THAT HE AND ZELDA ONCE BATHED IN THE HOTEL'S PULITZER FOUNTAINS.)
IN THE END FITZGERALD'S PROTAGONISTS SETTLE FOR A SUITE. "'A SWELL SUITE,' WHISPERED JORDAN RESPECTFULLY, AND EVERYONE LAUGHED." OF COURSE, THEY DID! BECAUSE, AS FITZGERALD WROTE, EVERYTHING ABOUT THE PLAZA WAS SWELL—AND STILL IS.
SCOTT AND ZELDA WERE REGULAR VISITORS TO THE HOTEL IN REAL LIFE TOO, DINING AT ITS GRILL ROOM, WHICH FEATURES IN HIS SECOND NOVEL, *THE BEAUTIFUL AND THE DAMNED*. AND ONCE THEY'D MOVED AWAY FROM NEW YORK, THEY WOULD STAY HERE WHEN THEY WERE IN TOWN, ENTERTAINING FRIENDS IN THE PALM COURT.

Ernest Hemingway & Karen Blixen

Often credited with introducing the word safari to the English language, Hemingway made his first month-long trip to Africa and specifically Kenya in December 1933, an experience that inspired his nonfiction book, *The Green Hills of Africa*, and two major short stories, *The Snows of Kilimanjaro* for *Esquire* and *The Short Happy Life of Francis Macomber* for *Cosmopolitan*. He stayed at The Norfolk and drank in its bar, though he does not actually mention it by name in either story. But in the subsequent movie of *The Short Happy Life...*, retitled *The Macomber Affair*, starring Gregory Peck and Joan Bennett as a couple who might have been loosely inspired by Scott and Zelda Fitzgerald, or indeed Hemingway and his then wife Pauline (née Pfeiffer), there is a scene at the hotel, where Macomber and the guide he is traveling with meet to plan their safari.

Hemingway never met Karen Blixen, though he knew of her work and was acquainted with her husband Bror von Blixen-Finecke. The Blixens' marriage did not last, and they separated in 1921, eight years after their marriage. Her book, *Out of Africa*, published under the pseudonym Isak Dinesen, tells the story of the farm she and Bror bought, which she later ran alone until she was forced to sell up in 1931. Hemingway is on record as having said that she would have been more deserving of the Nobel Prize in Literature than he was.

Above, the Mount Kenya Safari Club in Nanyuki, on the equator line 120 miles north of Nairobi.

Agatha Christie

Agatha Christie claimed to have "seen" Hercule Poirot twice in her lifetime: Once lunching in The Savoy and once on a boat in the Canary Islands.

The curtain was first raised on *The Mousetrap* in London's West End in 1952. Six years later, in April 1958, Agatha Christie, together with 1,000 prestigious guests at The Savoy Hotel, was celebrating her play's record of the longest stage run (2,239 performances in six years). Four years later, the crime writer chose The Savoy again to cut a gigantic mousetrap cake to mark *The Mousetrap*'s tenth anniversary. In 1973, the eighty-three-year-old Agatha Christie would come back to The Savoy to celebrate the twenty-one years of continuous performances of her play at the Ambassadors Theatre. No play in the world had ever run so long.
Even after the writer's death in 1976, the major anniversaries of *The Mousetrap* kept on being celebrated at The Savoy; in November 1977, the twenty-fifth anniversary in the presence of Prime Minister James Callaghan, and in 2004, the fifty-two years of the play at St. Martin's Theatre. The Covid-19 pandemic, however, put the performances on hold. But just for a while, as it reopened again in June 2021.

"She had sat next to Bond
and chattered vivaciously about
'what shows he had recently seen in town'
and 'didn't he think the Savoy Grill was the nicest place for supper.
One saw so many interesting people
– actresses and people like that".

Ian Fleming
QUANTUM OF SOLACE

Ian Fleming

As a young intelligence officer during World War II, Ian Fleming was among the officers serving at Château Frontenac during the 1943 conference. It had the code name Quadrant and was organized to plan D-Day and the Normandy Landings (pp. 200–1).
Ian Fleming was also among the 1,500 Royal Navy officers and code breakers stationed at The Hamilton Princess in Bermuda. The hotel had been requisitioned for war services and was used as a listening post. All correspondence sent to or from Europe was examined by Imperial Censorship staff based at the Hamilton Princess Hotel, and suspect items were intercepted and photographed, a process that "led to the identification of several German spies, among them George Nicolaus and Joachim Ruge."

Fleming is reckoned to have found inspiration for Dr. No's lair in the hotel's aquarium-lined Gazebo Bar. His short story *Quantum of Solace*, published in 1959, which bears no relation beyond its title to the posthumous movie of that name, is partly set on the island.
Back home, The Savoy and its American Bar were among Fleming's favorite haunts. He mentioned the hotel in several of his books including *Dr. No*, *For Your Eyes Only*, and *Diamonds Are Forever*. Dusko Popov, a Serbian playboy and triple agent code-named Tricycle, became a Savoy Hotel full-time guest during World War II, giving Ian Fleming an inspiration for his James Bond character.
In 1971, the seventh James Bond film *Diamonds are Forever* was released. Sean Connery chose The Savoy Hotel for his press conference (above).

Vladimir Nabokov

WEALTHY FROM THE SUCCESS OF *LOLITA*, VLADMIR NABOKOV AND HIS WIFE, VÉRA, TOOK UP RESIDENCE IN A LAKE VIEW JUNIOR SUITE ON THE SIXTH FLOOR OF WHAT IS NOW FAIRMONT LE PALACE MONTREUX IN 1961, AND LIVED HERE UNTIL HIS DEATH IN 1997.
IT WAS A PERIOD THAT SAW THE PUBLICATION OF FOUR MORE NOVELS—*PALE FIRE*, *ADA OR ARDOUR*, *TRANSPARENT THINGS* AND *LOOK AT THE HARLEQUINS*, AS WELL AS THE FRAGMENT *THE ORIGINAL OF LAURA*, AND NUMEROUS SHORT STORIES, POEMS, AND TRANSLATION OF CLASSICS FROM HIS NATIVE RUSSIAN, NOTABLY PUSHKIN'S NOVEL IN VERSE, *EVGENY ONEGIN*.

Kay Thompson

Best known for her performance as the Diana Vreeland-like magazine editor in the Audrey Hepburn and Fred Astaire musical, *Funny Face*, Kay Thompson was also an accomplished writer. The creator of *Eloise*, a series of children's books about a very demanding little girl who lives at The Plaza, is pictured left besides a portrait of her character by the book's illustrator, Hilary Knight. The portrait, stolen once, still hangs in the lobby today.

It's been said that Kay Thompson was inspired by her goddaughter Liza Minelli, who spent part of her childhood as a resident of the hotel with her mother Judy Garland, stepfather Sid Luft (see the three of them, right, in their suite in 1956) and half-siblings Lorna and Joey.

One of the first things she learned to do as a child, she has said, was to pick up the phone and call room service: "Otherwise we'd have starved." To Minelli, Thompson's books were for adults, not children. Eloise was "a kid alone in this huge hotel" compelled to find "ways to entertain herself."

CINEMA

In December 1954, Richard Burton promotes Robert Rossen's movie *Alexander the Great* by posing for the press against the plaque of the eponymous king, in a suite at The Savoy Hotel, London.

Hollywood of the North

For almost as long as directors have seen movies, they've been making them around Banff and Lake Louise, drawn by the stupendous mountain scenery.
In 1942, Betty Grable met her future husband Harry James (opposite) in Banff during the filming of Springtime in the Rockies, which was not only shot at Chateau Lake Louise, but set there too.
Two years later, the Banff National Park stood in for Yorkshire and Norway in Son of Lassie above, right, starring Peter Lawford.
And, as early as 1921, the silent movie Cameron of the Royal Mounted was partly filmed in Banff National Park (above, left).
Above, middle, John Barrymore and Camilla Horn in Eternal Love (1929), directed by Ernst Lubitsch and set in the Swiss Alps, but filmed in Banff National Park and around Chateau Lake Louise, where the cast stayed, establishing its reputation as the Hollywood of the North. Some of the Swiss guides recruited by Canadian Pacific Hotels, among them Rudolph Aemmer, Bruno Engler, and Edmond Petrig, had secondary careers as stuntmen.

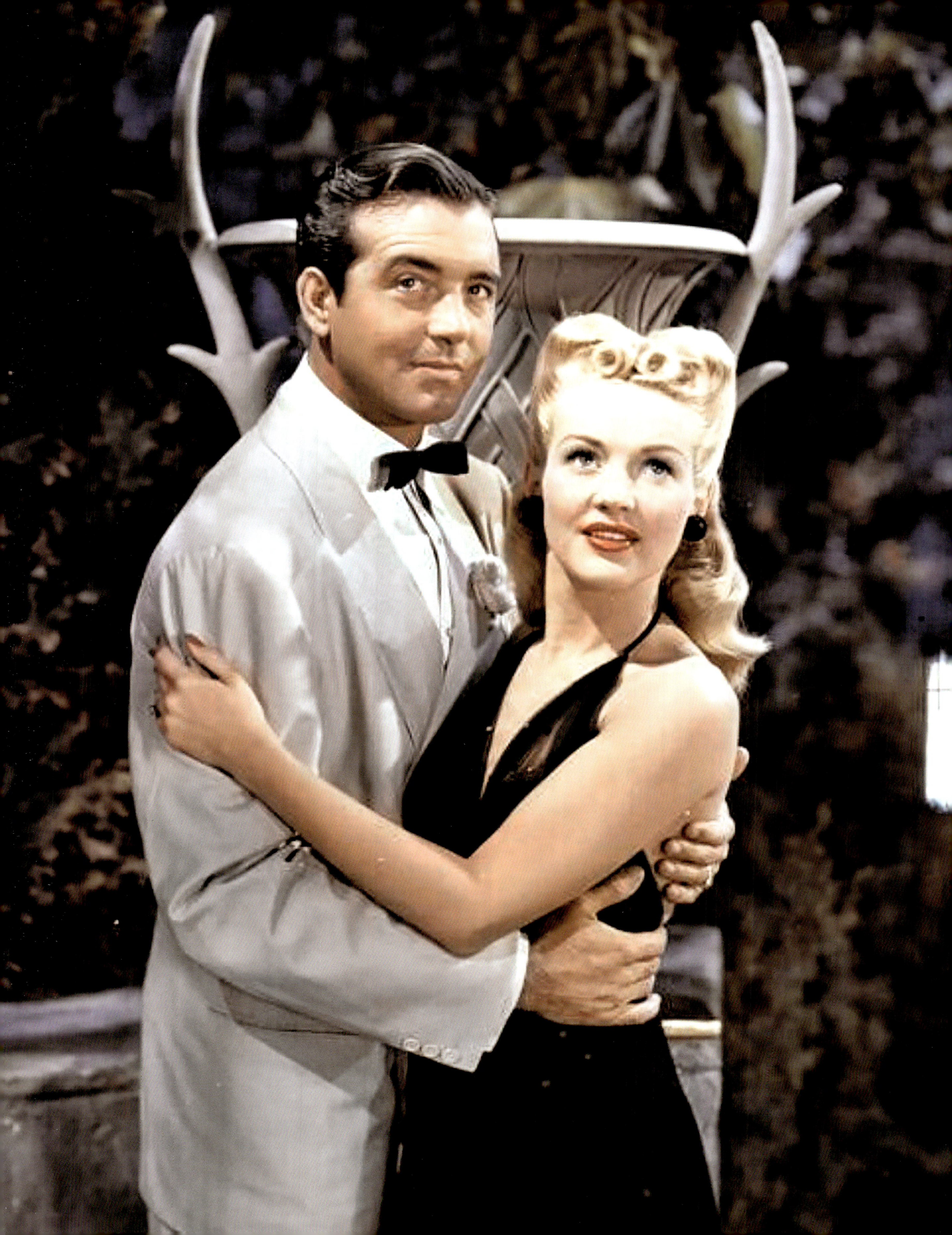

"I guess it doesn't really matter
where I point the camera;
we are absolutely surrounded by scenery."

Otto Preminger

Robert Mitchum and Marilyn Monroe in *River of No Return* (1954), a Western directed by Otto Preminger. The action was located in the north-western states of the United States, but the movie was filmed in the Banff and Jasper National Parks and around Lake Louise, and the cast and crew stayed at the Banff Springs Hotel.

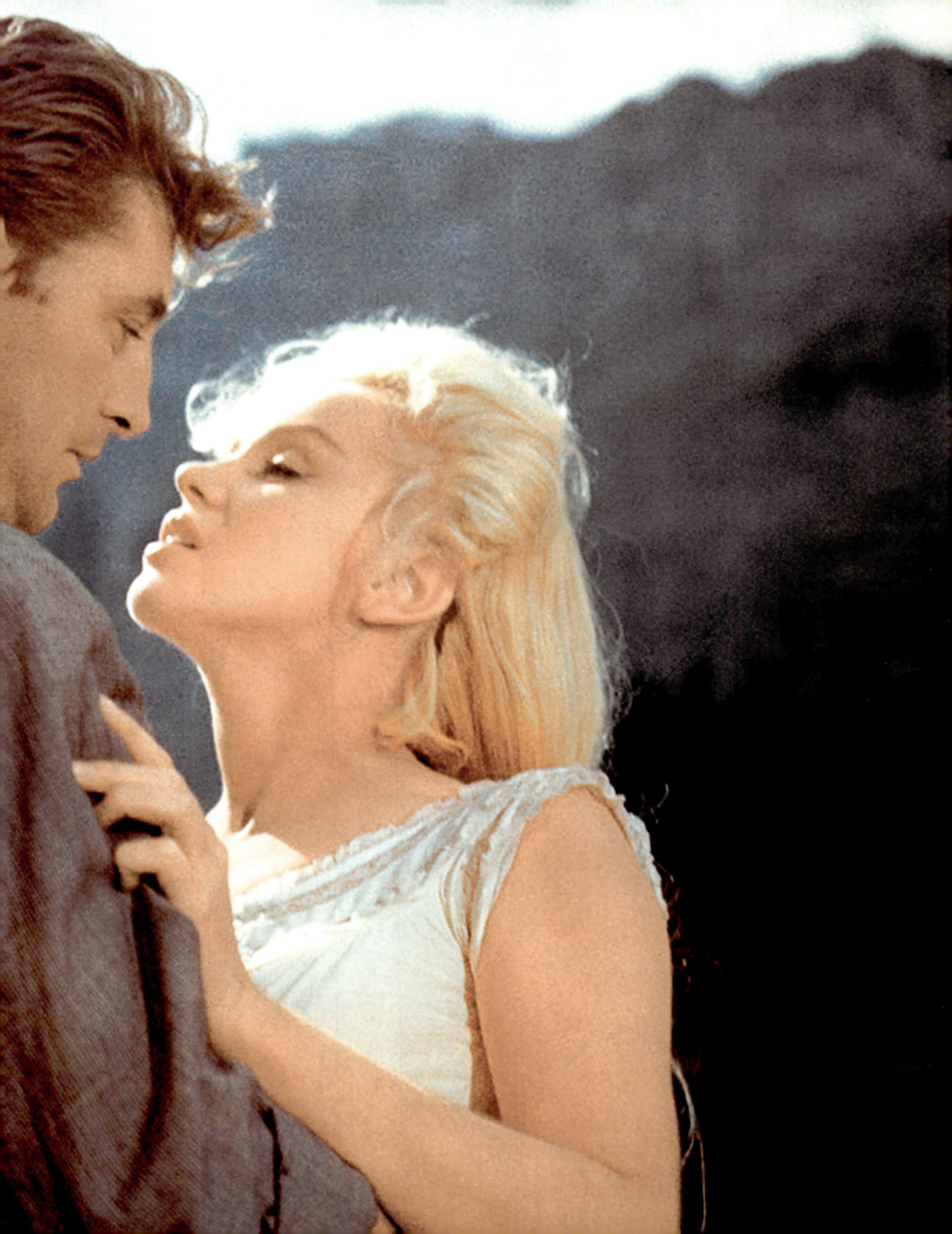

"This is the most beautiful place in the world."

William Holden
IN 1959 WHEN HE FIRST SAW WHAT WOULD BECOME THE MOUNT KENYA SAFARI CLUB.

Hollywood in Africa

BACK IN THE 1960S, FAIRMONT MOUNT KENYA SAFARI CLUB WAS AMONG THE MOST EXCLUSIVE PLACES ONE COULD STAY. MEMBERSHIP OF THE CLUB WAS BY INVITATION ONLY, AND NO WONDER, FOR ITS OWNERS WERE THE HOLLYWOOD ACTOR WILLIAM HOLDEN (STAR OF *SUNSET BOULEVARD* AND *SABRINA*), THE OIL MAGNATE RAY RYAN, AND THE SWISS FINANCIER CARL HIRSCHMANN.
"THIS IS THE MOST BEAUTIFUL PLACE IN THE WORLD," HOLDEN HAD SAID WHEN HE FIRST SET EYES ON THE ESTATE, WHICH LIES 125 MILES (OR A SHORT FLIGHT, BECAUSE OF COURSE, IT HAS ITS OWN AIRSTRIP) FROM NAIROBI. HAVING BOUGHT IT, HE AND HIS PARTNERS HAD NO TROUBLE IN RECRUITING MEMBERS, AMONG THEM CHARLIE CHAPLIN, WINSTON CHURCHILL, BING CROSBY, DAVID LEAN, STEVE MCQUEEN, AND THE MAHARAJA OF JAIPUR.
INEVITABLY, THEY MADE MOVIES HERE TOO, SUCH AS *THE LION* (1962), STARRING HOLDEN AND CAPUCINE, PHOTOGRAPHED OPPOSITE.
THE ACTOR, DIRECTOR, AND CHOREOGRAPHER, CHARLES O'CURRAN, SEEN LEFT WITH ELVIS PRESLEY ON THE SET OF *BLUE HAWAII*, WAS ANOTHER MEMBER, HENCE THE CLUB LOGO ON THE BREAST POCKET OF HIS BLAZER.

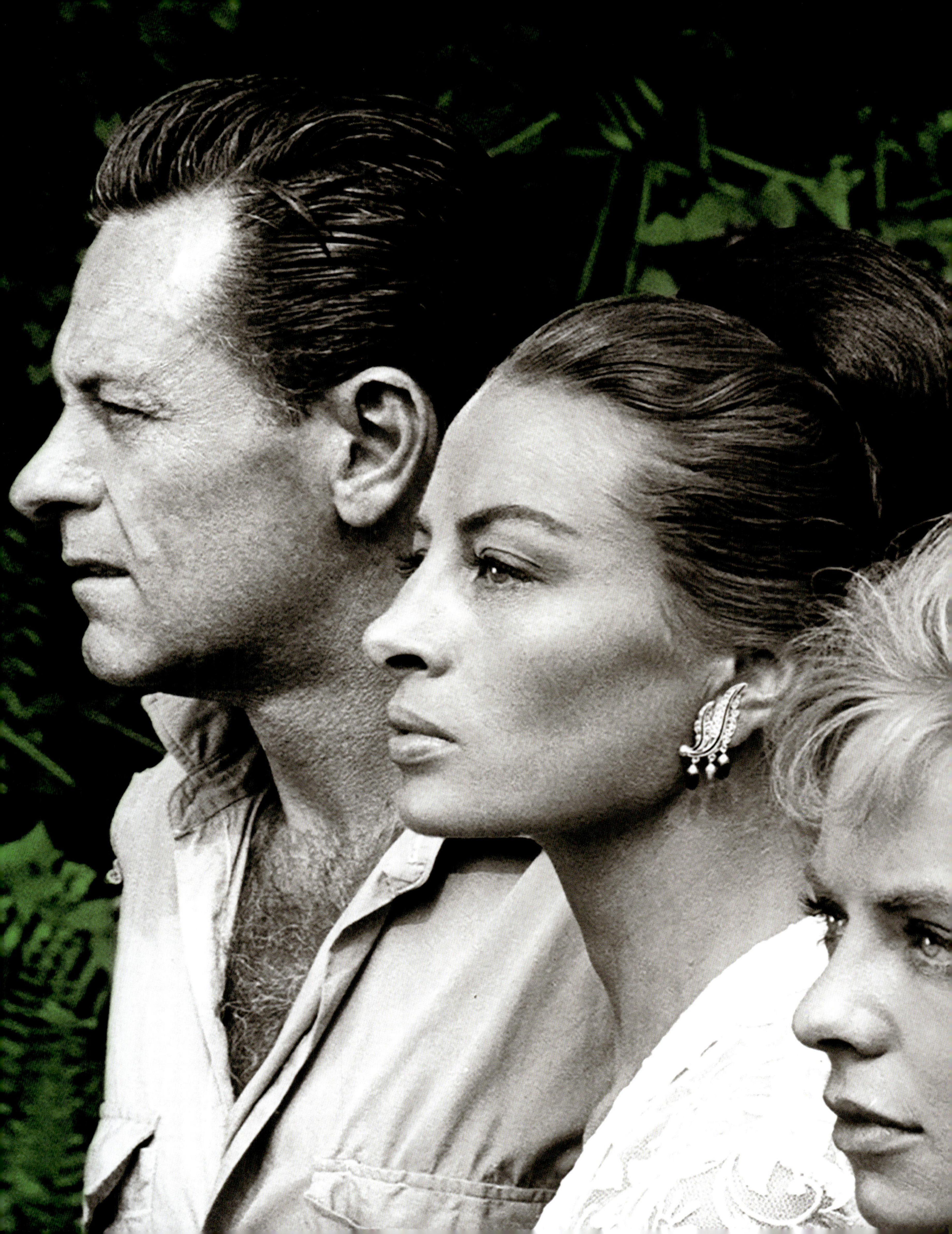

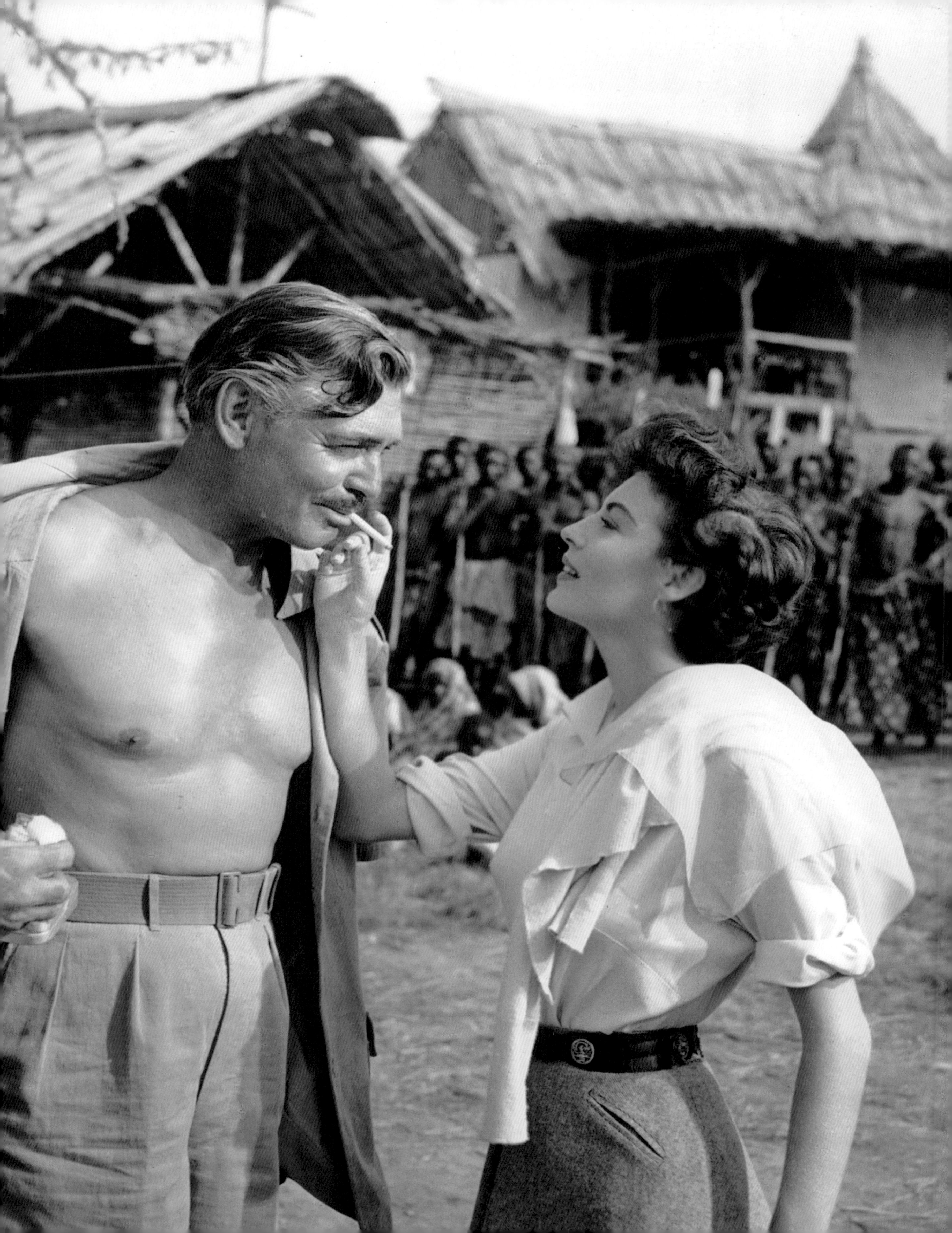

"Mogambo had three things that interested me.

John Ford,
Clark Gable,
and a trip to Africa with expenses paid.

If Mogambo had been made in Arizona,
I wouldn't have done it."

Grace Kelly

Clark Gable, Grace Kelly & Ava Gardner

CLARK GABLE AND AVA GARDNER (OPPOSITE) AND GRACE KELLY (TOP) IN *MOGAMBO* (1963), DIRECTED BY JOHN FORD. IT WAS SHOT AT VARIOUS LOCATIONS IN KENYA, ONE IN MOUNT KENYA SAFARI CLUB, WHERE MGM HAD BUILT A STUDIO, AS WELL AS IN THE CONGO AND IN UGANDA. BUT PRINCIPAL PHOTOGRAPHY COINCIDED WITH THE MAU MAU UPRISING, SO FORD AND THE PRINCIPAL CAST PREFERRED TO STAY IN NAIROBI, SOME OF THEM AT THE NORFOLK, FROM WHICH THEY WERE FLOWN TO THE SHOOT ONLY WHEN NEEDED. GABLE AND KELLY ARE REPORTED TO HAVE HAD AN AFFAIR ON SET.

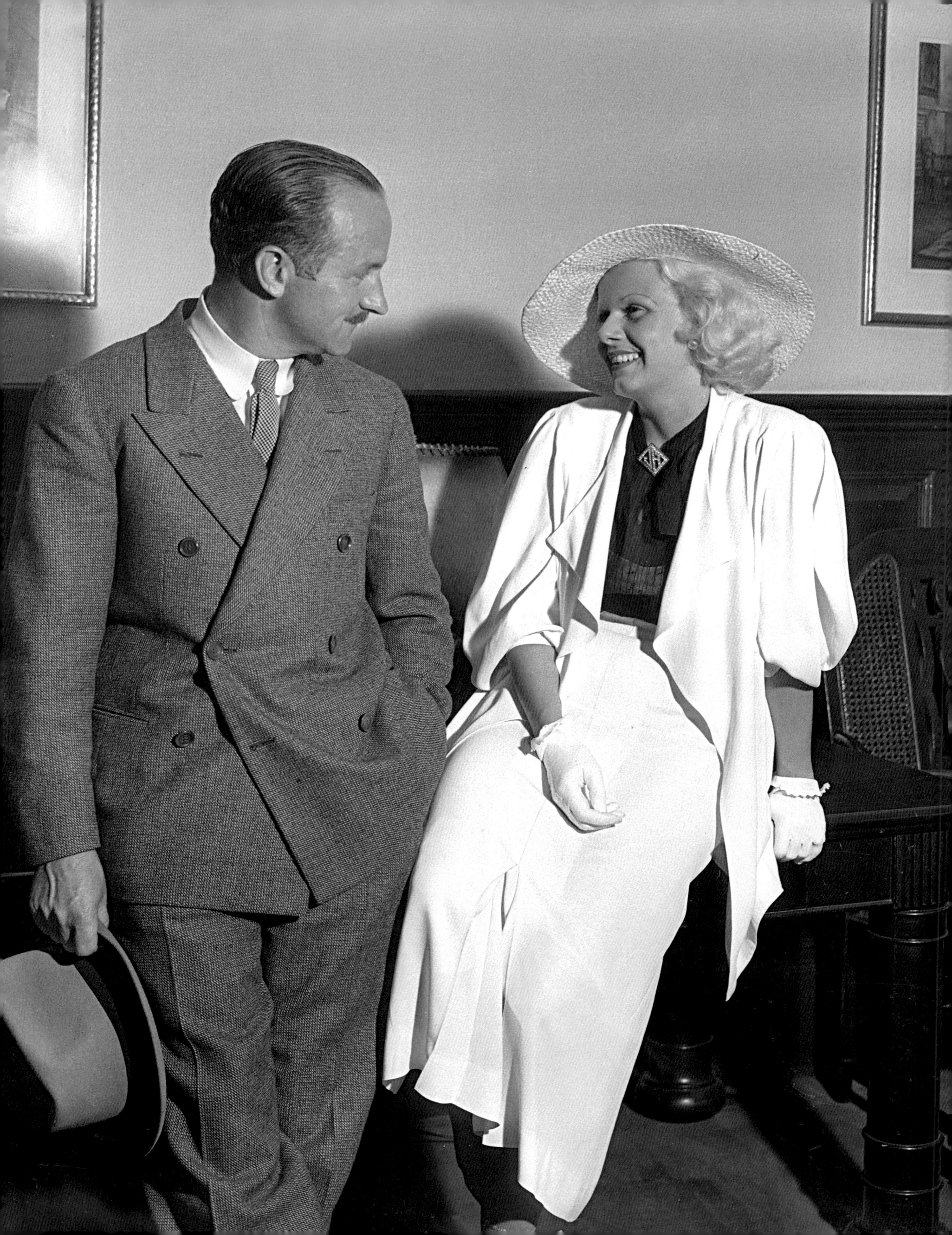

Hollywood at the Beach

Of all the places Greta Garbo lived in the United States, the one she stayed at the longest was what is now Fairmont Miramar Hotel & Bungalows in Santa Monica. Metro-Goldwyn-Mayer (MGM) brought her to Hollywood in 1925, putting her up in a studio with a kitchenette, a bathroom, and a sea view at the hotel's then newly built Palisades Wing.

She liked it so much that she stayed for three or four years, driving herself to the studio in a small car she had bought. One day, she was caught doing sixty miles-per-hour in a ten-miles-per-hour area. Louis B. Mayer, MGM's founder, called Santa Monica's chief of police to try to avert the jail sentence she was threatened with, and it was commuted to a ten-dollar fine. Garbo, who was thrifty by nature, "frowned" when she learned of his intervention. "Ten dollars—that's forty kronen! Why didn't you let me go to jail?" she exclaimed. I only have six dollars and a half in my purse. Take that, and I will pay the rest later." She kept her licence too. "We always cater to the picture people," the police chief is reported to have said. "We want them to be happy with us."

Jean Harlow, pictured left with the cinematographer Harold Rosson, was another regular at the Miramar. So were Marilyn Monroe and James Stewart. Humphrey Bogart, Cary Grant, and Antony Quinn were habitués of its nightclub. The hotel was also the set of numerous movies like *The Blue Dahlia* (1946) starring Veronica Lake (above).

256 — 257

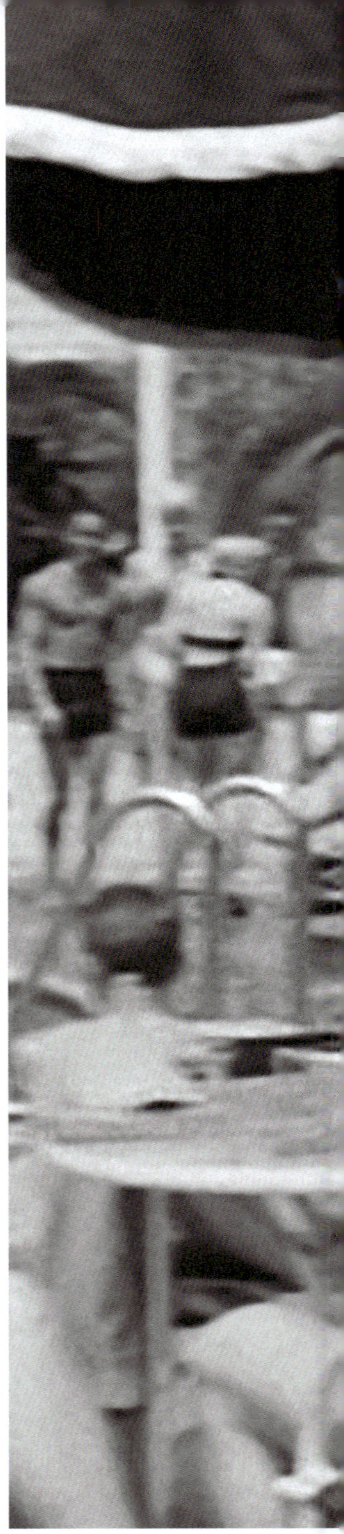

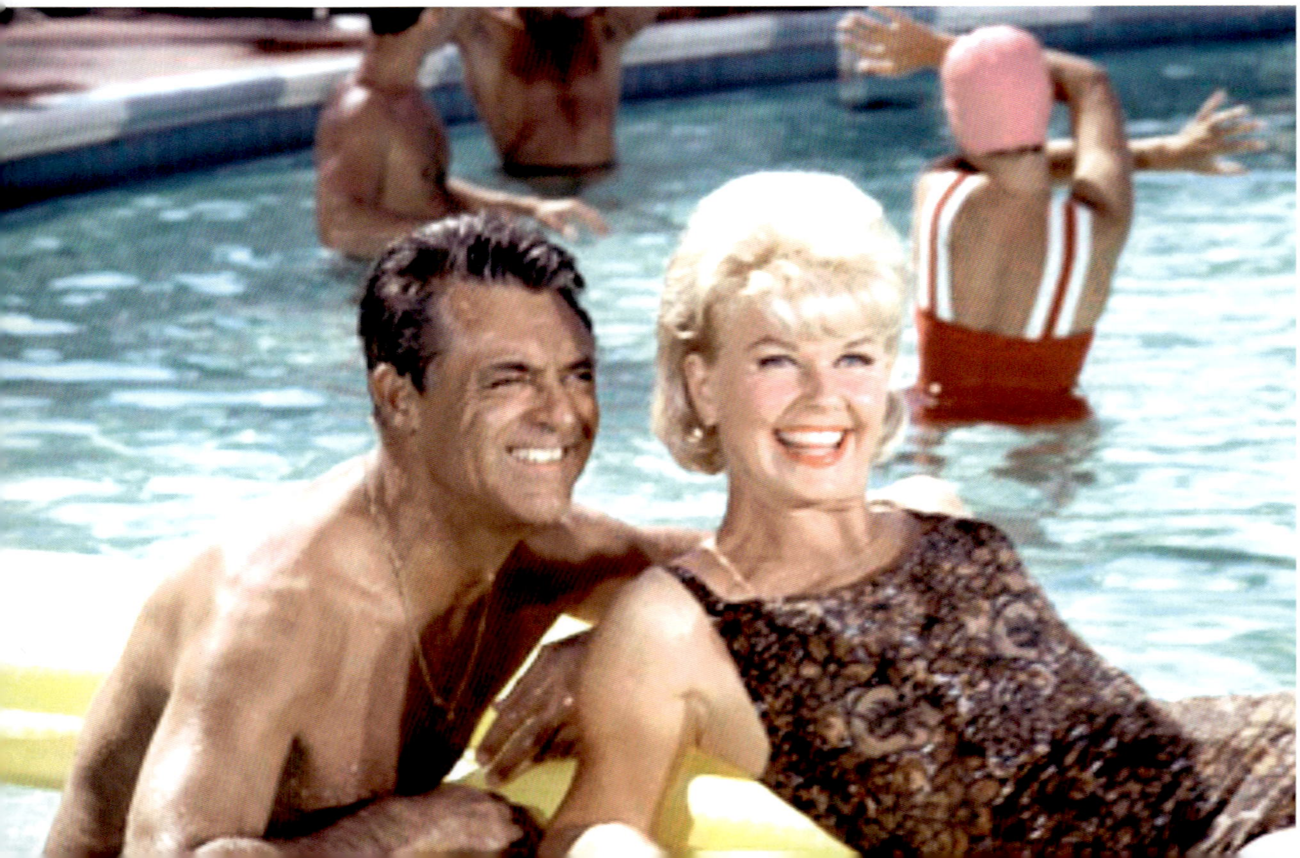

Cary Grant, Doris Day & Marylin Monroe

ABOVE, MARILYN MONROE AT THE MIRAMAR ON THE SET OF *LET'S MAKE IT LEGAL* (1951).

OPPOSITE, DORIS DAY AND CARY GRANT IN THE MIRAMAR POOL WHILE FILMING *THAT TOUCH OF MINK* (1962).

Orson Welles

In May 1941, on the evening that *Citizen Kane* opened in San Francisco, its director and star Orson Welles (pictured), then just twenty-five, found himself in an elevator at the Fairmont with William Randolph Hearst, the publishing tycoon whose own life bore some similarities to Kane's. (And whose fabulously extravagant home, Hearst Castle at San Simeon, had been designed by Julia Morgan, the architect who remodeled the Fairmont after the San Francisco earthquake.)
Offended by the idea that he might be perceived to have inspired the movie, Hearst had taken numerous steps to discredit its young director and delay the movie's release by banning any mention of or advertising for it in the media he owned, and thereby discouraging theaters from programming it. So, there was a distinct froideur between them. Welles reminded him that Hearst had been a friend of his father's, and invited him to the premiere. Hearst bluntly declined. "Charles Foster Kane would have accepted," he quipped as the publisher walked away.
Welles's third major motion picture, *The Lady from Shanghai* (1947), in which he also starred, this time alongside Rita Hayworth (pictured). Welles uses a recurring shot of the Bay Bridge from the top of Sacramento, which was taken from the steps of the Fairmont.

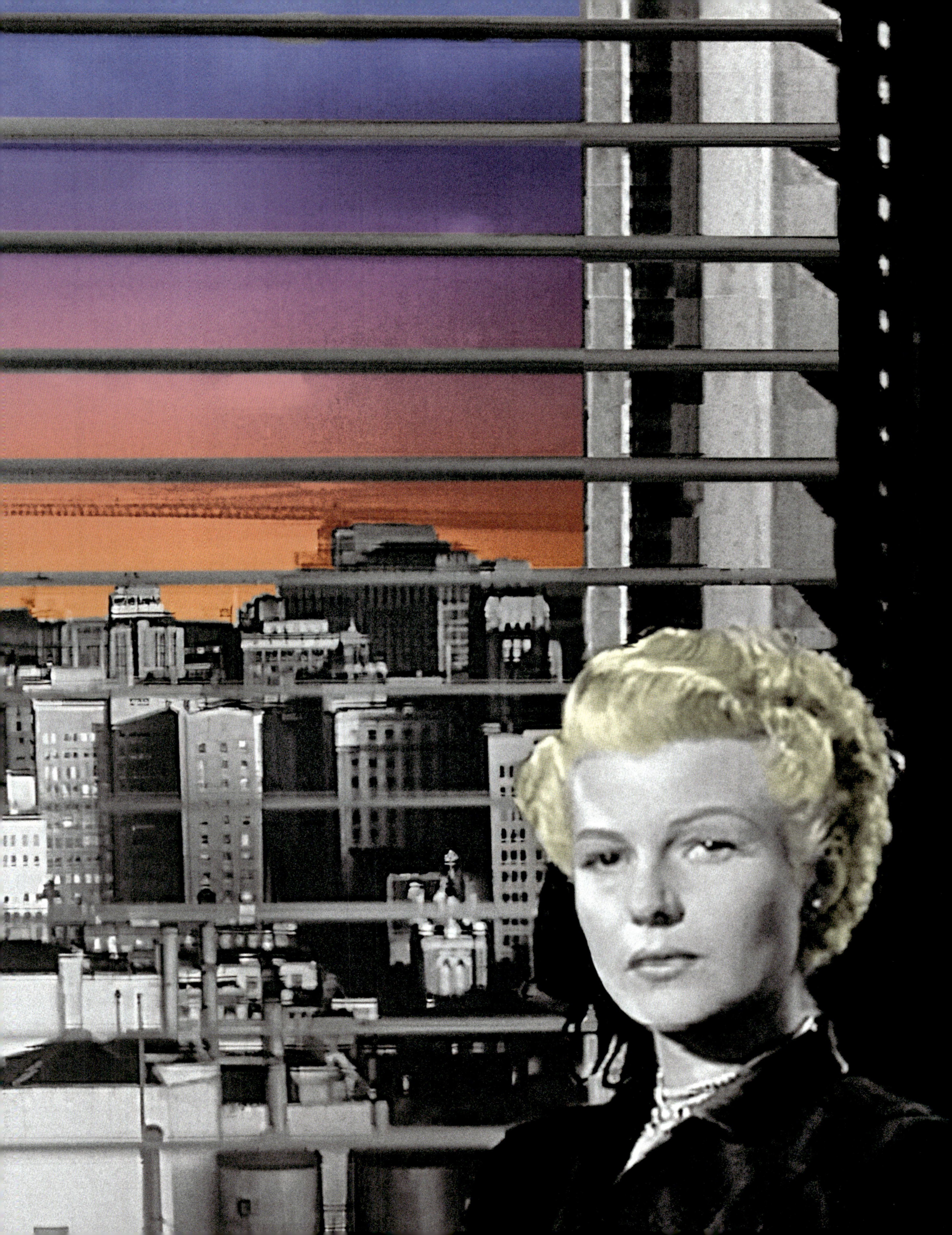

Alfred Hitchcock

Alfred Hitchcock was a regular at several hotels now managed by Fairmont, including The Savoy and was photographed at The Plaza in New York (opposite), Royal York in Toronto, and at Banff Springs. He also featured them in several of his movies. He selected The Plaza for the setting of Roger Thornhill's abduction in *North by Northwest* (3). Château Frontenac makes an appearance in *I Confess* (1) and the Fairmont San Francisco can be seen in *Vertigo* (2).

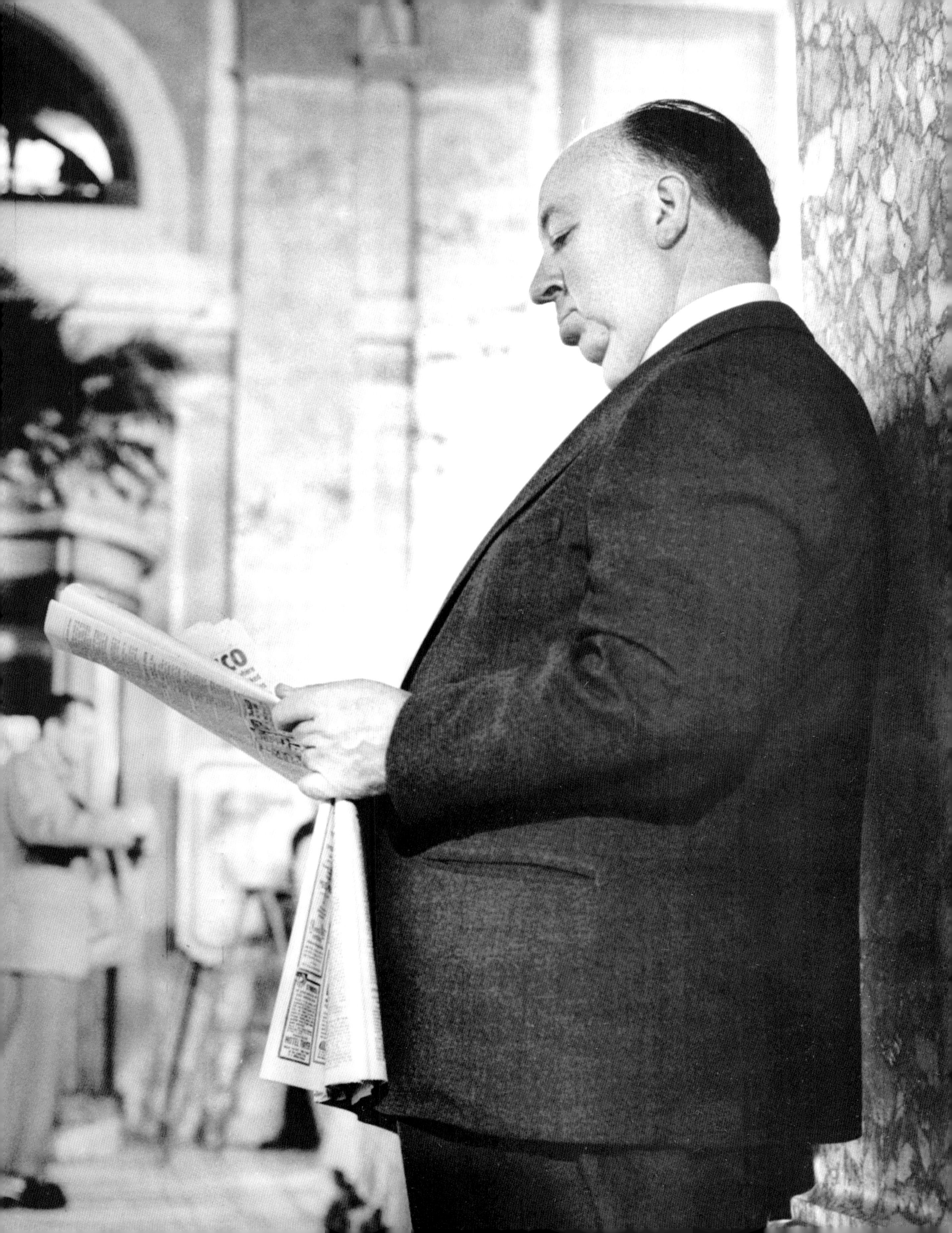

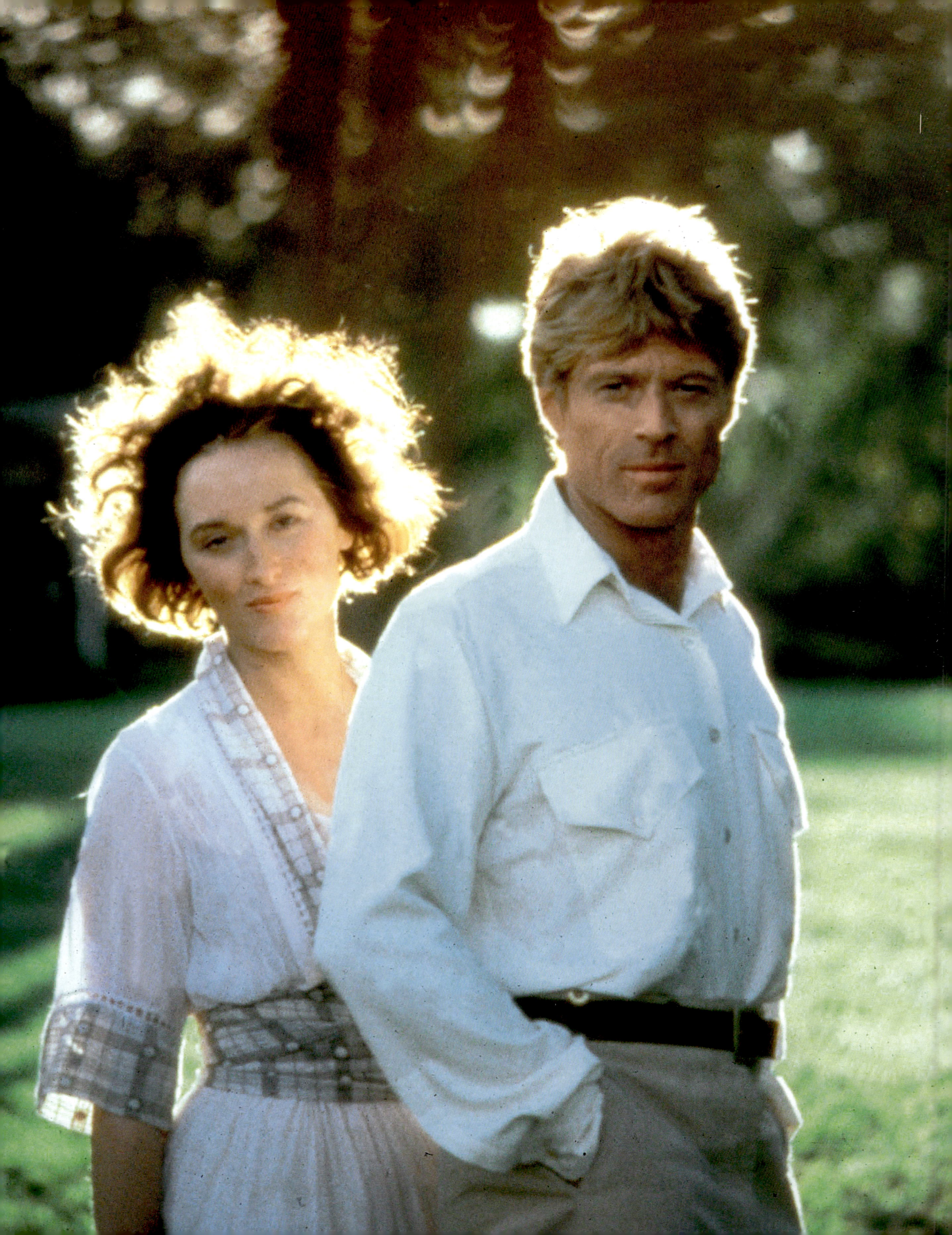

Sydney Pollack

When Sydney Pollack filmed the legendary movie *Out of Africa* (1985) in Kenya, Meryl Streep and Robert Redford (opposite), like all the other members of the cast, stayed at The Norfolk Hotel in Nairobi. So did the Danish Baroness Karen Blixen—played by Meryl Streep—when she first arrived in Kenya seven decades before.
Sydney Pollack and Robert Redford, with Barbra Streisand at The Plaza Hotel, New York (right) on the set of *The Way We Were* (1973).
Sydney Pollack and Tom Cruise two decades later in front of the Copley Plaza, Boston, on the set of *The Firm*, 1993 (left).

264 — 265

Luc Besson

FAIRMONT LE MONTREUX PALACE HAS SERVED AS THE LOCATION FOR A NUMBER OF MOVIES. IN 2000, LUC BESSON SPENT TEN DAYS THERE FILMING *KISS OF THE DRAGON* (ABOVE), STARRING BRIDGET FONDA AND JET LI.
IT HAD EARLIER SERVED AS THE SANATORIUM BERGHOF IN LUCHINO VISCONTI'S 1982 MOVIE OF THOMAS MANN'S NOVEL *THE MAGIC MOUNTAIN*. SIR PETER USTINOV USED IT AS A LOCATION IN HIS COMEDY *LADY L* (1965), STARRING SOPHIA LOREN, PAUL NEWMAN, AND DAVID NIVEN.

Steven Spielberg

The opening scenes of Steven Spielberg's *Empire of the Sun* (1987) were shot in Shanghai and Fairmont Peace Hotel can be seen across the Huangpu River. It appears again, when Jim (played by the young Christian Bale) signals to the Japanese fleet in Morse code.

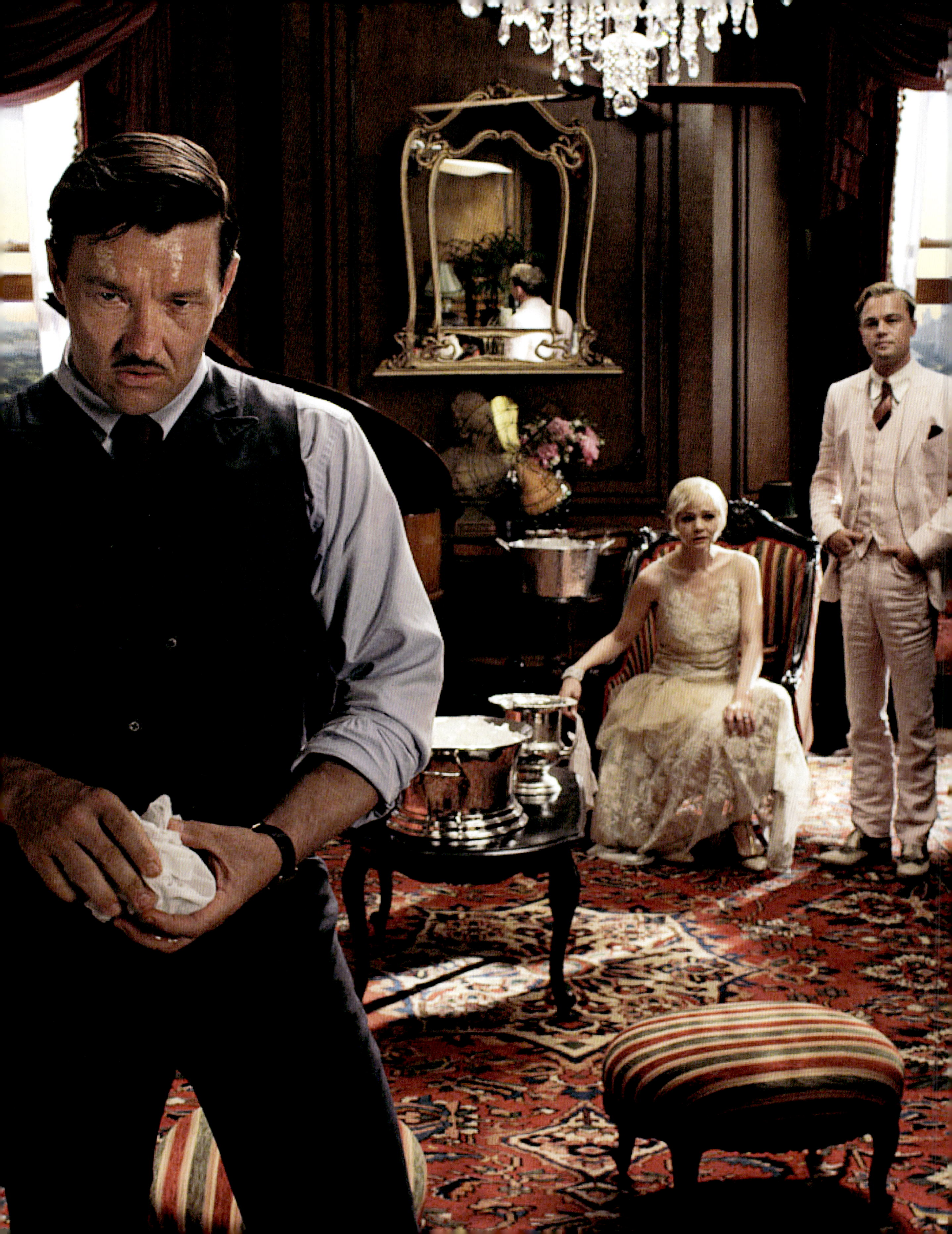

Fitzgerald on Film

Following Baz Lurhmann's 2013 movie of *The Great Gatsby*, starring Leonardo DiCaprio, Carey Mulligan, and Joel Edgerton (left), The Plaza commissioned Catherine Martin, the Oscar-winning production designer of the movie to design a Gatsby Suite for the hotel, with decor that, in her words, "F. Scott Fitzgerald and his character Jay Gatsby would be at home in—a dramatic deco space that evokes the danger, the sexiness, the glamour and a certain nostalgia for the hedonistic days of the 1920s, while still encapsulating all the comforts expected at The Plaza."

The novel had previously been filmed by Jack Clayton in 1974, starring Robert Redford and Mia Farrow, and based on a screenplay by Francis Ford Coppola (right).

"This is a film for today and of today, which is merely set in 1925," Clayton said, telling his art director, John Box, that he thought, "The film should have a golden look ... I intend to keep going through the film a constant feeling of extreme heat ... I want people to perspire all the time and I want even to see stains on people's dresses. It is a part of the story, the heat."

MUSIC

Music has played an integral role in the history of Fairmont. The Savoy was built with the riches amassed by the impresario Richard D'Oyly Carte, who built London's Palace and Savoy theaters, the latter adjoining the hotel. The hotel was the meeting point of the superstars of the time, opera composers and singers Giacomo Puccini, Richard Strauss, Igor Stravinsky, or Nellie Melba after which Escoffier's famous Peach was named were all clients of the hotel. In 1925, George Gershwin gave the British premiere of *Rhapsody in Blue* in what is now the hotel's Beaufort Bar.

Le Montreux Palace also saw music as integral to its very creation, and when it was built in 1906, its belle-époque building incorporated a theater and music salon so its guests could enjoy concerts and other musical entertainment. Richard Strauss lived there from 1947 to 1949, composing his *Duet-Concertino* for clarinet and bassoon. This musical tradition never faded away, Le Montreux palace being a favorite place for artists to stay during the city's annual Jazz Festival.

When it comes to exemplary jazz credentials, there are not many hotels to compete with Fairmont Royal York in Toronto, where the likes of Count Basie, Eartha Kitt, Ella Fitzgerald, Louis Armstrong, Pearl Bailey, and Peggy Lee have all performed in its Imperial Room. Or The Plaza's art-deco Persian Room, which counts John Coltrane, Miles Davis, Duke Ellington, and Billie Holiday among the jazz legends who have played there. The Rose Club, which replaced it, remains a nightclub of legend.

Then, there is the Fairmont in San Francisco, whose Venetian Room hosted a supper club where the likes of Nat King Cole, Marlene Dietrich, Ella Fitzgerald, and Bobby Short have played, not to mention James Brown and Tony Bennett, who first sang "I Left My Heart in San Francisco" here in 1961.

It is such an institution that Fairmont Dallas has its own Venetian Room, a recreation of the San Francisco original, complete with gigantic chandeliers, gilt moldings, and Italianate murals. It was inaugurated in 1969 by Jack Jones, and since then, artists from Jerry Lewis to Johnny Mathis, from Bernadette Peters to Ike and Tina Turner, and Sonny and Cher have sung from its stage.

If the Century Plaza in Los Angeles was not a place for concerts, it has always been in the spotlight of musicians due to the countless parties of the cinema, fashion, and music industries that the hotel hosted since it was built in 1966. Among its guests, David Bowie, Rod Stewart, John Lennon, and Mick Jagger (right) in 1974.

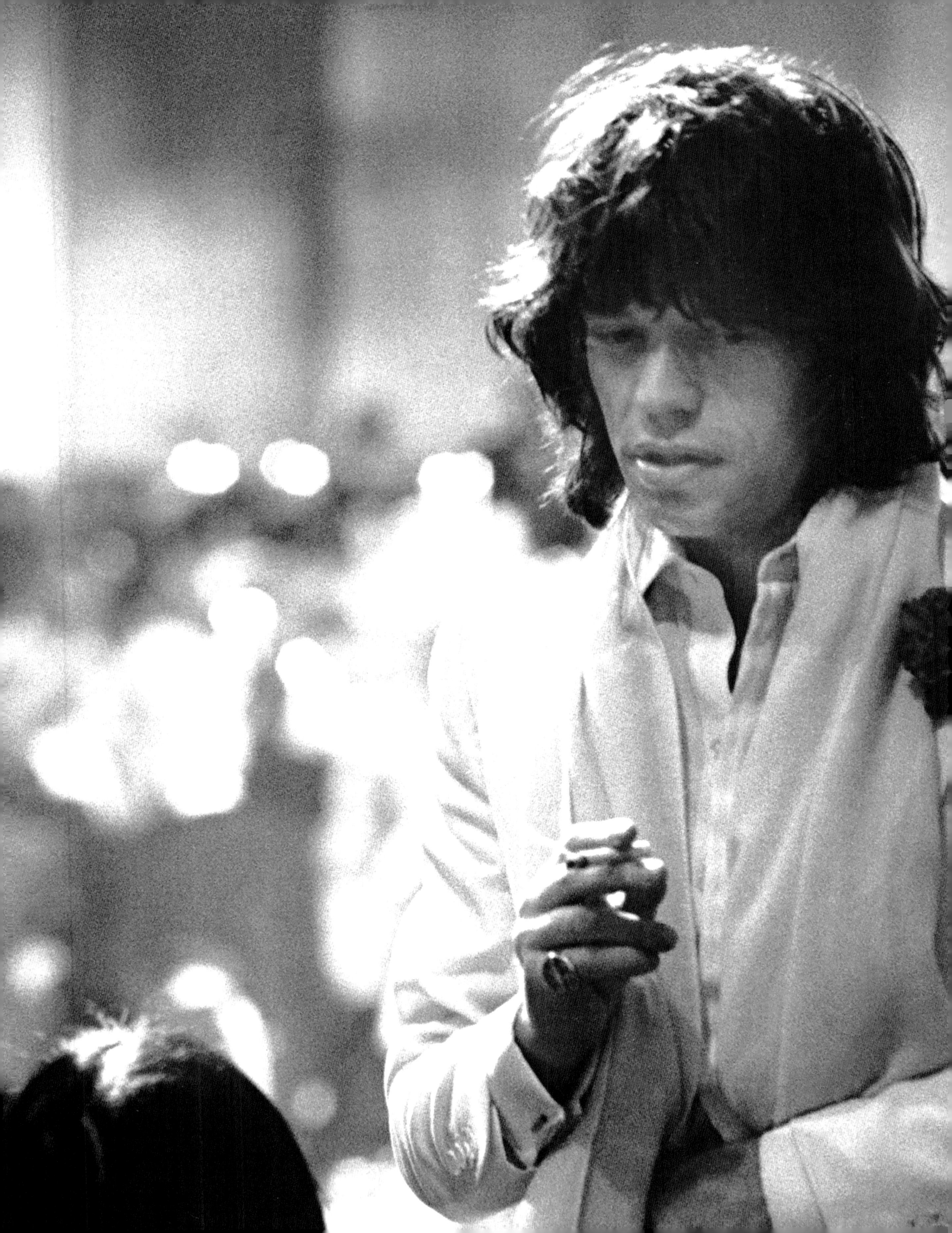

Johnny Cash

THE AMERICAN COUNTRY SINGER IS AT THE SAVOY HOTEL IN LONDON IN 1959 TO MEET THE PRESS. AT THE FAIRMONT SAN FRANCISCO IN 1965, HE PERFORMED IN THE VENETIAN ROOM.

The Supremes

FLORENCE BALLARD, MARY WILSON, AND DIANA ROSS HOPPING IN FRONT OF THE FAIRMONT SAN FRANCISCO WHERE THEY WOULD PERFORM FOR THREE WEEKS IN MAY 1966.

Igor Stravinsky

September 11, 1965, the Russian-born composer meets the press at The Savoy to announce a farewell performance at the London Royal Festival Hall that would become a legend: to stop the recalls and applause, the composer-conductor came back on stage wearing his hat and coat.

Bob Dylan

Bob Dylan at a press conference at The Savoy, London, May 1966. The year before, his precursory video clip *Subterranean Home-sick Blues*, was filmed in the street behind The Savoy Hotel and would soon become a point of reference in the music industry.

The Beatles

Having had their booking turned down by every other hotel, the Beatles spent six days at The Plaza in 1964. It wasn't that the Fab Four had a reputation for bad behavior then—they didn't. Rather, it was the hotel managements feared their screaming fans, and the lengths they would go to get near their idols, via the fire escape and housekeeping stairs (opposite). It was an unsuspecting concierge who accepted a large box and had it delivered to the band's suite. Inside were two adoring girls.
Above, over the past half-century, Fairmont Queen Elizabeth in Montreal has attracted numerous royals and celebrities. But the event that brought it the most worldwide attention was John Lennon and Yoko Ono's second Bed In, in 1969, when they spent a week in room 1742, now a suite named after them, and recorded "Give Peace a Chance."

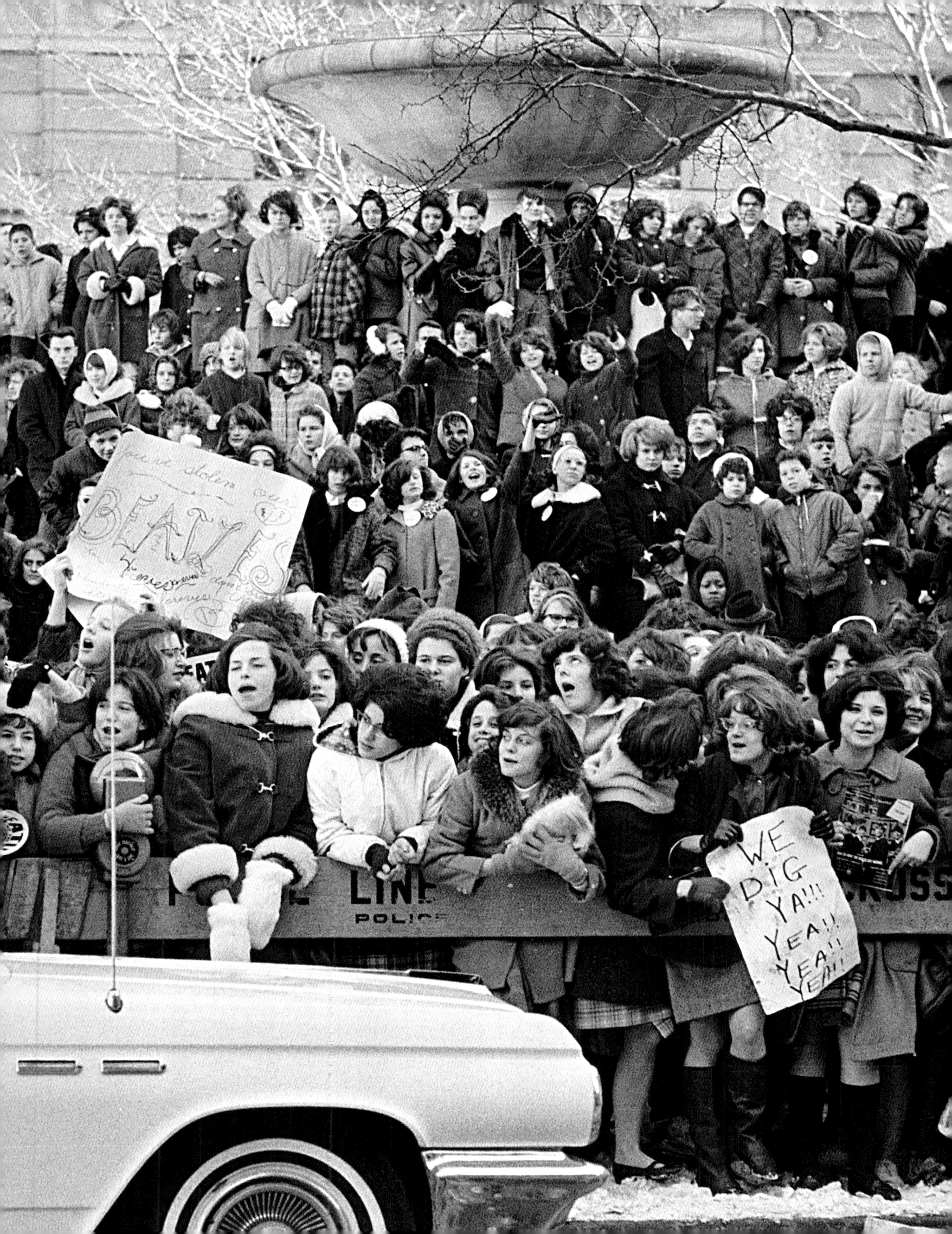
WE
DIG
YA!!!
YEA!!
YEA!!
YEA!!
POLICE

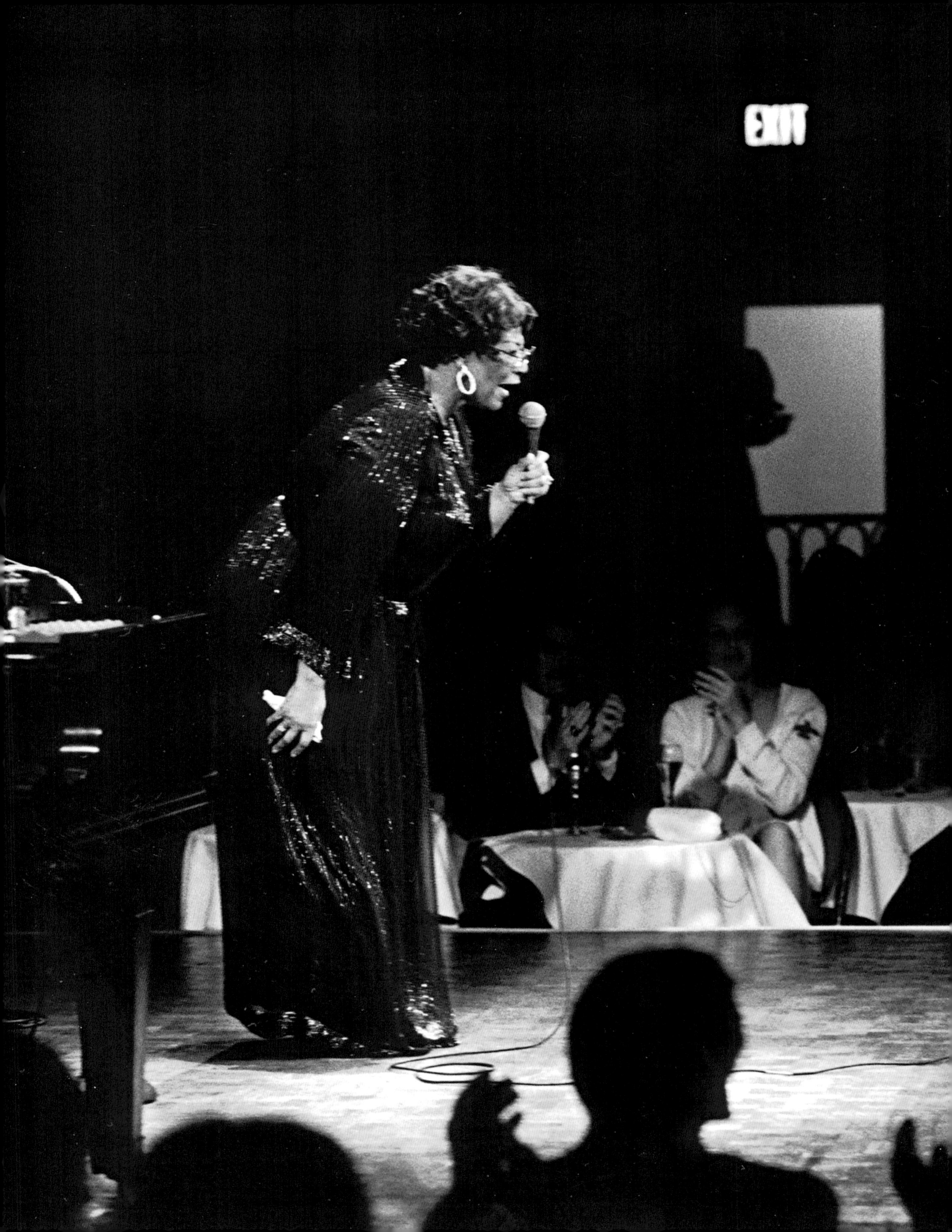
EXIT

Louis Armstrong & Tony Bennett

Louis Armstrong—who performed at the Claremont Hotel in Berkeley, at the Fairmont San Francisco, and in 1956 at the Savoy Hotel—came back to London in 1970 to be presented with his portrait, painted by the singer Tony Bennett (above).

When in 2018, the ninety-one-year-old Tony Bennett inaugurated the street named after him in San Francisco, he descended the Fairmont Hotel's facade on a rope. His 1961 concert in the Venitian Room of the hotel was very popular.

Tony Bennett's pianist, Ralph Sharon, had found in his drawer a pile of songs given to him years earlier by the aspiring songwriters George Cory and Douglass Cross.

"On top of the pile was a song called
I Left My Heart in San Francisco,
and Ralph took it along because that's where we were headed
[...]
I was happy to have a special song for my San Francisco show
because I'd never performed in that town
and had heard that if audiences didn't know you,
they didn't warm up to you quickly.

Ralph wrote up a great chart, and I sang it on opening night at the Fairmont Hotel.

It really went over like gang-busters.
It might have ended right there, but as fate would have it,
local Columbia reps heard the song at rehearsal that afternoon and loved it...
On January 23, 1962, I recorded San Francisco in one take.

That song helped make me a world citizen.
It allowed me to live, work and sing in any city on the globe.
It changed my whole life."

Tony Bennett

Ella Fitzgerald

American jazz vocalist Ella Fitzgerald (opposite) sings in front of an audience sitting at the tables of the Venetian Room of the Fairmont Hotel, Dallas, March 1980. She repeated her performance in 1982 just a few days after Dizzy Gillepsie, and also in 1985. She was a frequent entertainer of the Fairmont San Francisco where she had concerts in 1963, 1969, 1983, and 1985. In 1974, she performed at the Royal York in Toronto and came back in 1983 and 1984 when she sang in front of 300 children.

Tina Turner

In 1980, Tina Turner performed at the Fairmont Royal York and in both the Venetian rooms of the Fairmont Dallas (wearing her mythical golden stage outfit by the adulated stylist Bob Mackie) and the Fairmont San Francisco where she would keep on performing for four years in a row (1980–83).

Sonny & Cher

Sonny and Cher, who had performed at the Century Plaza the year before, were welcomed by the Canadian public at the Royal York Toronto in 1971 (top). "Humor has been added in large quantities to the performances of the husband-and-wife team of Sonny and Cher. The pair opened last night at the Royal York Hotel's Imperial Room and inaugurated that nightspot's new state facilities. Their new act is likened to that of the Smothers Brothers and they made the difficult transition from pop singers to polished nightclub entertainers with amazing success," read the *Toronto Star*, September 17, 1971.

The Ramones

In 1977, the Ramones (bottom) played in the Georgian Room of the Olympic Hotel in Seattle, before a private event organized by two recently graduated students from Roosevelt High. As the *Seattle Times* reported: "It likely was the loudest musical group ever to grace this grand old landmark that in its heyday was the center of Seattle high society." Needless to say, there were complaints to the front desk.

Prince

Prince came three times to perform at the Montreux Jazz Festival in 2007, 2009, and 2013. Every time a guest of the Montreux Palace, he rehearsed with his group in 2009 at the Petit Palais, the hotel's Belle-Époque pavilion on the Geneva Lake. One night after a show, he sat at the Grand Piano in the Grand Hall and played a private concert for a lucky few.
Above, Prince's last concert at the Montreux Jazz Festival, July 15, 2013.

"If you want peace of mind, come to Montreux"

Freddy Mercury

Freddy Mercury & Queen

Freddy Mercury stayed at the Montreux Palace while recording the Queen albums *Jazz*, *Hot Space*, and *It's a Kind of Magic* at the Mountain Studios. Mercury loved Montreux so much that he finally settled in the city and, together with his group, bought the legendary recording studios in 1979. Numerous guests of the Montreux Palace such as Iggy Pop or Michael Jackson—who stayed at the hotel for two weeks in 1997—came to record their albums there.
Freddy Mercury's statue over the Geneva Lake, a tribute of the Montreux city to its very special guest.

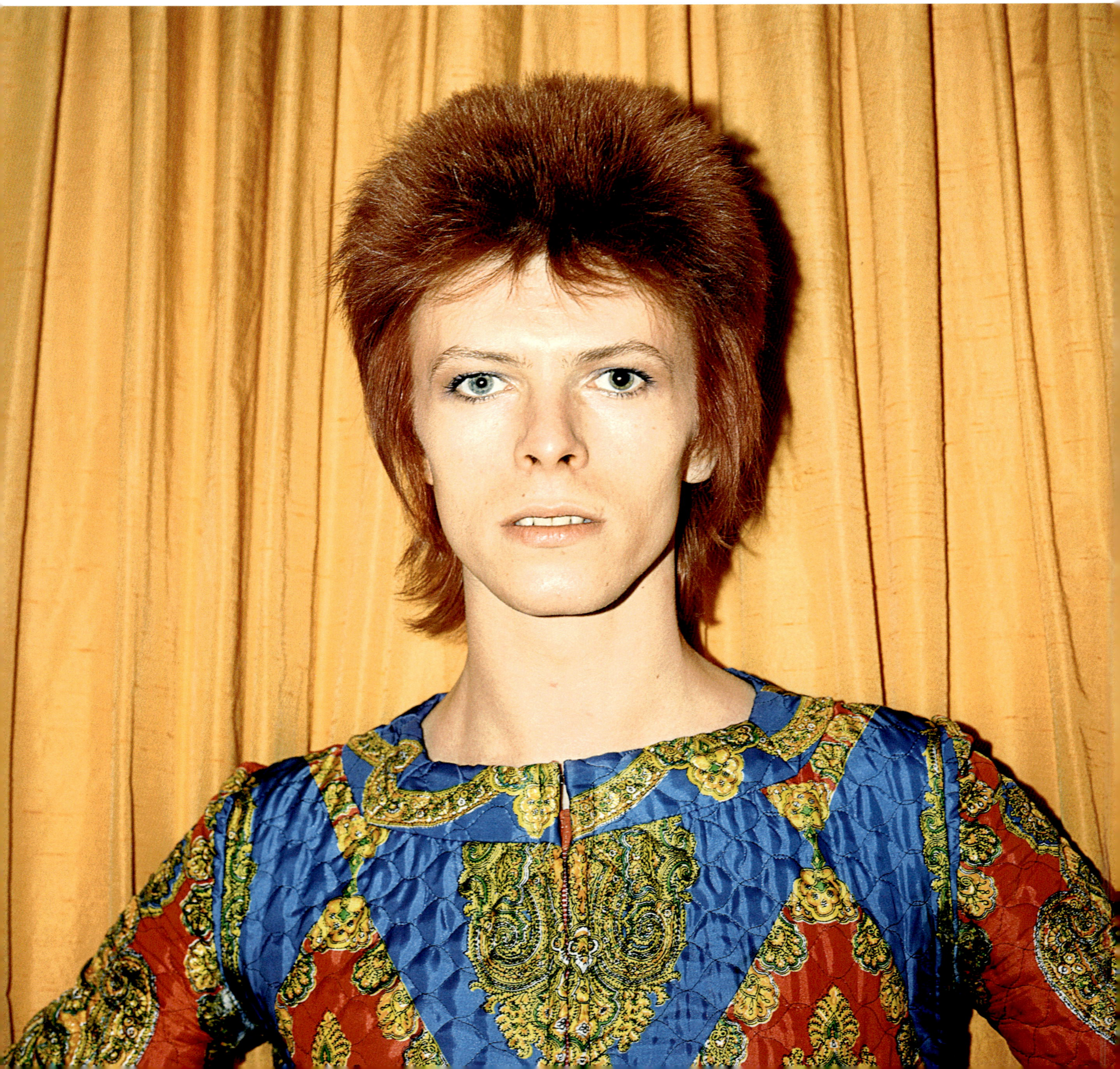

David Bowie

Just like Freddy Mercury, David Bowie fell in love with Montreux where he finally settled and used Freddy Mercury's Mountain Studios. Host of the Montreux Palace when he was performing at the Montreux Jazz Festival, he created the poster of the 1995 edition. This was a long time after he first came to present his show *Ziggy Stardust* in New York and had a press conference in his suite at The Plaza (opposite).

Madonna & Rihanna

In the 2000s, Madonna, then married to the British director Guy Ritchie, was living in London. She had been spotted at The Savoy as well at the Evening Standard Film Awards at The Savoy Hotel. In 1990, she was already a frequent guest of The Plaza in New York: she attended the Martha Graham Dance Company's 64th Season opening night Gala in October, and was with Warren Betty in June of that year.

Rihanna—portrayed above behind Madonna at The Plaza during a Gucci charity dinner in November 2008—also stayed at The Savoy in 2011 while working on her album *Talk That Talk*, which was partially recorded in the hotel.

FA SH ION

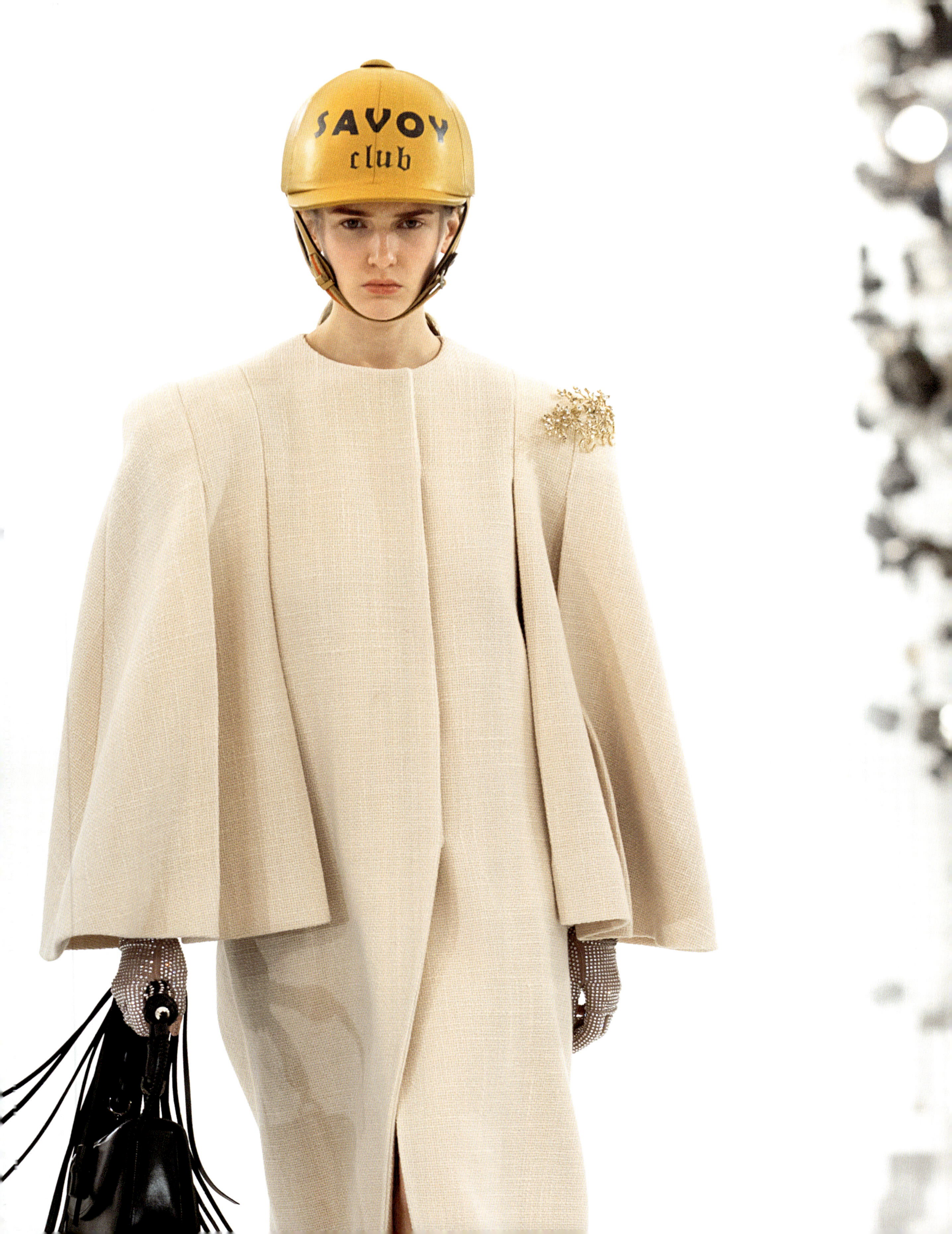
SAVOY
club

"Osa Johnson introduces African influence as a new fashion note in millinery.

As an explorer and producer of wildlife movies, she captured many novel style ideas in the jungle, inspired by the richness of color and shape as well as by the strange life of animals and natives.

Here we see a chapeau adorned with an African wild turkey wing, a color blend of gold, light brown, dark brown and orange, on a velvet hat of African 'Masai brown', a new color of her own creation.

With it goes a very sheer French veil."

NEW YORK TIMES, 1939

Fashion Trendsetters

WHEN OSA JOHNSON AND HER HUSBAND MARTIN, A COUPLE OF ADVENTURERS FROM KANSAS, ARRIVED IN NAIROBI AT THE START OF THEIR EXPLORATION OF THE KENYAN AND CONGOLESE WILDERNESS IN 1921, THEY HEADED FIRST FOR THE HOTEL THAT IS NOW FAIRMONT THE NORFOLK. OVER THE NEXT DECADES, THEY WENT ON TO MAKE FOUR LONG SAFARIS, DOCUMENTING WHAT THEY SAW BOTH IN PHOTOGRAPHS AND MOVIES, WHICH LED TO THE FEATURE FILMS *WILD AFRICAN ANIMALS* (1923), *SIMBA* (1928), *BABOONA* (1935), AND THE BESTSELLING BOOK *I MARRIED ADVENTURE* (1940). OSA ALSO BECAME SOMETHING OF A FASHION ICON, HENCE THE COVER OF THE JANUARY 1926 ISSUE OF *VOGUE*, WHERE SHE IS PICTURED SITTING ASTRIDE A ZEBRA (ABOVE).

Guccio Gucci

SON OF A FLORENTINE LEATHER WORKER, THE TWENTY-YEAR-OLD GUCCIO GUCCI TRAVELED TO LONDON AND FOUND A JOB AS A LIFT BOY AT THE SAVOY (CA. 1899). TWO DECADES LATER—AFTER AN EDUCATION GLEANED BY SCRUTINIZING THE INTERNATIONAL GUEST HANDBAGS, LUGGAGE, AND ACCESSORIES—HE RETURNED TO HIS NATIVE FLORENCE AND FOUNDED IN 1921 THE LEATHER GOODS COMPANY AND NOW FASHION HOUSE GUCCI.
WHEN IN 2013, GUCCI REINVENTED ITS 1947 BAMBOO HANDBAG, PHOTOGRAPHER BENJAMIN GRILLON SHOT ITS ADVERTISING CAMPAIGN AT THE SAVOY, IN ONE OF THE HOTEL'S GREEN-LACQUERED LIFTS (OPPOSITE). FOR THE 100 YEARS OF THE BRAND, GUCCI'S CREATIVE DIRECTOR ALESSANDRO MICHELE DECLARED: "THE MYTH OF FOUNDATION IS REINHABITED IN THE LIGHT OF THE PRESENT." BESIDES EQUESTRIAN REFERENCES OR THE ICONIC GG CANVAS, THE DESIGNER ILLUSTRATED THE SAVOY KEYSTONE STORY THROUGH A NEW TRADEMARK, THE "SAVOY CLUB" BLOCK LETTERS TURN INTO A NEW POP PATTERN (SEE PREVIOUS PAGE).

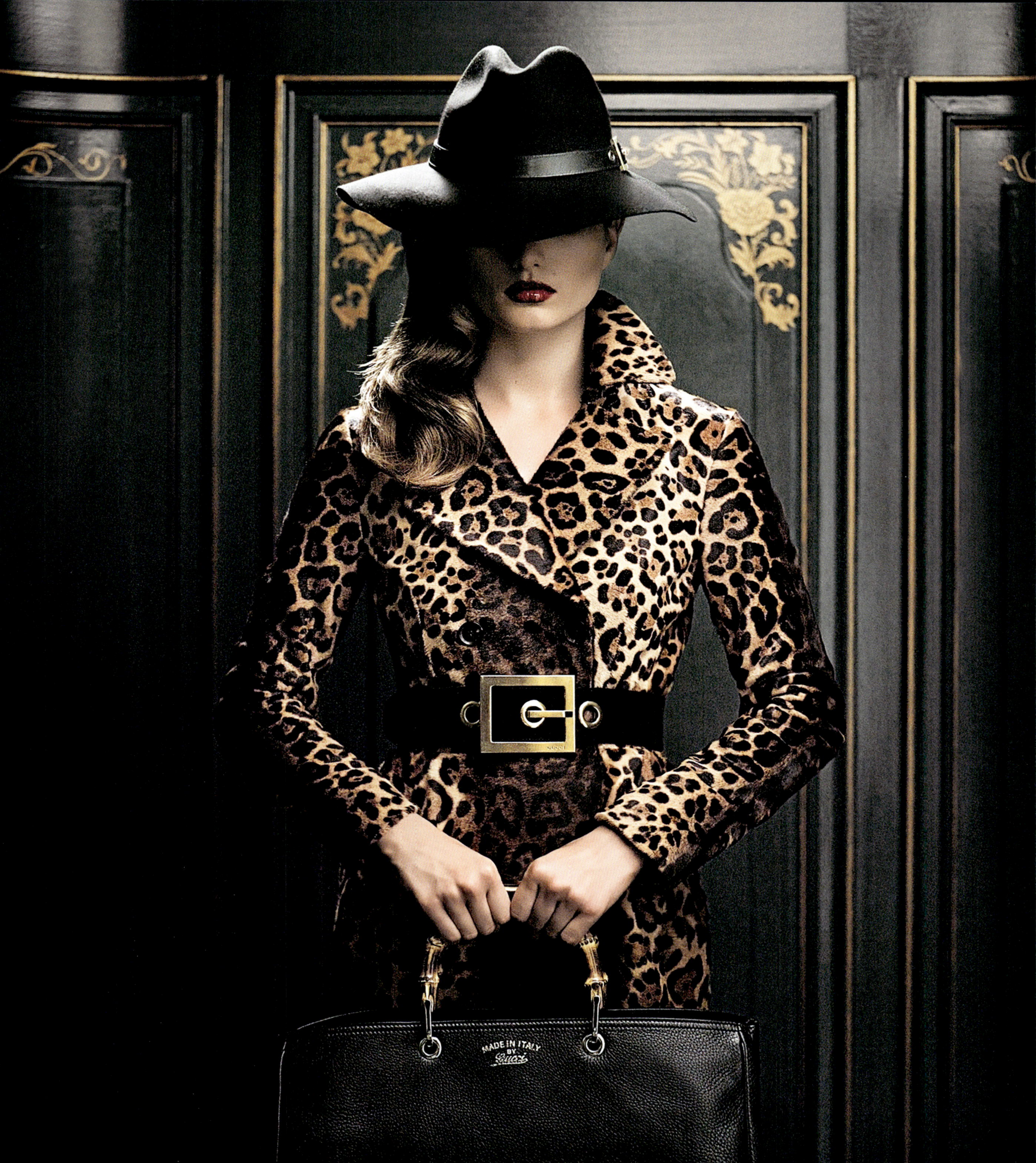
MADE IN ITALY
BY
Gucci

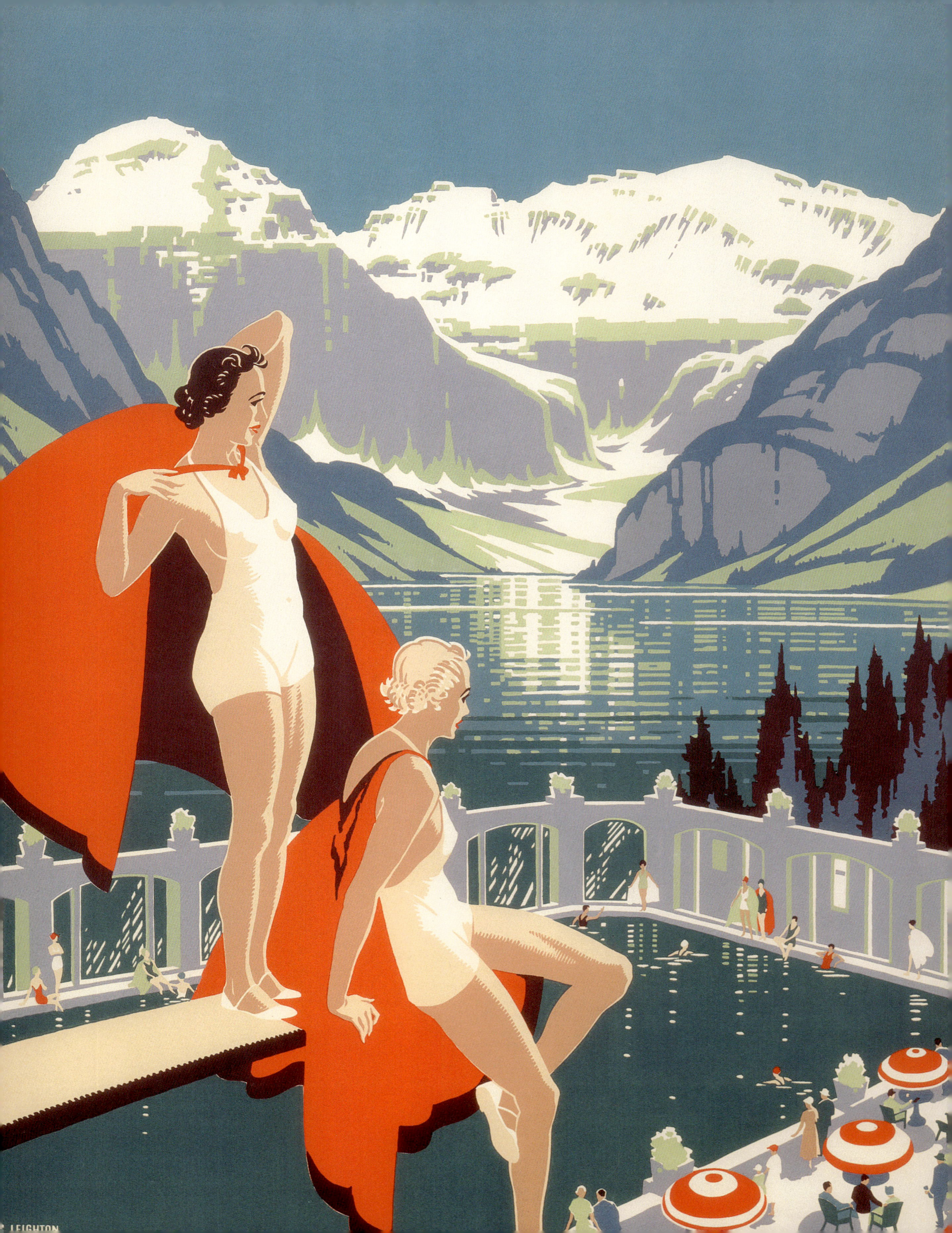
LEIGHTON

Resort Wear

Chateau Lake Louise and the Banff Springs Hotel welcomes a new generation of visitors, after attracting intrepid explorers, naturalists, and sportsmen in the early years. Wise to the fact that guests new to the experience of traveling to unfamiliar terrains might not know what to pack, Canadian Pacific published a handy guide for visitors entitled *What Shall I Wear At Banff Springs Hotel / Chateau Lake Louise?* "The spacious public rooms and gracious dining rooms" of its hotels, it advised, "invite lovely clothes," so while "comfort" and "casual" were fine during the day, something smarter was called for at dinner. But the company recognized that not every guest would want to invest in the necessary kit required for the various activities its hotels offered. So "sterilized bathing suits [could] be rented at each hotel pool." And guests were invited to "outfit" themselves for horse riding "at the housekeeper's office."

Opposite: Poster advertising Chateau Lake Louise's pool, Alberta, 1938. Above: Models pose for *Vogue* by the pool at what is now Fairmont Southampton, Bermuda, in 1975.

New York Fashion Week

Fashion may not have been foremost in the minds of many Europeans in 1943, but in New York, Eleanor Lambert, a public relations executive who had been instrumental in establishing the New York Dress Institute had an ingenious idea.

With Paris, historically the center of all that was fashionable, under occupation, New York was able to shine. Lambert's big idea was what she called Press Week, an event held at The Plaza—obviously—at which designers, journalists, and photographers could all be brought together in one place. To guarantee a good turnout of reporters from across the country, Lambert offered to cover their expenses. So, as Time magazine reported, "Not only did the editors show up, but when the fashion magazines released their next issues, they were full of American designers." Indeed, fifty-three domestic designers showed their collections for that season. And thus, the idea of Fashion Week was born, as was the idea of American fashion.

Among those who participated was the fashion entrepreneur Hattie Carnegie, pictured above, wearing what was described as an "eye-catching bodice of black and pink striped satin, and a slim black crepe skirt." She continued to show at The Plaza—in 1946, one of her models (opposite) was photographed wearing a blue crepe evening dress of Forstmann wool, a fur hat by John Frederics and jewelry by Carnegie herself—a tradition that continues to this day.

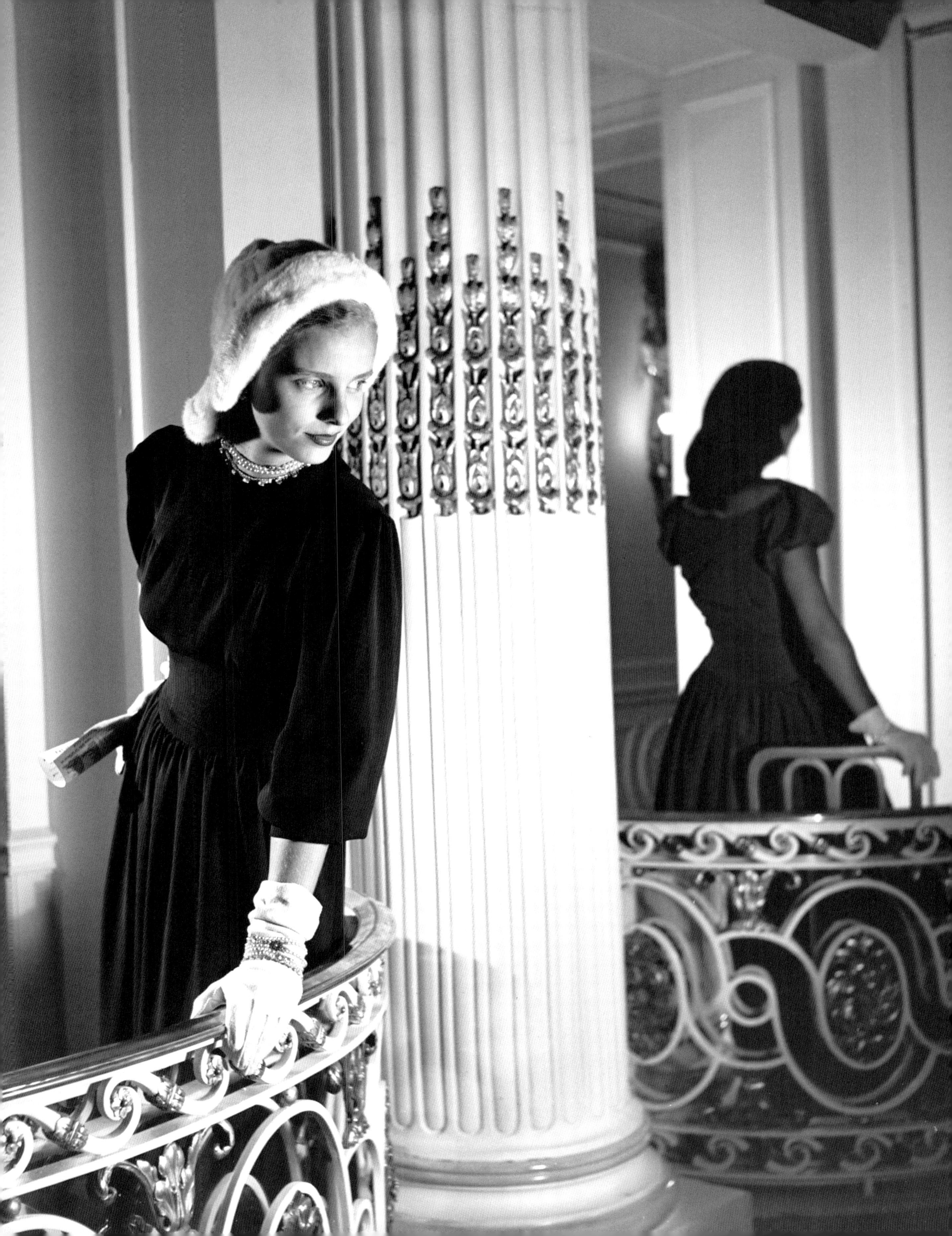

"'I've always had this idea for a black-and-white ball,'
Truman Capote continued,
explaining that he'd always loved the black-and-white scene
at the racetrack in My Fair Lady.
Also, he said that he loved the ballroom in The Plaza
and [had] always wanted to have a party there."

Katharine Graham
TRUMAN CAPOTE'S PUBLISHER

The Art of the Costume

THE POWER BROKER AND CITY PLANNER AMANDA BURDEN, DRESSED (ABOVE) IN ONE OF CECIL BEATON'S ORIGINAL COSTUMES FOR THE ASCOT RACECOURSE SCENE OF *MY FAIR LADY*, WHICH SHE HAD HIRED TO WEAR TO TRUMAN CAPOTE'S BLACK AND WHITE BALL AT THE PLAZA, NOVEMBER 1966. (SHE IS ACCOMPANIED BY ONE OF HER BROTHERS.)
AUDREY HEPBURN (OPPOSITE), STAR OF THE MOVIE *MY FAIR LADY*, WITH ITS COSTUME DESIGNER, CECIL BEATON, PHOTOGRAPHED AT THE PRESS RECEPTION FOR THE MOVIE AT THE SAVOY, JANUARY 1965. THIS TIME, HOWEVER, SHE IS WEARING A DRESS OF EMERALD-GREEN SHANTUNG SILK, BY HER FAVORITE DESIGNER, GIVENCHY.

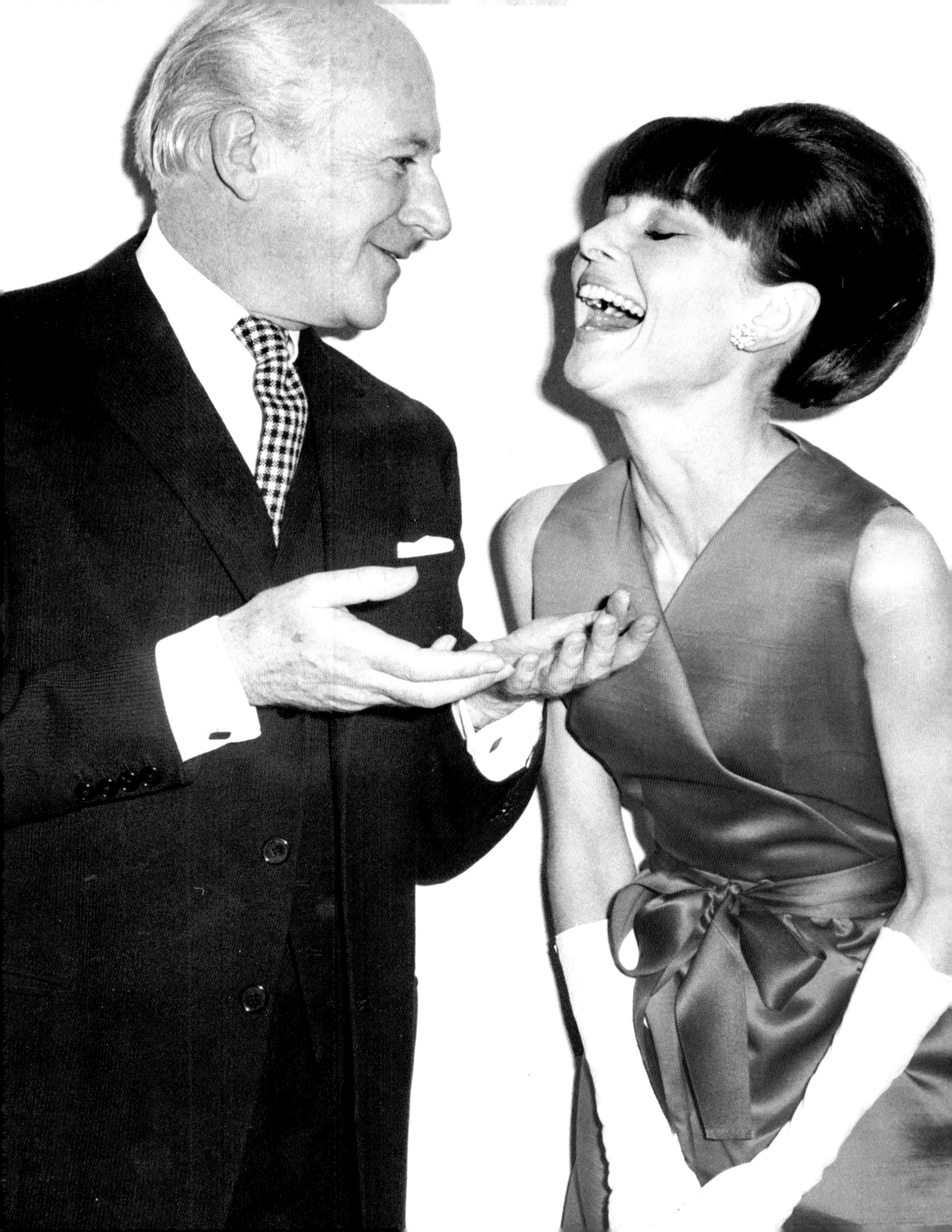

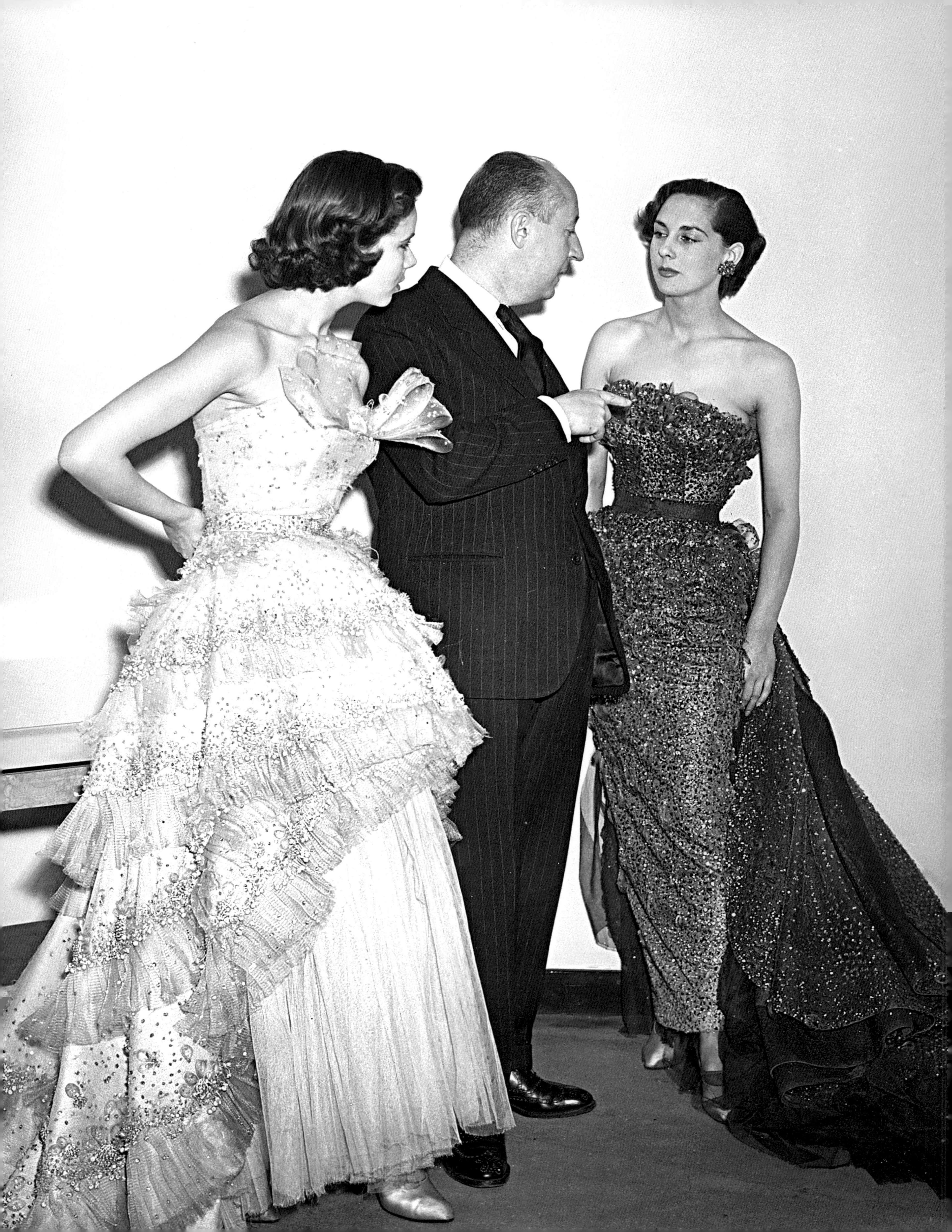

Christian Dior

On April 24, 1950, Christian Dior held his first fashion show in London at The Savoy. He had just launched his new Vertical line, and the show featured eighty outfits, and eight of his fourteen house models, one of whom, Jean Dawnay (photographed with Dior, opposite) was British. It was watched by an audience of more than a thousand (afterward there was a "secret" show for the then Queen Elizabeth and Princess Margaret), and such a success that he opened a shop in London two years later, establishing licensing deals with British manufacturers producing not just clothing, but underwear and jewellery.

Whenever Marlene Dietrich stayed at The Savoy, she requested a dozen pink roses and a bottle of Dom Perignon. She also liked to wear Dior. When she was approached by Alfred Hitchcock to star in his movie *Stage Fright*, she made it clear that she would only wear his clothes: "No Dior, no Dietrich." Above, she is at The Savoy for the press conference of the movie, which opened in London in 1950.

Little Black Dresses

The American model and actress Emily Ratajkowski arrives at Harper's Bazaar's party for Carine Roitfeld at The Plaza, September 2016 (above).

Marylin Monroe at The Savoy to promote her movie *The Prince and the Showgirl* in July 1956 (opposite), along with her co-star Laurence Olivier and accompanied by her then husband, Arthur Miller. She caused a sensation by wearing a wool crêpe cocktail dress by James G Alanos for Bergdorf Goodman that revealed her midriff through a panel of sheer chiffon. She caused another flurry of excitement when promoting the same movie in New York at The Plaza. This time the strap on her velvet sheath snapped, a story that made the front pages of newspapers across the country. Breaking news indeed. It later turned out it wasn't a wardrobe malfunction at all. Wise to the stir it would cause, the designer had intended it all along.

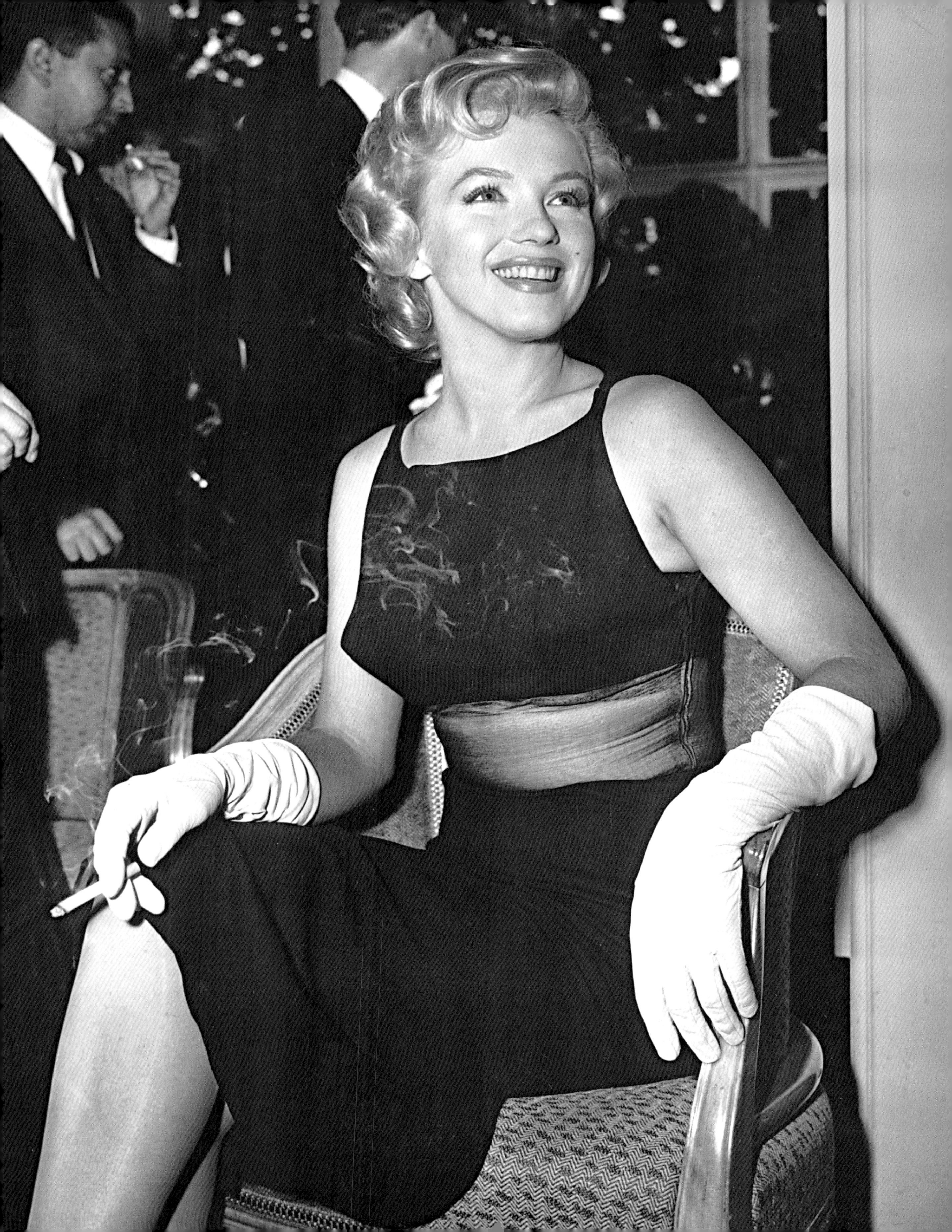

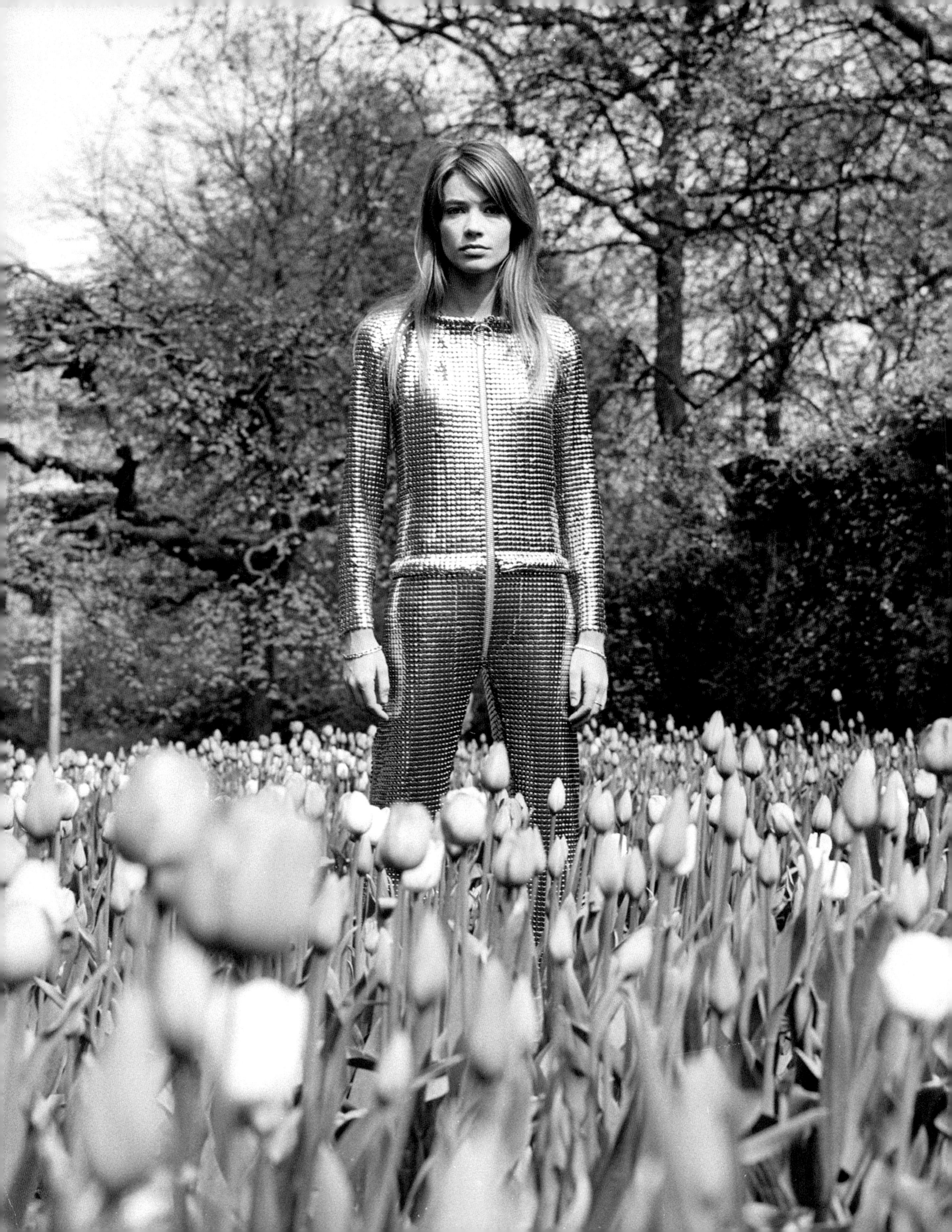

Fashion Avant-Garde

Expected by the British audience as much for her look as for her music, French singer-songwriter Françoise Hardy has performed at The Savoy Hotel for several years in a row since 1965. "I remember a concert at The Savoy in London, where Burt Bacharach (great American composer) then very fashionable, had come to hear me sing. It was a great honor for me so I decided to go and greet him. I still had my stage outfit by Courrèges on, the most beautiful stage outfit I have ever owned. Sober, very elegant. A top, some white trousers, and little white boots. But at the time, it was out of question to admit in a restaurant room like the one of The Savoy a woman wearing trousers. They did not allow me in…". For her last assignment in 1968, she had commissioned a custom-made outfit from Paco Rabanne (opposite) Her space-age chain-mail jumpsuit weighed almost ninety pounds and proved much too heavy to endorse. The singer though stuck to her intention to perform in it but was not able to move and needed help to leave the stage.
American supermodel Jerry Hall (above) poses in a window seat at The Savoy Hotel, 1985.

PA RTI ES

"I have always observed in almost every situation—

and I have been in almost every situation —
that people tend to cling to their own types.

The very rich people, for instance,
tend to like the company of very rich people.
The international social set likes international socialites.
Writers writers, artists artists.

I have thought for years that it would be interesting
to bring these disparate people together
and see what happens."

Truman Capote
ON PLANNING HIS BLACK AND WHITE BALL AT THE PLAZA IN 1966.
OPPOSITE, THE BALL PHOTOGRAPHED BY ELLIOTT ERWITT.

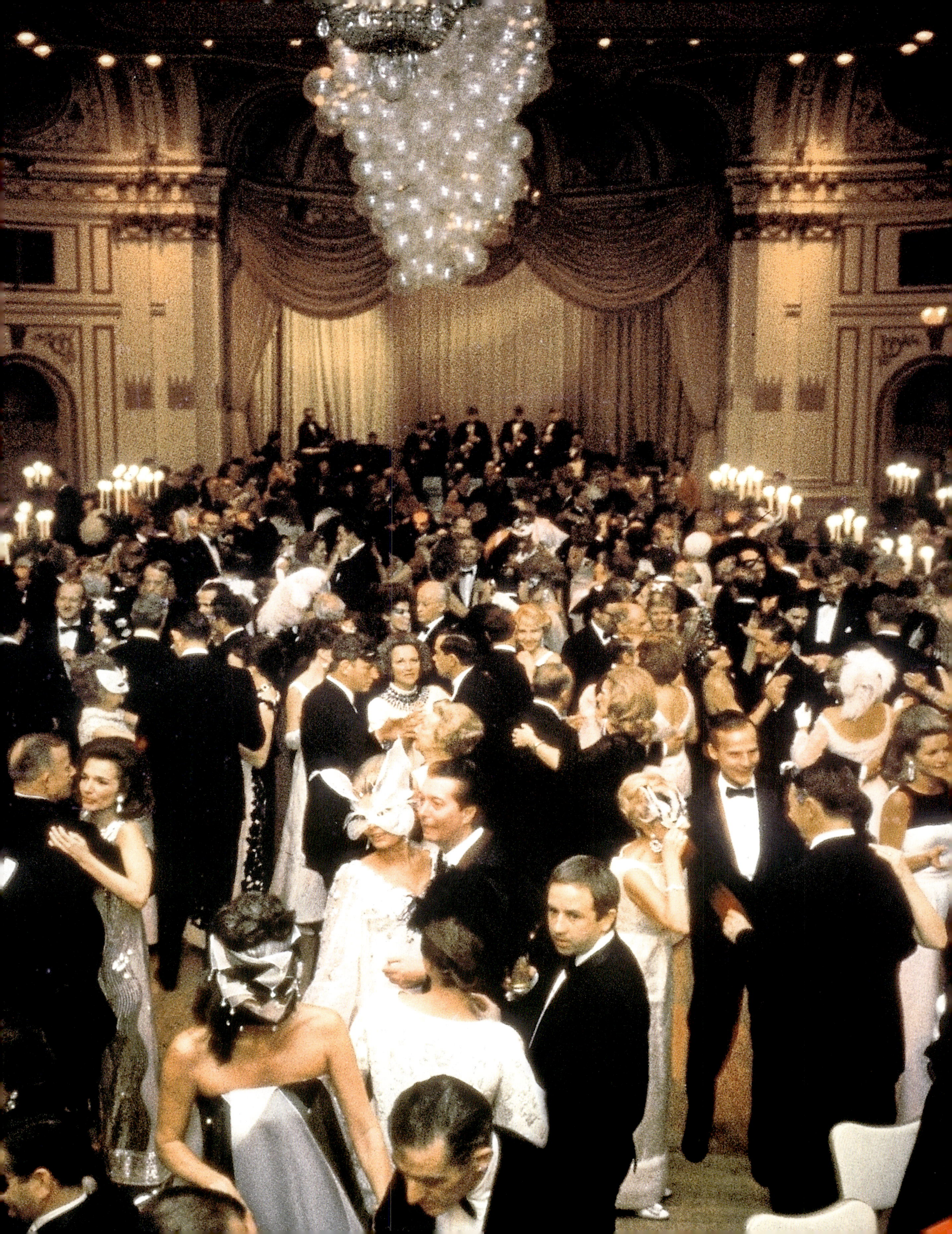

In July 1905, the American millionaire and architect George Kessler hosted one of the most spectacular parties London has ever witnessed in honor of King Edward VII. The original courtyard at The Savoy (now the Lancaster Room) was flooded, and the surrounding walls concealed by scenery behind painted scenes of Venice. Amid the water, stood (rather than floated) a giant gondola capable of seating twenty-four diners, who were served a twelve-course banquet by a team of waiters dressed as gondoliers, who accessed the "boat" via a "Venetian" bridge.
The other decorations included 12,000 carnations, 400 paper lanterns, and 100 live doves. There were also fish in the water and swans afloat on it, but unfortunately the powder used to tint the water proved toxic to both. Toward the end of the meal, a baby elephant, on loan from the London Zoo, arrived bearing a giant cake on its back. After which peaches and glacé fruits were served from the backs of three lions carved from ice. And if that were not entertainment enough, there were Gaiety Girls to toast the monarch, after which the most celebrated tenor of the time, Enrico Caruso, sang "O Sole Mio."

"Here, each night,
under the spell of a perfect symphonic orchestra
and rainbow-tinted lights,
sparkles the brilliant social life of Banff…

Beautiful women in gowns,
that will be fashionable next winter.
Distinguished looking men,
with the stamp of foreign courts about them.
Faces familiar in society pages and international news.

A stunning Spanish girl and a famous painter.
A diamond studded dowager and a British army officer.
And, because some are always just coming or just going,
men and women in smart travelling clothes."

BANFF SPRINGS HOTEL PAMPHLET, 1932

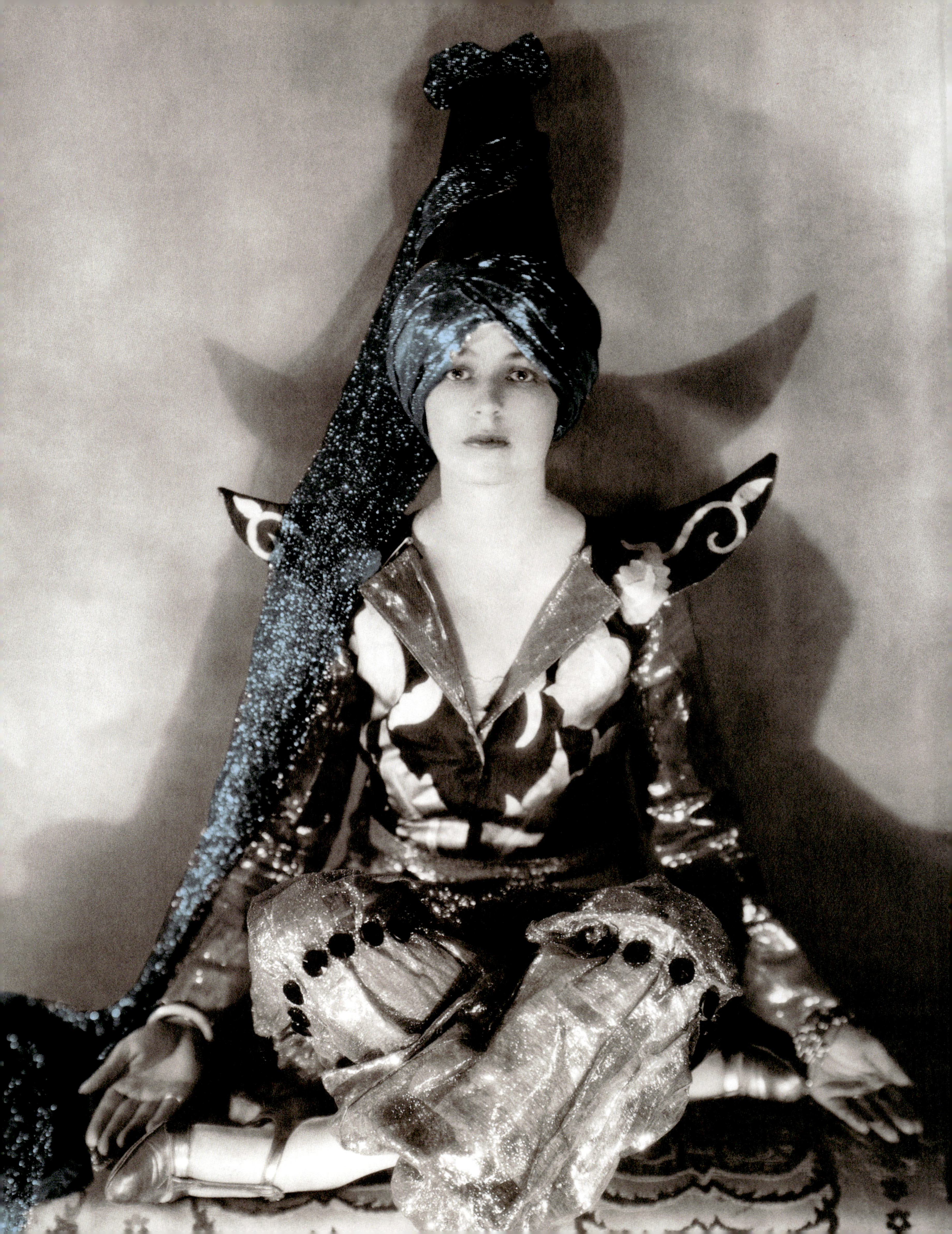

"The Persian fête for the benefit of the Big Sisters' organisations, which took place last night at The Plaza, under the sponsorship of Mrs. William K. Vanderbilt II, was one of the most unusual charity entertainments of the season. The Plaza ballroom and the adjoining rooms were transformed by means of Oriental hangings and lanterns," reported the New York Times on December 20, 1924.

Opposite, Jeanne Jacqueline Harper, whose daughter became the artist Niki de Saint Phalle, poses for Edward Steichen, then chief photographer at Vogue, in a costume designed by William Weaver for an Orientalist ballet choreographed for the evening by Ned Wayburn.

In 1925, Sir Bhupinder Singh, Maharajah of Patiala, threw an extravagant dinner at The Savoy, where the desserts were served by waiters from the backs of animals sculpted in ice (above). The hotel was popular with the Indian aristocracy, who would spend their summers in London, and Sir Bhupinder, a former captain of the Indian cricket team, became a regular, arriving in a cavalcade of twenty Rolls-Royces. In 1930, he took over an entire floor in order to accommodate his retinue of fifty, and the hotel installed a silver bathtub at his request.

Sir Victor Sassoon held a succession of fabulous fancy-dress parties at the Cathay (now Fairmont Peace) Hotel in Shanghai. This one, in January 1935, had a circus theme. The ballroom was transformed into a big (or circus) tent, and Sir Victor came dressed as the ringmaster, in a scarlet coat, top hat and false moustache, with a whip in his hand. The guests pictured here—Mr. Cord Squarey, Miss Ethelwynne Spence, and Mr. David Cox—came as clowns. Others were acrobats. One woman was swathed in furs as a performing seal, apparently quite a convincing one. Another, "Mrs. Winter was so realistic as the 'tattooed lady'," wrote the *North China Herald*, "that it was almost impossible that the designs and hieroglyphics that adorned her would all wash off in the morning."

Even that was not as sensational as the Shipwreck Party he gave in 1933, however. On that occasion, guests were asked to dress as though they were abandoning a sinking ship. One couple arrived naked, on the grounds that they had been taking a shower when the alarm was sounded.

Princess Grace of Monaco

The Quebec Winter Carnival of 1969 opened with a Grand Ball in eighteenth-century costume at Château Frontenac, at which the guest of honor was Princess Grace of Monaco.

Despite the fact that Great Britain was at war—World War I had broken out four months earlier—The Savoy nevertheless hosted a fancy dress ball just before Christmas in 1914 (above).
"I think you need cheering up. And I'm going to give you a ball," the writer Truman Capote told his publisher, Katharine Graham, in the summer of 1966.
Among the 500 friends he invited was Lee Radziwill, pictured opposite dancing with Capote at the ball, which took place in November 1966.

"Everyone stood back when Jerry, [the choreographer Jerome] Robbins, danced with Betty [Lauren] Bacall.

When they started out in a corner, people were dancing everywhere.

But the two of them were so superb that the dance floor just cleared."

Princess Lee Radziwill
JACQUELINE KENNEDY'S SISTER AND DEAR FRIEND OF TRUMAN CAPOTE.

From left, Principessa Luciana Pignatelli, Peter Gimbel and Contessa Crespi at Truman Capote's Black and White Ball

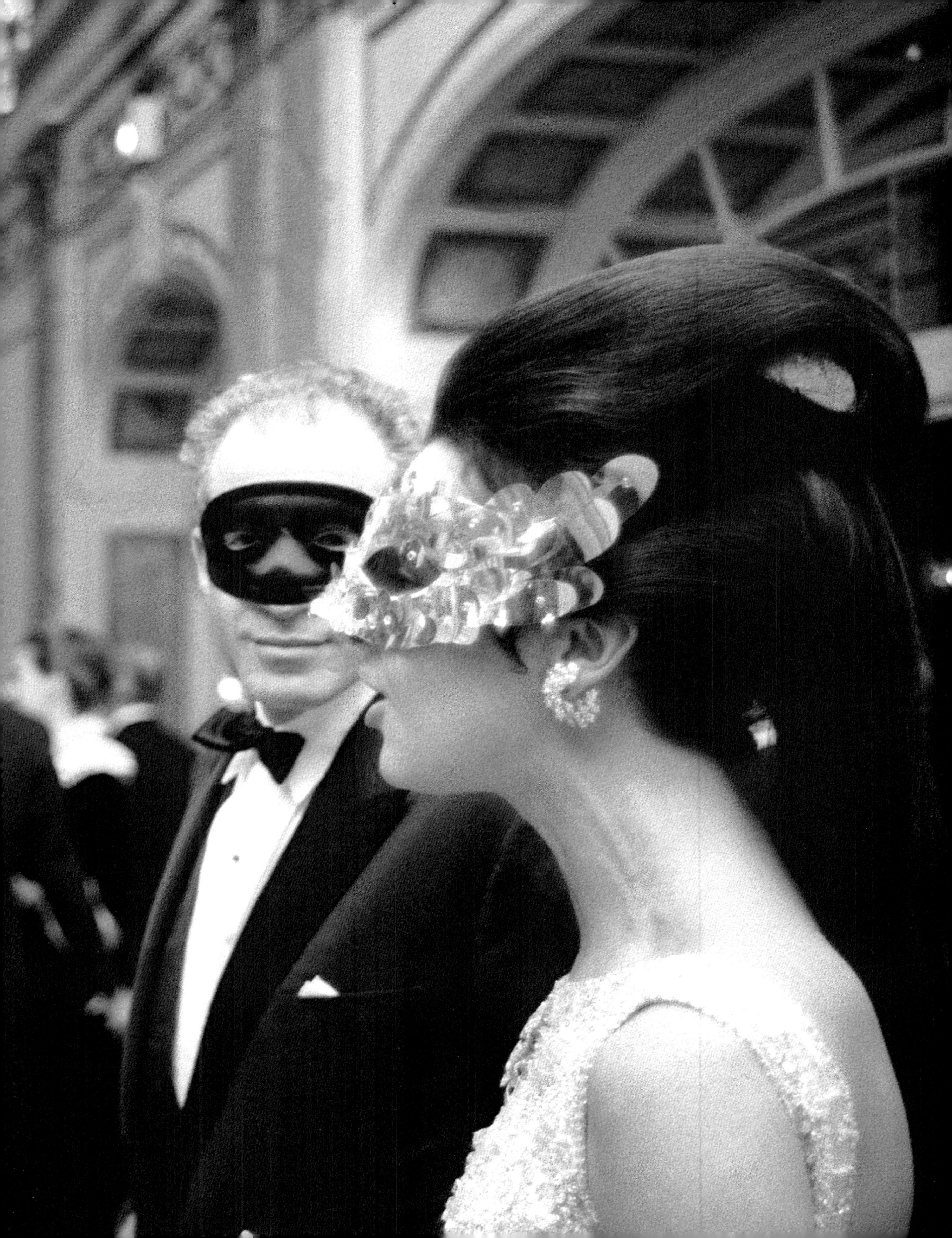

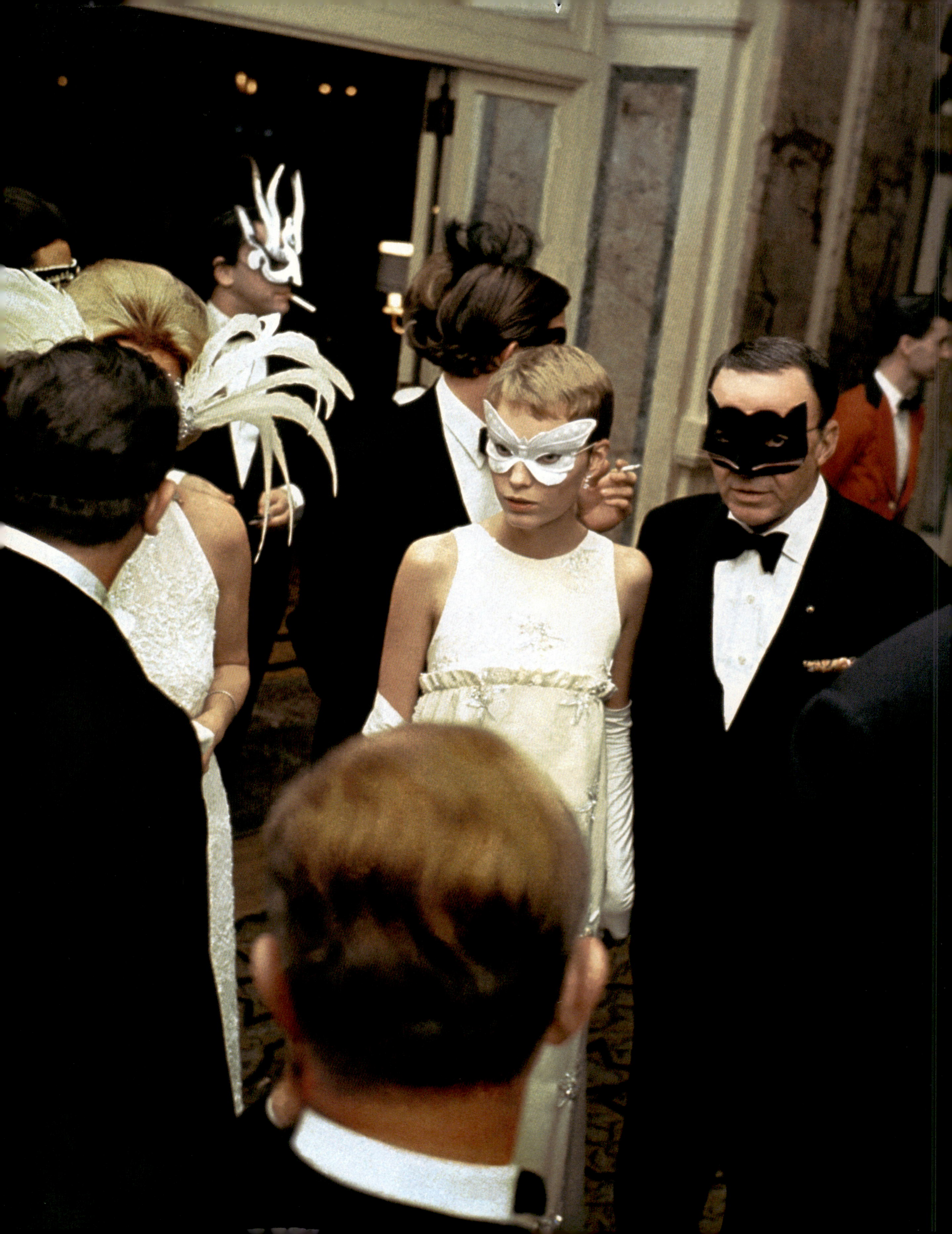

Mia Farrow & Franck Sinatra

Mia Farrow and Frank Sinatra photographed by Elliott Erwitt (opposite) Truman Capote's Black and White Ball.

Marisa Berenson

Marisa Berenson (above) the 52nd Annual Pioneer of the Year Awards at Century Plaza Hotel in Los Angeles, December 1990.

Nicole Mitchell & Eddie Murphy

NICOLE MITCHELL AND EDDIE MURPHY'S WEDDING RECEPTION AT THE PLAZA HOTEL, MARCH 18, 1993. THE SINGER JAMES BROWN AND THE ACTOR BRUCE LEE WERE AMONG THEIR GUESTS.

Lawford & Patricia Kennedy

The Hollywood actor Peter Lawford and Patricia Kennedy (sister of JFK) at their Plaza wedding on April 24, 1954.

Gigi Hadid & Kendall Jenner

The two American supermodels were captured at a party held at The Plaza for the fashion eminence Carine Roitfeld and the photographer Jean-Paul Goude to celebrate Harper's Bazaar's September 2016 issue.

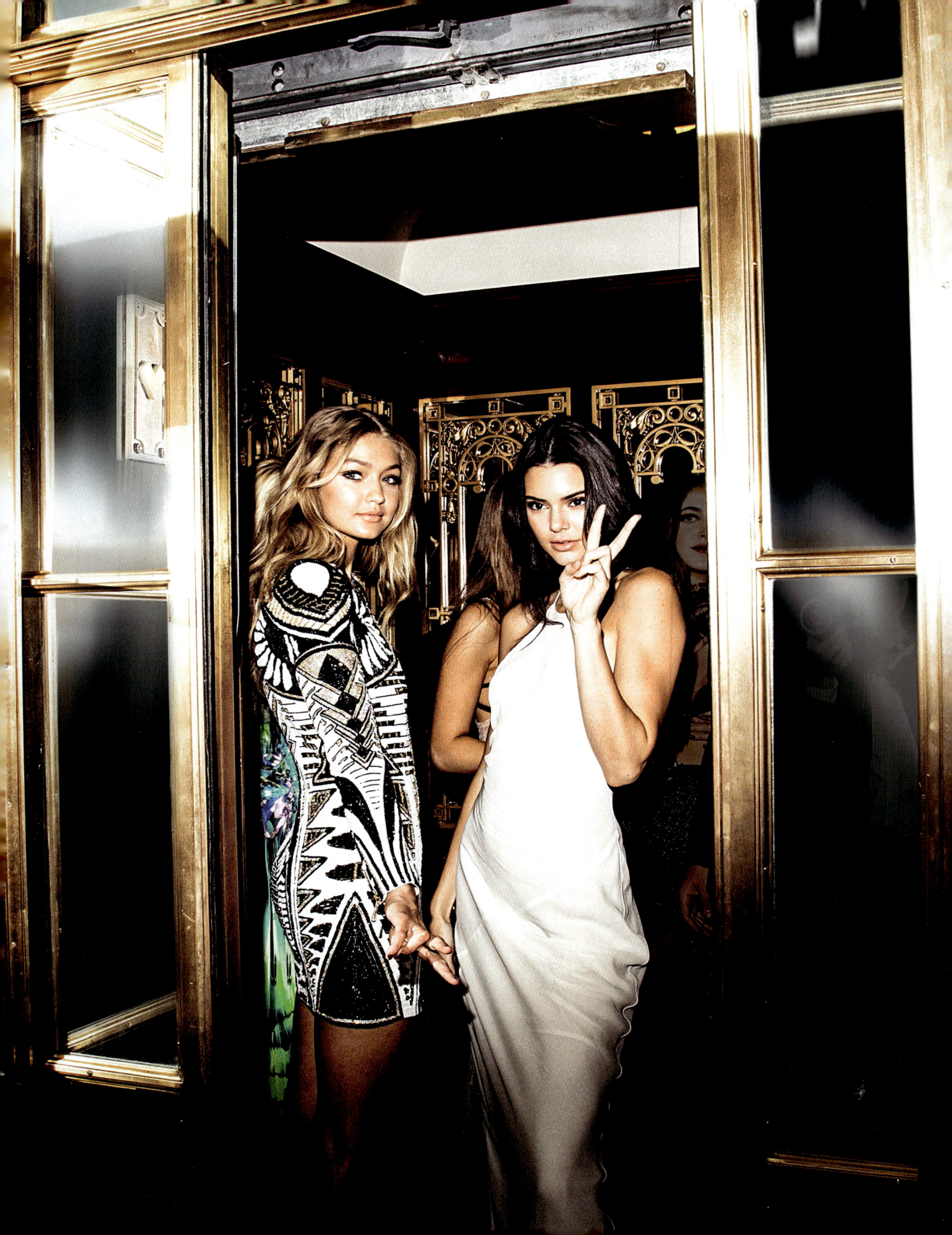

DESPITE SERIOUS RESEARCH, SOME AUTHORS OR COPYRIGHT HOLDERS OF PHOTOGRAPHS AND/OR WORKS REPRODUCED IN THIS VOLUME COULD NOT BE IDENTIFIED. WHOSOEVER BELIEVES HE HAS RIGHTS TO ENFORCE IS ASKED TO CONTACT THE PUBLISHER.

CREDITS

ORIGINS

COVER (INSET): RIGHTS RESERVED / CANADIAN NATIONAL RAILWAYS
COVER (BACKGROUND) RIGHTS RESERVED
PP. 6-7: RIGHTS RESERVED / ACCOR ARCHIVES
P. 8: GIOVANNI BOLDINI / FINE ARTS MUSEUM OF SAN FRANCISCO / GIFT OF MRS. VANDERBILT ADAMS
P. 9: W.A. COOPER / LIBRARY AND ARCHIVES CANADA / SIR WILLIAM VAN HORNE FONDS / A182603
P. 10: UBC LIBRARY / THE CHUNG COLLECTION
P. 11: LOOK AND LEARN / BREDGEMAN IMAGES
P. 14: UBC LIBRARY / THE CHUNG COLLECTION
P. 15 ABOVE: BYRON HARMON / UNIVERSITY OF ALBERTA LIBRARIES
P. 15 BELOW: HUBERT KANG
P. 16: WIKICOMMONS / KIM PAYANT
P. 17 ABOVE: MARY SCHAFFER FONDS / ARCHIVES AND LIBRARY, WHYTE MUSEUM OF THE CANADIAN ROCKIES
P. 17 BELOW: MATHIAS LÖVSTRÖM
P. 18: BYRON HARMON / MARY SCHAFFER FONDS / ARCHIVES AND LIBRARY, WHYTE MUSEUM OF THE CANADIAN ROCKIES
P. 19 ABOVE: CASPAR DAVID FRIEDRICH, HAMBURGER KUNSTHALLE, HAMBURG, GERMANY / BRIDGEMAN IMAGES
P. 19 BELOW: RIGHTS RESERVED
PP. 20-21: BYRON HARMON / UNIVERSITY OF ALBERTA LIBRARIES
P. 22: A.J. MELHUISH / NATIONAL PORTRAIT GALLERY, LONDON
PP. 22-23: H.R.H. THE PRINCESS LOUISE / NATIONAL GALLERY OF CANADA
P. 24: ALBERT BIERSTADT / PHOTO12 / ALAMY / ART COLLECTION
PP. 24-25: JOHN A. FRASER (1838-1898) / NATIONAL GALLERY OF CANADA
PP. 26-27: BYRON HARMON / MARY SCHAFFER FONDS / ARCHIVES AND LIBRARY, WHYTE MUSEUM OF THE CANADIAN ROCKIES
P. 27: BYRON HARMON FONDS / ARCHIVES AND LIBRARY, WHYTE MUSEUM OF THE CANADIAN ROCKIES.
PP. 28-29: CODY FITZGERALD
P. 30: COURTESY OF LIBRARIES AND CULTURAL RESOURCES DIGITAL COLLECTIONS, UNIVERSITY OF CALGARY
P. 31 ABOVE: JOHN HENRY WALKER / M930.50.1.142 / © MUSÉE MCCORD
P. 31 BELOW: KEVIN MUELLER
P. 32: COURTESY OF LIBRARIES AND CULTURAL RESOURCES DIGITAL COLLECTIONS, UNIVERSITY OF CALGARY
P. 33 LEFT: MARY SCHAFFER FONDS / ARCHIVES AND LIBRARY, WHYTE MUSEUM OF THE CANADIAN ROCKIES
P. 33 RIGHT: EDWARD FEUZ FONDS / ARCHIVES AND LIBRARY, WHYTE MUSEUM OF THE CANADIAN ROCKIES
P. 34 LEFT: MARY M. VAUX (PHILADELPHIA, USA) / ARCHIVES AND LIBRARY, WHYTE MUSEUM OF THE CANADIAN ROCKIES
P. 34 RIGHT: GIFT OF CHARLES C. REID, BANFF, ALBERTA, 1986 / WHYTE MUSEUM OF THE CANADIAN ROCKIES
P. 35: MARY SCHAFFER FONDS / ARCHIVES AND LIBRARY, WHYTE MUSEUM OF THE CANADIAN ROCKIES
PP. 36-37: AGATHE BERNARD
P. 38: CRHA / EXPORAIL, CANADIAN PACIFIC RAILWAY COMPANY FONDS
P. 39 ABOVE: BRIGDEN'S STUDIOS. COURTESY OF LIBRARIES AND CULTURAL RESOURCES DIGITAL COLLECTIONS, UNIVERSITY OF CALGARY
P. 39 BELOW: AGEFOTOSTOCK / DARWIN WIGGET
P. 40 ABOVE: RIGHTS RESERVED / FAIRMONT CHATEAU MONTEBELLO ARCHIVES
P. 40 BELOW: PHOTO12 / ALAMY / HNASE18STOCKIMO
P. 41: RIGHTS RESERVED / FAIRMONT CHATEAU MONTEBELLO ARCHIVES

P. 42 LEFT: J. FRED SPALDING / UNIVERSITY OF ALBERTA LIBRARIES
P. 42 RIGHT: G. MORRIS TAYLOR / UNIVERSITY OF ALBERTA LIBRARIES
P. 43 ABOVE: UNIVERSITY OF ALBERTA LIBRARIES
P. 43 BELOW: POWEROFFOREVER / GETTY IMAGES
P. 44 ABOVE: RIGHTS RESERVED / HOTEL CLAREMONT ARCHIVES
P. 44 BELOW: GIORGIO TROVATO / UNSPLASH
P. 45: RIGHTS RESERVED / HOTEL CLAREMONT ARCHIVES
P. 46: RICHARD BERHENDT
P. 47 ABOVE: RIGHTS RESERVED
P. 47 BELOW: HUBERT KANG
PP. 48-49: AURIMAGES_P12 / MANUEL COHEN
P. 50 TOP: BYRON HARMON / BYRON HARMON FONDS / ARCHIVES AND LIBRARY, WHYTE MUSEUM OF THE CANADIAN ROCKIES
P. 50 MIDDLE: RIGHTS RESERVED / ACCOR ARCHIVES
P. 50 BOTTOM: RIGHTS RESERVED
P. 51 ABOVE: PHOTO12 / ALAMY / BYGONE COLLECTION
P. 51 ABOVE: CADEN NICKEL
P. 52 BELLOW: ERIC CUVILLIER
P. 52 BELOW: RIGHTS RESERVED
P. 53 ABOVE: CHARLIE GRIEVES COOK
P. 53 BELOW: RIGHTS RESERVED / ACCOR ARCHIVES
P. 54 LEFT: CRHA / EXPORAIL, CANADIAN PACIFIC RAILWAY COMPANY FONDS
P. 54 RIGHT: CANADIAN PACIFIC RAILWAY COMPANY / UNIVERSITY OF BRITISH COLUMBIA LIBRARY
P. 55 ABOVE: LIBRARY AND ARCHIVES CANADA / C-029447 (DETAIL)
P. 55 BELOW: NEIL COOPER / UNSPLASH
P. 56 TOP: CRHA / EXPORAIL, CANADIAN PACIFIC RAILWAY COMPANY FONDS
P. 56 MIDDLE: CANADIAN PACIFIC RAILWAY COMPANY. CANADIAN PACIFIC HOTELS / UNIVERSITY OF BRITISH COLUMBIA LIBRARY
P. 56 BOTTOM: JASPER-YELLOWHEAD MUSEUM AND ARCHIVES / GST #11897 3312 RR0001
P. 57 ABOVE: BYRON HARMON / UNIVERSITY OF ALBERTA LIBRARIES
P. 57 BELOW: CAVAN IMAGES / GETTY IMAGES
PP. 58-59: CANADIAN MUSEUM OF IMMIGRATION AT PIER 21
P. 60 ABOVE: PHOTO12 / ALAMY / CBW
P. 60 BELOW: RIGHTS RESERVED
P. 61 LEFT: CANADIAN PACIFIC STEAMSHIPS LIMITED / UNIVERSITY OF BRITISH COLUMBIA LIBRARY
P. 61 RIGHT: AURIMAGES_P12 / MANUEL COHEN
P. 62 ABOVE: RIGHTS RESERVED / FAIRMONT MANOIR RICHELIEU ARCHIVES
P. 62 BELOW: HUBERT KANG
P. 63 LEFT: PHOTO12 / ALAMY / PICTURES NOW
P. 63 RIGHT: BIBLIOTHÈQUE ET ARCHIVES NATIONALES DU QUÉBEC
P. 64 ABOVE: RIGHTS RESERVED
P. 64 BELOW: RIGHTS RESERVED
P. 65: PHOTO12 / ALAMY / MATTEO OMIED
P. 66: RIGHTS RESERVED
P. 67 ABOVE: COURTESY OF LIBRARIES AND CULTURAL RESOURCES DIGITAL COLLECTIONS, UNIVERSITY OF CALGARY
P. 67 BELOW: WIKIWAND / SKOOKUM1
PP. 68-69: ROB ATKINS / GETTY IMAGES
P. 70: PHOTO12 / ALAMY / STOCK IMAGERY
P. 71: CRHA / EXPORAIL, CANADIAN PACIFIC RAILWAY COMPANY FONDS
P. 72: RIGHTS RESERVED
P. 73 LEFT: PHOTO12 / ALAMY / CPA MEDIA PTE LTD
P. 73 RIGHT: JIM HEIMANN COLLECTION / ARCHIVE PHOTOS / GETTY IMAGES

P. 74: RIGHTS RESERVED
P. 75: PHOTO12 / ALAMY / TOURING THE WORLD IN THE 20S AND 30S
P. 76: SHUTTERSTOCK
P. 77: IRVING BROWNING / THE NEW YORK HISTORICAL SOCIETY / GETTY IMAGES
P. 78 LEFT (1): PHOTO12 / ALAMY / MARC SCHECHTER
P. 78 RIGHT (2): RIGHTS RESERVED / FAIRMONT SANYA HAITANG BAY ARCHIVES
P. 78 RIGHT (3): RIGHTS RESERVED / FAIRMONT HERITAGE PLACE ACAPULCO ARCHIVES
P. 78 RIGHT (4): PHOTO12 / ALAMY / RUPERT SAGAR-MUSGRAVE
P. 78 RIGHT (5): RIGHTS RESERVED / FAIRMONT ORCHID ARCHIVES
P. 78 RIGHT (6): RIGHTS RESERVED / FAIRMONT SANUR BEACH ARCHIVES
P. 79: UNIVERSITY OF BRITISH COLUMBIA LIBRARY / THE CHUNG COLLECTION
P. 80 LEFT: ALAMY / PICTORIAL PRESS LTD
P. 80 RIGHT: RIGHTS RESERVED
P. 81: JOE KELLY / ALIFEIIMAGINED
P. 82 LEFT: ABC PHOTO ARCHIVES / DISNEY GENERAL ENTERTAINMENT CONTENT / GETTY IMAGES
P. 82 RIGHT: POPPERFOTO VIA GETTY IMAGES / GETTY IMAGES
P. 83: ALISDAIR MACDONALD / DAILY MIRROR / MIRRORPIX / GETTY IMAGES
PP. 84-85: PHOTO12 / ALAMY / PICTURES NOW
P. 86: JEAN PAGES / CONDÉ NAST / SHUTTERSTOCK
P. 87: WILLIAM R. DERRICK / SMITHSONIAN AMERICAN ART MUSEUM
P. 88: LIBRARY OF CONGRESS
P. 89: BETTMANN / GETTY IMAGES
P. 90: RIGHTS RESERVED
PP. 90-91: THE SEATTLE PUBLIC LIBRARY
PP. 92-93: NIALL CLUTTON
P. 93: PHOTO12 / ALAMY / AMORET TANNER
P. 94: P. PIEL / ULLSTEIN BILD / GETTY IMAGES
P. 95 TOP: RIGHTS RESERVED / FAIRMONT GRAND HOTEL KIEV ARCHIVES
P. 95 BOTTOM: RIGHTS RESERVED / FAIRMONT HOTEL VIER JAHRESZEITEN HAMBURG
P. 96: RIGHTS RESERVED
P. 97: RIGHTS RESERVED / MONTREUX PALACE ARCHIVES
PP. 98-99: CSTMC / CN COLLECTION
P. 100 LEFT: RIGHTS RESERVED
P. 100 RIGHT: YOUSUF KARSH / CAMERA PRESS
P. 101: RICHARD W. RUMMEL / LIBRARY AND ARCHIVES CANADA
P. 102: ALAMY / MICHAEL WHEATLEY
P. 103: CSTM ARCHIVES
P. 104: W.J. OLIVER. COURTESY OF LIBRARIES AND CULTURAL RESOURCES DIGITAL COLLECTIONS, UNIVERSITY OF CALGARY
P. 105: BYRON HARMON / UNIVERSITY OF ALBERTA LIBRARIES
P. 106: UBC LIBRARY / THE CHUNG COLLECTION
P. 107: PHOTO12 / ALAMY / CITY OF TORONTO ARCHIVES / WILLIAM JAMES FAMILY FONDS
P. 108 LEFT: BRITISH COLUMBIA ARCHIVES / ROYAL BC MUSEUM / B-00171
P. 108 RIGHT: PHOTO12 / ALAMY / JSMIMAGES
P. 109: UNIVERSITY OF BRITISH COLUMBIA LIBRARY. RARE BOOKS AND SPECIAL COLLECTIONS. UNO LANGMANN FAMILY COLLECTION OF B.C. PHOTOGRAPHS. UL_1628_0067
P. 110: CSTM COLLECTION / X-44744
P. 111: RIGHTS RESERVED / FAIRMONT MOSCOU ARCHIVES

ARCHITECTURE

P. 114 (1): Walter Wilcox / Digital Collections, University of Calgary

P. 114 (2): Digital Collections, University of Calgary

P. 114 (3): Digital Collections, University of Calgary

P. 114 (4): Digital Collections, University of Calgary

P. 114 (5): University of Alberta Libraries

P. 114 (6): Byron Harmon / Digital Collections, University of Calgary

P. 114 (7): Byron Harmon / Digital Collections, University of Calgary

P. 115: J.H. Clarke / Digital Collections, University of Calgary

P. 116: Digital Collections, University of Calgary

P. 117: Digital Collections, University of Calgary

P. 118: West Production / Fairmont Maldives Sirru Fen Fushi Archives

P. 119: Yash / Fairmont Maldives Sirru Fen Fushi Archives

P. 120 top: Rights reserved / Fairmont Taghazout Bay Archives

P. 120 middle: Rights reserved / Fairmont Scottsdale Princess Archives

P. 120 bottom: © Mohamed Jannat / Fairmont Royal Palm Marrakech Archives

P. 120 background: Sam Schooler

P. 121: Rights reserved / Fairmont Royal Palm Marrakech Archives

P. 122 left: Matthew Millman / Fairmont San Francisco Archives

P. 122 right: Gary Parker

P. 123 above: Rights reserved / Fairmont Mara Safari Club Archives

P. 123 below: Rights reserved / Fairmont Mara Safari Club Archives

PP. 124-125: AscentXmedia / iStock

P. 126: University of British Columbia / The Chung Collection

P. 127 top: Cinzia Orsini

P. 127 middle: David Wilson

P. 127 bottom: Rights reserved / Fairmont Heritage Place - Franz Klammer Lodge Archives

P. 128 (1): Roberto Machado Noa / LightRocket / Getty Images

P. 128 (2): Photo12 / Alamy / James Schwabel

P. 128 (3): Age / CSP_sainaniritu

P. 128 (4): Photo12 / Alamy / David J. Mitchell

P. 128 (5): Photo12 / Alamy / Todd Bannor

P. 128 (6): Rights reserved / Fairmont Windsor Park Archives

P. 129: Photo12 / Alamy / Chon Kit Leong

P. 130 (1): Photo12 / Alamy / Pictures Now

P. 130 (2): University of Alberta Libraries

P. 130 (3): MP-0000.158.96 / © Museum McCord

P. 130 (4): Photo12 / Alamy / Science History Images

P. 130 (5): UBC Library / The Chung Collection

P. 130 (6): Saj Shafique

P. 130 (7): akg-images

P. 130 (8): Rights reserved / Fairmont Chicago Archives

P. 131: British Columbia, Special Services Branch / Royal BC Museum

P. 132 above: Rights reserved / Fairmont Peace Hotel Archives

P. 132 below: Rights reserved / Fairmont Peace Hotel Archives

P. 133: Photo12 / Alamy

P. 134: Rights reserved / Fairmont Claremont Berkeley Archives

P. 135 above: Photo12 / Alamy / Touring the world in the 20s and 30s

P. 135 below: University of Alberta Libraries

P. 136 left: Rights reserved /Studio 27 / Fairmont Sonoma Mission Inn & Spa archives

P. 136 right: Rights reserved / Fairmont Grand Del Mar Archives

P. 137 above left: Rights reserved / Fairmont Royal Pavilion Archives

P. 137 above right: Christina Leme

P. 137 below: Paul Berthelon Bravo

PP. 138-139: Rights reserved / Carton House Archives

P. 140 above: Jack Hardy / Carton House Archives

P. 140 below: Rights reserved / Fairmont Copley Plaza Archives

P. 141: Nadine Shaabana

P. 142 above: Tony Bock / Toronto Star via Getty Images

P. 142 below: View Pictures / Universal Images Group / Getty Images

P. 143: Rights reserved / The Plaza New York Archives

P. 144: Kimberly Person / Into Dust Photography / Fairmont Olympic Seattle Archives

P. 145: Udo Bernhart / picture alliance

P. 146: William Lorton

P. 147: Jonathan Gazze

PP. 148-149: Paola Bertoletti

P. 150: Joginder Singh / Fairmont Jaipur Archives

P. 151 left: Rights reserved / STX Landscape Architects

P. 151 right: Rights reserved / The Peace Hotel Archives

P. 152 left: Rights reserved / Fairmont Ajman Archives

P. 152 right: Rights reserved

P. 153: Matthew Millman / Fairmont San Francisco Archives

P. 154: Eric Cuvillier / Fairmont Nile City Archives

P. 155 left: © Paul Thuysbaert / Fairmont Riyadh Archives

P. 155 right above: Eric Cuvillier / Fairmont Dubai The Palm Archives

P. 155 right below: Heather Shevlin

P. 156 above: Rights reserved / Katara Hospitality

P. 156 below: Hubert Kang

P. 157: Stocklib / Muhammad Abrar Sharif

P. 158 above left: Rights reserved / Studio Three Twenty One

P. 158 above right: Eric Cuvillier / The Savoy Hotel archives

P. 158 bottom right: Rights reserved / Fairmont Ambassador Seoul Archives

P. 159: Rory Daniel / Fairmont Beijing Archives

P. 160: WOW / Fairmont Chengdu Archives

P. 161: Rights reserved / Carton House Archives

PP. 162-163: Archives du MSTC

P. 164 top left: Rights reserved

P. 164 top right: Terry Uy / Fairmont Makati Archives

P. 164 middle left: Getty Images

P. 164 middle right: © Paul Thuysbaert / Fairmont Bab Al Bahr Archives

P. 164 bottom: Henry Kalen Collection / University of Manitoba Archives

P. 165: George Rose / Getty Images

P. 166 left: Rights reserved / Fairmont Istanbul

P. 166 right: Rights reserved / Fairmont Rabat

P. 167 above: Rights reserved / Fairmont Nanjing Archives

P. 167 below: Rights reserved / Fairmont Wuhan Archives

P. 168 above left: Marco Chow / Fairmont Jakarta Archives

P. 168 above right: Rights reserved / Fairmont Amman Archives

P. 168 below: Paul Thuysbaert / Fairmont Riyadh Archives

P. 169: Rights reserved / Fairmont Maldives - Sirru Fen Fushi Archives

P. 170: Jacques Elboustany / Fairmont Ramla Riyadh Archives

P. 171: Rights reserved / Monica Barros Le Touriste

PP. 172-173: Architect: Jean Nouvel. Associate architect: DJ Architectes Associés

P. 173: Albert Watson

P. 174: Pedro E. Guerrero Estate

P. 175 left: Pedro E. Guerrero Estate

P. 175 right: Rights reserved

P. 176: View MoMA #257 (detail), Wedding Chapel for Claremont Hotel (Berkeley, California). Scheme 2, Unbuilt Project. Drawing #5731.001, ink, pencil, and colored pencil on paper. Frank Lloyd Wright Foundation Archives (The Museum of Modern Art | Avery Architectural & Fine Arts Library, Columbia University)

P. 177 left: View From Air, Arthur Miller house (Roxbury, Connecticut). Unbuilt Project. Drawing #5719.001, ink, pencil, and colored pencil on paper. Frank Lloyd Wright Foundation Archives (The Museum of Modern Art | Avery Architectural & Fine Arts Library, Columbia University)

P. 177 right: Photo12 / ABC / PA images

P. 178 left: Rights reserved / Mark Yurkiv

P. 178 right: David Ng Collection, Courtesy of National Archives of Singapore

P. 179: Masano Kawana / Fairmont Singapore Archives

P. 180 above: Cité de l'architecture / Fonds Jean Ginsberg / Spélugues building complex, 1971-75, Monte-Carlo (Reinhard Müller-Metge, José and Jean Notari, Herbert Weisskamp, architects). Photo Michel Moch, N.D.

P. 180 below: Rights reserved / Fairmont Nanjing Archives

P. 181 above left: Jesus Alonso / Fairmont Quasar Istanbul Archives

P. 181 above right: Alamy / Agefotostock/ Douglas Williams

P. 181 below: Rights reserved / Fairmont Washington Archives

P. 182 top: Rights reserved / Fairmont Century Plaza Archives

P. 182 middle: Rights reserved / Fairmont Century Plaza Archives

P. 182 bottom: Coll. Okinawa Soba

P. 183: Julius Shulman © J. Paul Getty Trust. Getty Research Institute, Los Angeles

PP. 184-185: Courtesy LMN Architects

PP. 186-187: Eric Cuvillier / Fairmont Baku Flame Towers Archives

SOUL

pp. 190-191: Percy Lewis Pocock / W & D Downey / The Print Collector / Getty Images

p. 192 left: Peter and Catharine Whyte Fonds / Archives and Library, Whyte Museum of the Canadian Rockies

p. 192 right: Bettmann / Getty Images

p. 193: National Film Board of Canada / Library and Archives Canada / PA-211004

p. 194: J Walter Green / AP

p. 195: Jayne Fincher / Princess Diana Archive / Getty Images

p. 196 left: George Pimentel / WireImage / Getty Images

p. 196 right: PA Images / Alamy / David Cheskin

p. 197: Nathan Denette / The Canadian Press via AP

pp. 198-199: Yousuf Karsh / Camera Press

p. 200: National Film Board of Canada / Library and Archives Canada / C-011429

p. 201 top: Photo12 / Ann Ronan Picture Library

p. 201 middle: Photo12 / Alamy / Heritage Image Partnership Ltd

p. 201 bottom: Keystone / Hulton Archive / Getty Images

p. 202: Photo12 / Alamy / Keystone Press

p. 203 left: Photo12 / Alamy / Allstar Picture Library Ltd

p. 203 right: Carl Bigelow / MediaNews Group / Oakland Tribune via Getty Images

p. 204: Ted Grant

p. 205: Deanne Fitzmaurice / San Francisco Chronicle / Hearts Newspaper via Getty Images

p. 206: Bettmann / Getty Images

p. 207 top: Peter Heimsath / Shutterstock

p. 207 bottom: David Hume Kennerly / Getty Images

p. 208: NARA / White House Photographic Collection

p. 209: Photo12 / Alamy / dpa picture alliance

pp. 210-211: Photo12 / Alamy / American Photo Archive

pp. 212-213: Rory Daniel

p. 214: Cole Freeman

p. 215: AP Photo / Eric Risberg

p. 216: West Production / Fairmont Mayakoba Archives

p. 217: Eric Cuvillier / Fairmont Fen Surri Archives

pp. 218-219: © Family of Lawren S. Harris / The Thomson Collection at the Art Gallery of Ontario

p. 220: James Whistler / MET, New York

pp. 220-221: Claude Monet / Musée des Beaux-Arts de Lyon / Photo12 / Alamy / Peter Horree

p. 222: © Succession Picasso 2022 / Bridgeman Images

pp. 222-223: Solomon R. Guggenheim Foundation, New York. Rights reserved

p. 224: Cecil Beaton / Condé Nast / Shutterstock

pp. 224-225: Dmitri Kessel / The LIFE Picture Collection / Shutterstock

p. 226: J. Bess Studios / Chester Dale papers / Archives of American Art, Smithsonian Institution

p. 227 above: Oskar Kokoschka / Private Collection / Akg-images

p. 227 below: Oskar Kokoschka / Private Collection / Akg-images

p. 228: Bernard Gotfryd / Getty Images

p. 229 top: Prudence Cuming Associates © Damien Hirst and Science Ltd. All rights reserved ADAGP, 2021

p. 229 middle: Prudence Cuming Associates © Damien Hirst and Science Ltd. All rights reserved ADAGP, 2021

p. 229 bottom: Julian Opie / Rights reserved / Accor Archives

p. 230 above: Slim Aarons / Hulton Archive / Getty Images

p. 230 below: Photo12 / Alamy / Endless Travel

p. 231 above: Martin Parr / Magnum Photos

p. 231 below: Martin Parr / Magnum Photos

p. 232: Annie Leibovitz / Trunk Archive

p. 233 left: Jessica Craig Martin / Trunk Archive

p. 233 right: Courtesy the artist and Marian Goodman Gallery / Copyright: Nan Goldin

pp. 234-235: Philippe Halsman / Magnum Photos

p. 236: Universal History Archive / Universal Images Group via Getty Images

p. 237 above: Photo12 / Alamy / Pictorial Press Ltd

p. 237 below: Photo12 / Alamy / United Archives GmbH

p. 238 left: Photo12 / Alamy / Archive Pics

p. 238 right: Corey Stovin / Fairmont Empress Archives

p. 239 left: Universal History Archive / Universal Images Group via Getty Images

p. 239 right: Canadian Pacific Steamships / University of British Columbia Library

p. 240 left: Stereo-Travel Co. / Library of Congres

p. 240 right: Hulton Archive / Getty Images

p. 241 top: Rights reserved / Accor Archives

p. 241 middle: Alamy / Granger Historical Picture Archive

p. 241 bottom: Earl Theisen / Getty Images

p. 242: Bentley Archive / Popperfoto / Getty Images

p. 243: Terry Disney / Express / Hulton Archive / Getty Images

p. 244: Walter Mori / Mondadori via Getty Images

p. 245 left: Bettmann / Getty Images

p. 245 right: Bettmann / Getty Images

pp. 246-247: IMAGO / United Archives

p. 248 top left: Egbert O. Taylor Fonds / Archives and Library, Whyte Museum of the Canadian Rockies

p. 248 top right: Collection Christophel © Joseph M Schenck Productions / Feature Productions

p. 248 bottom: Photo12 / Alamy / Entertainment Pictures

p. 249: Photo12 / Alamy / Pictorial Press Ltd

pp. 250-251: Photo12 / Alamy / Moviestore Collection Ltd

p. 252 left: Rights reserved / Mount Kenya Safari Club Archives

p. 252 right: Rights reserved / Mount Kenya Safari Club Archives

p. 253: 20th Century Fox / Archive Photos / Moviepix / Getty Images

p. 254: Metro-Goldwyn-Mayer / Archives Photos / Moviepix / Getty Images

p. 255: Gene Lester / Getty Images

p. 256: Bettmann / Getty Images

p. 257: Photo12 / Alamy / United Archives GmbH

p. 258: Photo12 / Alamy / Pictorial Press Ltd

pp. 258-259: Photo12 / Alamy / Landmark Media © 20th Century Fox

p. 260: Photo12 / Alamy / Masheter Movie Archive

p. 261: Columbia Pictures

p. 262 top: Mondadori via Getty Images

p. 262 middle: Collection Christophel © Paramount

p. 262 bottom: Photo12 / 7e Art / MGM

p. 263: Photo12 / Alamy / Masheter Movie Archive

p. 264: Photo12 / Alamy / Moviestore Collection Ltd

p. 265 left: François Duhamel / Paramount Pictures / Photo12 / Alamy

p. 265 right: James Garrett / New York Daily News Archive via Getty Images

p. 266: Collection Christophel © Twentieth Century Fox Film Corporation / Patrick Camboulive

p. 267: Photo12 / Alamy / Moviestore Collection Ltd

p. 268: Photo12 / Alamy / Picture Lux The Hollywood Archive

p. 269: CBS Photo Archive via Getty Images

pp. 270-271: Ron Galella / Premium Archive / Getty Images

p. 272: Daily Herald / Mirrorpix via Getty Images

p. 273: Bettmann / Getty Images

p. 274: Erich Auerbach / Hulton Archive / Getty Images

p. 275: Fiona Adams / Redferns / Getty Images

p. 276: Photo12 / Alamy / Mirrorpix / Trinity Mirror

p. 277: Bettmann / Getty Images

p. 278: Tad Hershorn / Hulton Archive / Getty Images

p. 279: Photo12 / Mirrorpix

p. 280: Dick Darrell / Toronto Star Photograph Archive

p. 281 above: Toronto Star Photograph Archive, Courtesy of Toronto Public Library

p. 281 below: Neil Hubbard

p. 282: © 2013, Studio Edouard Curchod, Rights reserved

p. 283: Photo12 / Alamy / Nathan Daws

p. 284: Michael Ochs Archives / Getty Images

p. 285: Theo Wargo / WireImage via Getty Images

pp. 286-287: Greg Avenel

p. 288: Andre-Edouard Marty / Vogue / Condé Nast

p. 289: Benjamin Grillon / Agence Triptyque / Styling: Katie Shillingford / Model: Andrea Diaconu

p. 290: A.C. Leighton / University of British Columbia / The Chung Collection

p. 291: Kourken Pakchanian / Condé Nast / Shutterstock

p. 292: Bettmann / Getty Images

p. 293: Genevieve Naylor/Corbis via Getty Images

p. 294: Santi Visalli / Getty Images

p. 295: George Elam / Daily Mail / Shutterstock

p. 296: Fred Ramage / Keystone / Hulton Archive / Getty Images

p. 297: Bert Hardy / Picture Post / Hulton Archive / Getty Images

p. 298: Photo12 / Alamy / DC / Media Punch Inc.

p. 299: Douglas Miller / Hulton Archive / Getty Images

p. 300: Daily Herald / Mirrorpix / Getty Images

p. 301: John Downing / Getty Images

pp. 302-303: Elliott Erwitt / Magnum Photos

p. 304: Rights reserved

p. 305: University of British Columbia / The Chung Collection

p. 306: Edward Steichen / Condé Nast / Shutterstock

p. 307: Hulton-Deutsch Collection / Corbis via Getty Images

p. 308: Rights reserved

p. 309: Rights reserved

p. 310: Photo12 / Alamy / Beryl Peters Collection

p. 311: Santi Visalli / Getty Images

pp. 312-313: Lawrence Fried / Iconic Images

p. 314: Eliott Erwitt / Magnum Photos

p. 315: Ron Galella / Ron Galella Collection via Getty Images

p. 316: Photo12 / Alamy / Adam Scull

p. 317: Bettmann / Getty images

pp. 318-319: Amy Lombard / The New York Times-REDUX-REA

P. 22: Princess Louise Caroline Alberta, Duchess of Argyll, photograph by A.J. Melhuish, 1871, National Portrait Gallery, London

P. 215: AP Photo/Eric Risberg

P. 23: H.R.H. The princess Louise, *View from the Window of the Governor-General's Quarters, the Citadel, Quebec*, 1882, National Gallery of Canada, Acc. #14638.14

PP. 218-219: Lawren S. Harris, *Untitled Mountain Landscape*, c. 1928, oil on canvas. Art Gallery of Ontario

P. 25: Fraser, John A., *Summit Lake near Lenchoile, Bow River, Canadian Pacific Railway*, 1886, National Gallery of Canada, Acc. #28063

P. 295: Audrey & Cecil Beaton at The Savoy Hotel in London, January 19th 1965. Photo12 / Alamy / PA Images

P. 197: Nathan Denette / The Canadian Press via AP

P. 306: Portrait of Mrs. Fal de Saint Phalle wearing a Persian costume, *Vogue*, February 15, 1925. Edward Steichen / Condé Nast / Shutterstock

322 — 323

ACKNOWLEDGMENTS

Skira would like to extend a special thanks to Susan Sarandon for her beautifully written description of grandest of stories at Fairmont hotels.

We would also like to warmly thank to the authors of this book, Claire Wrathall and Claire-Marie Angelini-Thiennot, for capturing the atmosphere and universe of Fairmont.

A special acknowledgment for the historians, archivists, and staff across Fairmont properties without whom this book would not have been possible.

Skira is also very grateful to the teams at Glenbow Museum, Whyte Museum of the Canadian Rockies for their involvement.

We would also like to thank the everyone who contributed to the iconographic research for their help and insight, especially William Annesley (Marian Goodman Projects), Elizabeth Kundert-Cameron and Maura Knox (Whyte Museum of the Canadian Rockies), Isabelle Czerwonka, Timothée Viale (Gagosian), Chantal Guérin (Expo-Rail, the Canadian Railway Museum) Marcia Mordfield (Ingenium), and Jacqueline M. E. Vincent (Brechin Imaging Services).

A special thanks across time goes to James Graham Fair and his daughters, Virginia and Theresa, for imagining the foundations and spirit of Fairmont, as well as to all the guests who have made the history of the hotels, especially Princess Louise and the British Royal Family, Tony Bennet, David Bowie, Truman Capote, Agatha Christie, Christian Dior, Bob Dylan, Greta Garbo, Guccio Gucci, Alfred Hitchcock, Grace Kelly, the Kennedys, Annie Leibovitz, John Lennon & Yoko Ono, Freddy Mercury, Marylin Monroe, Vladimir Nabokov, F. Scott Fitzgerald, Andy Warhol, Oscar Wilde, and many more.

Chief Creative Officer
Jean-Guilhem Lamberti

Creative Director
Claire-Marie Thiennot

Art Director and Colorization Artist
Axel Vagnard

Project Lead
Angela Kara Tan

Global Vice President, Fairmont Brand
Mansi Vagt

Text and research by
Claire Wrathall
and Claire-Marie Thiennot

Journalist and Researcher
Janice Tober

Éditions Skira Paris
14, rue Serpente
75006 Paris
France
www.skira.net

Senior Editor
Nathalie Prat-Couadau

Editorial Coordination
María Laura Ribadeneira
assisted by Anna Koch

Editorial and Commercial Assistant
Meryl Mason

Iconographic Research
Nathalie Rosenblum
assisted by Béatrice Constanty
and Dominique Kervran

Copy Editing
Kim Scott

Layout
Felicidad Studio

Color Separation
Litho Art New, Turin

Printed by Graphius, in Ghent, Belgium
Legal deposit January 2022

ISBN 978-2-37074-171-4
© Accor, 2021
© Éditions Skira Paris, 2021

All right reserved.
No part of this publication may be reproduced, stored in a retrieval system, or transmitted in any form or by any means, electronic, mechanical, photocopying, recording, or otherwise, without prior consent of the publishers.

31327007172901